NASB
HANDY CONCORDANCE

NASB

HANDY CONCORDANCE

A COMPACT
CONCORDANCE
TO THE
NEW AMERICAN
STANDARD BIBLE

Regency
Reference Library
Zondervan Publishing House
Grand Rapids, Michigan

NASB HANDY CONCORDANCE
Copyright © 1979 by THE LOCKMAN FOUNDATION

Regency Reference Library is an imprint of Zondervan
Publishing House, 1415 Lake Drive, S.E.,
Grand Rapids, Michigan 49506

Library of Congress Cataloging in Publication Data

New American standard concordance to the Old and New
   Testaments.
   NASB handy concordance.

   Reprint. Originally published: c1979.
   Previously published as: New American standard Bible
concordance to the Old and New Testaments : La Habra, Calif. :
Foundation Press Publications, publisher for the Lockman
Foundation. 1972.
   1. Bible–Concordances, English–New American standard
I. Title: N.A.S.B. handy concordance.
BS425.N383   1984   220.5'2053   84-13204
ISBN 0-310-45252-X

Printed in the United States of America

84   85   86   87   88   89   90 / 10   9   8   7   6   5   4   3   2   1

To Dorothy Carter
From Sis, Murphy
1989

This is a collection of the principal **proper nouns** and **key words** in Scripture. The following format is used: Descriptive phrases and references are listed under each **proper noun**. If the descriptive phrases are numbered, this indicates different individuals or identities. **Key words** are immediately followed by explanatory words or synonyms. Under each **key word** examples are listed with text and reference. The **key word** is abbreviated in the text to its first letter, e.g., "abide" is "a". Variants add suffixes, e.g., "abides" appears as "**a-s**" and "abiding" appears as "**a-ing**".

A

AARON

brother of Moses	Ex 4:14
spokesman for Moses	
	Ex 4:28;7:1-2
as priest	Ex 28:1;29:44
rod of	Num 17:8; Heb 9:4
critical of Moses	Num 12:1
death	Deut 10:6

ABADDON

1 *region of dead*	Job 26:6
	Prov 15:11
2 *angel of bottomless pit*	
	Rev 9:11

ABANDON *leave*

LORD has **a-ed** us	Judg 6:13
not **a** His people	1 Sam 12:22
a the remnant	2 Kin 21:14
not **a** my soul to	Ps 16:10
not **a** His people	Ps 94:14
a-ed My inheritance	Jer 12:7
a my soul to Hades	Acts 2:27

ABASE *humble*

man will be **a-ed**	Is 2:11
lofty will be **a-d**	Is 10:33
a the haughtiness	Is 13:11
a-d before all	Mal 2:9

ABATE *decrease*

water was **a-ed**	Gen 8:8
his vigor **a-ed**	Deut 34:7

ABBA *father*

A! Father	Mark 14:36
we cry out, **A**!	Rom 8:15

ABED-NEGO

friend of Daniel	Dan 1:6
Hebrew name Azariah	Dan 1:7
faithful to God	Dan 3:16,17
cast into furnace	Dan 3:20

ABEL

son of Adam	Gen 4:2
shepherd	Gen 4:2

favored by God   Gen 4:4
righteous   Matt 23:35
slain by Cain   Gen 4:8

ABHOR *despise, detest*

associates **a** me   Job 19:19
greatly **a**-red Israel   Ps 78:59
nations will **a** him   Prov 24:24
To the One **a**-red   Is 49:7
A what is evil   Rom 12:9

ABIB

early name of first month of
    Hebrew calendar   Ex 34:18
month of Passover and
    Unleavened Bread   Deut 16:1

ABIDE *remain, stay*

LORD **a**-s forever   Ps 9:7
a in Thy tent   Ps 15:1
a in the shadow   Ps 91:1
wrath of God **a**-s   John 3:36
a in My word   John 8:31
unless you **a** in Me   John 15:7
a in My love   John 15:9
now **a** faith   1 Cor 13:13
word...LORD **a**-s   1 Pet 1:25
love of God **a**   1 John 3:17
God **a**-s in us   1 John 4:12

ABIGAIL

1 *wife of Nabal*   1 Sam 25:3
   kind to David   1 Sam 25:18ff
   wife of David   1 Sam 25:42
2 *daughter of Nahash*
    2 Sam 17:25

ABIHU

son of Aaron   Ex 6:23
priest   Ex 24:1-11
disobeyed God   Lev 10:1
judged by God   Lev 10:2

ABIJAH

1 *son of Samuel*   1 Sam 8:2
2 *son of Becher*   1 Chr 7:8
3 *son of Jeroboam*   1 Kin 14:1
4 *king of Judah*   2 Chr 12:16
5 *line of Eleasar*   1 Chr 24:10
6 *Hezekiah's mother*   2 Chr 29:1
7 *priest*   Neh 10:7;12:4

ABILITY *power, strength*

According to their **a**   Ezra 2:69

a for serving   Dan 1:4
a to conceive   Heb 11:11

ABIMELECH

1 *king of Gerar*   Gen 20:1-18
2 *king of Gerar*   Gen 26:1ff
3 *king of Shechem*   Judg 9:1ff
4 *priest*   1 Chr 18:16
5 *Psalm title*   Ps 34

ABIRAM

opposed Moses   Num 16:1ff
judged by God   Num 16:25ff

ABISHAI

brother of Joab   1 Sam 26:6
warrior of David   1 Chr 18:22
aided Abner's assassination
    2 Sam 3:30

ABLE *qualified*

a to judge   1 Kin 3:9
a from these stones   Matt 3:9
I am **a** to do   Matt 9:28
Him who is **a**   Matt 10:28
a to separate us   Rom 8:39
what you are **a**   1 Cor 10:13
a to comprehend   Eph 3:18
be **a** to teach   2 Tim 2:2
a to save Him   Heb 5:7
One who is **a**   James 4:12
a to open   Rev 5:3

ABNER

Saul's commander   1 Sam 17:55
loyal to David   2 Sam 3:12ff
killed by Joab   2 Sam 3:27
mourned by David   2 Sam 3:32

ABODE *habitation*

a of righteousness   Jer 31:23
Our **a** with him   John 14:23
their proper **a**   Jude 6

ABOLISH

not come to **a**   Matt 5:17
a-ing in His flesh   Eph 2:15
who **a**-ed death   2 Tim 1:10

ABOMINABLE *detestable*

committed **a** deeds   Ps 14:1
your beauty **a**   Ezek 16:25
a idolatries   1 Pet 4:3
unbelieving and **a**   Rev 21:8

ABOMINATION *hated thing*

a to the Egyptians	Ex 8:26
a into your house	Deut 7:26
seen their a-s	Deut 29:17
a to the LORD	Prov 3:32
all their a-s	Ezek 33:29
a of desolation	Matt 24:15
a-s of the earth	Rev 17:5

ABOUND *excel, plentiful*

faithful man will a	Prov 28:20
May your peace a	Dan 4:1
a in hope	Rom 15:13
a-ing in the work	1 Cor 15:58
affection a-s	2 Cor 7:15
all grace a	2 Cor 9:8

ABOVE *over*

exalted a the heavens	Ps 57:5
disciple is not a	Matt 10:24
I am from a	John 8:23
a every name	Phil 2:9
exalts himself a	2 Thess 2:4
gift is from a	James 1:17

ABRAHAM

covenant	Gen 17:1-8
promise of Isaac	Gen 17:19
asked the Lord	Gen 18:22ff
offers Isaac	Gen 22:9,10
death	Gen 25:8
righteousness of	Rom 4:3-9

ABRAHAM'S BOSOM

rabbinic terminology	
for Paradise	Luke 16:22

ABRAM

called of God	Gen 12:1-3
rescued Lot	Gen 14:14-16
covenant with God	Gen 15:18
name changed	Gen 17:5

ABSALOM

son of David	2 Sam 13:1
popular	2 Sam 15:6
his revolt	2 Sam 15:1-2
slain by Joab	2 Sam 18:15

ABSENT *being away*

we are a from	Gen 31:49
a in body	1 Cor 5:3
a from the Lord	2 Cor 5:6
a from the body	2 Cor 5:8

ABSTAIN *refrain from*

a from wine	Num 6:3
a-ing from foods	1 Tim 4:3
a from wickedness	2 Tim 2:19
a from fleshly lusts	1 Pet 2:11

ABUNDANCE *plenty, surplus*

seven years of a	Gen 41:34
a of all things	Deut 28:47
a of Thy house	Ps 36:8
a of peace	Ps 72:7
a of counselors	Prov 24:6
he who loves a	Eccl 5:10
delight yourself in a	Is 55:2
one has an a	Luke 12:15
the a of grace	Rom 5:17

ABUNDANT *enough, plenteous*

come...find a water	2 Chr 32:4
a righteousnes	Job 37:23
a in loving kindness	Ps 86:5
comfort is a	2 Cor 1:5

ABUNDANTLY *plenteous*

they may breed a	Gen 8:17
Populate the earth a	Gen 9:7
will prosper you a	Deut 30:9
drip upon man a	Job 36:28

ABUSE (n) *insulting speech*

hurling a at Him	Matt 27:39
was hurling a	Luke 23:39

ABUSE (v) *hurt, molest*

a-d her all night	Judg 19:25
uncircumcised...a me	1 Chr 10:4

ABUSIVE *filthy, vulgar*

a speech from your	Col 3:8
strife, a language	1 Tim 6:4

ABYSS *deep, depth*

depart into the a	Luke 8:31
descend into the a	Rom 10:7
angel of the a	Rev 9:11
key of the a	Rev 20:1

ACCEPT *receive*

a the work of	Deut 33:11
a good from God	Job 2:10
the LORD a-ed Job	Job 42:9
a-ed no chastening	Jer 2:30
hear the word and a	Mark 4:20
God has a-ed him	Rom 14:3
a one another	Rom 15:7

ACCEPTABLE *pleasing*

my heart Be a	Ps 19:14
sacrifice, a to God	Rom 12:1
a to the saints	Rom 15:31
now is the a time	2 Cor 6:2
to God an a service	Heb 12:28
sacrifices a to God	1 Pet 2:5

ACCESS *approach, entry*

grant you free a	Zech 3:7
our a in one Spirit	Eph 2:18

ACCOMPANY *attach to, follow*

who a my lord	1 Sam 25:27
a-ied the king	2 Sam 19:40
a-ied by trumpets	2 Chr 5:13
that a salvation	Heb 6:9

ACCOMPLISH *perform, realize*

a-ed deliverance	1 Sam 11:13
shall a my desire	1 Kin 5:9
God...a-es *all things*	Ps 57:2
has a-ed His wrath	Lam 4:11
a-ed redemption	Luke 1:68
a His work	John 4:34
I am a-ing a work	Acts 13:41
when sin is a-ed	James 1:15
man can a much	James 5:16

ACCORD *agreement, union*

one a to fight	Josh 9:2
voices...with one a	Acts 4:24
one a in Solomon's	Acts 5:12
multitudes with one a	Acts 8:6
one a they came	Acts 12:20

ACCORDING

a to your word	Gen 30:34
Moses did; a to all	Ex 40:16
a to our sins	Ps 103:10
a to his deeds	Matt 16:27
a to the revelation	Rom 16:25
heirs a to promise	Gal 3:29
a to His riches	Phil 4:19

ACCOUNT (n) *reckoning*

the a of the heavens	Gen 2:4
On whose a *has* this	Jon 1:8
settled a-s with	Matt 25:19
who will give an a	Heb 13:17

ACCOUNT (v) *reckon*

do not a *this* sin	Num 12:11

Thou hast taken a of	Ps 56:8
I am a-ed wicked	Job 9:29
are a-ed as nothing	Dan 4:35

ACCURATELY *correctly*

teaching a...things	Acts 18:25
handling a...word	2 Tim 2:15

ACCURSED *damned*

camp of Israel a	Josh 6:18
be *thought* a	Is 65:20
Depart...a ones	Matt 25:41
let him be a	Gal 1:8
in greed, a children	2 Pet 2:14

ACCUSATION *charge of wrong*

wrote an a against	Ezra 4:6
find a ground of a	Dan 6:4
What a do you	John 18:29
a against my nation	Acts 28:19
Do not receive an a	1 Tim 5:19

ACCUSE *testify against*

a-d his brother	Deut 19:18
a-s you in judgment	Is 54:17
He was being a-d	Matt 27:12
a-ing...vehemently	Luke 23:10
a you before the	John 5:45
alternately a-ing	Rom 2:15
not a-d of dissipation	Titus 1:6
unjustly a-ing us	3 John 10

ACCUSER *complainant*

they act as my a-s	Ps 109:4
instructing his a-s	Acts 23:30
when the a-s stood	Acts 25:18
a of our brethren	Rev 12:10

ACHAIA

province of Greece	Acts 18:12
	Rom 15:26; 1 Cor 16:15

ACHAN

stole from Jericho	Josh 7:1
executed by people	Josh 7:25

ACKNOWLEDGE *confess*

I a-d my sin	Ps 32:5
all your ways a Him	Prov 3:6
Pharisees a them all	Acts 23:8
see fit to a God	Rom 1:28

ACQUAINTED *become familiar*

a with all my ways	Ps 139:3

a with grief   Is 53:3

ACQUAINTANCE *friend*

a-s are...estranged Job 19:13
dread to my a-s Ps 31:11
removed my a-s far Ps 88:8
relatives and a-s Luke 2:44
And all His a-s Luke 23:49

ACQUIRE *get, purchase*

a property in it Gen 34:10
have a-d Ruth Ruth 4:10
a wise counsel Prov 1:5
You have a-d riches Ezek 28:4
Do not a gold Matt 10:9

ACQUIT *declare innocent*

not a me of my guilt Job 10:14
A me of hidden *faults* Ps 19:12
You will not be a-ted Jer 49:12

ACT (n) *deed, work*

a destestable a Lev 20:13
mighty a-s as Thine Deut 3:24
every abominable a Deut 12:31
the a-s of Solomon 1 Kin 11:41
over the rebellious a Mic 7:18

ACT (v) *behave*

they refuse to a Prov 21:7
I a-ed ignorantly 1 Tim 1:13
So speak and so a James 2:12
are a-ing faithfully 3 John 5

ACTION *behavior, work*

a-s are weighed 1 Sam 2:3
a-s of a...harlot Ezek 16:30
plan or a should be Acts 5:38
gird your minds for a 1 Pet 1:13

ADAM

1 *first man* Gen 2:20
 fall of man Gen 3:6,7
 type of Christ Rom 5:14
 compared to Jesus 1 Cor 15:22
2 *site in Jordan Valley* Josh 3:16

ADAR

twelfth month of Hebrew
 calendar Ezra 6:15
month of Purim Esth 3:7;39:19ff

ADD

a to your yoke 1 Kin 12:11

a-ing to the wrath Neh 13:18
not a to His words Prov 30:6
if anyone a-s to them Rev 22:18

ADJURE *charge solemnly*

many times...I a 1 Kin 22:16
I a you, O daughters Song 3:5
I a you by Jesus Acts 19:13

ADMINISTRATION

a of the province Dan 3:12
healings, helps, a-s 1 Cor 12:28
in our a of this 2 Cor 8:20
a of the mystery Eph 3:9

ADMONISH *warn*

prophets...had a-ed Neh 9:26
How shall I a you Lam 2:13
not cease to a each Acts 20:31
able also to a one Rom 15:14
a-ing one another Col 3:16
a the unruly 1 Thess 5:14
a him as a brother 2 Thess 3:15

ADONIJAH

1 *son of David* 2 Sam 3:4
 aspired to throne 1 Kin 1:5ff
 pardoned 1 Kin 1:52ff
 executed 1 Kin 2:25
2 *Levite* 2 Chr 17:8
3 *of the restoration* Neh 10:16

ADOPTION *acceptance*

spirit of a as sons Rom 8:15
to whom belongs...a Rom 9:4
receive the a as sons Gal 4:5
predestined us to a Eph 1:5

ADORN *array, clothe*

A yourself with Job 40:10
as a bride a-s herself Is 61:10
a-ed with beautiful Luke 21:5
women to a 1 Tim 2:9
a the doctrine of God Titus 2:10
a-ed with gold Rev 17:4
as a bride a-ed Rev 21:2

ADULTERER

a and the adulteress Lev 20:10
eye of the a waits Job 24:15
associate with a-s Ps 50:18
a-s, nor effeminate 1 Cor 6:9
a-s God will judge Heb 13:4

ADULTERESS

a shall surely be   Lev 20:10
a who flatters with   Prov 2:16
mouth of an a   Prov 22:14
You a wife, who   Ezek 16:32
they are a-es   Ezek 23:45
shall be called an a   Rom 7:3

ADULTERY

shall not commit a   Ex 20:14
man who commits a   Lev 20:10
a-ies of faithless   Jer 3:8
worn out by a-ies   Ezek 23:43
committed a with her   Matt 5:28
woman commits a   Matt 5:32
Do not commit a   Luke 18:20
eyes full of a   2 Pet 2:14

ADVANCE ahead, beyond

old, a-d in age   Gen 24:1
a-d in *years*   1 Sam 17:12
have told you in a   Matt 24:25
both a-d in years   Luke 1:7
a-ing in Judaism   Gal 1:14

ADVANTAGE benefit, profit

lead surely to a   Prov 21:5
What a does man   Eccl 1:3
Wisdom has the a   Eccl 10:10
a that I go away   John 16:7
what a has the Jew   Rom 3:1
no a be taken of us   2 Cor 2:11
sake of *gaining an a*   Jude 16

ADVERSARY foe, opponent

an a to your a-ies   Ex 23:22
an a to Solomon   1 Kin 11:14
Lest my a-ies rejoice   Ps 13:4
a-ies and my enemies   Ps 27:2
redeemed...from the a   Ps 78:42
crush his a-ies   Ps 89:23
there are many a-ies   1 Cor 16:9
consume the a-ies   Heb 10:27
Your a, the devil   1 Pet 5:8

ADVERSITY distress, misfortune

death and a   Deut 30:15
not accept a   Job 2:10
relief from...a   Ps 94:13
falls into a   Prov 13:17
A pursues sinners   Prov 13:21

ADVICE counsel

forsook the a   1 Kin 12:13

a of the young   2 Chr 10:14
a of the cunning   Job 5:13
they took his a   Acts 5:40
have followed my a   Acts 27:21

ADVISER counselor

with his a Ahuzzath   Gen 26:26
Pharaoh's wisest a-s   Is 19:11

ADVOCATE defender, witness

my a is on high   Job 16:19
A with the Father   1 John 2:1

AFFECTION devotion, love

set His a to love   Deut 10:15
in your own a-s   2 Cor 6:12
a of Christ Jesus   Phil 1:8
fond a for you   1 Thess 2:8

AFFLICT (v) oppress, trouble

a with hard labor   Ex 1:11
not a any widow   Ex 22:22
Egyptians...a-ed us   Deut 26:6
bind him to a him   Judg 16:5
the wicked a them   2 Sam 7:10
They a-ed his feet   Ps 105:18
He was a-ed   Is 63:9
will a no longer   Nah 1:12
were sick or a-ed   Acts 5:16
are a-ed in every   2 Cor 4:8
those who a you   2 Thess 1:6
a-ed, ill-treated   Heb 11:37

AFFLICTED (n) troubled

save an a people   2 Sam 22:28
to catch the a   Ps 10:9
justice to the a   Ps 82:3
LORD supports the a   Ps 147:6
days of the a   Prov 15:15
O a one   Is 54:11
good news to the a   Is 61:1

AFFLICTION oppression

my a and the toil   Gen 31:42
the land of my a   Gen 41:52
the bread of a   Deut 16:3
LORD saw the a   2 Kin 14:26
Thou didst see the a   Neh 9:9
afflicted in their a   Job 36:15
Look upon my a   Ps 25:18
a severe a   Eccl 6:2
a or persecution   Mark 4:17
healed of her a   Mark 5:29
a-s await me   Acts 20:23

out of much a   2 Cor 2:4
great ordeal of a   2 Cor 8:2
to suffer a   1 Thess 3:4

AFRAID *dreading, fearful*

a because...naked   Gen 3:10
a to look at God   Ex 3:6
a and fainthearted   Deut 20:8
Whoever is a   Judg 7:3
a of the terror   Ps 91:5
not a of the snow   Prov 31:21
a to swear   Eccl 9:2
a of man who dies   Is 51:12
a to take Mary   Matt 1:20
were a of Him   Mark 11:18
Do not be a, Mary   Luke 1:30
a of those who kill   Luke 12:4
a of the people   Luke 22:2
a, lest the serpent   2 Cor 11:3
Do not be a   Rev 1:17

AGABUS

prophet   Acts 11:28;21:10

AGE *period, year*

David reached old a   1 Chr 23:1
a should speak   Job 32:7
either in this a   Matt 12:32
the end of the a   Matt 13:40
sons of this a are   Luke 16:8
in the a-s to come   Eph 2:7
hidden...past a-s   Col 1:26
in the present a   Titus 2:12

AGED *old*

Wisdom is...a men   Job 12:12
a are among us   Job 15:10
refined, a wine   Is 25:6
Paul, the a   Philem 9

AGONY *anguish*

a has seized me   2 Sam 1:9
A like...childbirth   Jer 50:43
in a in this flame   Luke 16:24
in a He was praying   Luke 22:44
the a of death   Acts 2:24

AGREE *consent*

if two of you a   Matt 18:19
did you not a   Matt 20:13
Jews had already a-d   John 9:22
have a-d together   Acts 5:9
words...Prophets a   Acts 15:15
a with sound words   1 Tim 6:3

AGREEMENT *accord*

an a in writing   Neh 9:38
Saul was in hearty a   Acts 8:1
a has the temple   2 Cor 6:16
three are in a   1 John 5:8

AGRIPPA

1 *Herod Agrippa I see* **HEROD**
2 *Herod Agrippa II see* **HEROD**

AHAB

1 *son of Omri*   1 Kin 16:29
  king of Israel   1 Kin 16:28
  married Jezebel   1 Kin 16:31
  idolater   1 Kin 16:33
2 *false prophet*   Jer 29:21,22

AHASUERUS

1 *Persian king, Xerxes I*
       Ezra 4:6 Book of Esther
2 *father of Darius the Mede*
       Dan 9:1

AHAZ

1 *son of Jotham*   2 Kin 15:38
  king of Judah   2 Kin 16:2
2 *line of Jonathan*   1 Chr 8:35

AHIJAH/AHIAH

1 *prophet of Shiloh*   1 Kin 14:2
2 *of Issachar*   1 Kin 15:27
3 *son of Jerahmeel*   1 Chr 2:25
4 *the Pelonite*   1 Chr 11:36
5 *under Nehemiah*   Neh 10:26

AHIMELECH

1 *high priest*   1 Sam 22:16
  gave bread and sword
    to David   1 Sam 21:1-9
2 *Hittite*   1 Sam 26:6,7

AHITHOPHEL

counselor of David   2 Sam 15:22
       1 Chr 27:33

AI

place near Bethel   Gen 12:8
defeat of Israelites   Josh 7:5
captured   Josh 8:23,29

AIJALON

1 *city of refuge*   Josh 10:12
  valley   Josh 19:42
  Levitical city   Josh 21:24
2 *Zebulunite town*   Judg 12:12

AIR

AIR *breeze, sky*

no a can come	Job 41:16
They pant for a	Jer 14:6
birds of the a	Matt 6:26
not beating the a	1 Cor 9:26
speaking into the a	1 Cor 14:9
power of the a	Eph 2:2
the Lord in the a	1 Thess 4:17

ALABASTER *whitish stone*

stones, and a	1 Chr 29:2
pillars of a	Song 5:15
brought an a vial	Luke 7:37

ALARM (n) *danger, warning*

when you blow an a	Num 10:5
The a of war	Jer 4:19
shout of a at noon	Jer 20:16
a on My...mountain	Joel 2:1

ALARM (v) *frighten, warn*

he is not a-ed	Job 40:23
interpretation a you	Dan 4:19
thoughts a-ed him	Dan 5:6
being much a-ed	Acts 10:4
in no way a-ed by	Phil 1:28

ALERT (n) *watch*

be on the a	Matt 24:42
be a and sober	1 Thess 5:6

ALERT (v) *be watchful*

keeping a in it	Col 4:2
let us be a	1 Thess 5:6

ALEXANDER

1 *son of Simon of Cyrene*	
	Mark 15:21
2 *of priestly family*	Acts 4:6
3 *Ephesian Jew*	Acts 19:33
4 *apostate teacher*	1 Tim 1:20
5 *enemy of Paul*	2 Tim 4:14

ALEXANDRIAN

1 *of Alexandria*	Acts 6:9
2 *ship*	Acts 27:6;28:11
3 *Apollos*	Acts 18:24

ALIEN *foreigner, stranger*

love for the a	Deut 10:19
give it to the a	Deut 14:21
Our houses to a-s	Lam 5:2
a-s in a foreign land	Acts 7:6
no longer...a-s	Eph 2:19

he lived as an a	Heb 11:9
I urge you as a-s	1 Pet 2:11

ALIENATE *estrange*

Lest I be a-d	Jer 6:8
a this choice *portion*	Ezek 48:14
were formerly a-d	Col 1:21

ALIVE

Is your father still a	Gen 43:7
down a to Sheol	Num 16:33
go down a to Sheol	Ps 55:15
may keep a a heifer	Is 7:21
when He was...a	Matt 27:63
heard...He was a	Mark 16:11
presented Himself a	Acts 1:3
yet the spirit is a	Rom 8:10
all shall be made a	1 Cor 15:22
made us a together	Eph 2:5
a in the spirit	1 Pet 3:18
I am a forevermore	Rev 1:18

ALLEGIANCE *loyalty*

pledged a to King	1 Chr 29:24
he pledged his a	Ezek 17:18

ALLIANCE *agreement*

formed a marriage a	1 Kin 3:1
after an a is made	Dan 11:23

ALLIED *joined*

a...by marriage	2 Chr 18:1
throne of...a	Ps 94:20

ALLOT *apportion, divide*

only a it to Israel	Josh 13:6
a Him a portion	Is 53:12
a-ted to each...faith	Rom 12:3

ALLOTMENT *portion*

an a from Pharaoh	Gen 47:22
as a perpetual a	Num 18:19
Jacob is the a	Deut 32:9
set apart the...a	Ezek 48:20

ALLOW *permit*

not a the destroyer	Ex 12:23
whether his body a-s	Lev 15:3
a Thy Holy One	Ps 16:10
Nor a Thy Holy One	Acts 2:27
not be a-ed to live	Acts 22:22
a you to be tempted	1 Cor 10:13
not a a woman	1 Tim 2:12

ALMIGHTY *all-powerful*

I am God A	Gen 17:1
vision of the A	Num 24:4
A has afflicted me	Ruth 1:21
limits of the A	Job 11:7
A was yet with me	Job 29:5
destruction from...A	Joel 1:15
Lord God, the A	Rev 4:8
the A, reigns	Rev 19:6

ALMOND

a and plane trees	Gen 30:37
shaped like a *blossoms*	Ex 37:19
and it bore ripe a-s	Num 17:8

ALMS *charity*

therefore you give a	Matt 6:2
a may be in secret	Matt 6:4
a to the *Jewish*	Acts 10:2
bring a to my nation	Acts 24:17

ALONE

So He let him a	Ex 4:26
Leave me a, for my	Job 7:16
not live on bread a	Matt 4:4
He was praying a	Luke 9:18
I am not a *in it*	John 8:16
receiving but you a	Phil 4:15
and not by faith a	James 2:24

ALOUD *joyful, piercing*

crying a as she	2 Sam 13:19
read a from the book	Neh 13:1
I will cry a	Ps 77:1
Sing a with gladness	Jer 31:7
The king called a	Dan 5:7
began to weep a	Acts 20:37

ALPHA

first letter of Gr. alphabet	Rev 1:8
title of Jesus Christ	Rev 21:6
expresses eternalness of God	Rev 22:13

ALTAR *place of sacrifice*

offerings on the a	Gen 8:20
Moses built an a	Ex 17:15
fire on the a	Lev 6:9
Gideon built an a	Judg 6:24
erect an a to	2 Sam 24:18
go to the a of God	Ps 43:4
a-s may become waste	Ezek 6:6
offering at the a	Matt 5:23

a that sanctifies	Matt 23:19
golden a of incense	Heb 9:4
we have an a	Heb 13:10
horns of the golden a	Rev 9:13

ALWAYS *ever, forever*

fear the LORD...a	Deut 14:23
He will not a strive	Ps 103:9
fear of the LORD a	Prov 23:17
a loses his temper	Prov 29:11
will I a be angry	Is 57:16
I am with you a	Matt 28:20
poor you a have	Mark 14:7
Rejoice in the Lord a	Phil 4:4
a be with...Lord	1 Thess 4:17
I shall a be ready	2 Pet 1:12

AMALEKITES

descendants of Esau	Gen 36:12
tribe in Negev and Sinai	
	Ex 17:8,9;Num 14:25
	1 Sam 15:7;1 Chr 4:43

AMASA

1 son of Abigail	1 Chr 2:17
Absalom's commander	
	2 Sam 17:25
pardoned	2 Sam 19:13
2 an Ephraimite	2 Chr 28:12

AMAZED *astonished, astounded*

are a at His rebuke	Job 26:11
a at His teaching	Mark 1:22
heard Him were a	Luke 2:47
were a and marveled	Acts 2:7
whole earth was a	Rev 13:3

AMAZEMENT *astonishment*

a came upon them	Luke 4:36
with wonder and a	Acts 3:10

AMAZIAH

1 king of Judah	2 Kin 12:21
son of Joash	2 Kin 14:1
2 a Simeonite	1 Chr 4:34
3 son of Hilkiah	1 Chr 6:45
4 a priest of Bethel	Amos 7:10

AMBASSADOR *envoy*

a-s of peace weep	Is 33:7
a-s for Christ	2 Cor 5:20
an a in chains	Eph 6:20

AMBITION *design, intention*

out of selfish a	Phil 1:17

9

AMBITION

a to lead a quiet	1 Thess 4:11
jealousy...selfish **a**	James 3:14

AMBUSH (n) *cover, hiding place*

a for the city	Josh 8:2
rise from *your* **a**	Josh 8:7
Israel set men in **a**	Judg 20:29
a...behind them	2 Chr 13:13
Place men in **a**	Jer 51:12

AMBUSH (v) *lie in wait*

going to **a** the city	Josh 8:4
a the innocent	Prov 1:11
a their own lives	Prov 1:18

AMEN *so be it*

people shall say, **A**	Deut 27:16
the LORD forever! **A**	Ps 89:52
glory forever...**A**	Phil 4:20
the **A**, the faithful	Rev 3:14
A, Come, Lord Jesus	Rev 22:20

AMMONITES

tribes E of Jordan	Gen 19:38
defeated Israel	Judg 3:13
hired Arameans	2 Sam 10:6
fought against Judah	2 Kin 24:2

AMNON

eldest son of David	2 Sam 3:2
raped his sister	2 Sam 13:2ff
ordered killed	2 Sam 13:28

AMON

1 *Ahab's governor*	1 Kin 22:26
2 *king of Judah*	2 Kin 21:18-26
3 *of the Nethinims*	Neh 7:59
4 *Egyptian deity*	Jer 46:25

AMORITES

tribe on both sides of Jordan
Gen 15:16; Ex 24:11; Deut 1:27
Judg 11:23; Amos 2:9

AMOS

prophet to Israel Book of Amos

AMOUNT *measure*

daily **a** of bricks	Ex 5:19
a of your valuation	Lev 27:23
large **a** of bronze	1 Chr 18:8

ABRAM

1 *father of Moses*	Ex 6:18-20
	1 Chr 23:13
2 *son of Bani*	Ezra 10:34

ANAK/ANAKIM

pre-Israelite tribe of Palestine
Num 13:22-33
giants Deut 2:10; Josh 14:15

ANANIAS

1 *deceived Jerusalem church*	
	Acts 5:1-5
2 *Damascus Christian*	
	Acts 9:10,17
3 *high priest*	Acts 23:2

ANCESTORS *forefathers*

blessings of my **a**	Gen 49:26
the **a** have set	Deut 19:14
iniquities of their **a**	Jer 11:10

ANCHOR

they weighed **a**	Acts 27:13
they cast four **a**-s	Acts 27:29
an **a** of the soul	Heb 6:19

ANCIENT *aged, old*

of the **a** mountains	Deut 33:15
the records are **a**	1 Chr 4:22
keep to the **a** path	Job 22:15
O **a** doors	Ps 24:9
A of Days	Dan 7:9
the **a**-s were told	Matt 5:21
from **a** generations	Acts 15:21
not spare the **a** world	2 Pet 2:5

ANDREW

fisherman	Matt 4:18
brother of Peter	Matt 4:18
receives Jesus	John 1:40-42
apostle	Luke 6:14

ANGEL *divine messenger*

send His **a** before	Gen 24:7
a-s...were ascending	Gen 28:12
an **a** to Jerusalem	1 Chr 21:15
bread of **a**-s	Ps 78:25
Praise Him, all His **a**-s	Ps 148:2
a of His presence	Is 63:9
a who was speaking	Zech 4:4
give His **a**-s charge	Matt 4:6
a Gabriel was sent	Luke 1:26
they are like **a**-s	Luke 20:36
two **a**-s in white	John 20:12
like the face of an **a**	Acts 6:15
as an **a** of light	2 Cor 11:14
worship of the **a**-s	Col 2:18
entertained **a**-s	Heb 13:2

God did not spare **a-s**   2 Pet 2:4
a of the church   Rev 2:1

ANGEL OF THE LORD

a called to Abraham   Gen 22:15
a took his stand   Num 22:22
I have seen the a   Judg 6:22
a said to Elijah   2 Kin 1:3
a destroying   1 Chr 21:12
a encamps around those   Ps 34:7
a admonished Joshua   Zech 3:6
a commanded him   Matt 1:24
a appeared to Joseph   Matt 2:13
a...opened the gates   Acts 5:19

ANGER *indignation, wrath*

My a will be kindled   Ex 22:24
Moses' a burned   Ex 32:19
from His burning a   Deut 13:17
a with their idols   1 Kin 16:13
a kills the simple   Job 5:2
not turn back His a   Job 9:13
not rebuke me in Thine a   Ps 6:1
a is but for a moment   Ps 30:5
He who is slow to a   Prov 14:29
a man *given* to a   Prov 22:24
a of the LORD   Is 5:25
sun go down...a   Eph 4:26
put...aside: a   Col 3:8
slow to a   James 1:19

ANGRY *enraged, indignant*

Why are you a   Gen 4:6
king became very a   Esth 1:12
lest He become a   Ps 2:12
a man stirs up strife   Prov 29:22
a beyond measure   Is 64:9
and a no more   Ezek 16:42
a with his brother   Matt 5:22
Be a...do not sin   Eph 4:26
a with this generation   Heb 3:10

ANGUISH *distress, pain*

writhed in great a   Esth 4:4
My heart is in a   Ps 55:4
land of distress and a   Is 30:6
A has seized us   Jer 6:24
and a of heart   2 Cor 2:4

ANIMAL *beast, creature*

from man to a-s   Gen 6:7
lies with an a   Ex 22:19
the fat of the a   Lev 7:25

wild **a-s** of the field   Jer 27:6
a blemished a   Mal 1:14
four-footed **a-s**   Acts 10:12
like unreasoning **a-s**   2 Pet 2:12

ANNA

prophetess   Luke 2:36

ANNAS

high priest   Luke 3:2
  John 18:13ff

ANNIHILATE *destroy*

to a all the Jews   Esth 3:13
My enemy **a-d** them   Lam 2:22
to destroy and a   Dan 11:44
let it be **a-d**   Zech 11:9

ANNOUNCE *proclaim*

Who **a-s** peace   Is 52:7
I shall a My words   Jer 18:2
a-ing to...disciples   John 20:18
a-d...the Righteous   Acts 7:52

ANNUL *dismiss, make void*

he shall a her vow   Num 30:8
husband has **a-ed**   Num 30:12
not a Thy covenant   Jer 14:21
a-s one of the least   Matt 5:19

ANOINT *sprinkle oil upon*

a them and ordain   Ex 28:41
a Aaron and his sons   Ex 30:30
LORD **a-ed** you king   1 Sam 15:17
a-ed my head with oil   Ps 23:5
a the most holy *place*   Dan 9:24
has **a-ed** My body   Mark 14:8
did not a My head   Luke 7:46
and **a-ed** my eyes   John 9:11
a-ed...feet of Jesus   John 12:3
a-ed Him...Spirit   Acts 10:38
a-ing him with oil   James 5:14

ANOINTED (adj) *consecrated*

if the a priest sins   Lev 4:3
not touch My a   1 Chr 16:22
a cherub who   Ezek 28:14
the two a ones   Zech 4:14

ANOINTED (n) *consecrated one*

walk before My a   1 Sam 2:35
he is the LORD'S a   1 Sam 24:10
against His a   Ps 2:2

ANOINTING

ANOINTING (adj) *consecration*

spices for the **a** oil   Ex 25:6
shall be a holy **a** oil   Ex 30:31
for the LORD'S **a** oil   Lev 10:7

ANOINTING (n) *consecration*

a shall qualify them   Ex 40:15
a from the Holy   1 John 2:20
His **a** teaches you   1 John 2:27

ANSWER (n) *response*

consider what **a** I   1 Chr 21:12
the king sent an **a**   Ezra 4:17
Who gives a right **a**   Prov 24:26
amazed at...His **a-s**   Luke 2:47

ANSWER (v) *respond*

anyone who will **a** you   Job 5:1
The LORD **a-ed** me   Ps 118:5
king **a-ed** and said   Dan 2:8
Jesus **a-ing** said   Matt 3:15
who **a-s** back to God   Rom 9:20

ANT *insect*

to the **a**, O sluggard   Prov 6:6
a-s are not a strong   Prov 30:25

ANTELOPE *animal*

Like an **a** in a net   Is 51:20

ANTICHRIST *foe of Christ*

a-s have arisen   1 John 2:18
This is the **a**   1 John 2:22
the *spirit* of the **a**   1 John 4:3
deceiver and the **a**   2 John 7

ANTIOCH

city in Syria   Acts 6:5;11:19,26
city in Asia Minor   Acts 13:14
    Acts 14:19

ANTIPAS

1 *Pergamum martyr*   Rev 2:13
2 *Herod Antipas see* **HEROD**

ANXIETY *sorrow*

a because of my sin   Ps 38:18
There is a **a** by the sea   Jer 49:23
casting all your **a**   1 Pet 5:7

ANXIOUS *concern, worry*

and become **a** for us   1 Sam 9:5
not be **a** in...drought   Jer 17:8
my spirit is **a** to   Dan 2:3

not be **a** for your life   Matt 6:25
not be **a** for tomorrow   Matt 6:34
be **a** beforehand   Mark 13:11
a can add a *single*   Luke 12:25
Be **a** for nothing   Phil 4:6

APART *separate*

So they set **a** Kedesh   Josh 20:7
tear their fetters **a**   Ps 2:3
a from your Father   Matt 10:29
a from Him nothing   John 1:3
a from Me you can   John 15:5
faith **a** from works   Rom 3:28

APOLLOS

Alexandrian Jew   Acts 18:24
taught at Ephesus   Acts 18:25
taught at Corinth   1 Cor 3:4,6

APOSTASY *faithlessness*

a-ies are numerous   Jer 5:6
Turned away in...**a**   Jer 8:5
I will heal their **a**   Hos 14:4
unless the **a** comes   2 Thess 2:3

APOSTLE *sent with authority*

the twelve **a-s**   Matt 10:2
named as **a-s**   Luke 6:13
called *as* an **a**   Rom 1:1
an **a** of Gentiles   Rom 11:13
fit to be called an **a**   1 Cor 15:9
men are false **a-s**   2 Cor 11:13
He gave some **a-s**   Eph 4:11
Jesus, the **A** and   Heb 3:1
a-s of the Lamb   Rev 21:14

APOSTLESHIP *office of apostle*

received grace and **a**   Rom 1:5
seal of my **a**   1 Cor 9:2
Peter in *his* **a** to   Gal 2:8

APPAREL *clothing, garment*

of gold on your **a**   2 Sam 1:24
majestic in His **a**   Is 63:1
men...in dazzling **a**   Luke 24:4
put on his royal **a**   Acts 12:21

APPEAL *ask, entreat*

standing and **a-ing**   Acts 16:9
I **a** to Caesar   Acts 25:11
Paul **a-ed** to be held   Acts 25:21
a-ed to...Emperor   Acts 25:25
a to him as a father   1 Tim 5:1
love's sake I...**a**   Philem 9

APPEAR *become visible*

LORD a-ed to Abram   Gen 12:7
glory of the LORD a-ed   Ex 3:2
a-ed on the wings   2 Sam 22:11
and a-ed to many   Matt 27:53
first a-ed to Mary   Mark 16:9
who, a-ing in glory   Luke 9:31
a-ed to them tongues   Acts 2:3
we must all a before   2 Cor 5:10
a-ing of the glory   Titus 2:13
shall a a second time   Heb 9:28
Chief Shepherd a-s   1 Pet 5:4
not a-ed as yet   1 John 3:2

APPEARANCE *countenance*

handsome in...a   Gen 39:6
the a of the angel   Judg 13:6
at the outward a   1 Sam 16:7
a is blacker than soot   Lam 4:8
lapis lazuli in a   Ezek 1:26
they neglect their a   Matt 6:16
judge according to a   John 7:24
a of His coming   2 Thess 2:8
a of the locusts   Rev 9:7

APPEASE *moderate, mollify*

I will a him   Gen 32:20
wise man will a it   Prov 16:14
have a-ed My wrath   Zech 6:8

APPETITE *desire, hunger*

our a is gone   Num 11:6
a of the young lions   Job 38:39
man of *great* a   Prov 23:2
a is not satisfied   Eccl 6:7
enlarged his a like   Hab 2:5
whose god is *their* a   Phil 3:19

APPLE *fruit*

as the a of the eye   Ps 17:8
Like a-s of gold   Prov 25:11
Refresh me with a-s   Song 2:5
touches the a of His   Zech 2:8

APPOINT *assign, commission*

shall a *as a penalty*   Ex 21:23
I will a over you   Lev 26:16
who a-ed Moses   1 Sam 12:6
to a their relatives   1 Chr 15:16
a magistrates and   Ezra 7:25
there is a harvest a-ed   Hos 6:11
a-ed elders for them   Acts 14:23
a-ed a preacher and   1 Tim 2:7

For the Law a-s men   Heb 7:28

APPORTION *distribute*

a the inheritance   Num 34:29
a this land   Josh 13:7
He a-s our fields   Mic 2:4

APPROPRIATE *suitable*

blessing a to him   Gen 49:28
eat at the a time   Eccl 10:17
a to repentance   Acts 26:20

APPROVAL *consent*

loved the a of men   John 12:43
give hearty a to   Rom 1:32
men of old gained a   Heb 11:2

APPROVE *accept, attest*

the Lord does not a   Lam 3:36
too pure to a evil   Hab 1:13
standing by a-ing   Acts 22:20
and a-ed by men   Rom 14:18
present yourself a-d   2 Tim 2:15

AQUILA

a *native of Pontus*   Acts 18:2
Corinthian Christian   Acts 18:18
co-worker with Paul   Rom 16:3

ARAB

1 *town in Judah*   Josh 15:52
2 *ethnic identity*   1 Kin 10:15
    Neh 2:19; Is 13:20

ARABAH

1 *desert steppe*   Is 35:1,6
    Jer 52:7
2 *Jordan rift valley*   Deut 1:1
    Josh 3:17
3 *Dead Sea*   Josh 3:16
    2 Kin 14:25

ARABIA

land SE of Palestine   Is 21:13
    Ezek 30:5; Gal 1:17;4:25

ARAM

1 *son of Shem*   Gen 10:22,23
2 *Syria and N Mesopotamia*
    Num 23:7; 1 Kin 11:25
    2 Kin 13:19; Is 7:8

ARAMAIC

Semitic language   2 Kin 18:26
    Ezra 4:7; Is 36:11; Dan 2:4

ARAMEANS

tribes of Aram   2 Sam 8:5
     1 Kin 20:16; 2 Kin 24:2

ARARAT

mountain range of Armenia
Gen 8:4; 2 Kin 19:37; Jer 51:27

ARAUNAH

*Jebusite owner of threshing
    floor on Mt. Moriah*
     2 Sam 24:16,18
*David purchases threshing floor
    for altar and later temple*
     2 Sam 24:23,24

also **Ornan**

ARCHANGEL

voice of *the* **a**   1 Thess 4:16
But Michael the **a**   Jude 9

ARCHELAUS *see* HEROD

ARCHER *bowman*

the **a-s** hit him   1 Sam 31:3
a-s shot king Josiah 2 Chr 35:23
a-s equipped with bows Ps 78:9
an **a** who wounds   Prov 26:10

ARCHIPPUS

Colossian Christian   Col 4:17
co-worker with Paul   Philem 2

AREOPAGUS

hill and council in Athens
     Acts 17:19,22

ARGUE *dispute, question*

I will **a** my ways   Job 13:15
hastily to **a** *your case* Prov 25:8
Pharisees...a with   Mark 8:11
scribes **a-ing** with   Mark 9:14
a-ing with the...*Jews* Acts 9:29

ARGUMENT *disagreement*

Please hear my **a**   Job 13:6
mouth are no **a-s**   Ps 38:14
a arose among them Luke 9:46

ARIEL

1 *a Moabite*   2 Sam 23:20
     1 Chr 11:22
2 *applied to Jerusalem* Is 29:1ff
3 *sent by Ezra*   Ezra 8:16

ARISE *rise, stand*

A, walk about the   Gen 13:17
Abraham **arose** early Gen 19:27
will **a** and play   Deut 31:16
you have **a-n** early 1 Sam 29:10
arose and tore his robe Job 1:20
when God **a-s**   Job 31:14
A, O Lord; save me   Ps 3:7
Though war **a**   Ps 27:3
A, my darling   Song 2:13
a-n *anyone* greater Matt 11:11
false prophets will **a** Matt 24:11
arose from the dead Acts 10:41
A, and be baptized Acts 22:16
a from the dead   Eph 5:14
arose loud voices   Rev 11:15

ARISTARCHUS

Thessalonian Christian Acts 20:4
     Acts 27:2
co-worker with Paul   Col 4:10
     Philem 24

ARK *chest, vessel*

a *of gopher wood*   Gen 6:14
into the **a** of Noah   Gen 7:9
a of acacia wood   Ex 37:1
a of the covenant   Josh 4:7
Noah entered the **a** Matt 24:38
a of His covenant   Rev 11:19

ARM (n) *part of body*

the everlasting **a-s** Deut 33:27
a without strength   Job 26:2
a-s of the wicked   Ps 37:17
His holy **a** have gained Ps 98:1
a seal on your **a**   Song 8:6
be carried in the **a-s**   Is 60:4
took...in His **a-s**   Mark 10:16
with an uplifted **a**   Acts 13:17

ARM (v) *mobilize*

A men from among Num 31:3
a-ed for battle   Num 32:29
a-ed with iron   2 Sam 23:7
a yourselves also   1 Pet 4:1

ARMAGEDDON

see HAR-MAGEDON

ARMED (adj) *mobilized*

the **a** men went   Josh 6:13
their **a** camps   1 Sam 28:1
So the **a** men left 2 Chr 28:14

like an a man — Prov 6:11

ARMOR *protective device*

a joint of the a — 1 Kin 22:34
strip off his outer a — Job 41:13
all his a on which — Luke 11:22
put on...a of light ⌠ Rom 13:12
full a of God — Eph 6:11

ARMY *host, war*

not go out with the a — Deut 24:5
like the a of God — 1 Chr 12:22
a ready for battle — 2 Chr 26:11
officers of the a — Neh 2:9
forth with our a-ies — Ps 60:10
exceedingly great a — Ezek 37:10
a-ies...in heaven — Rev 19:14
and against His a — Rev 19:19

ARNON

river in Gilead — Num 21:13
valley in Moab — Deut 2:24

AROMA *odor*

a soothing a — Gen 8:21
his a has not changed — Jer 48:11
through us...sweet a — 2 Cor 2:14
a from life to life — 2 Cor 2:16
as a fragrant a — Eph 5:2

AROUSE *raise, stir*

A Thyself to help me — Ps 59:4
a-s for you the spirits — Is 14:9
a-d one from the north — Is 41:25
He will a *His* zeal — Is 42:13
LORD has a-d the spirit — Jer 51:11
Jews a-d the devout — Acts 13:50

ARRANGE *set in order*

a what belongs on it — Ex 40:4
shall a the pieces — Lev 1:8
he a-d the wood — 1 Kin 18:33
thus he had a-d it — Acts 20:13

ARRAY (n) *arrangement, order*

went up in martial a — Ex 13:18
in battle a — Josh 4:12
Worship...in holy a — 1 Chr 16:29
holy a, from the womb — Ps 110:3

ARRAY (v) *adorn, clothe*

Israel a-ed for battle — Judg 20:20
let them a the man — Esth 6:9
A yourselves before — Job 33:5
God so a-s the grass — Matt 6:30

a-ed Him in a purple — John 19:2

ARREST *restrain*

he a-ed Jeremiah — Jer 37:13
Herod had John a-ed — Matt 14:3
and clubs to a Me — Matt 26:55
proceeded to a Peter — Acts 12:3

ARROGANCE *pride*

your a has come — 2 Kin 19:28
Pride and a and — Prov 8:13
a of the proud — Is 13:11
a, pride, and fury — Is 16:6
a of your heart — Jer 49:16
you boast in your a — James 4:16

ARROGANT *proud*

a men have risen up — Ps 86:14
But a fool is a — Prov 14:16
a toward the LORD — Jer 48:26
Knowledge makes a — 1 Cor 8:1
boastful, a, revilers — 2 Tim 3:2
speaking...a *words* — 2 Pet 2:18

ARROW *dart, missile*

shot an a past him — 1 Sam 20:36
a-s of the Almighty — Job 6:4
a cannot make him — Job 41:28
make ready their a — Ps 11:2
broke the flaming a-s — Ps 76:3
sword and a sharp a — Prov 25:18
tongue is a deadly a — Jer 9:8
target for the a — Lam 3:12
deadly a-s of famine — Ezek 5:16

ART *craft*

with their secret a-s — Ex 7:22
the perfumers' a — 2 Chr 16:14

ARTAXERXES

Persian king — Ezra 4:7,8;7:1,12
Neh 2:1;5:14

ARTEMIS

Greek goddess — Acts 19:24ff

ARTICLE *object, vessel*

a-s of silver — Gen 24:53
any wooden a — Lev 11:32
of every precious a — Hos 13:15
every a of ivory — Rev 18:12

ASA

1 king of Judah — 1 Kin 15:8-14
2 Chr 14:8-16

2 *a Levite*   1 Chr 9:16

ASCEND *go up*

a into the hill   Ps 24:3
If I a to heaven   Ps 139:8
Who has **a-ed** into   Prov 30:4
breath of man **a-s**   Eccl 3:21
has **a-ed** into heaven   John 3:13
Son of Man **a-ing**   John 6:62
a-ed to the Father   John 20:17
who **a-ed** far above   Eph 4:10

ASCENT *hill, rise*

by the a of Heres   Judg 8:13
a of the...Olives   2 Sam 15:30

ASCRIBE *attribute*

have **a-d** to David   1 Sam 18:8
A to the LORD   1 Chr 16:28
a righteousness to   Job 36:3

ASH

but dust and **a-es**   Gen 18:27
from the a heap   1 Sam 2:8
a-es on her head   2 Sam 13:19
a-es were poured   1 Kin 13:5
proverbs of **a-es**   Job 13:12
repent in dust and **a-es** Job 42:6
garland instead of **a-es** Is 61:3
roll in **a-es**   Jer 6:26
sackcloth and **a-es**   Luke 10:13
a-es of a heifer   Heb 9:13

ASHAMED *embarrassed*

naked and were not a   Gen 2:25
Let me never be a   Ps 71:1
a of Me...My words   Mark 8:38
a when He comes   Luke 9:26
not a of the gospel   Rom 1:16
a of the testimony   2 Tim 1:8
God is not a   Heb 11:16
let him not feel a   1 Pet 4:16

ASHDOD

Philistine city   Josh 15:47
                  1 Sam 5:1,6; Amos 1:8

ASHER

1 *eighth son of Jacob* Gen 35:26
                             Gen 49:20
2 *tribe of Israel*   Num 1:41
                  Num 13:13; Rev 7:6
3 *town in Palestine*   Josh 17:7

ASHERAH

Canaanite goddess and symbol
                  Deut 16:21; Judg 6:25
Asherim (pl)
                  1 Kin 14:15; Mic 5:14
Asheroth (pl)
                  Judg 3:7; 2 Chr 19:3

ASHKELON

Philistine city   Judg 1:18
2 Sam 1:20; Jer 47:5; Zeph 2:4

ASHTORETH

1 *Near Eastern goddess*
                  1 Kin 11:5,33; 2 Kin 23:13
Ashtaroth (pl)   Judg 2:13
                  1 Sam 7:4; 31:10
2 *town of Bashan, Manasseh*
                  Deut 1:4; Josh 13:12

ASIA

Roman province of Asia Minor
                  Acts 6:9; Rom 16:5; Rev 1:4

ASK *appeal, beg, inquire*

whatever you a   Ruth 3:11
Two things I **a-ed**   Prov 30:7
A a sign for yourself   Is 7:11
a for the ancient paths   Jer 6:16
A rain from the LORD   Zech 10:1
Give to him who **a-s**   Matt 5:42
A, and it shall be   Matt 7:7
a...believing   Matt 21:22
pray and a, believe   Mark 11:24
Jews a for signs   1 Cor 1:22
let him a of God   James 1:5

ASLEEP *death, rest*

sound a...exhausted   Judg 4:21
they fall a   Ps 90:5
not died, but is a   Matt 9:24
in the stern, a   Mark 4:38
Lazarus...fallen a   John 11:11
said this, he fell a   Acts 7:60
fallen a in Jesus   1 Thess 4:14

ASSAIL *attack*

will you a a man   Ps 62:3
Whoever **a-s** you   Is 54:15
storm was **a-ing** us   Acts 27:20

ASSEMBLE *gather*

a all the congregation   Lev 8:3

A the people to Me Deut 4:10
David a-ed all Israel 1 Chr 13:5
peoples may be a-ed Is 43:9
A...on the mountains Amos 3:9
I will...a all of you Mic 2:12
whole city a-ed to Acts 13:44
a-ed to make war Rev 19:19

ASSEMBLY *congregation*

holy a on the seventh Ex 12:16
the people of the a Lev 16:33
a before the rock Num 20:10
Or calls an a Job 11:10
a of the righteous Ps 1:5
hate the a of evildoers Ps 26:5
proclaim a solemn a Joel 2:15
I delight in...a-ies Amos 5:21
the a was divided Acts 23:7
general a and church Heb 12:23
comes into your a James 2:2

ASSOCIATE (n) *colleague*

All my a-s abhor me Job 19:19
high priest and...a-s Acts 5:21

ASSOCIATE (v) *identify with*

shall they a with 1 Kin 11:2
a with adulterers Ps 50:18
not a with a man Prov 22:24
dared to a with them Acts 5:13
but a with the lowly Rom 12:16
not a with him 2 Thess 3:14

ASSURANCE *confirmation*

no one has a of life Job 24:22
a of understanding Col 2:2
full a of hope Heb 6:11
full a of faith Heb 10:22
a of *things* hoped for Heb 11:1

ASSURE *confirm*

kingdom will be a-ed Dan 4:26
I a you before God Gal 1:20
shall a our heart 1 John 3:19

ASSYRIA

kingdom name from Asshur
        Gen 10:22; 1 Chr 1:17
empire in upper Mesopotamia
    2 Kin 19:17; Is 19:24; Jer 2:36

ASTONISHED *amazed*

will be a and hiss 1 Kin 9:8

a at His teaching Matt 22:33
listeners were a Mark 6:2
were utterly a Mark 7:37
they were all a Luke 1:63

ASTOUNDED *astonished*

prophets will be a Jer 4:9
a at the vision Dan 8:27
were completely a Mark 5:24

ASTRAY *erring, wandering*

a like a lost sheep Ps 119:176
leading *them* a Is 9:16
like sheep have gone a Is 53:6
led my people a Jer 23:32
lead the elect a Mark 13:22
a from the faith 1 Tim 6:21
go a in their heart Heb 3:10
My bond-servants a Rev 2:20

ATHALIAH

1 *daughter of Ahab* 2 Kin 8:26
  wife of Jehoram 2 Chr 22:2
  wicked 2 Kin 11:1
2 *a Benjamite* 1 Chr 8:26
3 *returned exile* Ezra 8:7

ATHENS

leading Greek city Acts 17:15ff

ATONEMENT *expiation*

by which a was made Ex 29:33
shall make a for him Lev 4:35
a before the LORD Lev 14:31
how can I make a 2 Sam 21:3
make a for iniquity Dan 9:24

ATONEMENT, DAY OF

see **DAY OF ATONEMENT**

ATTACK (n) *assault*

at the first a 2 Sam 17:9
king ready for the a Job 15:24
joined in the a Acts 24:9

ATTACK (v) *assault, fall upon*

lest he come and a Gen 32:11
adversary who a-s Num 10:9
and a-ed the camp Judg 8:11
a the Philistines 1 Sam 23:2
it a-ed the plant Jon 4:7
no man will a you Acts 18:10

ATTAIN *acquire*

I cannot a to it   Ps 139:6
woman a-s honor   Prov 11:16
worthy to a to that   Luke 20:35
a-ed righteousness   Rom 9:30
a to the resurrection   Phil 3:11

ATTEND *pay attention to*

a to your priesthood   Num 18:7
thousands were a-ing   Dan 7:10
who a regularly   1 Cor 9:13
a to...business   1 Thess 4:11
ears a to their prayer   1 Pet 3:12

ATTENDANT *helper, servant*

the a of Moses   Num 11:28
king's a-s, who served   Esth 2:2
a-s of...bridegroom   Mark 2:19

ATTENTION *heed, regard*

no a to false words   Ex 5:9
gives a to the word   Prov 16:20
pays a to falsehood   Prov 29:12
they do not pay a   Is 5:12
pay a to myths   1 Tim 1:4
a to the...reading   1 Tim 4:13

ATTIRE *covering, dress*

in his military a   2 Sam 20:8
cupbearers...a   2 Chr 9:4
Him in holy a   2 Chr 20:21

ATTITUDE *frame of mind*

see your father's a   Gen 31:5
a of the righteous   Luke 1:17
Have this a in   Phil 2:5
have a different a   Phil 3:15

AUGUSTUS

name of Caesar Octavianus
    Luke 2:1

see **CAESAR**

AUTHOR *source*

a of their salvation   Heb 2:10
a...perfecter of faith   Heb 12:2

AUTHORITY *power, right*

submit...to her a   Gen 16:9
put...your a on him   Num 27:20
Who gave Him a   Job 34:13
a over...day of death   Eccl 8:8
entrust him with your a   Is 22:21
as *one* having a   Matt 7:29

a on earth to forgive   Matt 9:6
a over unclean spirits   Matt 10:1
All a...given to Me   Matt 28:18
Son of Man has a   Luke 5:24
no a except from God   Rom 13:1
majesty, dominion...a   Jude 25
give a over...nations   Rev 2:26

AVENGE *revenge*

He will a the blood   Deut 32:43
the LORD a me   1 Sam 24:12
Shall I not a Myself   Jer 5:9
I will a their blood   Joel 3:21
a-ing our blood   Rev 6:10

AVENGER *revenger*

The blood a himself   Num 35:19
lest the a of blood   Deut 19:6
a of their evil deeds   Ps 99:8
God, an a who brings   Rom 13:4
Lord is *the* a   1 Thess 4:6

AVOID *refuse*

A it, do not pass by   Prov 4:15
a-ing...empty chatter   1 Tim 6:20

AWAIT *wait*

afflictions a me   Acts 20:23
a-ing...the revelation   1 Cor 1:7
who eagerly a Him   Heb 9:28

AWAKE *be attentive, watch*

awoke from his sleep   Gen 28:16
A, a, Deborah   Judg 5:12
Thy likeness when I a   Ps 17:15
dream when one a-s   Ps 73:20
arouse or a-n *my* love   Song 2:7
He a-ns My ear   Is 50:4
A, a, put on strength   Is 51:9
A, drunkards...weep   Joel 1:5
that I may a-n him   John 11:11
hour for you to a-n   Rom 13:11

AWARE *know, understand*

the lad was not a   1 Sam 20:39
Will you not be a   Is 43:19
But Jesus, a of *this*   Matt 12:15
I was a that power   Luke 8:46

AWE *fear, reverence*

stand in a of Him   Ps 33:8
in a of Thy words   Ps 119:161
in a of My name   Mal 2:5
feeling a sense of a   Acts 2:43

AWESOME *fearful*

How **a** is this place Gen 28:17
angel of God, very **a** Judg 13:6
great and **a** God Neh 1:5
God is **a** majesty Job 37:22
As **a** as an army Song 6:4
a day of the LORD Joel 2:31

AXE *cutting tool*

his **a**, and his hoe 1 Sam 13:20
hammer nor **a** 1 Kin 6:7
a head fell into 2 Kin 6:5
a is already laid Luke 3:9

AZARIAH

1 *ancestor of Samuel*
  1 Chr 6:36
2 *official of Solomon* 1 Kin 4:2
3 *son of Nathan* 1 Kin 4:5
4 *prophet* 2 Chr 15:1-8
5 *two sons of king Jehoshaphat*
  2 Chr 21:2
6 *king of Judah,*
  also Uzziah
  2 Kin 15:1; 2 Chr 26:1
7 *high priest* 1 Chr 6:10
8 *family of Merari* 2 Chr 29:12
9 *son of Hilkiah* 1 Chr 6:13,14
10 *original name of Abed-nego*
  Dan 1:7
  the name of twelve other
  individuals in the OT

B

BAAL

1 *Canaanite god(s)* Num 22:41
  Judg 6:25; 1 Kin 18:40
2 *personal name* 1 Chr 8:30;5:5
3 *place name* 1 Chr 4:33

BAAL-HANAN

1 *king of Edom* Gen 36:38
2 *servant of David* 1 Chr 27:28

BAAL-HAZOR

mountain in central Palestine
  2 Sam 13:23

BAAL-HERMON

part of Mt. Hermon Judg 3:3
  1 Chr 5:23

BAAL-ZEBUB

god of Ekron 2 Kin 1:2,16
see also **BEELZEBUL**

BAASHA

king of Israel 1 Kin 15:16,32

BABEL *a city*

founded by Nimrod
  Gen 10:10;11:9
later called Babylon

BABES *infants*

From the mouth of...**b** Ps 8:2
abundance to their **b** Ps 17:14
woe...who nurse **b** Matt 24:19
as to **b** in Christ 1 Cor 3:1
like newborn **b** 1 Pet 2:2

BABY *infant*

b leaped...her womb Luke 1:41
b wrapped in cloths Luke 2:12
b as He lay Luke 2:16

BABYLON *city*

1 *on the Euphrates*
  2 Kin 17:24; Jer 20:4
  Ezek 29:18; Dan 4:29
2 *symbolic of godlessness*
  Rev 14:8;17:5

BACK *part of body*

you shall see My **b** Ex 33:23
turned his **b** to leave 1 Sam 10:9
law behind their **b-s** Neh 9:26
my sins behind Thy **b** Is 38:17

BAD *evil, wrong*

b report of the land Num 13:32
basket had very **b** figs Jer 24:2
if your eye is **b** Matt 6:23
b tree bears **b** fruit Matt 7:18
B company corrupts 1 Cor 15:33

BAG *sack*

fill their **b-s** Gen 42:25
in the shepherd's **b** 1 Sam 17:40
silver in two **b-s** 2 Kin 5:23
carrying *his* **b** of seed Ps 126:6
b of...weights Mic 6:11
b for *your* journey Matt 10:10
Carry no purse, no **b** Luke 10:4

19

BAGGAGE *bags, supplies*

stayed with the b 1 Sam 25:13
prepare...yourself b Ezek 12:4

BAKE *cook*

b-d unleavened bread Gen 19:3
b-d food for Pharaoh Gen 40:17
they b-d the dough Ex 12:39
B what you will b Ex 16:23
grain offering b-d Lev 2:4
b twelve cakes Lev 24:5
taste of cakes b-d Num 11:8
fire to b bread Is 44:15

BAKER *cook*

b for the king Gen 40:1
cooks and b-s 1 Sam 8:13
from the b-s' street Jer 37:21
oven heated by the b Hos 7:4

BALAAM

diviner Num 22:5-31;23:5
Josh 13:22; Rev 2:14

BALAK

king of Moab Num 22:4
Mic 6:5

BALANCE *scale*

shall have just b-s Lev 19:36
b-s...with my iniquity Job 6:2
False b is an Prov 11:1
mountains in a b Is 40:12

BALD *hairless*

if...head becomes b Lev 13:41
every head is b Jer 48:37
head was made b Ezek 29:18

BALDHEAD *hairless*

mocked him...you b 2 Kin 2:23

BALM *aromatic ointment*

b and myrrh Gen 37:25
a present, a little b Gen 43:11
no b in Gilead Jer 8:22
Gilead and obtain b Jer 46:11
Bring b for her pain Jer 51:8
honey, oil, and b Ezek 27:17

BALSAM *aromatic gum*

tops of the b trees 2 Sam 5:24
like a bed of b Song 5:13

BAN *set apart to God*

city...under the b Josh 6:17

destroy...under the b Josh 7:12
who violated the b 1 Chr 2:7
consign Jacob to the b Is 43:28

BAND *bond or group*

b-s *shall be* of silver Ex 27:10
skillfully woven b Ex 28:8
saw a marauding b 2 Kin 13:21
b of destroying angels Ps 78:49
b-s of the yoke Is 58:6

BANISH *exile*

b-ed one may not 2 Sam 14:14
assemble the b-ed Is 11:12
gaiety...is b-ed Is 24:11
where I shall b them Ezek 4:13

BANK *slope*

b of the Nile Gen 41:3
reeds by the b Ex 2:3
b of the river Ezek 47:7
herd rushed down...b Luke 8:33

BANNER *flag, standard*

set up our b-s Ps 20:5
b to those who fear Ps 60:4
b over me is love Song 2:4
as an army with b-s Song 6:4

BANQUET *dinner, feast*

b lasting seven days Esth 1:5
brought me to *his* b Song 2:4
lavish b for all Is 25:6
place of honor at b-s Matt 23:6
Herod...gave a b Mark 6:21

BAPTISM *symbolic washing*

Sadducees coming...b Matt 3:7
b of repentance Mark 1:4
b with which I am Mark 10:38
with the b of John Luke 7:29
a b to undergo Luke 12:50
through b into death Rom 6:4
one faith, one b Eph 4:5
buried with Him in b Col 2:12

BAPTIZE *symbolic washing*

b...Holy Spirit Matt 3:11
tax-gatherers...b-d Luke 3:12
Jesus also was b-d Luke 3:21
sent me to b in water John 1:33
b-ing more disciples John 4:1
b-d with the Holy Acts 1:5
each of you be b-d Acts 2:38

he arose and was **b-d** Acts 9:18
household...been **b-d** Acts 16:15
John **b-d** with the Acts 19:4
b-d into Jesus Christ Rom 6:3
b-d into Moses 1 Cor 10:2
b-d into one body 1 Cor 12:13
b-d for the dead 1 Cor 15:29

BAR *metal or block*

b-s of your yoke Lev 26:13
a **b** of gold Josh 7:21
like **b-s** of iron Job 40:18
earth with its **b-s** Jon 2:6

BARABBAS

robber Matt 27:16; Luke 23:18
released by Pilate Matt 27:26

BARAK

Deborah's commander Judg 4:6

BARBARIAN *non-Hellenic*

obligation...to **b-s** Rom 1:14
who speaks a **b** 1 Cor 14:11
b, Scythian, slave Col 3:11

BARE (adj) *barren, uncovered*

to cover *their* **b** flesh Ex 28:42
he went to a **b** hill Num 23:3
strips the forests **b** Ps 29:9
were naked and **b** Ezek 16:7

BARE (v) *expose, uncover*

foundations...laid **b** Ps 18:15
b-d His holy arm Is 52:10
foundation is laid **b** Ezek 13:14
opened and laid **b** Heb 4:13

BAREFOOT *without sandals*

priests walk **b** Job 12:19
gone naked and **b** Is 20:3

BAR-JESUS

magician Acts 13:6
also Elymas

BARLEY *grain*

land of wheat and **b** Deut 8:8
beginning...**b** harvest Ruth 1:22
stinkweed instead...**b** Job 31:40
has five **b** loaves John 6:9

BARN *farm building*

b-s are torn down Joel 1:17
seed still in the **b** Hag 2:19

wheat into the **b** Matt 3:12
nor gather into **b-s** Matt 6:26
tear down my **b-s** Luke 12:18

BARNABAS

Cyprian by birth Acts 4:36
introduced Paul Acts 9:27
co-worker with Paul Acts 13:2,7
separated from Paul Acts 15:39

BARREN *childless, sterile*

Sarai was **b** Gen 11:30
but Rachel was **b** Gen 29:31
wrongs the **b** woman Job 24:21
Shout...O **b** one Is 54:1
Blessed are the **b** Luke 23:29

BARTHOLOMEW

apostle Matt 10:3; Luke 6:14
Acts 1:13

BARTIMAEUS

healed by Jesus Mark 10:46

BARUCH

1 *scribe* Jer 36:26;43:6
2 *priest* Neh 3:20
3 *a Judean* Neh 11:5

BASE *dishonorable*

a **b** thought Deut 15:9
b things of...world 1 Cor 1:28

BASEMATH

1 *Esau's wife* Gen 26:34
2 *Esau's wife* Gen 36:3,4
3 *daughter of Solomon*
1 Kin 4:15

BASHAN

land E of Jordan Num 21:33
John 13:11; Is 2:13

BASIN *bowl, vessel*

blood...in the **b** Ex 12:22
b-s...of pure gold 1 Chr 28:17
a *sacrificial* **b** Zech 9:15
water into the **b** John 13:5

BASKET *container*

got him a wicker **b** Ex 2:3
b among the reeds Ex 2:5
b of summer fruit Amos 8:1
seven large **b-s** full Mark 8:8
twelve **b-s** *full* Luke 9:17

let down in a b 2 Cor 11:33

BATH *measure of capacity*

two thousand **b-s** 1 Kin 7:26
100 **b-s** of oil Ezra 7:22
only one b *of wine* Is 5:10
a tenth of a b from Ezek 45:14

BATHE *wash*

wash his clothes and b Lev 15:5
b his body in water Num 19:7
saw a woman **b-ing** 2 Sam 11:2
B-d in milk Song 5:12

BATHSHEBA

wife of Uriah 2 Sam 11:3
taken by David 2 Sam 11:4
wife of David 2 Sam 11:27
mother of Solomon 2 Sam 12:24

BATTLE (n) *conflict, war*

b is the LORD'S 1 Sam 17:47
b is...God's 2 Chr 20:15
scents the b from afar Job 39:25
with strength for b Ps 18:39
noise of b is in Jer 50:22
another king in b Luke 14:31
horses prepared for b Rev 9:7

BATTLE (v) *fight*

b against the sons Judg 20:14
drew near to b 1 Sam 7:10
about to go to b 1 Chr 12:19
nations...to b Zech 14:2

BEACH *coast*

multitude...on the b Matt 13:2
Jesus stood on the b John 21:4
down on the b Acts 21:5

BEAM *log*

like a weaver's b 2 Sam 21:19
one was felling a b 2 Kin 6:5
b-s, the thresholds 2 Chr 3:7
b-s of His...chambers Ps 104:3

BEAR (n) *animal*

b came and took 1 Sam 17:34
b robbed of...cubs Prov 17:12
the b will graze Is 11:7
resembling a b Dan 7:5

BEAR (v) *sustain*

too great to b Gen 4:13

bore you on eagles' Ex 19:4
not b false witness Ex 20:16
LORD...**b-s** our burden Ps 68:19
b their iniquities Is 53:11
b the penalty Ezek 23:49
she will b a Son Matt 1:21
John **bore** witness John 1:15
If I *alone* b witness John 5:31
it **b-s** much fruit John 12:24
you *will* b witness John 15:27
b-ing His own cross John 19:17
b fruit for God Rom 7:4
Spirit...**b-s** witness Rom 8:16
b the image of 1 Cor 15:49
B...another's burdens Gal 6:2
b the sins of many Heb 9:28
bore our sins 1 Pet 2:24

BEARD *whiskers*

infection...on the b Lev 13:29
seized *him* by...b 1 Sam 17:35
shaved...their **b-s** 2 Sam 10:4
until your **b-s** grow 1 Chr 19:5

BEARER *carrier*

the **b-s** of the ark 2 Sam 6:13
strength of...**b-s** Neh 4:10
b of good news Is 40:9

BEAST *animal, creature*

God formed every b Gen 2:19
Noah and all the **b-s** Gen 8:1
eliminate harmful **b-s** Lev 26:6
b-s of the fields Lev 26:22
But now ask the **b-s** Job 12:7
b of the forest Ps 50:10
b also had four heads Dan 7:6
they worshiped the b Rev 13:4
mark of the b Rev 16:2

BEAT *hit, strike*

b-ing a Hebrew Ex 2:11
b out what she Ruth 2:17
b-ing tambourines Ps 68:25
B your plowshares Joel 3:10
b Him with their Matt 26:67
b-ing His head with Mark 15:19
b-ing his breast Luke 18:13
b-en us in public Acts 16:37
stopped **b-ing** Paul Acts 21:32
b-en with rods 2 Cor 11:25

BEAUTIFUL *lovely, pleasing*

daughters...were **b**   Gen 6:2
Rachel was **b**   Gen 29:17
foliage of **b** trees   Lev 23:40
Most **b** among women   Song 1:8
Branch...will be **b**   Is 4:2
Your **b** sheep   Jer 13:20
enter the **B** Land   Dan 11:41
How **b** are the feet   Rom 10:15

BEAUTIFUL GATE *see* GATES OF JERUSALEM

BEAUTY

Your **b**...is slain   2 Sam 1:19
behold the **b** of the LORD   Ps 27:4
Zion...perfection of **b**   Ps 50:2
b is vain   Prov 31:30
see the King in His **b**   Is 33:17

BED *pallet*

My **b** will comfort me   Job 7:13
make my **b** swim   Ps 6:6
remember...on my **b**   Ps 63:6
in **b** with a fever   Matt 8:14
take up your **b**   Matt 9:6
lamp...under a **b**   Mark 4:21

BEDROOM *sleeping area*

and into your **b**   Ex 8:3
you speak in your **b**   2 Kin 6:12
his nurse in the **b**   2 Chr 22:11

BEELZEBUL

N.T. prince of the demons
   Matt 12:27; Luke 11:15
see also **BAAL-ZEBUB**

BEERSHEBA

well/town in Negev   Gen 21:31
   Judg 20:1
home of Abraham   Gen 22:19
home of Isaac   Gen 26:23

BEFOREHAND *prior*

do not be anxious **b**   Mark 13:11
anointed My body **b**   Mark 14:8
God announced **b**   Acts 3:18
prepared **b** for glory   Rom 9:23

BEG *appeal, ask*

children wander...**b**   Ps 109:10
b-s during...harvest   Prov 20:4

b You to look at   Luke 9:38
I am ashamed to **b**   Luke 16:3
who used to sit and **b**   John 9:8
b-ging them...leave   Acts 16:39

BEGET *bring into being, sire*

Rock who **begot**   Deut 32:18
whom you shall **b**   2 Kin 20:18
begotten the...dew   Job 38:28
I have **begotten** Thee   Ps 2:7
who **b-s** a wise son   Prov 23:24
have **begotten** Thee   Acts 13:33

BEGINNING *origin, starting*

In the **b** God created   Gen 1:1
from **b** to end   1 Sam 3:12
b was insignificant   Job 8:7
fear of the LORD...**b**   Ps 111:10
The **b** of the gospel   Mark 1:1
In the **b** was the Word   John 1:1
This **b** of *His* signs   John 2:11
He is the **b**   Col 1:18
the **b** and the end   Rev 21:6

BEGOTTEN (adj) *born one*

b from the Father   John 1:14
the only **b** God   John 1:18
gave His only **b** Son   John 3:16
only **b** Son of God   John 3:18
offering...only **b**   Heb 11:17
sent His only **b** Son   1 John 4:9

BEHALF *sake of*

atonement on his **b**   Lev 5:6
the Father on your **b**   John 16:26
I ask on their **b**   John 17:9
one man to die on **b**   John 18:14
be sin on our **b**   2 Cor 5:21

BEHAVE *act*

David **b-d** himself   1 Sam 18:30
b-ing as a madman   1 Sam 21:14
b properly as in   Rom 13:13
blamelessly we **b-d**   1 Thess 2:10

BEHAVIOR *conduct*

instruction in wise **b**   Prov 1:3
reverent in their **b**   Titus 2:3
holy...in all *your* **b**   1 Pet 1:15
the **b** of their wives   1 Pet 3:1

BEHEADED *cut off*

killed him and **b** him   2 Sam 4:7
John **b** in the prison   Matt 14:10

23

BEHEADED

John, whom I b   Mark 6:16
b because of the   Rev 20:4

BEHEMOTH

hippopotamus   Job 40:15

BEHOLD *look, see*

upright will b His face   Ps 11:7
b the works of the LORD   Ps 46:8
we beheld His glory   John 1:14
b the Son of Man   John 6:62
may b My glory   John 17:24
b-ing as in a mirror   2 Cor 3:18
No one has beheld   1 John 4:12
B, I stand at the door   Rev 3:20

BEING *existence, life*

man became a living b Gen 2:7
a...b coming up   1 Sam 28:13
wisdom in the...b   Job 38:36
truth in the...b   Ps 51:6
four living b-s   Ezek 1:5
resembled a...b   Dan 10:16

BEL

Babylonian god, related to Baal
     Jer 50:2;51:44

BELIEVE *have faith, trust*

he b-d in the LORD   Gen 15:6
did not b in God   Ps 78:22
naive b-s everything   Prov 14:15
you b that I am able   Matt 9:28
ask in prayer, b-ing   Matt 21:22
repent and b   Mark 1:15
they b-d...Scripture   John 2:22
whoever b-s in Him   John 3:16
will you b My words   John 5:47
who b-s has eternal   John 6:47
men will b in Him   John 11:48
b in the light   John 12:36
not see, and *yet* b-d   John 20:29
b-d were of one heart   Acts 4:32
B in the Lord Jesus   Acts 16:31
Abraham b-d God   Rom 4:3
how shall they b   Rom 10:14
love...b-s all   1 Cor 13:7
whom I have b-d   2 Tim 1:12
comes to God must b   Heb 11:6
demons also b   James 2:19
do not b every spirit   1 John 4:1

BELIEVERS *faithful ones*

all the circumcised b Acts 10:45

example to all the b 1 Thess 1:7
toward you b   1 Thess 2:10

BELL

a b...a pomegranate   Ex 39:26
b-s of the horses   Zech 14:20

BELLY *stomach*

On your b...you go   Gen 3:14
crawls on its b   Lev 11:42
b of the sea monster Matt 12:40

BELOVED *dearly loved*

b of the LORD dwell Deut 33:12
gives to His b *even*   Ps 127:2
b is like a gazelle   Song 2:9
This is My b Son   Matt 3:17
your upbuilding, b 2 Cor 12:19
stand firm...my b   Phil 4:1
faithful and b brother   Col 4:9
Luke, the b physician Col 4:14
slave, a b brother   Philem 16
This is My b Son   2 Pet 1:17
the called, b in God   Jude 1

BELSHAZZER

ruler of Babylon   Dan 5:1;7:1

BELT *waistband*

the b of the strong   Job 12:21
leather b about his   Matt 3:4
no money in their b   Mark 6:8
Paul's b and bound   Acts 21:11

BELTESHAZZER

Daniel's Babylonian name
    Dan 1:7;2:26;5:12;10:1

BENAIAH

1 *son of Jehoiada*   2 Sam 8:18
  captain of David 2 Sam 23:23
2 *Levitical singer* 1 Chr 15:18,20
3 *a priest*   1 Chr 15:24;16:5
common name of a number of
  people in Israel

BENEFIT *blessing, profit*

no return for the b 2 Chr 32:25
forget none of His b-s Ps 103:2
His b-s toward me   Ps 116:12
the b of circumcision Rom 3:1

BEN-HADAD

name of three kings of Aram
  1 Kin 15:18; 2 Kin 6:24;13:22

BEN-HINNOM, VALLEY OF
see **HINNOM VALLEY**

BENJAMIN
1 *son of Jacob*	Gen 35:18
2 *tribe*	Num 2:22
3 *of clan of Jediael*	1 Chr 7:10
4 *of the restoration*	Neh 3:23

BENJAMIN GATE see GATES OF JERUSALEM

BEREA
city in Macedonia visited by Paul Acts 17:10,13

BEREAVE *deprive, make sad*
be **b-d** of you both Gen 27:45
b...of your children Lev 26:22
I will **b** them Jer 15:7
longer **b** your nation Ezek 36:14

BERNICE
daughter of Herod Agrippa I Acts 25:13,23

BERODACH-BALADAN
king of Babylon 2 Kin 20:12
also **Merodach-Baladan**

BESEECH *ask earnestly*
LORD, I **b** Thee Ps 116:4
do save, we **b** Thee Ps 118:25
leper came...**b-ing** Mark 1:40
b the Lord of the Luke 10:2

BESIEGE *assail, surround*
When you **b** a city Deut 20:19
enemies **b** them 2 Chr 6:28
was **b-ing** Jerusalem Jer 32:2
b-d...with bitterness Lam 3:5

BESTOWED *granted*
b...royal majesty 1 Chr 29:25
that the Spirit was **b** Acts 8:18
which He freely **b** Eph 1:6
b on Him the name Phil 2:9
Every good thing **b** James 1:17
love the Father has **b** 1 John 3:1

BETHANY
1 *E of Jerusalem* Matt 21:17
home of Mary, Martha and
Lazarus John 11:1,18
2 *where John baptized* John 1:28

BETHEL
town in Benjamin Gen 12:8
N of Jerusalem Josh 8:17

BETHESDA
pool in Jerusalem John 5:2

BETH-HORON
1 *famous battle site*
pass NW of Jerusalem Josh 10:10,11
2 *two towns at both ends of*
mountain pass Josh 16:3,5

BETHLEHEM
1 *town S of Jerusalem* Gen 35:19
home of Ruth and Boaz Ruth 4:11
birthplace of Jesus Matt 2:1
2 *Zebulunite village* Josh 19:15

BETH-PEOR
Moabite city Deut 4:46;34:6

BETHPHAGE
village on the Mount of Olives Matt 21:1; Mark 11:1

BETHSAIDA
village on Sea of Galilee Mark 8:22; Luke 9:10
home of Philip, Andrew and Peter John 1:44

BETH-SHEAN, BETH-SHAN
city at junction of Jezreel and Jordan valleys Josh 17:11
1 Kin 4:12; 1 Chr 7:29

BETH-SHEMESH
1 *city of Judah* Josh 15:10
2 *Issachar border city* Josh 19:22
3 *city of Naphtali* Josh 19:38

BETRAY *break faith, disloyal*
do not **b** the fugitive Is 16:3
wine **b-s** the haughty Hab 2:5
how to **b** Him Mark 14:11
one...will **b** Me Mark 14:18
Judas, you are **b-ing** Luke 22:48

BETROTH *promise to wed*

You shall **b** a wife   Deut 28:30
I will **b** you to Me   Hos 2:19
Mary had been **b-ed** Matt 1:18
I **b-ed** you to one   2 Cor 11:2

BEWARE *be careful, watch*

B of practicing   Matt 6:1
B of the scribes   Mark 12:38
B of the leaven   Luke 12:1
b...false circumcision   Phil 3:2

BEYOND *over and above*

it was **b** measure   Gen 41:49
remove...**b** Babylon   Acts 7:43
tempted **b** what   1 Cor 10:13
b their ability   2 Cor 8:3

b all that we ask   Eph 3:20
and **b** reproach   Col 1:22

BEZER

1 *son of Zophah*   1 Chr 7:37
2 *city of refuge*   Josh 20:8

BIG *large*

on the **b** toes   Ex 29:20
Pharaoh...a **b** noise   Jer 46:17
gave a **b** reception   Luke 5:29

BILDAD

one of Job's friends   Job 2:11
Job 18:1;42:9

BILHAH

1 *Rachel's servant*   Gen 29:29
  Jacob's concubine   Gen 30:3,4
2 *Simeonite town*   1 Chr 4:29

BIND *fasten, secure*

bound his son Isaac   Gen 22:9
were **b-ing** sheaves   Gen 37:7
b them as a sign   Deut 6:8
b-s up their wounds   Ps 147:3
B up the testimony   Is 8:16
b up the brokenhearted Is 61:1
shall **b** on earth   Matt 16:19
and **bound** Him   John 18:12
bound...a thousand   Rev 20:2

BIRD *fowl*

let **b-s** fly above   Gen 1:20
eat any clean **b**   Deut 14:20
b-s of the heavens   Ps 8:8

Flee *as* a **b** to   Ps 11:1
snare of a **b** catcher   Hos 9:8
b-s...*have* nests   Luke 9:58

BIRTH *act of being born*

A time to give **b**   Eccl 3:2
You gave me **b**   Jer 2:27
b of Jesus Christ   Matt 1:18
rejoice at his **b**   Luke 1:14
a man blind from **b**   John 9:1
in pain to give **b**   Rev 12:2

BIRTHDAY *day of birth*

was Pharaoh's **b**   Gen 40:20
Herod's **b** came   Matt 14:6
his **b**...banquet   Mark 6:21

BIRTHRIGHT *first-born rights*

First sell me your **b** Gen 25:31
He took away my **b** Gen 27:36
sold his own **b**   Heb 12:16

BITE

serpent **bit** any man Num 21:9
it **b-s** like a serpent Prov 23:32
if you **b**...one another Gal 5:15

BITHYNIA

*territory on the Bosporus in Asia
Minor*   Acts 16:7; 1 Pet 1:1

BITTER *painful, unpleasant*

b with hard labor   Ex 1:14
waters of Marah...**b** Ex 15:23
b speech *as* their arrow Ps 64:3
substitute **b** for sweet   Is 5:20
Strong drink is **b**   Is 24:9
fresh and **b** *water* James 3:11

BITTERNESS *unpleasantness*

in the **b** of my soul   Job 10:1
because of the **b**   Is 38:15
full of cursing and **b** Rom 3:14
all **b**...be put away   Eph 4:31
no root of **b**   Heb 12:15

BLACK *dark*

sky grew **b** with   1 Kin 18:45
darkness and **b** gloom Job 3:5
I am **b** but lovely   Song 1:5
behold, a **b** horse   Rev 6:5
sun became **b**   Rev 6:12

BLAME *fault, responsibility*

let me bear the **b**	Gen 43:9
bear the **b**...forever	Gen 44:32

BLAMELESS *faultless*

show Thyself **b**	2 Sam 22:26
just *and* **b** man is a	Job 12:4
His way is **b**	Ps 18:30
b will inherit good	Prov 28:10
a **b** conscience	Acts 24:16
holy and **b** before Him	Eph 1:4
in the Law, found **b**	Phil 3:6
spotless and **b**	2 Pet 3:14
b with great joy	Jude 24

BLASPHEME *curse*

enemies...to **b**	2 Sam 12:14
name is continually **b-d**	Is 52:5
This *fellow* **b-s**	Matt 9:3
b-s...Holy Spirit	Mark 3:29
force them to **b**	Acts 26:11
name of God is **b-d**	Rom 2:24
taught not to **b**	1 Tim 1:20
b-d the God of	Rev 16:11

BLASPHEMY *cursing, profanity*

b against the Spirit	Matt 12:31
b-ies they utter	Mark 3:28
You...heard the **b**	Mark 14:64
man...speaks **b-ies**	Luke 5:21
stone You...for **b**	John 10:33
words and **b-ies**	Rev 13:5

BLAST *burst*

the **b** of Thy nostrils	Ex 15:8
b with the ram's horn	Josh 6:5
a trumpet **b** of war	Jer 49:2

BLAZING *burning*

LORD...a **b-ing** fire	Ex 3:2
furnace of **b** fire	Dan 3:6
and to a **b** fire	Heb 12:18

BLEMISH *imperfection, spot*

there is no **b** in you	Song 4:7
six lambs without **b**	Ezek 46:4
Himself without **b**	Heb 9:14
stains and **b-es**	2 Pet 2:13

BLESS (v) *bestow favor or praise*

God **b-ed** the...day	Gen 2:3
I will greatly **b** you	Gen 22:17
LORD **b-ed** the sabbath	Ex 20:11
and **b** Thine inheritance	Ps 28:9

LORD will **b** His people	Ps 29:11
B the LORD	Ps 103:2
generous will be **b-ed**	Prov 22:9
who **b-es** his friend	Prov 27:14
rise up and **b** her	Prov 31:28
b-ed of My Father	Matt 25:34
He **b-ed** *the* food	Mark 6:41
b...who curse you	Luke 6:28
while He was **b-ing**	Luke 24:51
you are **b-ed** if you	John 13:17
b...who persecute	Rom 12:14
we **b** *our* Lord	James 3:9

BLESSED (adj) *favored, happy*

b be God Most High	Gen 14:20
B are you, O Israel	Deut 33:29
B be the name of	Job 1:21
How **b** is the man	Ps 127:5
b...who finds wisdom	Prov 3:13
nations will call you **b**	Mal 3:12
B are the poor in	Matt 5:3
B are the gentle	Matt 5:5
B *is* the...kingdom	Mark 11:10
B among women *are*	Luke 1:42
more **b** to give	Acts 20:35
looking for...**b** hope	Titus 2:13

BLESSING (n) *God's favor*

you shall be a **b**	Gen 12:2
taken away your **b**	Gen 27:35
a **b** and a curse	Deut 11:26
curse into a **b**	Neh 13:2
b of the LORD be upon	Ps 129:8
showers of **b**	Ezek 34:26
pour out for you a **b**	Mal 3:10
fulness of the **b**	Rom 15:29
cup of **b** which we	1 Cor 10:16
inherit a **b**	1 Pet 3:9
honor and glory and **b**	Rev 5:12

BLIND (adj) *sightless*

misleads a **b** *person*	Deut 27:18
To open **b** eyes	Is 42:7
b...guides a **b** man	Matt 15:14
b beggar *named*	Mark 10:46
b man was sitting	Luke 18:35
I was **b**, now I see	John 9:25

BLIND (n) *without sight*

block before the **b**	Lev 19:14
I was eyes to the **b**	Job 29:15
the **b** receive sight	Matt 11:5
a guide to the **b**	Rom 2:19

BLIND (v) *make sightless*

b-s the clear-sighted   Ex 23:8
bribe to **b** my eyes   1 Sam 12:3
has **b-ed** the minds   2 Cor 4:4
darkness has **b-ed**   1 John 2:11

BLINDNESS *sightlessness*

madness and with **b**   Deut 28:28
struck them with **b**   2 Kin 6:18
every horse...with **b**   Zech 12:4

BLOOD

Whoever sheds man's **b**   Gen 9:6
bridegroom of **b**   Ex 4:25
b shall be a sign   Ex 12:13
not eat...any **b**   Lev 3:17
land is filled with **b**   Ezek 9:9
b did not reveal   Matt 16:17
covenant in My **b**   Luke 22:20
sweat...drops of **b**   Luke 22:44
drinks My **b** abides   John 6:56
Field of **B**   Acts 1:19
the moon into **b**   Acts 2:20
justified by His **b**   Rom 5:9
sharing in the **b**   1 Cor 10:16
redemption...His **b**   Eph 1:7
cleansed with **b**   Heb 9:22
b, as of a lamb   1 Pet 1:19
the sea became **b**   Rev 8:8
b of the saints   Rev 17:6

BLOODGUILTINESS

no **b** on his account   Ex 22:2
b is upon them   Lev 20:11
b shall be forgiven   Deut 21:8
Deliver me from **b**   Ps 51:14

BLOODSHED *killing, murder*

abhors the man of **b**   Ps 5:6
Men of **b** hate   Prov 29:10
the **b** of Jerusalem   Is 4:4
give you over to **b**   Ezek 35:6
b follows **b**   Hos 4:2

BLOSSOM *bloom*

the almond tree **b-s**   Eccl 12:5
Israel will **b** and sprout   Is 27:6
arrogance has **b-ed**   Ezek 7:10
fig tree should not **b**   Hab 3:17

BLOT *erase*

I will **b** out man   Gen 6:7
b me...from Thy book   Ex 32:32

b out their name   Deut 9:14
sin be **b-ted** out   Neh 4:5
b out all my iniquities   Ps 51:9
works...be **b-ted** out   Ezek 6:6

BLOW *forcible stroke*

gave Jesus a **b**   John 18:22
give Him **b-s**   John 19:3
inflicted many **b-s**   Acts 16:23

BLUE *color*

tent of **b** and purple   Ex 26:36
ephod all of **b**   Ex 28:31
royal robes of **b**   Esth 8:15

BOANERGES

name of James and John
   Mark 3:17

BOAST (n) *bragging*

soul shall make its **b**   Ps 34:2
the **b** of our hope   Heb 3:6

BOAST (v) *brag, glory*

B no more so   1 Sam 2:3
b in the LORD   Ps 34:2
who **b-s** of his gifts   Prov 20:14
not **b** about tomorrow   Prov 27:1
let not a rich man **b**   Jer 9:23
b in God   Rom 2:17
who **b** in the Law   Rom 2:23
b...my weaknesses   2 Cor 12:9
it **b-s** of great things   James 3:5

BOASTFUL *proud*

b shall not stand   Ps 5:5
insolent, arrogant, **b**   Rom 1:30
b pride of life   1 John 2:16

BOASTING *bragging*

Where is your **b**   Judg 9:38
Where then is **b**   Rom 3:27
our **b** about you   2 Cor 9:3
all such **b** is evil   James 4:16

BOAT *watercraft*

slip by like reed **b-s**   Job 9:26
left the **b** and their   Matt 4:22
Peter got out of...**b**   Matt 14:29
filled both of the **b-s**   Luke 5:7
disciples into the **b**   John 6:22

BOAZ

1 *husband of Ruth*   Ruth 4:13

grandfather of David
Ruth 4:17ff
2 temple pillar   2 Chr 3:17

BODY corpse, flesh

b cleaves to the earth   Ps 44:25
lamp of the b   Matt 6:22
perfume upon My b   Matt 26:12
this is My b   Mark 14:22
did not find His b   Luke 24:23
b of sin...done away   Rom 6:6
redemption of our b   Rom 8:23
present your b-ies   Rom 12:1
b-ies are members   1 Cor 6:15
b is a temple   1 Cor 6:19
you are Christ's b   1 Cor 12:27
b to be burned   1 Cor 13:3
absent from the b   2 Cor 5:8
one b and one Spirit   Eph 4:4
building up of the b   Eph 4:12
wives as...own b-ies   Eph 5:28
transform the b   Phil 3:21
b be preserved   1 Thess 5:23
bore...sins in His b   1 Pet 2:24

BODYGUARD guard, protector

captain of the b put   Gen 40:4
you my b for life   1 Sam 28:2

BOIL (n) sore, swelling

when...has a b   Lev 13:18
b-s of Egypt   Deut 28:27
smote Job with sore b-s   Job 2:7

BOIL (v) cook, heat

not b a kid in its   Ex 34:26
we b-ed my son   2 Kin 6:29
fire causes water to b   Is 64:2
b the guilt offering   Ezek 46:20

BOISTEROUS clamorous, loud

woman of folly is b   Prov 9:13
of noise, You b town   Is 22:2
will drink, and be b   Zech 9:15

BOLD brave, fearless

wicked man...b face   Prov 21:29
righteous are b as   Prov 28:1
I may not be b   2 Cor 10:2

BOLDNESS confidence

word of God with b   Acts 4:31
b and...access   Eph 3:12

with b the mystery   Eph 6:19

BOND band, restraint

neither b nor free   2 Kin 14:26
b of the covenant   Ezek 20:37
with b-s of love   Hos 11:4
in the b of peace   Eph 4:3
eternal b-s under   Jude 6

BONDAGE servitude, slavery

Israel sighed...b   Ex 2:23
the b of iniquity   Acts 8:23
sold into b to sin   Rom 7:14

BOND-SERVANT servant, slave

b-s of...Most High   Acts 16:17
Paul, a b of Christ   Rom 1:1
ourselves as your b-s   2 Cor 4:5
b...be quarrelsome   2 Tim 2:24
b of God...apostle   Titus 1:1
His b-s...serve Him   Rev 22:3

BONDSLAVE servant, slave

state of His b   Luke 1:48
a b of Jesus Christ   Col 4:12
Urge b-s to be subject   Titus 2:9
use it as b-s of God   1 Pet 2:16

BONE

now b of my b-s   Gen 2:23
the b-s of Joseph   Josh 24:32
my b-s are dismayed   Ps 6:2
rottenness in his b-s   Prov 12:4
tongue breaks the b   Prov 25:15
can these b-s live   Ezek 37:3
dead men's b-s   Matt 23:27
Not a b...be broken   John 19:36

BOOK scroll

in a b as a memorial   Ex 17:14
blot me...from Thy b   Ex 32:32
found the b of the   2 Kin 22:8
seal up the b   Dan 12:4
not contain the b-s   John 21:25
names are in the b   Phil 4:3
worthy to open the b   Rev 5:2
Lamb's b of life   Rev 21:27

BOOK OF LIFE

God's book with names
  of righteous   Ps 69:28
    Phil 4:3; Rev 13:8;17:8;20:15

BOOTHS *shelters*

b for his livestock   Gen 33:17
live in **b** for seven   Lev 23:42
in **b** during the feast Neh 8:14

BOOTHS, FEAST OF
see FEASTS

BOOTY *loot, plunder*

b that remained   Num 31:32
Swift is the **b**   Is 8:1
divide the **b** with   Is 53:12
have his *own* life as **b** Jer 38:2

BORDER *boundary*

enlarge your **b-s**   Ex 34:24
b of...city of refuge Num 35:26
the Jordan as *a* **b**   Deut 3:17
God extends your **b** Deut 12:20
peace in your **b-s**   Ps 147:14

BORN *brought into life*

man is **b** for trouble   Job 5:7
mountains were **b**   Ps 90:2
child will be **b** to us   Is 9:6
land be **b** in one day   Is 66:8
b King of the Jews   Matt 2:2
those **b** of women   Luke 7:28
b not of blood   John 1:13
unless one is **b** again John 3:3
b of the Spirit   John 3:6
to one untimely **b**   1 Cor 15:8
b...to a living hope   1 Pet 1:3
loves is **b** of God   1 John 4:7

BORROW *use temporarily*

if a man **b-s** *anything* Ex 22:14
you shall not **b**   Deut 28:12
b-s and does not pay Ps 37:21
wants to **b** from you Matt 5:42

BOSOM *breast*

iniquity in my **b**   Job 31:33
take fire in his **b**   Prov 6:27
to Abraham's **b**   Luke 16:22
the **b** of the Father John 1:18

BOTHER *pester*

conscience **b-ed**   1 Sam 24:5
you **b** the woman   Matt 26:10
worried and **b-ed**   Luke 10:41
this widow **b-s** me   Luke 18:5

BOTTOMLESS *without bottom*

key of the **b** pit   Rev 9:1
he opened the **b** pit Rev 9:2

BOUGH *branch*

Joseph is a fruitful **b** Gen 49:22
b-s of leafy trees   Lev 23:40
cedars...with its **b-s** Ps 80:10
nested in its **b-s**   Ezek 31:6

BOUND (adj) *fastened, tied*

Foolishness is **b** up Prov 22:15
cast **b** into the...fire Dan 3:24
A wife is **b** as long 1 Cor 7:39

BOUND (n) *boundary, limit*

utmost **b** of...hills Gen 49:26
set **b-s** for the people Ex 19:12
b-s...the mountain Ex 19:23

BOUNDARY *border, limit*

b-ies of the peoples Deut 32:8
b of light and   Job 26:10
the **b-ies** of the earth Ps 74:17
set for the sea its **b** Prov 8:29
the **b** of the widow Prov 15:25

BOUNTY *generous gift*

to his royal **b**   1 Kin 10:13
crowned...with Thy **b** Ps 65:11
over the **b** of the LORD Jer 31:12

BOW (n) *rainbow*

set My **b** in the cloud Gen 9:13

BOW (n) *shooting device*

his **b** remained firm Gen 49:24
a **b** of bronze   2 Sam 22:35
not trust in my **b**   Ps 44:6
b-s are shattered   Jer 51:56

BOW (v) *bend, worship*

nations **b** down to   Gen 27:29
Israel **b-ed** in   Gen 47:31
to Him you shall **b** 2 Kin 17:36
My soul is **b-ed** down Ps 57:6
B Thy heavens, O LORD Ps 144:5
nations will **b** down Zeph 2:11
He **b-ed** His head   John 19:30
every knee shall **b** Rom 14:11

BOWELS *entrails, innards*

a disease of your **b** 2 Chr 21:15

smote him in his **b**   2 Chr 21:18
b gushed out   Acts 1:18

BOWL *dish, jug*

golden **b** is crushed   Eccl 12:6
from sacrificial **b-s**   Amos 6:6
dips with Me in...**b**   Mark 14:20
b-s full of the wrath   Rev 15:7

BOX *container*

b with the golden   1 Sam 6:11
sashes, perfume **b-es**   Is 3:20
Judas had the...**b**   John 13:29

BOX *type of tree*

b tree and the cypress   Is 41:19

BOY *child, lad*

she left the **b**   Gen 21:15
let the **b-s** live   Ex 1:17
b will lead them   Is 11:6
Traded a **b** for a harlot   Joel 3:3
b was cured at once   Matt 17:18

BRACELETS *armlets*

two **b** for her wrists   Gen 24:22
armlets and **b**   Num 31:50
earrings, **b**, veils   Is 3:19

BRAMBLE *briar*

trees said to the **b**   Judg 9:14
fire...from the **b**   Judg 9:15

BRANCH *bough*

David a righteous **B**   Jer 23:5
b-es *fit* for scepters   Ezek 19:11
beautiful **b-es** and   Ezek 31:3
birds...in its **b-es**   Luke 13:19
b-es of the palm   John 12:13
b...not bear fruit   John 15:2
you are the **b-es**   John 15:5
be holy, the **b-es**   Rom 11:16

BREACH *break*

For every **b** of trust   Ex 22:9
Lord had made a **b**   Judg 21:15
closed up the **b**   1 Kin 11:27
that no **b** remained   Neh 6:1
Heal its **b-s**   Ps 60:2

BREAD *food*

eat unleavened **b**   Ex 12:20
rain **b** from heaven   Ex 16:4

He will bless your **b**   Ex 23:25
b of the Presence   Ex 25:30
not live by **b** alone   Deut 8:3
ravens brought...**b**   1 Kin 17:6
b of heaven   Ps 105:40
satisfy...with **b**   Ps 132:15
b *eaten* in secret   Prov 9:17
eat the **b** of idleness   Prov 31:27
Cast your **b**...waters   Eccl 11:1
not live on **b** alone   Matt 4:4
Give us...daily **b**   Matt 6:11
gives you the true **b**   John 6:32
I am the **b** of life   John 6:35

BREAK *divide, shatter*

b down your pride   Lev 26:19
never **b** My covenant   Judg 2:1
broke the pitchers   Judg 7:20
soft tongue **b-s** the   Prov 25:15
reed He will not **b**   Is 42:3
I broke your yoke   Jer 2:20
B...fallow ground   Hos 10:12
waves were **b-ing**   Mark 4:37
she broke the vial   Mark 14:3
their nets *began* to **b**   Luke 5:6
b-ing the Sabbath   John 5:18
did not **b** His legs   John 19:33
your **b-ing** the Law   Rom 2:23

BREAST *bosom*

orphan from the **b**   Job 24:9
upon my mother's **b-s**   Ps 22:9
b-s are like...fawns   Song 7:3
b-s...never nursed   Luke 23:29
reclining on Jesus' **b**   John 13:23
girded across His **b**   Rev 1:13

BREASTPIECE *breast covering*

a **b** and an ephod   Ex 28:4
make a **b** of judgment   Ex 28:15
they bound the **b**   Ex 39:21

BREASTPLATE *breast armor*

righteousness like a **b**   Is 59:17
b of faith and love   1 Thess 5:8
like **b-s** of iron   Rev 9:9

BREATH *air, spirit, wind*

the **b** of life   Gen 2:7
days are *but* a **b**   Job 7:16
man is a mere **b**   Ps 39:11
b came into them   Ezek 37:10
give **b** to the image   Rev 13:15

BREATHE *inhale and exhale*

Abraham **b-d** his last   Gen 25:8
such as **b** out violence   Ps 27:12
garden **b**...*fragrance*   Song 4:16
b on these slain   Ezek 37:9
He **b-d** His last   Mark 15:39
He **b-d** on them   John 20:22

BRETHREN *brothers*

beating...his **b**   Ex 2:11
b from all the nations   Is 66:20
His **b** Will return   Mic 5:3
b, why do you injure   Acts 7:26
sinning aginst...**b**   1 Cor 8:12
dangers...false **b**   2 Cor 11:26
Peace be to the **b**   Eph 6:23
faithful **b** in Christ   Col 1:2
the love of the **b**   1 Thess 4:9
b...not grow weary   2 Thess 3:13
my **b**, do not swear   James 5:12
our lives for the **b**   1 John 3:16
accuser of our **b**   Rev 12:10

BRIAR *thistle, thorn*

b-s and thorns will come   Is 5:6
land will be **b-s**   Is 7:24
grapes from a **b** bush   Luke 6:44

BRIBE *illegal gift*

b blinds...clear-sighted   Ex 23:8
nor take a **b**   Deut 10:17
who hates **b-s** will   Prov 15:27
b corrupts the heart   Eccl 7:7
Everyone loves a **b**   Is 1:23

BRICK *clay block*

they used **b** for stone   Gen 11:3
straw to make **b** as   Ex 5:7
deliver...quota of **b-s**   Ex 5:18
burning incense on **b-s**   Is 65:3

BRIDE *newlywed*

as a **b** adorns herself   Is 61:10
the voice of the **b**   Jer 7:34
b out of her *bridal*   Joel 2:16
He who has the **b**   John 3:29
b...of the Lamb   Rev 21:9

BRIDEGROOM *newlywed*

a **b** of blood to me   Ex 4:25
As a **b** decks himself   Is 61:10
voice of the **b**   Jer 7:34
attendants of the **b**   Matt 9:15
out to meet the **b**   Matt 25:1

BRIDLE (n) *head harness*

My **b** in your lips   2 Kin 19:28
a **b** for the donkey   Prov 26:3
up to the horses' **b-s**   Rev 14:20

BRIDLE (v) *control*

not **b** his tongue   James 1:26
man, able to **b**   James 3:2

BRIGHT *shining*

b in the skies   Job 37:21
night is as **b** as   Ps 139:12
B eyes gladden   Prov 15:30
b cloud...them   Matt 17:5
b light...flashed   Acts 22:6
the **b** morning star   Rev 22:16

BRIMSTONE *sulfur*

b and fire from   Gen 19:24
b and burning wind   Ps 11:6
rained fire and **b**   Luke 17:29
tormented with...**b**   Rev 14:10
lake of fire and **b**   Rev 20:10

BRING *carry, lead*

shall **b** forth children   Gen 3:16
Cain **brought**...offering   Gen 4:3
b two of every *kind*   Gen 6:19
B the ark of God   1 Sam 14:18
Kings with **b** gifts   Ps 68:29
B water for the thirsty   Is 21:14
B the whole tithe   Mal 3:10
b-ing...a paralytic   Matt 9:2
not...to **b** peace   Matt 10:34
brought forth a son   Luke 1:57
I **b** you good news   Luke 2:10
Law **b-s** about wrath   Rom 4:15
b-ing salvation   Titus 2:11

BROAD *wide*

into a **b** place   2 Sam 22:20
land was **b** and   1 Chr 4:40
the sea, great and **b**   Ps 104:25
dark in **b** daylight   Amos 8:9
way is **b** that leads to   Matt 7:13

BROKEN *crushed, separated*

My spirit is **b**   Job 17:1
A **b** and contrite heart   Ps 51:17
they have **b** Thy law   Ps 119:126
deeps were **b** up   Prov 3:20
silver cord is **b**   Eccl 12:6
bind up the **b**   Ezek 34:16
Scripture...be **b**   John 10:35

Not a bone...b   John 19:36
Branches were b off   Rom 11:19

BROKENHEARTED grieving

LORD is near to the b   Ps 34:18
He heals the b   Ps 147:3
sent me to bind...b   Is 61:1

BRONZE metal

implements of b   Gen 4:22
made a b serpent   Num 21:9
bend a bow of b   2 Sam 22:35
as walls of b   Jer 1:18
third kingdom of b   Dan 2:39
costly wood and b   Rev 18:12

BROOD group, offspring

b of sinful men   Num 32:14
You b of vipers   Matt 3:7
hen gathers her b   Luke 13:34

BROOK stream, wadi

stones from the b   1 Sam 17:40
by the b Cherith   1 Kin 17:5
deer pants for...b-s   Ps 42:1
wisdom...bubbling b   Prov 18:4

BROTHER male relative

Am I my b-'s   Gen 4:9
b-s were jealous   Gen 37:11
b-s may redeem   Lev 25:48
b-s to dwell together   Ps 133:1
b is born for   Prov 17:17
closer than a b   Prov 18:24
b-s of a poor man   Prov 19:7
reconciled to your b   Matt 5:24
b will deliver up b   Matt 10:21
behold, His...b-s   Matt 12:46
not forgive his b   Matt 18:35
My b and sister   Mark 3:35
b of yours was dead   Luke 15:32
left...wife or b-s   Luke 18:29
not even His b-s   John 7:5
b shall rise again   John 11:23
b goes to law with b   1 Cor 6:6
my b to stumble   1 Cor 8:13
yet hates his b   1 John 2:9

BROTHERHOOD

the covenant of b   Amos 1:9
love the b, fear God   1 Pet 2:17

BRUISE (n) wound

for wound, b for b   Ex 21:25

Only b-s, welts, and raw   Is 1:6
the b He has inflicted   Is 30:26

BRUISE (v) batter, crush

b him on the heel   Gen 3:15
b-s me with a tempest   Job 9:17

BRUTAL fierce, vicious

hand of b men   Ezek 21:31
b, haters of good   2 Tim 3:3

BUD blossom, a sprout

flax was in b   Ex 9:31
put forth b-s   Num 17:8
the b blossoms   Is 18:5

BUFFET beat

I b my body   1 Cor 9:27
Satan to b me   2 Cor 12:7

BUILD construct, form

Noah built an altar   Gen 8:20
let us b...a city   Gen 11:4
b for Me a house   1 Chr 17:12
b-ing...house of God   2 Chr 3:3
built high places   2 Chr 33:19
has built up Zion   Ps 102:16
Unless the LORD b-s   Ps 127:1
a time to b up   Eccl 3:3
built his house upon   Matt 7:24
I will b My church   Matt 16:18
able to b you up   Acts 20:32
being built together   Eph 2:22
stones...being built   1 Pet 2:5

BUILDER fashioner, maker

Solomon's b-s   1 Kin 5:18
b-s had laid the   Ezra 3:10
the b-s rejected   Matt 21:42
as a wise master b   1 Cor 3:10
architect and b is   Heb 11:10

BUILDING structure

reconstructing this b   Ezra 5:4
b that was in front   Ezek 41:12
what wonderful b-s   Mark 13:1
you are...God's b   1 Cor 3:9
have a b from God   2 Cor 5:1
whole b, being fitted   Eph 2:21

BULB part of plant

a b and a flower   Ex 25:33
b-s and their branches   Ex 25:36

BULL animal

b of the sin offering   Lev 4:20

33

b without blemish   Ezek 45:18
blood of **b-s** and   Heb 10:4

BULRUSH *marsh plant*

b in a single day   Is 9:14
b-es by the Nile   Is 19:7
palm branch or **b**   Is 19:15

BUNDLE *package*

b...*was* in his sack   Gen 42:35
the **b** of the living   1 Sam 25:29
in **b-s** to burn   Matt 13:30

BURDEN (n) *load, weight*

b-s of the Egyptians   Ex 6:6
the **b** of the people   Num 11:17
I am a **b** to myself   Job 7:20
who daily bears our **b**   Ps 68:19
b-s hard to bear   Luke 11:46
Bear one another's **b-s**   Gal 6:2

BURDEN (v) *weigh down*

b-ed Me with your sins   Is 43:24
were **b-ed** excessively   2 Cor 1:8
not **b** you myself   2 Cor 12:16
the church be **b-ed**   1 Tim 5:16

BURIAL *interment*

give me a **b** site   Gen 23:4
even have a *proper* **b**   Eccl 6:3
to prepare Me for **b**   Matt 26:12
b custom of the Jews   John 19:40

BURN *consume, kindle*

Jacob's anger **b-ed**   Gen 30:2
bush was **b-ing**   Ex 3:2
Thine anger **b** against   Ex 32:11
Moses' anger **b-ed**   Ex 32:19
did not **b** any cities   Josh 11:13
jealousy **b** like fire   Ps 79:5
to **b** their sons   Jer 7:31
not to **b** the scroll   Jer 36:25
will **b** up the chaff   Luke 3:17
b-ed in their desire   Rom 1:27
my body to be **b-ed**   1 Cor 13:3
works will be **b-ed**   2 Pet 3:10
lake of fire...**b-s**   Rev 19:20

BURNING

Thy **b** anger   Ex 15:7
shall bewail the **b**   Lev 10:6
b lips and a wicked   Prov 26:23
b heat of famine   Lam 5:10
b anger of the LORD   Zeph 2:2

BURNISHED *polished*   8

gleamed like **b** bronze   Ezek 1:7
feet...like **b** bronze   Rev 1:15

BURNT OFFERINGS
see **OFFERINGS**

BURST *break*

great deep **b** open   Gen 7:11
wine will **b** the skins   Luke 5:37
b his fetters   Luke 8:29
he **b** open   Acts 1:18

BURY *place in earth*

b-ied at...old age   Gen 15:15
that I may **b** my dead   Gen 23:4
b-ied the bones of   Josh 24:32
go and **b** my father   Matt 8:21
dead to **b** their own   Matt 8:22
devout...**b-ied** Stephen   Acts 8:2
that He was **b-ied**   1 Cor 15:4
b-ied...in baptism   Col 2:12

BUSH *shrub*

boy under...the **b-s**   Gen 21:15
the **b** was burning   Ex 3:2
who dwelt in the **b**   Deut 33:16
like a **b** in the desert   Jer 17:6

BUSINESS *occupation, work*

until I...told my **b**   Gen 24:33
carry on the *king's* **b**   Esth 3:9
another to his **b**   Matt 22:5
attend to your...**b**   1 Thess 4:11
engage in **b**   James 4:13

BUSYBODIES *meddlers*

no work...like **b**   2 Thess 3:11
gossips and **b**   1 Tim 5:13

BUTTER

steps...bathed in **b**   Job 29:6
smoother than **b**   Ps 55:21
milk produces **b**   Prov 30:33

BUYER *purchaser*

Bad, bad, says the **b**   Prov 20:14
the **b** like the seller   Is 24:2
Let not the **b** rejoice   Ezek 7:12

BYSTANDERS *onlookers*

b...said to Peter   Matt 26:73
the **b** heard it   Mark 15:35

BYWORD *contemptible*

b among all peoples   1 Kin 9:7
a proverb and a b   2 Chr 7:20
He has made me a b   Job 17:6
b among the nations   Ps 44:14

C

CAESAR

1 *Roman emperor* Matt 22:17,21
    Mark 12:14, John 19:12
2 *Augustus*   Luke 2:1
3 *Tiberius*   Luke 3:1
    John 19:12
4 *Claudius*   Acts 11:28;17:7
    Acts 18:2
5 *Nero*   Acts 25:12;26:32
    Phil 4:22

CAESAREA

Roman coastal city   Acts 8:40
    Acts 10:1;21:16;25:4

CAESAREA PHILIPPI

city at base of Mt. Hermon
    Matt 16:13; Mark 8:27

CAIAPHAS

high priest   Matt 26:57
Luke 3:2;John 11:49ff;Acts 4:6

CAIN

son of Adam   Gen 4:1
tiller of the ground   Gen 4:2
killed his brother   Gen 4:8
marked by sign   Gen 4:15

CAKE *type of bread*

and make bread c-s   Gen 18:6
took one unleavened c Lev 8:26
make me a...c   1 Kin 17:13

CALAMITY *adversity, trouble*

day of my c   2 Sam 22:19
sorry over the c   1 Chr 21:15
palate discern c-ies   Job 6:30
c from God is   Job 31:23
stumble in *time of* c Prov 24:16
beginning to work c   Jer 25:29
relents concerning c   Jon 4:2

CALCULATE *count*

shall c from the year Lev 25:50

c the cost   Luke 14:28
c the...beast   Rev 13:18

CALEB

1 *aide to Moses*   Num 13:30
   son of Jephunneh Num 32:12
   received Hebron   Josh 14:13
2 *son of Hezron*   1 Chr 2:18
3 *son of Hur*   1 Chr 2:50

CALF *animal*

tender and choice c   Gen 18:7
into a molten c   Ex 32:4
c and the young lion   Is 11:6
skip about like c-ves   Mal 4:2
bring the fattened c Luke 15:23
blood of...c-ves   Heb 9:12

CALL *address, summon, name*

God c-ed the light day Gen 1:5
c upon the name   Gen 4:26
c-s up the dead   Deut 18:11
LORD was c-ing...boy 1 Sam 3:8
c fine gold my trust Job 31:24
c upon the LORD   Ps 18:3
those who c evil good   Is 5:20
c His name Immanuel   Is 7:14
You shall c Me   Jer 3:19
who is c-ed Christ   Matt 1:16
to c the righteous   Matt 9:13
c-s his own sheep   John 10:3
c Me Teacher and   John 13:13
God has not c-ed 1 Thess 4:7
c-s...a prophetess   Rev 2:20

CALLING *summoning*

the c of assemblies   Is 1:13
the c of God   Rom 11:29
For consider your c 1 Cor 1:26
with a holy c   2 Tim 1:9
His c and choosing   2 Pet 1:10

CALM *still*

be c, have no fear   Is 7:4
sea may become c   Jon 1:11
it became perfectly c Matt 8:26
you ought to keep c Acts 19:36

CAMEL *animal*

dismounted...the c   Gen 24:64
his wives upon c-s   Gen 31:17
a garment of c-'s hair Matt 3:4
c...eye of a needle   Matt 19:24

clothed with c-'s hair Mark 1:6

CAMP (n) *lodging area*

This is God's c   Gen 32:2
people out of the c   Ex 19:17
outside the c seven   Num 31:19
pitch c-s, and place   Ezek 4:2
the c of the saints   Rev 20:9

CAMP (v) *settle*

you shall c in front   Ex 14:2
they shall also c   Num 1:50
God walks in...c   Deut 23:14
Israel c-ed at Gilgal   Josh 5:10
I will c against you   Is 29:3
c around My house   Zech 9:8

CANA

Galilean town   John 2:1,11;4:46

CANAAN

1 *son of Ham*   Gen 9:18,25
2 *Syro-Palestine*   Gen 13:12
    Gen 42:5; Ex 16:35; Ps 105:11
3 *language (Hebrew)*   Is 19:18
    see also HEBREW
    see also JUDEAN

CANAL *water way*

c-s will emit a stench   Is 19:6
rivers and wide c-s   Is 33:21
the Nile c-s dry   Ezek 30:12
in front of the c   Dan 8:3

CAPERNAUM

city on Sea of Galilee
    Matt 4:13, Luke 4:23
    John 6:24,59

CAPHTOR

Crete   Deut 2:23; Jer 47:4
    Amos 9:7

see also CRETE

CAPITAL *top part of column*

height of the other c   1 Kin 7:16
c on the top of each   2 Chr 3:15
c-s...were on top   2 Chr 4:12

CAPITAL *city*

Susa the c   Esth 2:3

CAPPADOCIA

province in Asia Minor
    Acts 2:9; 1 Pet 1:1

CAPTAIN *leader*

c of the bodyguard   Gen 39:1
the c-s of hundreds   Num 31:14
c of the host of   Josh 5:14
the c of the ship   Acts 27:11

CAPTIVE *prisoner*

first-born of the c   Ex 12:29
slain and the c-s   Deut 32:42
restores His c people   Ps 14:7
hast led c *Thy* c-s   Ps 68:18
release to the c-s   Luke 4:18
every thought c   2 Cor 10:5
having been held c   2 Tim 2:26

CAPTIVITY *imprisonment*

restore you from c   Deut 30:3
land of their c   2 Chr 6:37
had come from the c   Ezra 8:35
had survived the c   Neh 1:2
destined for c   Rev 13:10

CAPTURE *seize, take*

they c-d and looted   Gen 34:29
c-d all his cities   Deut 2:34
Can anyone c him   Job 40:24
it c-s nothing at all   Amos 3:5

CARAVAN *expedition*

a c of Ishmaelites   Gen 37:25
The c-s of Tema   Job 6:19
O c-s of Dedanites   Is 21:13

CARCASS *corpse*

down upon the c-es   Gen 15:11
one who touches...c   Lev 11:39
c-es shall be food   Deut 28:26
c of the lion   Judg 14:8
c-es of their...idols   Jer 16:18

CARE (n) *concern*

into the c of...sons   Gen 30:35
put him in my c   Gen 42:37
friends and receive c   Acts 27:3
c for one another   1 Cor 12:25

CARE (v) *have concern for*

He c-d for him   Deut 32:10
No one c-s for...soul   Ps 142:4
c for My sheep   Ezek 34:12
and took c of him   Luke 10:34
take c of the church   1 Tim 3:5
He c-s for you   1 Pet 5:7

CAREFUL *watchful, on guard*

I not be **c** to speak   Num 23:12
c to observe all   Deut 6:25
you shall be **c** to do   Deut 8:1
be **c** not to drink   Judg 13:4
be **c** how you walk   Eph 5:15

CARELESS *thoughtless*

a fool is...**c**   Prov 14:16
food, and **c** ease   Ezek 16:49
that every **c** word   Matt 12:36

CARGO *merchandise*

and they threw the **c**   Jon 1:5
to unload its **c**   Acts 21:3
no one buys...**c**-es   Rev 18:11

CARMEL

1 *range of hills*   1 Kin 18:42
  2 Kin 4:25; Jer 46:18
2 *town in Judah*   1 Sam 15:12
  1 Sam 25:5,40

CARPENTER *craftsman*

c-s and stonemasons   2 Sam 5:11
to the masons and **c**-s   Ezra 3:7
this the **c**-'s son   Matt 13:55
c, the son of Mary   Mark 6:3

CARRY *bear*

LORD...**c**-ied you   Deut 1:31
c an ephod before   1 Sam 2:28
Spirit...will **c** you   1 Kin 18:12
c *them* in His bosom   Is 40:11
our sorrows He **c**-ied   Is 53:4
c-ied away...diseases   Matt 8:17
C no purse, no bag   Luke 10:4
the cross to **c**   Luke 23:26
c out the desire of   Gal 5:16

CART *wagon*

So Moses took the **c**-s   Num 7:6
the cows to the **c**   1 Sam 6:7
sin as if with **c** ropes   Is 5:18
his **c** and his horses   Is 28:28

CARVE (v) *cut, fashion*

he **c**-d all the walls   1 Kin 6:29
who **c** a resting place   Is 22:16
c-d with cherubim   Ezek 41:18
its maker had **c**-d it   Hab 2:18

CARVED (adj) *cut, etched*

with **c** engravings   1 Kin 6:29

c image of the idol   2 Chr 33:7
abdomen is **c** ivory   Song 5:14

CAST *throw*

one who **c**-s a spell   Deut 18:11
Joshua **c** lots for   Josh 18:10
c Thy law behind   Neh 9:26
c *lots* for the orphans   Job 6:27
c My words behind   Ps 50:17
Do not **c** me away   Ps 51:11
c you out of My sight   Jer 7:15
c-ing...insult   Mark 15:32
will **c** out demons   Mark 16:17
c Him out of...city   Luke 4:29
c fire upon...earth   Luke 12:49
clothing they **c** lots   John 19:24
c-ing all your anxiety   1 Pet 5:7
but **c** them into hell   2 Pet 2:4
c their crowns before   Rev 4:10

CATCH *seize, trap*

shall **c** his wife   Judg 21:21
to **c** the afflicted   Ps 10:9
c...with her eyelids   Prov 6:25
C the foxes for us   Song 2:15
caught in My snare   Ezek 12:13
will be **c**-ing men   Luke 5:10
unable to **c** Him   Luke 20:26
caught in adultery   John 8:3
who **c**-es the wise   1 Cor 3:19
if a man is **caught**   Gal 6:1
child was **caught** up   Rev 12:5

CATTLE *domestic animals*

c and creeping things   Gen 1:24
the first-born of **c**   Ex 12:29
defect from the **c**   Lev 22:19
c on a thousand hills   Ps 50:10
no **c** in the stalls   Hab 3:17

CAUSE (n) *purpose, reason*

the **c** of the just   Ex 23:8
to death without a **c**   1 Sam 19:5
place my **c** before God   Job 5:8
hate me without a **c**   Ps 69:4
wounds without **c**   Prov 23:29
c a man shall leave   Matt 19:5
hated...without a **c**   John 15:25

CAUSE (v) *make*

I **c** My name to be   Ex 20:24
c Israel to inherit   Deut 1:38
has **c**-d His name   Ezra 6:12

CAUSE

c His face to shine   Ps 67:1
speech c you to sin   Eccl 5:6
who c dissensions   Rom 16:17
was c-ing the growth   1 Cor 3:6

CAVE *shelter*

buried him in the c   Gen 25:9
escaped to the c   1 Sam 22:1
by fifties in a c   1 Kin 18:4
mountains and c-s   Heb 11:38
hid...in the c-s   Rev 6:15

CEASE *stop*

you shall c *from labor*   Ex 23:12
poor will never c   Deut 15:11
He makes wars to c   Ps 46:9
C...consideration   Prov 23:4
make this proverb c   Ezek 12:23
c-d to kiss My feet   Luke 7:45
tongues, they will c   1 Cor 13:8
pray without c-ing   1 Thess 5:17

CEDAR *tree, wood*

with the c wood   Lev 14:6
c-s beside the waters   Num 24:6
all the c-s of Lebanon   Is 2:13
the height of c-s   Amos 2:9

CELEBRATE *rejoice*

may c a feast to Me   Ex 5:1
you shall c it in   Lev 23:41
C the Passover   2 Kin 23:21
all Israel were c-ing   1 Chr 13:8
to c *the feast*   2 Chr 30:23

CENSER *incense container*

c-s for yourselves   Num 16:6
his c in his hand   Ezek 8:11
holding a golden c   Rev 8:3
angel took the c   Rev 8:5

CENSUS *population roll*

c of...congregation   Num 1:2
number of the c   1 Chr 21:5
c which...David   2 Chr 2:17
the first c taken   Luke 2:2
in the days of the c   Acts 5:37

CENT *money*

paid up the last c   Matt 5:26
sparrows...for a c   Matt 10:29
amount to a c   Mark 12:42

CENTURION *captain*

Jesus said to the c   Matt 8:13

summoning the c   Mark 15:44
soldiers and c-s   Acts 21:32
gave orders to the c   Acts 24:23

CEPHAS

apostle Peter   John 1:42
     1 Cor 1:12;15:5; Gal 2:11

CERTAINTY *sureness*

know with c that   Josh 23:13
c of the words   Prov 22:21
you know with c   Eph 5:5

CERTIFICATE *permit, record*

a c of divorce   Deut 24:1
a c of divorce   Matt 5:31
c of debt   Col 2:14

CHAFF *husk*

consumes them as c   Ex 15:7
c which the wind blows   Ps 1:4
make the hills like c   Is 41:15
c from the summer   Dan 2:35
burn up the c   Matt 3:12

CHAIN *band*

bound...bronze c-s   Judg 16:21
he drew c-s of gold   1 Kin 6:21
whose hands are c-s   Eccl 7:26
was bound with c-s   Luke 8:29
c-s fell off his hands   Acts 12:7
great c in his hand   Rev 20:1

CHALDEA

S Babylonia   Jer 50:10;51:24
                             Ezek 23:15

CHALDEANS

inhabitants of Chaldea
Gen 11:28; 2 Kin 24:2; Job 1:17
     Jer 24:5; Dan 5:11; Hab 1:6

CHAMBER *room*

entered his c   Gen 43:30
in his cool roof c   Judg 3:20
c-s of the storehouse   Neh 10:38
bridegroom...his c   Ps 19:5
to the c-s of death   Prov 7:27
out of her *bridal* c   Joel 2:16
c-s in the heavens   Amos 9:6

CHAMPION *fighter*

c, the Philistine   1 Sam 17:23
a Savior and a C   Is 19:20
like a dread c   Jer 20:11

38

CHANGE (n) *alteration*

gave **c-s** of garments	Gen 45:22
had a **c** of heart	Ex 14:5
two **c-s** of clothes	2 Kin 5:23
Until my **c** comes	Job 14:14
a **c** of law	Heb 7:12

CHANGE (v) *alter, transform*

and **c-d** my wages	Gen 31:7
He **c-s** a wilderness	Ps 107:35
c-d their glory	Jer 2:11
Ethiopian **c** his skin	Jer 13:23
He who **c-s** the times	Dan 2:21
LORD **c-d** His mind	Amos 7:6
I, the LORD, do not **c**	Mal 3:6
shall all be **c-d**	1 Cor 15:51

CHANNEL *furrow*

Who has cleft a **c**	Job 38:25
c-s of water appeared	Ps 18:15
heart is *like* **c-s**	Prov 21:1
sent out its **c-s**	Ezek 31:4

CHANT *sing*

David **c-ed**...this	2 Sam 1:17
Jeremiah **c-ed** a	2 Chr 35:25
daughters...shall **c**	Ezek 32:16

CHARACTER

| and proven **c**, hope | Rom 5:4 |
| Let your **c** be free | Heb 13:5 |

CHARGE (n) *responsibility*

under Joseph's **c**	Gen 39:23
keep the **c** of the LORD	Lev 8:35
c of his household	Matt 24:45
allotted to your **c**	1 Pet 5:3

CHARGE (n) *accusation*

far from a false **c**	Ex 23:7
bring **c-s** against	Acts 19:38
c against God's elect	Rom 8:33

CHARGE (n) *cost*

| gospel without **c** | 1 Cor 9:18 |

CHARGE (v) *command*

Abimelech **c-d** all	Gen 26:11
I **c-d** your judges	Deut 1:16
Moses **c-d** us with a	Deut 33:4
I solemnly **c** you	1 Tim 5:21

CHARGE (v) *exact a price*

| not **c** him interest | Ex 22:25 |

| **c** that to my account | Philem 18 |

CHARIOT *wagon*

Joseph prepared...**c**	Gen 46:29
appeared a **c** of fire	2 Kin 2:11
Some *boast* in **c-s**	Ps 20:7
c-s of God are myriads	Ps 68:17
Thy **c-s** of salvation	Hab 3:8
I will cut off the **c**	Zech 9:10
and sitting in his **c**	Acts 8:28

CHARIOTEERS *warriors*

David killed 700 **c**	2 Sam 10:18
7,000 **c** and 40,000	1 Chr 19:18
with horses and **c**	Ezek 39:20

CHARITY *alms*

give that...as **c**	Luke 11:41
and give to **c**	Luke 12:33
deeds of...**c**	Acts 9:36

CHARM *beauty*

| A bribe is a **c** | Prov 17:8 |
| with *all* your **c-s** | Song 7:6 |

CHASE *drive, pursue*

Egyptians **c-d** after	Ex 14:9
will **c** your enemies	Lev 26:7
one **c** a thousand	Deut 32:30
c-ing...Philistines	1 Sam 17:53
be **c-d** like chaff	Is 17:13

CHASTE *pure*

| **c**...behavior | 1 Pet 3:2 |
| kept themselves **c** | Rev 14:4 |

CHASTEN *discipline*

Man is also **c-ed**	Job 33:19
Nor **c** me in Thy wrath	Ps 6:1
c-ed every morning	Ps 73:14
who **c-s** the nations	Ps 94:10

CHASTISE *punish*

| Thou hast **c-d** me | Jer 31:18 |
| I will **c** all of them | Hos 5:2 |

CHATTER *babbling*

| worldly...empty **c** | 1 Tim 6:20 |
| avoid...empty **c** | 2 Tim 2:16 |

CHEAT *deceive*

| your father has **c-ed** | Gen 31:7 |
| **c** with...scales | Amos 8:5 |

CHEBAR
river in Babylonia Ezek 3:15
Ezek 10:15

CHEDORLAOMER
king of Elam Gen 14:9,17

CHEEK *part of face*
slapped me on the c Job 16:10
Your c-s are lovely Song 1:10
tears are on her c-s Lam 1:2
hits you on the c Luke 6:29

CHEERFUL
and be c Job 9:27
joyful heart...a c Prov 15:13
c heart...feast Prov 15:15
God loves a c giver 2 Cor 9:7
Is anyone c James 5:13

CHEMOSH
god of Moab Judg 11:24
1 Kin 11:7;Jer 48:13

CHERETHITES
1 *tribe on Philistine plain*
1 Sam 30:14; Ezek 25:16
Zeph 2:5
2 *David's bodyguards*
2 Sam 8:18;15:18;1 Kin 1:38
1 Chr 18:17

CHERISH *love*
or the wife you c Deut 13:6
the wife he c-s Deut 28:54
men c themselves Acts 24:15
c-s it, just as Christ Eph 5:29

CHERUB *celestial being*
He rode on a c 2 Sam 22:11
one c...ten cubits 1 Kin 6:26
c stretched out his Ezek 10:7

CHERUBIM *plural of Cherub*
He stationed the c Gen 3:24
c had *their* wings Ex 37:9
enthroned *above*...c 2 Sam 6:2
c appeared to have Ezek 10:8

CHEST *box*
the priest took a c 2 Kin 12:9
money in the c 2 Kin 12:10
levies...into the c 2 Chr 24:10

CHEW *eat*
which c the cud Lev 11:4
before it was c-ed Num 11:33

CHIEF *head, prominent*
c-s of the sons of Gen 36:15
the c-s of Edom Gen 36:43
of the thirty c men 2 Sam 23:13
c of the magicians Dan 4:9
C Shepherd appears 1 Pet 5:4

CHILD
c grew...weaned Gen 21:8
Train up a c in Prov 22:6
discipline from the c Prov 23:13
c will be born to us Is 9:6
with c by the Holy Matt 1:18
take the C and His Matt 2:13
He called a c to Matt 18:2
saying, "C, arise Luke 8:54
a woman with c 1 Thess 5:3

CHILDBIRTH
multiply...pain in c Gen 3:16
as of a woman in c Ps 48:6
pains of c come Hos 13:13
suffers the pains of c Rom 8:22

CHILDLESS
I am c, and the heir Gen 15:2
They shall die c Lev 20:20
c among women 1 Sam 15:33
and died c Luke 20:29

CHILDREN
pain...bring forth c Gen 3:16
Are these all the c 1 Sam 16:11
compassion on *his* c Ps 103:13
C are a gift Ps 127:3
c rise up end bless Prov 31:28
c were dashed to Nah 3:10
slew all the male c Matt 2:16
stones to raise up c Matt 3:9
c...against parents Matt 10:21
and become like c Matt 18:3
bringing c to Him Mark 10:13
if c, heirs Rom 8:17
C, obey your parents Eph 6:1
My little c 1 John 2:1
kill her c with Rev 2:23

CHINNERETH/
CHINNEROTH
1 *lake* Num 34:11; Josh 12:3

also **Sea of Galilee**
also **Lake of Gennesaret**
also **Sea of Tiberius**
2 *city of Naphtali*   Deut 3:17
                              Josh 19:35
3 *plain near Galilee*
                   Josh 11:2; 1 Kin 15:20

CHISLEV
ninth month of Hebrew
calendar   Neh 1:1;Zech 7:1

CHOICE *option or best*

Saul, a c...*man*   1 Sam 9:2
c men of Israel   2 Sam 10:9
And eat its c fruits   Song 4:16
God made a c among   Acts 15:7
God's gracious c   Rom 11:5
His c of you   1 Thess 1:4

CHOIR *chorus*

c proceeded to the   Neh 12:38
two c-s took their   Neh 12:40

CHOKE *stifle*

riches c the word   Matt 13:22
began to c him   Matt 18:28
thorns...c-d it   Mark 4:7
c-d with worries   Luke 8:14

CHOOSE *select, take*

C men for us   Ex 17:9
whom the LORD c-s   Num 16:7
C wise...discerning   Deut 1:13
He c-s our inheritance   Ps 47:4
refuse evil and c good   Is 7:15
not God c the poor   James 2:5

CHOP *cut*

who c-s your wood   Deut 29:11
c-ped down...altars   2 Chr 34:7
C down the tree   Dan 4:14

CHOSE *selected*

Lot c for himself   Gen 13:11
God has c-n you   Deut 7:6
I c David to be   1 Kin 8:16
when I c Israel   Ezek 20:5
c twelve of them   Luke 6:13
has c-n the weak   1 Cor 1:27
He c us in Him   Eph 1:4

CHOSEN *elected, selected*

Moses His c one   Ps 106:23
My c *one in whom*   Is 42:1
Israel My c *one*   Is 45:4
c ones shall inherit   Is 65:9
My Son, *My* C One   Luke 9:35
c of God, holy and   Col 3:12
of *His* c angels   1 Tim 5:21
you are a c race   1 Pet 2:9

CHRIST *Messiah*

birth of Jesus C was   Matt 1:18
C should suffer and   Luke 24:46
both Lord and C   Acts 2:36
fellow heirs with C   Rom 8:17
are one body in C   Rom 12:5
preach C crucified   1 Cor 1:23
judgment seat of C   2 Cor 5:10
ambassadors for C   2 Cor 5:20
faith in C Jesus   Gal 2:16
as sons through Jesus C   Eph 1:5
to live is C   Phil 1:21
C, who is our life   Col 3:4
dead in C shall   1 Thess 4:16
coming of...C   2 Thess 2:1
C...high priest   Heb 9:11
Advocate...Jesus C   1 John 2:1
with C for a thousand   Rev 20:4

CHRISTIAN *follower of Christ*

first called C-s in   Acts 11:26
me to become a C   Acts 26:28
suffers as a C   1 Pet 4:16

CHRONICLES *book of register*
1 *of kings of Israel*
                     1 Kin 14:19;15:31
                     2 Kin 14:28;15:26
2 *of kings of Judah*
                     1 Kin 14:29;15:23
                     2 Kin 15:36;24:5
3 *of kings of Media/Persia*
                              Esth 10:2

CHURCH *a called out assembly*

I will build my c   Matt 16:18
tell it to the c   Matt 18:17
shepherd the c   Acts 20:28
c-es of the Gentiles   Rom 16:4
together as a c   1 Cor 11:18
woman...speak in c   1 Cor 14:35
to the c-es of Judea   Gal 1:22

CHURCH

Christ...head of the c   Eph 5:23
persecutor of the c   Phil 3:6
c of the living God   1 Tim 3:15
Spirit says to the c-es   Rev 2:11

CILICIA

region in SE Asia Minor
                    Acts 15:41;21:39;27:5

CINNAMON *spice*

and of fragrant c   Ex 30:23
myrrh, aloes and c   Prov 7:17
and c and spice   Rev 18:13

CIRCLE *area*

sleeping inside...c   1 Sam 26:7
He has inscribed a c   Job 26:10
did not sit in the c   Jer 15:17

CIRCUIT *course*

on the c to Bethel   1 Sam 7:16
its c to the other end   Ps 19:6

CIRCULATE *spread*

proclamation was c-d   Ex 36:6
LORD'S people c-ing   1 Sam 2:24
to c a proclamation   2 Chr 30:5

CIRCUMCISE *be pure or cut off*

every male...be c-d   Gen 17:10
Abraham c-d his son   Gen 21:4
C then your heart   Deut 10:16
God will c...heart   Deut 30:6
C yourselves to the LORD   Jer 4:4
came to c the child   Luke 1:59
c-d the eighth day   Phil 3:5

CIRCUMCISION *act of purity*

because of the c   Ex 4:26
c is...of the heart   Rom 2:29
if you receive c   Gal 5:2
if I still preach c   Gal 5:11
we are the *true* c   Phil 3:3
c made without hands   Col 2:11
those of the c   Titus 1:10

CIRCUMSTANCE *condition*

spoken in right c-s   Prov 25:11
may know...my c-s   Eph 6:21
peace in every c   2 Thess 3:16
of humble c-s   James 1:9

CISTERN *reservoir*

a c collecting water   Lev 11:36

water from your...c   Prov 5:15
wheel at the c is   Eccl 12:6
prophet from the c   Jer 38:10

CITADEL *fortress*

c of the king's   1 Kin 16:18
in the c of Susa   Dan 8:2
c-s of Jerusalem   Amos 2:5
Proclaim on the c-s   Amos 3:9
tramples on our c-s   Mic 5:5

CITIES OF REFUGE

1 *Kedesh in Naphtali*   Josh 20:7
2 *Shechem in Ephraim*   Josh 20:7
3 *Hebron (Kiriath-arba)*
                         Josh 20:7
4 *Bezer in Reuben*   Josh 20:8
5 *Ramoth-gilead in Gad*
                         Josh 20:8
6 *Golan in Manasseh*   Josh 20:8

CITIZEN *resident*

your fellow c-s   Ezek 33:12
fellow c-s who talk   Ezek 33:30
c-s called him   Luke 19:14
c of no insignificant Acts 21:39
fellow c-s with the   Eph 2:19

CITY

Build...a c   Gen 11:4
burned...their c-ies   Num 31:10
die in my own c   2 Sam 19:37
glad the c of God   Ps 46:4
LORD guards the c   Ps 127:1
the C of Destruction   Is 19:18
the C of Truth   Zech 8:3
a c called Nazareth   Matt 2:23
into the holy c   Matt 4:5
the c was stirred   Matt 21:10
c, shake off the dust Luke 9:5
He has prepared a c   Heb 11:16
I saw the holy c   Rev 21:2

CLAIM *demand*

Let darkness...c it   Job 3:5
Do not c honor in   Prov 25:6
c-ing to be someone   Acts 8:9

CLAN *family, tribe*

c of the household   Judg 9:1
and by your c-s   1 Sam 10:19
among...c-s of Judah   Mic 5:2
I will make the c-s   Zech 12:6

CLAP *applaud*

c-ped their hands | 2 Kin 11:12
c-s his hands among | Job 34:37
rivers c their hands | Ps 98:8
trees...will c | Is 55:12

CLAUDIA

Roman Christian | 2 Tim 4:21

CLAUDIUS

Roman Emperor
Acts 11:28;18:2
see CAESAR

CLAUDIUS LYSIAS

Roman tribune Acts 22:28;23:26

CLAY

dwell in houses of c | Job 4:19
Father, We are the c | Is 64:8
c in the potter's hand | Jer 18:6
the c to his eyes | John 9:6

CLEAN *cleansed, washed*

animals that are not c | Gen 7:2
eat in a c place | Lev 10:14
pronounce him c | Lev 13:28
Create in me a c heart | Ps 51:10
make yourselves c | Is 1:16
You can make me c | Matt 8:2
things are c for you | Luke 11:41
c because of the word | John 15:3

CLEANSE *purify, wash*

To c the house then | Lev 14:49
c the house of the 2 | Chr 29:15
I have c-d my heart | Prov 20:9
I am willing; be c-d | Matt 8:3
the lepers are c-d | Matt 11:5
not eat unless they c | Mark 7:4
let us c ourselves | 2 Cor 7:1
C...you sinners | James 4:8
blood...c-s us | 1 John 1:7

CLEAR *make free* or *plain*

c away many nations | Deut 7:1
C the way for the LORD | Is 40:3
c His threshing floor | Matt 3:12
Christ had made c | 2 Pet 1:14
river...c as crystal | Rev 22:1

CLEAVE *cling, divide*

shall c to his wife | Gen 2:24
tongue c-s to my jaws | Ps 22:15

c to Thy testimonies | Ps 119:31
c the earth with rivers | Hab 3:9
shall c to his wife | Eph 5:31

CLEFT *crevice*

in the c of the rock | Judg 15:8
the c-s of the cliffs | Is 2:21
who live in the c-s | Obad 3

CLEOPAS

disciple of Christ | Luke 24:18

CLEVER *smart*

c in their own sight | Is 5:21
cleverness of the c | 1 Cor 1:19

CLIFF *crag*

nest is set in the c | Num 24:21
On the c he dwells | Job 39:28
c-s are a refuge | Ps 104:18

CLIMB *ascend*

I will c the palm tree | Song 7:8
the one who c-s | Jer 48:44
c-ed...a sycamore | Luke 19:4
c-s up...other way | John 10:1

CLING *cleave*

and c to Him | Deut 13:4
c to the LORD | Josh 23:8
My soul c-s to Thee | Ps 63:8
Stop c-ing to Me | John 20:17
c to what is good | Rom 12:9

CLOAK *coat, mantle*

Give me the c | Ruth 3:15
neither bread nor c | Is 3:7
fringe of His c | Matt 9:20
Wrap your c around | Acts 12:8

CLOSE *shut, stop*

and the LORD c-d | Gen 7:16
floodgates...were c-d | Gen 8:2
earth c-d over them | Num 16:33
have c-d their eyes | Acts 28:27
every mouth...c-d | Rom 3:19
c-s his heart | 1 John 3:17

CLOTH *fabric*

spread over *it* a c | Num 4:6
is wrapped in a c | 1 Sam 21:9
with embroidered c | Ezek 16:10
in the linen c | Mark 15:46

CLOTHE *array, dress*

C me with skin | Job 10:11

43

meadows are **c-d** with Ps 65:13
O Zion; **C** yourself Is 52:1
naked...you **c-d** Me Matt 25:36
are splendidly **c-d** Luke 7:25
c-d with power from Luke 24:49
c...with humility 1 Pet 5:5
c-d in the white robes Rev 7:13

CLOTHES *garments*

c of her captivity Deut 21:13
your **c** have not worn Deut 29:5
and worn-out **c** on Josh 9:5
and changed his **c** 2 Sam 12:20
without wedding **c** Matt 22:12
And tearing his **c** Mark 14:63

CLOTHING *clothes, raiment*

reduce...her **c** Ex 21:10
c did not wear out Deut 8:4
purple are their **c** Jer 10:9
and the body than **c** Matt 6:25
in sheep's **c** Matt 7:15
His **c** *became* white Luke 9:29
sister is without **c** James 2:15

CLOUD *mist*

set My bow in the **c** Gen 9:13
in a pillar of **c** Ex 13:21
c where God was Ex 20:21
c covered...mountain Ex 24:15
c for a covering Ps 105:39
voice came out...**c** Mark 9:7
Son...coming in **c-s** Mark 13:26
in a **c** with power Luke 21:27
and a **c** received Him Acts 1:9

CLUB *weapon*

went...with a **c** 2 Sam 23:21
C's are...as stubble Job 41:29
Like a **c** and a Prov 25:18
with swords and **c-s** Matt 26:47

CLUSTER *collection*

c-s produced ripe Gen 40:10
c-s of raisins 1 Sam 25:18
breasts are...**c-s** Song 7:7
gather the **c-s** Rev 14:18

COAL *charcoal*

breath kindles **c-s** Job 41:21
man walk on hot **c-s** Prov 6:28
burning **c** in his hand Is 6:6
heap burning **c-s** Rom 12:20

COAST

c of the Great Sea Josh 9:1
along the **c** of Asia Acts 27:2

COASTLAND

inhabitants of this **c** Is 20:6
to the **c-s** of Kittim Jer 2:10
c-s shake at the Ezek 26:15
c-s of the nations Zeph 2:11

COAT *cloak*

opening...**c** of mail Ex 28:32
with his **c** torn 2 Sam 15:32
have your **c** also Matt 5:40

COBRA *snake*

deadly poison of **c-s** Deut 32:33
To the venom of **c-s** Job 20:14
tread upon the...**c** Ps 91:13

COCK *bird*

The strutting **c** Prov 30:31
before a **c** crows Matt 26:34
c shall not crow John 13:38

COFFIN *bier*

in a **c** in Egypt Gen 50:26
and touched the **c** Luke 7:14

COHORT *military unit*

the whole *Roman* **c** Matt 27:27
called the Italian **c** Acts 10:1
of the Augustan **c** Acts 27:1

COIN *money*

Show Me the **c** Matt 22:19
woman...loses one **c** Luke 15:8
He poured out...**c-s** John 2:15

COLD *cool*

covering against the **c** Job 24:7
Like the **c** of snow Prov 25:13
cup of **c** water Matt 10:42
love will grow **c** Matt 24:12
neither **c** nor hot Rev 3:15

COLLAPSE *fall*

grass **c-s** into the flame Is 5:24
pathways will **c** Ezek 38:20
ancient hills **c-d** Hab 3:6

COLLEAGUES *co-workers*

the rest of his **c** Ezra 4:7
and your **c** Ezra 6:6

COLLECT *exact, take*

c-ed his strength	Gen 48:2
cistern **c-ing** water	Lev 11:36
c captives like sand	Hab 1:9
C no more than	Luke 3:13
c-ed a tenth from	Heb 7:6

COLLECTION *acquisition*

let your c *of idols*	Is 57:13
no **c-s** be made	1 Cor 16:2

COLOSSAE

city in Asia Minor	Col 1:2

COLT *foal*

camels and their **c-s**	Gen 32:15
Even on a c	Zech 9:9
and a c with her	Matt 21:2
on a donkey's c	John 12:15

COLUMN *pillar, text*

in a c of smoke	Judg 20:40
and marble **c-s**	Esth 1:6
read three...**c-s**	Jer 36:23

COME

C, let us build	Gen 11:4
C, let us worship	Ps 95:6
All came from...dust	Eccl 3:20
your king is **c-ing**	Zech 9:9
Thy kingdom c	Matt 6:10
C to Me, all who	Matt 11:28
children to c to Me	Mark 10:14
not c...temptation	Mark 14:38
Son of Man **c-ing**	Luke 21:27
Father...hour has c	John 17:1
His judgment has c	Rev 14:7
I am **c-ing** quickly	Rev 22:20

COMFORT (n) *consolation*

mourning without c	Job 30:28
c in my affliction	Ps 119:50
he will give you c	Prov 29:17
c of the Holy Spirit	Acts 9:31
and God of all c	2 Cor 1:3
your c and salvation	2 Cor 1:6

COMFORT (v) *console, cheer*

relatives came to c	1 Chr 7:22
Thy rod...they c me	Ps 23:4
I, am He who **c-s** you	Is 51:12
To c all who mourn	Is 61:2
he is being **c-ed**	Luke 16:25
c one another	1 Thess 4:18

COMFORTER *consoler*

Sorry **c-s** are you all	Job 16:2
c-s, but I found none	Ps 69:20
She has no c	Lam 1:9
Where will I seek **c-s**	Nah 3:7

COMING (n) *arrival*

Joseph's c at noon	Gen 43:25
the day of His c	Mal 3:2
be the sign of Your c	Matt 24:3
c of the Son of Man	Matt 24:37
Christ's at His c	1 Cor 15:23
c of the Lord is	James 5:8
the promise of His c	2 Pet 3:4

COMMAND (n) *order*

the c of the LORD	Lev 24:12
disobeyed the c	1 Kin 13:21
to the king's c	2 Chr 35:10
no c of the Lord	1 Cor 7:25
could not bear the c	Heb 12:20

COMMAND (v) *declare, order*

I **c-ed** you not to eat	Gen 3:11
may c his children	Gen 18:19
speak all that I c you	Ex 7:2
bring all that I c	Deut 12:11
the angel...**c-ed**	Matt 1:24
c that these stones	Matt 4:3
c-s even the winds	Luke 8:25
c-ing the jailer	Acts 16:23

COMMANDER *captain, general*

the **c-s** of Israel	Judg 5:9
c of Saul's army	2 Sam 2:8
his chariot **c-s**	1 Kin 9:22
and Joab was the c	1 Chr 27:34
c for the peoples	Is 55:4
the C of the host	Dan 8:11
and the flesh of **c-s**	Rev 19:18

COMMANDMENT *instruction*

and keep My **c-s**	Ex 20:6
the Ten **C-s**	Ex 34:28
and keep His **c-s**	Josh 22:5
c of the LORD is pure	Ps 19:8
the c of your father	Prov 6:20
which is the great c	Matt 22:36
A new c I give	John 13:34
will keep My **c-s**	John 14:15
I have kept...**c-s**	John 15:10
not writing a new c	1 John 2:7
keep the **c-s** of God	Rev 14:12

COMMEND *praise, present*

So I c-ed pleasure Eccl 8:15
I c you to God Acts 20:32
food will not c us 1 Cor 8:8
to c ourselves again 2 Cor 3:1

COMMISSION *appoint*

c him in their sight Num 27:19
He c-ed Joshua Deut 31:23
king has c-ed me 1 Sam 21:2
c it against the people Is 10:6

COMMISSIONERS *supervisors*

and over them three c Dan 6:2
Then the c and satraps Dan 6:4

COMMIT *entrust, practice*

c-ted to Joseph's Gen 39:22
shall not c adultery Ex 20:14
have c-ted incest Lev 20:12
I c my spirit Ps 31:5
C your way to the LORD Ps 37:5
weary...c-ing iniquity Jer 9:5
Do not c adultery Luke 18:20
I c My spirit Luke 23:46
everyone who c-s sin John 8:34
who c-ted no sin 1 Pet 2:22

COMMON *ordinary, shared*

anyone of...c people Lev 4:27
place of the c people Jer 26:23
iron...with c clay Dan 2:41
had all things in c Acts 2:44
about our c salvation Jude 3

COMMONWEALTH *nation*

from the c of Israel Eph 2:12

COMMOTION *disturbance*

the noise of this c 1 Sam 4:14
great c out of the Jer 10:22
Why make a c and Mark 5:39

COMPANION *comrade, friend*

are you striking your c Ex 2:13
brought thirty c-s Judg 14:11
And a c of ostriches Job 30:29
c of fools will suffer Prov 13:20
your c and your wife Mal 2:14
Paul and his c-s Acts 13:13

COMPANY *assembly, group*

into three c-ies Judg 9:43

c of the godless Job 15:34
c will stone them Ezek 23:47
Bad c corrupts 1 Cor 15:33

COMPARE *contrast, liken*

none to c with Thee Ps 40:5
to what shall I c Matt 11:16
c the kingdom of Luke 13:20
be c-d with the glory Rom 8:18

COMPASS

outlines it with a c Is 44:13
four points of the c Dan 11:4

COMPASSION *concern, love*

God...grant you c Gen 43:14
whom I will show c Ex 33:19
in Thy great c Neh 9:19
have c on the poor Ps 72:13
have c on Zion Ps 102:13
His c-s never fail Lam 3:22
He felt c for them Matt 9:36
his father...felt c Luke 15:20
put on a heart of c Col 3:12
Lord is full of c James 5:11

COMPASSIONATE *loving*

your God is a c God Deut 4:31
c, Slow to anger Neh 9:17
He is gracious and c Joel 2:13
a gracious and c God Jon 4:2

COMPEL *force, press*

Egyptians c-led the Ex 1:13
c them to come in Luke 14:23
c...to be circumcised Gal 6:12

COMPETE *strive*

can you c with horses Jer 12:5
everyone who c-s 1 Cor 9:25
c-s as an athlete 2 Tim 2:5

COMPLAIN *murmur*

c-ed to Abimelech Gen 21:25
c in the bitterness Job 7:11
I will c and murmur Ps 55:17
Do not c, brethren James 5:9

COMPLAINT *grumbling*

c-s of...Israel Num 14:27
couch will ease my c Job 7:13
today my c is rebellion Job 23:2
hospitable...without c 1 Pet 4:9

COMPLETE (adj) *full, total*

a sabbath of c rest   Ex 35:2
be seven c sabbaths   Lev 23:15
not...a c destruction   Jer 5:10
you have been made c   Col 2:10
be perfect and c   James 1:4
joy may be made c   1 John 1:4

COMPLETE (v) *finish, fulfill*

God c-ed His work   Gen 2:2
C the week of this   Gen 29:27
C your work quota   Ex 5:13
your days are c   2 Sam 7:12
house...was c-d   2 Chr 8:16
thousand years are c-d   Rev 20:7

COMPOSE *write*

c words against you   Job 16:4
have c-ed songs for   Amos 6:5
The first account I c-d   Acts 1:1

COMPOSE *make calm*

c-d and quieted my   Ps 131:2
I c my soul   Is 38:13

COMPREHEND *understand*

which we cannot c   Job 37:5
speech...no one c-s   Is 33:19
and they did not c   Luke 18:34
darkness did not c   John 1:5

COMPULSION *coercion*

under c...let them go   Ex 6:1
as it were by c   Philem 14
not under c, but   1 Pet 5:2

CONCEAL *cover, hide*

man c-s knowledge   Prov 12:23
They do not *even* c it   Is 3:9
Do not c *it* but   Jer 50:2
was c-ed from them   Luke 9:45

CONCEIT *pride*

selfishness or empty c   Phil 2:3
he is c-ed   1 Tim 6:4
c-ed, lovers of   2 Tim 3:4

CONCEIVE *become pregnant*

Sarah c-d and bore a   Gen 21:2
c-d all this people   Num 11:12
sin my mother c-d me   Ps 51:5
she c-d and gave birth   Is 8:3
when lust has c-d   James 1:15

CONCERN *have care*

master does not c   Gen 39:8
the LORD was c-ed   Ex 4:31
Thou art c-ed about   Job 7:17
c-ed about the poor   John 12:6
is married is c-ed   1 Cor 7:33
not c-ed about oxen   1 Cor 9:9

CONCUBINE *secondary wife*

Ephraim...took a c   Judg 19:1
Now Saul had a c   2 Sam 3:7
king left ten c-s   2 Sam 15:16
three hundred c-s   1 Kin 11:3
in charge of the c-s   Esth 2:14

CONDEMN *discredit, judge*

c-ing the wicked   1 Kin 8:32
my mouth will c me   Job 9:20
he who c-s Me   Is 50:9
will c Him to death   Mark 10:33
do not c, and you   Luke 6:37
you c yourself   Rom 2:1
he stood c-ed   Gal 2:11
our heart c-s us   1 John 3:20

CONDEMNATION *judgment*

receive greater c   Mark 12:40
same sentence of c   Luke 23:40
Their c is just   Rom 3:8
no c...in Christ   Rom 8:1
c upon themselves   Rom 13:2
c...by the devil   1 Tim 3:6

CONDITION *state*

with you on this c   1 Sam 11:2
c-s were good in   2 Chr 12:12
c in which...called   1 Cor 7:20
or adds c-s to it   Gal 3:15

CONDUCT (n) *behavior*

queen's c...known   Esth 1:17
turn...*from his* c   Job 33:17
who are upright in c   Ps 37:14
sensual c of...men   2 Pet 2:7
holy c and godliness   2 Pet 3:11

CONDUCT (v) *behave*

c-s himself arrogantly   Job 15:25
c...same spirit   2 Cor 12:18
C...with wisdom   Col 4:5
c yourselves in fear   1 Pet 1:17

CONDUIT *channel*

c of the upper pool   2 Kin 18:17
at the end of the c   Is 7:3

47

CONFESS

CONFESS *acknowledge*

that he shall **c**	Lev 5:5
c-ing the sins of	Neh 1:6
c my transgressions	Ps 32:5
c Me before men	Matt 10:32
c-ing their sins	Mark 1:5
c with your mouth	Rom 10:9
If we **c** our sins	1 John 1:9
I will **c** his name	Rev 3:5

CONFESSION *admission*

praying and making **c**	Ezra 10:1
your **c** of the gospel	2 Cor 9:13
testified the good **c**	1 Tim 6:13
the **c** of our hope	Heb 10:23

CONFIDENCE *boldness, trust*

What is this **c**	2 Kin 18:19
they lost their **c**	Neh 6:16
LORD will be your **c**	Prov 3:26
proud **c** is this	2 Cor 1:12
c in me may abound	Phil 1:26
no **c** in the flesh	Phil 3:3

CONFINE *imprison, limit*

who were **c-d** in jail	Gen 40:5
he does not **c** it	Ex 21:29
be **c-d** in prison	Is 24:22
c-d in the court	Jer 33:1

CONFINEMENT *imprisonment*

c in his master's	Gen 40:7
he put me in **c**	Gen 41:10

CONFIRM *establish, strengthen*

LORD **c** His word	1 Sam 1:23
c Thine inheritance	Ps 68:9
c the work of our	Ps 90:17
C-ing the word of His	Is 44:26
c-ed...by the signs	Mark 16:20
who shall also **c** you	1 Cor 1:8

CONFIRMATION *verification*

and **c** of the gospel	Phil 1:7
an oath *given* as **c**	Heb 6:16

CONFLICT *contention*

one of great **c**	Dan 10:1
in **c** with the LORD	Jer 50:24
experiencing...**c**	Phil 1:30
source of...**c-s**	James 4:1

CONFORMED *being like*

c...image of His Son	Rom 8:29

CONFOUND *confuse*

LORD **c-ed** them	Josh 10:10
c their strategy	Is 19:3
c-ing the Jews	Acts 9:22

CONFRONT *challenge, face*

snares of death **c-ed**	2 Sam 22:6
Days of affliction **c**	Job 30:27
Arise, O LORD, **c** him	Ps 17:13
the elders **c-ed** *Him*	Luke 20:1

CONFUSE *perplex*

c their language	Gen 11:7
Send...and **c** them	Ps 144:6
They are **c-ed** by wine	Is 28:7

CONFUSION *disorder*

into great **c**	Deut 7:23
Jerusalem was in **c**	Acts 21:31
not *a* God of **c**	1 Cor 14:33

CONGREGATION *assembly*

all the **c** of Israel	Ex 12:3
c shall stone him	Num 15:35
strife of the **c**	Num 27:14
Bless God in the **c-s**	Ps 68:26
c of the godly ones	Ps 149:1
the **c** of the disciples	Acts 6:2
In the midst of the **c**	Heb 2:12

CONJURER *magician*

magician, **c** or	Dan 2:10
wise men *and the* **c-s**	Dan 56:15

CONQUER *be victorious*

c-ed all the country	Gen 14:7
but could not **c** it	Is 7:1
c through Him	Rom 8:37
out **c-ing**, and to **c**	Rev 6:2

CONSCIENCE *moral obligation*

David's **c** bothered	1 Sam 24:5
always a blameless **c**	Acts 24:16
also for **c'** sake	Rom 13:5
their **c** being weak is	1 Cor 8:7
faith with a clear **c**	1 Tim 3:9
seared in their own **c**	1 Tim 4:2
keep a good **c**	1 Pet 3:16

CONSECRATE *sanctify*

sons of Israel **c**	Ex 28:38
garments shall be **c-d**	Ex 29:21

c it and all its   Ex 40:9
C yourselves   Lev 11:44
c the fiftieth year   Lev 25:10
c-s his house as holy   Lev 27:14
he shall c his head   Num 6:11
C yourselves   Josh 3:5
have c-d this house   1 Kin 9:3

CONSECRATED *sanctified*

touch any c thing   Lev 12:4
c people to the LORD   Deut 26:19
there is c bread   1 Sam 21:4
c ones were purer   Lam 4:7
ate the c bread   Matt 12:4

CONSENT *agree*

Do not listen or c   1 Kin 20:8
entice you, Do not c   Prov 1:10
If you c and obey   Is 1:19
c-s to live with him   1 Cor 7:12

CONSIDER *observe, think*

were c-ed unclean   Neh 7:64
C my groaning   Ps 5:1
he who c-s the helpless   Ps 41:1
We are c-ed as sheep   Ps 44:22
day of adversity c   Eccl 7:14
c the work of His hands   Is 5:12
C the ravens, for   Luke 12:24
c your calling   1 Cor 1:26
He c-ed me faithful   1 Tim 1:12
c how to stimulate   Heb 10:24
c-ed...God is able   Heb 11:19

CONSIST *composed of*

reverence for Me c-s   Is 29:13
life c of his   Luke 12:15
does not c in words   1 Cor 4:20
c-ing of decrees   Col 2:14

CONSOLATION *comfort*

c-s of God too small   Job 15:11
Thy c-s delight my   Ps 94:19
is any c of love   Phil 2:1

CONSOLE *soothe*

Esau is c-ing himself   Gen 27:42
servants to c him   2 Sam 10:2
c-d...comforted   Job 42:11
c them concerning   John 11:19

CONSPIRACY *plot, scheme*

the c was strong   2 Sam 15:12
found c in Hoshea   2 Kin 17:4
from the c-ies of man   Ps 31:20

CONSPIRE *plot-against*

have c-d against me   1 Sam 22:8
c-d against my   2 Kin 10:9
c together against   Ps 83:3
Amos...c-d against   Amos 7:10

CONSTELLATION *stars*

a c in its season   Job 38:32
c-s Will not flash   Is 13:10

CONSTRUCT *build*

c a sanctuary for Me   Ex 25:8
c siegeworks   Deut 20:20

CONSTRUCTION *structure*

c of the sanctuary   Ex 36:3
it has been under c   Ezra 5:16
the c of the ark   1 Pet 3:20

CONSULT *confer*

c-ed with the elders   1 Kin 12:6
C the mediums   Is 8:19
Without c-ing Me   Is 30:2
people c their wooden   Hos 4:12
not...c with flesh   Gal 1:16

CONSUME *destroy, devour*

c-d...purchase price   Gen 31:35
the brush was not c-d   Ex 3:2
c-d the burnt offering   Lev 9:24
great fire will c us   Deut 5:25
c the cedars   Judg 9:15
Thou dost c as a moth   Ps 39:11
c-d by Thine anger   Ps 90:7
c-s his own flesh   Eccl 4:5
fire c-ing the stubble   Joel 2:5
Zeal...will c   John 2:17
c your flesh like fire   James 5:3

CONSUMING (adj) *destroying*

glory...like a c fire   Ex 24:17
the flame of a c fire   Is 29:6
our God is a c fire   Heb 12:29

CONTAIN *hold*

cannot c Thee   1 Kin 8:27
c the burnt offering   2 Chr 7:7
c-ing twenty...gallons   John 2:6
not c the books   John 21:25
is c-ed in Scripture   1 Pet 2:6

CONTEMPT *scorn*

He pours c on nobles   Job 12:21
With pride and c   Ps 31:18

treating Him with c   Luke 23:11
your brother with c   Rom 14:10

CONTEND *strive*

c with him in battle   Deut 2:24
c-ed...vigorously   Judg 8:1
c with the Almighty   Job 40:2
not c...without cause   Prov 3:30
Who will c with Me   Is 50:8
I will not c forever   Is 57:16
he c-ed with God   Hos 12:3
c...for the faith   Jude 3

CONTENT *satisfied*

Nor will he be c   Prov 6:35
c with your wages   Luke 3:14
c with weaknesses   2 Cor 12:10
have learned to be c   Phil 4:11
c with what you have   Heb 13:5

CONTENTION *strife*

object of c to our   Ps 80:6
puts an end to c-s   Prov 18:18
the c-s of a wife   Prov 19:13
Strife exists and c   Hab 1:3

CONTENTIOUS *quarrelsome*

a c...woman   Prov 21:19
with a c woman   Prov 25:24
inclined to be c   1 Cor 11:16

CONTINUE *persevere, persist*

My covenant may c   Mal 2:4
c in the grace of   Acts 13:43
Are we to c in sin   Rom 6:1
you c in the faith   Col 1:23
love of the brethren c   Heb 13:1

CONTRARY *against*

c to the command   Num 24:13
for the wind was c   Matt 14:24
grafted c to nature   Rom 11:24
c to the teaching   Rom 16:17
a gospel c to that   Gal 1:8
c to sound teaching   1 Tim 1:10

CONTRIBUTE *give*

Josiah c-d to the   2 Chr 35:7
c yearly one third   Neh 10:32
c-ing to their support   Luke 8:3
c-ing to...the saints   Rom 12:13

CONTRIBUTION *gift, offering*

to raise a c for Me   Ex 25:2

as a c to the LORD   Lev 7:14
c-s, the first fruits   Neh 12:44
a c for the poor   Rom 15:26
liberality of your c   2 Cor 9:13

CONTRITE *sorrowful*

broken and a c heart   Ps 51:17
humble and c of spirit   Is 66:2

CONTROL (n) *order, rule*

people were out of c   Ex 32:25
was it not under...c   Acts 5:4
your lack of self-c   1 Cor 7:5
children under c   1 Tim 3:4

CONTROL (v) *rule, subdue*

he c-ed himself and   Gen 43:31
Joseph could not c   Gen 45:1
Haman c-ed himself   Esth 5:10

CONTROVERSY *dispute*

wise man has a c   Prov 29:9
LORD has a c with the   Jer 25:31
shun foolish c-ies   Titus 3:9

CONVERSE *discuss*

they were c-ing   Luke 24:15
Stoic...were c-ing   Acts 17:18
and c with him   Acts 24:26

CONVERSION *change*

c of the Gentiles   Acts 15:3

CONVERTED *changed*

sinners will be c   Ps 51:13
unless you are c   Matt 18:3
perceive...and be c   John 12:40

CONVICT *condemn, judge*

one of you c-s Me   John 8:46
c...concerning sin   John 16:8
he is c-ed by all   1 Cor 14:24
to c all the ungodly   Jude 15

CONVINCED *persuaded*

c that John was a   Luke 20:6
c that neither death   Rom 8:38
c in the Lord Jesus   Rom 14:14
c of better things   Heb 6:9

CONVOCATION *conclave*

sabbath...a holy c   Lev 23:3
shall have a holy c   Num 29:7

CONVULSION *paroxysm*

threw him into a c   Mark 9:20

a c with foaming   Luke 9:39

COOK *prepare food*

Jacob had c-ed stew   Gen 25:29
you shall c and eat   Deut 16:7

COOL *cold*

in the c of the day   Gen 3:8
in his c roof chamber   Judg 3:20
who has a c spirit   Prov 17:27

COPPER *metal*

you can dig c   Deut 8:9
not acquire...c   Matt 10:9
widow...c coins   Luke 21:2

COPY *facsimile*

c of this law on a   Deut 17:18
c of...law of Moses   Josh 8:32
c of the edict   Esth 8:13
mere c of the true   Heb 9:24

CORBAN *offering*

C (that is to say   Mark 7:11

CORD *band, rope*

c-s of Sheol   2 Sam 22:6
c-s of affliction   Job 36:8
c-s of death   Ps 18:4
silver c is broken   Eccl 12:6
the c-s of falsehood   Is 5:18
a scourge of c-s   John 2:15

CORINTH

city in Greece   Acts 18:1
N.T. church site   1 Cor 1:1,2

CORNELIUS

centurion, believer   Acts 10:1ff

CORNER *angle, intersection*

the chief c stone   Ps 118:22
lurks by every c   Prov 7:12
on the street c-s   Matt 6:5
the chief c stone   Mark 12:10
four c-s of the earth   Rev 7:1

CORNER GATE *see* **GATES OF JERUSALEM**

CORNERSTONE *support stone*

who laid its c   Job 38:6
the c of her tribes   Is 19:13
costly c *for* the   Is 28:16
From them...the c   Zech 10:4

CORPSE *dead body*

made unclean by a c   Lev 22:4
Their c-s will rise   Is 26:19
a mass of c-s   Nah 3:3
boy...like a c   Mark 9:26

CORRECT *reprove*

c him with the rod   2 Sam 7:14
He who c-s a scoffer ·   Prov 9:7
C your son, and he   Prov 29:17
C me, O LORD   Jer 10:24
gentleness c-ing   2 Tim 2:25

CORRECTION *improvement*

Whether for c, or   Job 37:13
refused to take c   Jer 5:3
for reproof, for c   2 Tim 3:16

CORRUPT (adj) *evil, rotten*

the earth was c   Gen 6:11
detestable and c   Job 15:16
They are c   Ps 14:1
all of them, are c   Jer 6:28

CORRUPT (v) *make evil*

a bribe c-s the heart   Eccl 7:7
c-ed your wisdom   Ezek 28:17
have c-ed the covenant   Mal 2:8
Bad company c-s   1 Cor 15:33
harlot who was c-ing   Rev 19:2

CORRUPTION *decay, evil*

their c is in them   Lev 22:25
no negligence or c   Dan 6:4
from the flesh reap c   Gal 6:8
c that is in the world   2 Pet 1:4
slaves of c   2 Pet 2:19

COSMETICS *beautifying aids*

provided her with...c   Esth 2:9
the c for the women   Esth 2:12

COST *expense, price*

c of their lives   Num 16:38
let the c be paid   Ezra 6:4
calculate the c   Luke 14:28
water...without c   Rev 22:6

COSTLY *expensive*

redemption...is c   Ps 49:8
gold, silver, c stones   Dan 11:38
vial of...c perfume   Mark 14:3
pearls or c garments   1 Tim 2:9

COUCH bed, pallet

he went up to my c — Gen 49:4
falling on the c — Esth 7:8
dissolve my c with my — Ps 6:6
sprawl on their c-es — Amos 6:4

COUNCIL assembly

not enter into their c — Gen 49:6
the c of the holy ones — Ps 89:7
the c of My people — Ezek 13:9
to their c chamber — Luke 22:6
conferred with his c — Acts 25:12

COUNCIL

Sanhedrin — Matt 26:59
Jewish governing body
— Mark 15:1,43; Luke 23:50

COUNSEL (n) advice, opinion

I shall give you c — Ex 18:19
take c and speak up — Judg 19:30
To Him belong c — Job 12:13
not walk in the c — Ps 1:1
Listen to c and — Prov 19:20
chief priests took c — John 12:10
the c of His will — Eph 1:11

COUNSEL (v) advise

he c-ed rebellion — Deut 13:5
I c that all Israel — 2 Sam 17:11
How do you c me — 1 Kin 12:6
c you with My eye — Ps 32:8

COUNSELOR adviser

the king and his c-s — Ezra 7:15
c-s walk barefoot — Job 12:17
abundance of c-s — Prov 11:14
Wonderful C, Mighty — Is 9:6
who became His c — Rom 11:34

COUNT consider, number

c the stars, if you — Gen 15:5
could not be c-ed — 1 Kin 8:5
If I should c them — Ps 139:18
my prayer be c-ed — Ps 141:2
was c-ed among us — Acts 1:17
I c all...loss — Phil 3:8
as some c slowness — 2 Pet 3:9

COUNTENANCE appearance

why has your c fallen — Gen 4:6
LORD lift up His c — Num 6:26
light of Thy c — Ps 4:6
an angry c — Prov 25:23

COUNTRY land, region

Go forth from your c — Gen 12:1
up into the hill c — Deut 1:24
go out into the c — Song 7:11
them from the c-ies — Ezek 34:13
they are seeking a c — Heb 11:14

COUNTRYMAN

not hate...fellow c — Lev 19:17
among your c-en — Deut 17:15
a man and his c — Deut 25:11
my fellow c-en and — Rom 11:14

COURAGE heart, valor

he lost c — 2 Sam 4:1
and do not lose c — 2 Chr 15:7
let your heart take c — Ps 27:14
with justice and c — Mic 3:8
Take c, My son — Matt 9:2
Take c, it is I — Matt 14:27
c; I have overcome — John 16:33
we are of good c — 2 Cor 5:8

COURAGEOUS brave

Be strong and c — Deut 31:6
be strong and very c — Josh 1:7
I purpose to be c — 2 Cor 10:2

COURIER messenger

c-s went throughout — 2 Chr 30:6
letters...by c-s — Esth 3:13
One c runs to meet — Jer 51:31

COURSE area, extent, way

strong man to run his c — Ps 19:5
on its circular c-s — Eccl 1:6
I have finished the c — 2 Tim 4:7
the c of our life — James 3:6

COURT area, hall, tribunal

c of the tabernacle — Ex 27:9
c of the harem — Esth 2:11
a day in Thy c-s — Ps 84:10
c of the LORD'S house — Jer 26:2
c of the guardhouse — Jer 39:15
then you have law c-s — 1 Cor 6:4
drag you into c — James 2:6

COURTYARD compound

a well in his c — 2 Sam 17:18
c of the high priest — Matt 26:58
Peter...in the c — Mark 14:66

COVENANT *agreement*

establish My c	Gen 6:18
for a sign of a c	Gen 9:13
for an everlasting c	Gen 17:13
ark of the c	Num 10:33
My c of peace	Num 25:12
book of the c	2 Kin 23:2
Remember His c	1 Chr 16:15
who keep His c	Ps 103:18
I will make a new c	Jer 31:31
forsake the holy c	Dan 11:30
a c with Assyria	Hos 12:1
the blood of *My* c	Zech 9:11
cup...is the new c	Luke 22:20
c which God made	Acts 3:25
this is My c with	Rom 11:27
servants of a new c	2 Cor 3:6
strangers to the c-s	Eph 2:12
guarantee...better c	Heb 7:22
blood of the...c	Heb 13:20
ark of His c	Rev 11:19

COVER (n)

c of porpoise skin	Num 4:14
the c of a couch	Amos 3:12

COVER (v) *hide, protect*

and c up his blood	Gen 37:26
basket and c-ed it	Ex 2:3
Whose sin is c-ed	Ps 32:1
He will c you with	Ps 91:4
love c-s all	Prov 10:12
not c My face	Is 50:6
c-ed...with sackcloth	Jon 3:6
to the hills, C us	Luke 23:30
c a multitude of sins	James 5:20
love c-s a multitude	1 Pet 4:8

COVERING *canopy*

made...loin c-s	Gen 3:7
spread a cloud for a c	Ps 105:39
she mades c-s for	Prov 31:22
sackcloth their c	Is 50:3
given to her for a c	1 Cor 11:15
freedom as a c	1 Pet 2:16

COVET *crave, desire*

not c your neighbor's	Ex 20:17
You shall not c	Deut 5:21
I c-ed them and took	Josh 7:21
They c fields and then	Mic 2:2
c-ed no one's silver	Acts 20:33

COVETOUS *desirous*

the c and swindlers	1 Cor 5:10
c, nor drunkards	1 Cor 6:10

COW *animal*

came up seven c-s	Gen 41:2
c calves and does not	Job 21:10
c and the bear will	Is 11:7
you c-s of Bashan	Amos 4:1

CRAFTINESS *shrewd*

the wise in their c	1 Cor 3:19
not walking in c	2 Cor 4:2
by c in deceitful	Eph 4:14

CRAFTSMAN *artisan*

the hands of the c	Deut 27:15
all the c-men and	2 Kin 24:14
idol, a c casts it	Is 40:19
business to...c-men	Acts 19:24
c of any craft will	Rev 18:22

CRAG *protrusion, rock*

sharp c on the one	1 Sam 14:4
Upon the rocky c	Job 39:28
clefts of the c-s	Is 57:5

CRAVE *covet, desire*

day long he is c-ing	Prov 21:26
fig *which* I c	Mic 7:1
generation c-s for	Matt 12:39
should not c evil	1 Cor 10:6

CRAWLING *creeping*

venom of c things	Deut 32:24
beasts and the c	Acts 11:6
and c creatures	Rom 1:23

CREATE *form, make*

c-d the heavens	Gen 1:1
c-d man in His	Gen 1:27
C in me a clean	Ps 51:10
C-ing the praise of	Is 57:19
c new heavens	Is 65:17
one God c-d us	Mal 2:10
c-d...for good works	Eph 2:10
who c-d all things	Eph 4:24
Thou didst c all	Rev 4:11

CREATION

beginning of c	Mark 10:6
preach...to all c	Mark 16:15
whole c groans	Rom 8:22

beginning of c   2 Pet 3:4

CREATOR *Maker*

Remember...your C   Eccl 12:1
The C of Israel   Is 43:15
rather than the C   Rom 1:25
to a faithful C   1 Pet 4:19

CREATURE *created being*

every living c that   Gen 1:21
winged c will make   Eccl 10:20
and crawling c-s   Rom 1:23
in Christ...new c   2 Cor 5:17
as c-s of instinct   2 Pet 2:12

CREDITOR *lender*

not to act as a c to   Ex 22:25
every c shall release   Deut 15:2
Let the c seize all   Ps 109:11
My c-s did I sell you   Is 50:1

CREEP *crawl*

everything that c-s   Gen 1:25
that c on the earth   Ezek 38:20

CREEPING *crawling*

cattle and c things   Gen 1:24
c things and fish   1 Kin 4:33
c locust has eaten   Joel 1:4
c locust strips and   Nah 3:16

CRETANS

inhabitants of Crete   Acts 2:11
    Titus 1:12

CRETE

Mediterranean island
    Acts 27:7,21; Titus 1:5
see also **CAPHTOR**

CRIME *vice*

be a lustful c   Job 31:11
committed no c   Dan 6:22
full of bloody c-s   Ezek 7:23
not of such c-s   Acts 25:18

CRIMINAL *lawbreaker*

crucified...the c-s   Luke 23:33
imprisonment as a c   2 Tim 2:9

CRIMSON *deep red*

purple, c and violet   2 Chr 2:7
like c...be like wool   Is 1:18

CRIPPLED *lame*

a son c in his feet   2 Sam 4:4

enter life c or lame   Matt 18:8
bring...c and blind   Luke 14:21

CRISPUS

Corinthian Christian   Acts 18:8
    1 Cor 1:14

CROOKED *evil, twisted*

and c generation   Deut 32:5
to their c ways   Ps 125:5
What is c cannot be   Eccl 1:15
make c the straight   Acts 13:10
c and perverse   Phil 2:15

CROP *yield of produce*

old things from the c   Lev 25:22
c-s to the grasshopper   Ps 78:46
c began to sprout   Amos 7:1
share of the c-s   2 Tim 2:6

CROSS (n) *execution device*

take his c and   Matt 10:38
down from the c   Matt 27:40
to bear His c   Mark 15:21
take up his c daily   Luke 9:23
standing by the c   John 19:25
hanging Him on a c   Acts 5:30
c of Christ should   1 Cor 1:17
word of the c is   1 Cor 1:18
boast, except in the c   Gal 6:14
even death on a c   Phil 2:8
enemies of the c   Phil 3:18
blood of His c   Col 1:20
endured the c   Heb 12:2

CROSS (v) *pass over*

you c the Jordan   Deut 12:10
c-ed opposite Jericho   Josh 3:16
kept c-ing the ford   2 Sam 19:18
Jesus had c-ed over   Mark 5:21
c-ing over to   Acts 21:2

CROUCH *bow, stoop*

sin is c-ing at the   Gen 4:7
Beneath Him c the   Job 9:13
Nothing...but to c   Is 10:4

CROWD *multitude*

because of the c   Mark 2:4
c of tax-gatherers   Luke 5:29
they stirred up the c   Acts 17:8

CROWN (n) *royal emblem* or *top*

on the c of the head   Gen 49:26
the c of their king   2 Sam 12:30

he set the royal c	Esth 2:17
wife is the c of	Prov 12:4
gray head is a c	Prov 16:31
c of the drunkards	Is 28:3
a c of thorns	Matt 27:29
receive the c of life	James 1:12
c-s before the throne	Rev 4:10
golden c on His head	Rev 14:14

CROWN (v) *to place crown on*

c him with glory	Ps 8:5
Who c-s you with	Ps 103:4
head c-s you like	Song 7:5
c-ed him with glory	Heb 2:7

CRUCIFY *execution on cross*

scourge and c Him	Matt 20:19
Let Him be c-ied	Matt 27:22
Jesus...been c-ied	Matt 28:5
c your King	John 19:15
Paul was not c-ied	1 Cor 1:13
preach Christ c-ied	1 Cor 1:23
not have c-ied the	1 Cor 2:8
c-ied with Christ	Gal 2:20
world...c-ied to me	Gal 6:14
their Lord was c-ied	Rev 11:8

CRUEL *fierce, harsh*

their...c bondage	Ex 6:9
c man does...harm	Prov 11:17
compassion...is c	Prov 12:10
c and have no mercy	Jer 6:23
people has become c	Lam 4:3

CRUMBS *morsels*

dogs feed on the c	Matt 15:27
on the children's c	Mark 7:28

CRUSH *demolish, destroy*

a foot may c them	Job 39:15
saves...c-ed in spirit	Ps 34:18
lying tongue...c-es	Prov 26:28
by c-ing My people	Is 3:15
c-ed for our iniquities	Is 53:5
LORD was pleased To c	Is 53:10
who c the needy	Amos 4:1
c Satan under...feet	Rom 16:20

CRY (n) *scream, sob*

great and bitter c	Gen 27:34
the c of triumph	Ex 32:18
c has come to Me	1 Sam 9:16
Hear my c, O God	Ps 61:1

the c of Jerusalem	Jer 14:2
Jesus uttered a...c	Mark 15:37

CRY (v)

do not c for help	Job 36:13
c aloud in the night	Lam 2:19
His elect, who c	Luke 18:7
stones will c out	Luke 19:40
Jesus stood and c-ied	John 7:37

CRYSTAL *glass*

awesome gleam of c	Ezek 1:22
sea of glass like c	Rev 4:6
water...clear as c	Rev 22:1

CUB *whelp, young*

robbed of her c-s	2 Sam 17:8
She reared her c-s	Ezek 19:2
lioness, and lion's c	Nah 2:11

CUBIT *linear measure*

ark three hundred c-s	Gen 6:15
length was nine c-s	Deut 3:11
gallows fifty c-s high	Esth 5:14
the altar by c-s	Ezek 43:13
add a *single* c to	Matt 6:27

CUD *previously swallowed food*

chews the c	Lev 11:3
not chew c, it is	Lev 11:7
chews the c	Deut 14:6

CULT *religious, ritual*

be a c prostitute	Deut 23:17
male c prostitutes	1 Kin 14:24
male c prostitutes	2 Kin 23:7

CULTIVATE *till*

no man to c the	Gen 2:5
Eden to c it	Gen 2:15
and c vineyards	Deut 28:39
servants shall c	2 Sam 9:10
and c faithfulness	Ps 37:3

CUMMIN *plant for seasoning*

driven over c	Is 28:27
mint and dill and c	Matt 23:23

CUNNING *crafty*

he is very c	1 Sam 23:22
advice of the c	Job 5:13
harlot and c of heart	Prov 7:10

CUP *container*

into Pharaoh's c	Gen 40:11
My c overflows	Ps 23:5
the c of salvation	Ps 116:13
a c of consolation	Jer 16:7
c of cold water	Matt 10:42
let this c pass	Matt 26:39
washing of c-s and	Mark 7:4
gives you a c of	Mark 9:41
c...new covenant	Luke 22:20
c of blessing	1 Cor 10:16
eat...drink the c	1 Cor 11:26
c full of abominations	Rev 17:4

CUPBEARER *royal official*

c spoke to Pharaoh	Gen 41:9
his c-s, and his	1 Kin 10:5
c-s and their attire	2 Chr 9:4
c to the king	Neh 1:11

CURDS *butter, cheese*

he took c and milk	Gen 18:8
she brought him c	Judg 5:25
with honey and c	Job 20:17

CURE *become well*

c him of his leprosy	2 Kin 5:3
c you of your wound	Hos 5:13
they could not c him	Matt 17:16
that...time He c-d	Luke 7:21

CURSE (n) *condemning oath*

upon myself a c	Gen 27:12
c on Mount Ebal	Deut 11:29
c to My chosen ones	Is 65:15
they will become a c	Jer 44:12
will be no more c	Zech 14:11
become a c for us	Gal 3:13

CURSE (v) *verbally condemn*

who c-s you I will c	Gen 12:3
You shall not c God	Ex 22:28
not c a deaf man	Lev 19:14
c-d the...anointed	2 Sam 19:21
c-d the day of his *birth*	Job 3:1
began to c and	Mark 14:71
bless and c not	Rom 12:14
with it we c men	James 3:9

CURSED (adj) *under a curse*

C is the ground	Gen 3:17
C be Canaan	Gen 9:25

C is the man who	Deut 27:15
C...who trusts	Jer 17:5
C...who hangs	Gal 3:13

CURTAIN *covering, drape*

on the edge of the c	Ex 26:4
heaven like a *tent* c	Ps 104:2
c-s of your dwellings	Is 54:2
c-s of the land of	Hab 3:7

CUSH

1 *area of W Asia*	Gen 2:13
2 *patriarch*	Gen 10:6,8
3 *region S of Egypt*	2 Kin 19:9
	Is 20:3
4 *a Benjamite*	Ps 7:title

CUSTODY *prison, protection*

they put him in c	Num 15:34
into the c of Hegai	Esth 2:3
John...taken into c	Matt 4:12
holding Jesus in c	Luke 22:63

CUSTOM *manner or tax*

it became a c in	Judg 11:39
not pay tribute, c	Ezra 4:13
c, He entered the	Luke 4:16
burial c of the Jews	John 19:40
c-s...not lawful	Acts 16:21
c-s of our fathers	Acts 28:17
whom tax is *due*; c	Rom 13:7

CUT *destroy, divide*

did not c the birds	Gen 15:10
c off from the earth	Ex 9:15
c down their Asherim	Ex 34:13
LORD c off...lips	Ps 12:3
tongue will be c	Prov 10:31
C off your hair and	Jer 7:29
were c-ting branches	Matt 21:8
and c off his ear	Matt 26:51
were c to the quick	Acts 7:54
you...will be c off	Rom 11:22

CYMBAL *musical instrument*

castanets and c-s	2 Sam 6:5
loud-sounding c-s	1 Chr 15:16
with loud c-s	Ps 150:5
or a clanging c	1 Cor 13:1

CYPRESS *tree*

cedar and c timber	1 Kin 5:10
c and algum timber	2 Chr 2:8

Our rafters, **c-es**   Song 1:17
Wail, O **c**, for the   Zech 11:2

CYPRUS

Mediterranean island   Is 23:1
   Acts 11:19;15;39;21:16
see also **KITTIM**

CYRENE

NW African port   Mark 15:21
   Luke 23:26;Acts 2:10;11:20

CYRUS

king of Persia   2 Chr 36:22
   Is 45:1
decreed to rebuild Temple
   Ezra 1:1;5:13

D

DAGON

god of Philistines   Judg 16:23
   1 Sam 5:4; 1 Chr 10:10

DAMAGE (n) *destruction*

any **d** may be found   2 Kin 12:5
the **d-s** of the house   2 Kin 12:6
d and great loss   Acts 27:10
incurred this **d** and   Acts 27:21

DAMAGE (v) *destroy, hurt*

it will **d** the revenue   Ezra 4:13
and **d-ing** to kings   Ezra 4:15
enemy has **d-d**   Ps 74:3
Lest anyone **d** it   Is 27:3

DAMASCUS

city of Aram (Syria)   Gen 14:15
   2 Kin 5:12;Acts 9:3,27;26:20

DAN

1 *son of Jacob*   Gen 30:6;49:16
2 *tribal area*   Josh 19:40
   Judg 18:2
3 *city in N Palestine*   Josh 19:47

DANCE (n) *rhythmic movement*

timbrels...with **d-ing**   Ex 15:20
they sing in the **d-s**   1 Sam 29:5
shall rejoice in the **d**   Jer 31:13
music and **d-ing**   Luke 15:25

DANCE (v) *move rhythmically*

from those who **d-d**   Judg 21:23

David was **d-ing**   2 Sam 6:14
and a time to **d**   Eccl 3:4
Herodias **d-d** before   Matt 14:6

DANGER *peril*

not only is there a **d**   Acts 19:27
often in **d** of death   2 Cor 11:23
d-s from...Gentiles   2 Cor 11:26

DANIEL

1 *son of David and Abigail*
   1 Chr 3:1
2 *priest*   Ezra 8:2
3 *prophet*   Ezek 14:14;Dan 1:3
   also **Belteshazzar**

DARE *presume, risk*

who **d-s** rouse him up   Gen 49:9
who would **d** to risk   Jer 30:21
d from that day   Matt 22:46
did not **d** pronounce   Jude 9

DARIUS

1 *Darius the Mede*   Dan 5:31
2 *Darius I*   Ezra 4:5; Hag 1:1
3 *Darius II*   Neh 12:22

DARK *dim, shadow*

not in **d** sayings   Num 12:8
d places of the land   Ps 74:20
live in a **d** land   Is 9:2
it was still **d**   John 20:1
shining in a **d** place   2 Pet 1:19

DARKEN *obscure*

the land was **d-ed**   Ex 10:15
this that **d-s** counsel   Job 38:2
the stars are **d-ed**   Eccl 12:2
sun will be **d-ed**   Mark 13:24
their eyes be **d-ed**   Rom 11:10

DARKNESS *gloom, shadow*

blind...gropes in **d**   Deut 28:29
are silenced in **d**   1 Sam 2:9
illumines my **d**   2 Sam 22:29
that stalks in **d**   Ps 91:6
those who dwelt in **d**   Ps 107:10
as light excels in **d**   Eccl 2:13
people who walk in **d**   Is 9:2
light will rise in **d**   Is 58:10
into the outer **d**   Matt 22:13
those who sit in **d**   Luke 1:79
men loved the **d**   John 3:19
turn from **d** to light   Acts 26:18

DARKNESS

has light with **d**   2 Cor 6:14
unfruitful deeds of **d**   Eph 5:11
in Him there is no **d**   1 John 1:5
brother is in the **d**   1 John 2:9

DARLING *love*

you are, my **d**   Song 1:15
Arise, my **d**   Song 2:13
my **d**, My dove   Song 5:2

DATHAN

rebelled against Moses
     Num 16:12; Ps 106:17

DAUGHTER

d-s were born to them   Gen 6:1
if a man sells his **d**   Ex 21:7
inheritance to his **d**   Num 27:8
Kings' **d-s** are among   Ps 45:9
d-s of song   Eccl 12:4
destruction of the the **d**   Is 22:4
the **d** of my people   Jer 9:1
D rises up against   Mic 7:6
mother against **d**   Luke 12:53

DAUGHTER-IN-LAW

said to his **d** Tamar   Gen 38:11
nakedness of your **d**   Lev 18:15
said to Ruth her **d**   Ruth 2:22
D against her   Mic 7:6

DAVID

anointed   1 Sam 16:13
killed Goliath   1 Sam 17:50
fled from Saul   1 Sam 19:18
spared Saul   1 Sam 26:9
king of Judah and Israel
     2 Sam 2:4;5:3
covenant with God   2 Sam 7:8
death   1 Kin 2:10

DAWN (n) *daylight*

at the approach of **d**   Judg 19:25
caused the **d** to know   Job 38:12
rise before **d** and   Ps 119:147
wings of the **d**   Ps 139:9
As the **d** is spread   Joel 2:2

DAWN (v) *become light*

the day began to **d**   Judg 19:26
when morning **d-s**   Ps 46:5
a light **d-ed**   Matt 4:16
d toward the first   Matt 28:1
until the day **d-s**   2 Pet 1:19

DAY *light*

God called the light **d**   Gen 1:5
come on a festive **d**   1 Sam 25:8
d...LORD has made   Ps 118:24
what a **d** may bring   Prov 27:1
d-s of your youth   Eccl 12:1
a **d** of reckoning   Is 2:12
d of the LORD is near   Is 13:6
has despised the **d**   Zech 4:10
the **d** of His coming   Mal 3:2
Give us this **d**   Matt 6:11
raise...the last **d**   John 6:39
judge...the last **d**   John 12:48
the **d** of salvation   2 Cor 6:2
perfect it until the **d**   Phil 1:6
d of the Lord   1 Thess 5:2
d is as a thousand   2 Pet 3:8
tormented **d**...night   Rev 20:10

DAY OF ATONEMENT

month is the **d**   Lev 23:27
for it is a **d**   Lev 23:28

DAZZLING *blinding, bright*

My beloved is **d**   Song 5:10
Like **d** heat   Is 18:4
near...in **d** apparel   Luke 24:4

DEACONS *officer, server*

overseers and **d**   Phil 1:1
D likewise *must be*   1 Tim 3:8
let them serve as **d**   1 Tim 3:10
Let **d** be husbands   1 Tim 3:12
served well as **d**   1 Tim 3:13

DEAD *without life*

you are a **d** man   Gen 20:3
near to a **d** person   Num 6:6
dealt with the **d**   Ruth 1:8
forgotten as a **d** man   Ps 31:12
d do not praise   Ps 115:17
better than a **d** lion   Eccl 9:4
Your **d** will live   Is 26:19
not weep for the **d**   Jer 22:10
rising from the **d**   Mark 9:10
d shall hear the   John 5:25
resurrection of the **d**   Acts 23:6
d in your trespasses   Eph 2:1
first-born from the **d**   Col 1:18
living and the **d**   2 Tim 4:1
repentance...**d** works   Heb 6:1
to those who are **d**   1 Pet 4:6

I was d...I am alive | Rev 1:18
Hades gave up the d | Rev 20:13

DEAF *without hearing*

makes *him* dumb or d | Ex 4:11
not curse a d man | Lev 19:14
Like a d cobra | Ps 58:4
the d shall hear | Is 29:18
and *the* d hear | Matt 11:5
the d to hear | Mark 7:37
d and dumb spirit | Mark 9:25

DEAL *allot, barter, treat*

let us d wisely | Ex 1:10
have you d-t with us | Ex 14:11
nor d falsely | Lev 19:11
d-t with mediums | 2 Kin 21:6
who d treacherously | Ps 25:3
has d-t bountifully | Ps 116:7
who d faithfully | Prov 12:22
Everyone d-s falsely | Jer 6:13
when I have d-t | Ezek 20:44
has d-t with me | Luke 1:25

DEALINGS *actions, relations*

no d with anyone | Judg 18:7
no d with Samaritans | John 4:9
of the Lord's d | James 5:11

DEAR *beloved*

Is Ephraim My d son | Jer 31:20
my life...as d to | Acts 20:24
had become very d | 1 Thess 2:8

DEATH *without life*

d of the upright | Num 23:10
d encompassed me | 2 Sam 22:5
d for his own sin | 2 Chr 25:4
D rather than...pains | Job 7:15
no mention of Thee in d | Ps 6:5
cords of d encompassed | Ps 18:4
the shadow of d | Ps 23:4
escapes from d | Ps 68:20
doomed to d | Ps 102:20
d of His godly ones | Ps 116:15
who hate me love d | Prov 8:36
love is as strong as d | Song 8:6
He will swallow up d | Is 25:8
D cannot praise Thee | Is 38:18
no pleasure in the d | Ezek 18:32
d is better to me | Jon 4:3
let him be put to d | Matt 15:4
shall not taste d | Matt 16:28

to the point of d | Mark 14:34
passed out of d | John 5:24
he shall never see d | John 8:51
sickness is not unto d | John 11:4
the agony of d | Acts 2:24
d by hanging Him | Acts 10:39
d reigned from Adam | Rom 5:14
wages of sin is d | Rom 6:23
the law of sin and d | Rom 8:2
proclaim...Lord's d | 1 Cor 11:26
d, where...victory | 1 Cor 15:55
even d on a cross | Phil 2:8
He might taste d | Heb 2:9
it brings forth d | James 1:15
passed out of d | 1 John 3:14
Be faithful until d | Rev 2:10
had the name D | Rev 6:8
second d...no power | Rev 20:6

DEBATE *dispute*

d-d...themselves | Mark 1:27
dissention and d | Acts 15:2
had been much d | Acts 15:7

DEBORAH

1 *nurse of Rebekah* | Gen 35:8
2 *prophetess, judge* | Judg 4,5

DEBT *obligation*

and pay your d | 2 Kin 4:7
exaction of every d | Neh 10:31
sureties for d-s | Prov 22:26
forgive us our d-s | Matt 6:12

DEBTOR *borrower*

restores to the d | Ezek 18:7
forgiven our d-s | Matt 6:12
had two d-s | Luke 7:41
his master's d-s | Luke 16:5

DECAY *corruption*

own eyes see his d | Job 21:20
Holy Only to...d | Acts 2:27
did not undergo d | Acts 13:37

DECEASED *dead*

wife of the d shall | Deut 25:5
the widow of the d | Ruth 4:5
the name of the d | Ruth 4:10
the sister of the d | John 11:39

DECEIT *falsehood, deception*

full of curses and d | Ps 10:7

59

DECEIT

in whose spirit...no **d**   Ps 32:2
your tongue frames **d**   Ps 50:19
D is in the heart   Prov 12:20
he lays up **d**   Prov 26:24
Offspring of **d**   Is 57:4
houses are full of **d**   Jer 5:27
house of Israel...**d**   Hos 11:12
d, sensuality, envy   Mark 7:22
full of envy...**d**   Rom 1:29
the lusts of **d**   Eph 4:22
nor was any **d** found   1 Pet 2:22

DECEITFUL *false*

From a **d** tongue   Ps 120:2
the wicked are **d**   Prov 12:5
d are the kisses of   Prov 27:6
Charm is **d** and   Prov 31:30
The heart is more **d**   Jer 17:9
false apostles, **d**   2 Cor 11:13

DECEIVE *cheat, mislead*

have you **d-d** me   Gen 29:25
Jacob **d-d** Laban   Gen 31:20
d-s his companion   Lev 6:2
both stolen and **d-d**   Josh 7:11
Do not **d** me   2 Kin 4:28
who **d-s** his neighbor   Prov 26:19
Do not **d** yourselves   Jer 37:9
your heart had **d-d** you   Obad 3
they keep **d-ing**   Rom 3:13
Let no one **d** you   Eph 5:6
d-ing and being **d-d**   2 Tim 3:13

DECEIVER *liar*

as a **d** in his sight   Gen 27:12
as **d-s** and yet true   2 Cor 6:8
d and the antichrist   2 John 7

DECEPTION *falsehood*

their mind prepares **d**   Job 15:35
the hills are a **d**   Jer 3:23
last **d** will be worse   Matt 27:64
philosophy and empty **d**   Col 2:8
reveling in their **d-s**   2 Pet 2:13

DECEPTIVE *misleading*

wicked **d** wages   Prov 11:18
Do not trust in **d** words   Jer 7:4
d *stream* With water   Jer 15:18

DECISION *judgment, resolution*

d is from the LORD   Prov 16:33
in the valley of **d**   Joel 3:14

My **d** is to gather   Zeph 3:8
majority reached a **d**   Acts 27:12

DECLARE *explain, proclaim*

Moses **d-d** to...sons   Lev 23:44
d to Him the number   Job 31:37
d Thy faithfulness   Ps 30:9
mouth...**d** Thy praise   Ps 51:15
d Thy lovingkindness   Ps 92:2
Who has **d-d** *this*   Is 41:26
d-s the LORD   Amos 4:11
He will **d** all things   John 4:25
d-d the Son of God   Rom 1:4

DECLINE *decrease*

for the shadow to **d**   2 Kin 20:10
our days have **d-d**   Ps 90:9
for the day **d-s**   Jer 6:4

DECREASE *abate, subside*

the water **d-d** steadily   Gen 8:5
not let their cattle **d**   Ps 107:38
increase...I must **d**   John 3:30

DECREE (n) *judgment, order*

issued a **d** to rebuild   Ezra 5:13
and **d** of the king   Esth 2:8
devises mischief by **d**   Ps 94:20
only one **d** for you   Dan 2:9
delivering the **d-s**   Acts 16:4
to the **d-s** of Caesar   Acts 17:7

DECREE (v) *decide, determine*

been **d-d** against her   Esth 2:1
will also **d** a thing   Job 22:28
And rulers **d** justice   Prov 8:15
Seventy weeks...**d-d**   Dan 9:24

DEDICATE *consecrate, devote*

D yourselves today   Ex 32:29
I wholly **d** the silver   Judg 17:3
d-d by...David   1 Kin 7:51
David...**d-d** these   1 Chr 18:11
d-d part...the spoil   1 Chr 26:27
d-ing it to Him   2 Chr 2:4

DEDICATION *consecration*

the **d** of the altar   2 Chr 7:9
celebrated the **d** of   Ezra 6:16
d of the wall   Neh 12:27
d of the image   Dan 3:2
assembled for the **d**   Dan 3:3

DEDICATION, FEAST OF
see FEASTS

DEED *action* or *document*

What is this **d**	Gen 44:15
for our evil **d-s**	Ezra 9:13
blot out...loyal **d-s**	Neh 13:14
abominable **d-s**	Ps 14:1
I...sealed the **d**	Jer 32:10
prophet mighty in **d**	Luke 24:19
their **d-s** were evil	John 3:19
d-s of the flesh are	Gal 5:19
for every good **d**	Titus 3:1
I know your **d-s**	Rev 2:2

DEEP (adj) *far ranging*

d sleep falls on men	Job 4:13
Thy judgments are...**d**	Ps 36:6
casts into a **d** sleep	Prov 19:15
into **d** darkness	Jer 13:16
the well is **d**	John 4:11

DEEP (n) *abyss, depth*

fountains of the...**d**	Gen 7:11
the **d** lying beneath	Deut 33:13
surface of the **d** is	Job 38:30
D calls to **d**	Ps 42:7
The **d-s** also trembled	Ps 77:16
His wonders in the **d**	Ps 107:24
the springs of the **d**	Prov 8:28

DEER *animal*

besides **d**, gazelles	1 Kin 4:23
d pants for the water	Ps 42:1
lame will leap like a **d**	Is 35:6

DEFEAT *conquer, overthrow*

d-ed...and pursued	Gen 14:15
able to **d** them	Num 22:6
sons of Israel **d-ed**	Josh 12:7
d the Arameans	2 Kin 13:17
d-ed the Philistines	1 Chr 18:1
d-ed the entire army	Jer 37:10

DEFECT (n) *blemish, spot*

No one who has a **d**	Lev 21:18
one ram without **d**	Num 6:14
if it has any **d**	Deut 15:21
no **d** in him	2 Sam 14:25
in whom was no **d**	Dan 1:4

DEFECT (v) *rebel, disobey*

d to his master	1 Chr 12:19
many **d-ed** to him	2 Chr 15:9

you have deeply **d-ed**	Is 31:6

DEFEND *protect*

LORD of hosts will **d**	Zech 9:15
d-ed him and took	Acts 7:24
or else **d-ing** them	Rom 2:15
are **d-ing** ourselves	2 Cor 12:19

DEFENSE *protection*

d-s are **d-s** of clay	Job 13:12
the **d** of my life	Ps 27:1
Thou hast been a **d**	Is 25:4
the **d**...of the gospel	Phil 1:7

DEFILE *pollute, profane*

astray...**d-s** herself	Num 5:29
d-d the high places	2 Kin 23:8
d-d the priesthood	Neh 13:29
d-d Thy holy temple	Ps 79:1
your hands are **d-d**	Is 59:3
those **d** the man	Matt 15:18
is what **d-s** the man	Mark 7:20
conscience...is **d-d**	1 Cor 8:7
d-s the entire body	James 3:6

DEFILEMENT *filth*

her *interest*, for **d**	Ezek 22:3
from all **d** of flesh	2 Cor 7:1

DEFRAUD *deprive, wrong*

whom have I **d-ed**	1 Sam 12:3
To **d** a man	Lam 3:36
Do not **d**	Mark 10:19
no one keep **d-ing**	Col 2:18

DEITY *God, gods*

of strange **d-ies**	Acts 17:18
fulness of **D** dwells	Col 2:9

DELAY *hinder, linger, stall*

Do not **d** me	Gen 24:56
Moses **d-ed** to come	Ex 32:1
shall not **d** to pay	Deut 23:21
bridegroom...**d-ing**	Matt 25:5
Do not **d** to come	Acts 9:38
now why do you **d**	Acts 22:16
in case I am **d-ed**	1 Tim 3:15

DELICACIES *fancy foods*

eat of their **d**	Ps 141:4
Do not desire his **d**	Prov 23:3
Those who ate **d**	Lam 4:5

DELIGHT (n) *pleasure*

I have no **d** in you	2 Sam 15:26

DELIGHT

Will he take **d**	Job 27:10
his **d** is in the law	Ps 1:2
commandments...**d**	Ps 119:143
my **d** in the sons of	Prov 8:31
a just weight is His **d**	Prov 11:1
the **d** of kings	Prov 16:13
I took great **d**	Song 2:3
call the sabbath a **d**	Is 58:13
My **d** is in her	Is 62:4

DELIGHT (v) *desire*

LORD **d-ed** over you	Deut 28:63
d in...offerings	1 Sam 15:22
d to revere Thy name	Neh 1:11
d in the Almighty	Job 22:26
D yourself in the LORD	Ps 37:4
not **d** in sacrifice	Ps 51:16
Who **d** in doing evil	Prov 2:14
d in my ways	Prov 23:26
takes no **d** in fools	Eccl 5:4
I **d** in loyalty	Hos 6:6
d-s...unchanging love	Mic 7:18
d-ing...self-abasement	Col 2:18

DELIGHTFUL *pleasant*

d is a timely word	Prov 15:23
to find **d** words	Eccl 12:10
and how **d** you are	Song 7:6
Is he a **d** child	Jer 31:20

DELILAH

Philistine woman	Judg 16:4
enticed Samson	Judg 16:6-20

DELIVER *give, rescue, save*

come down to **d** them	Ex 3:8
d the manslayer	Num 35:25
My...power has **d-ed**	Judg 7:2
can this one **d**	1 Sam 10:27
He will **d** you	Job 5:19
d-ed my soul from	Ps 56:13
none who can **d**	Is 43:13
mind on **d-ing** Daniel	Dan 6:14
d us from evil	Matt 6:13
d Him up to you	Matt 26:15
d-ed over to death	2 Cor 4:11
The Lord will **d** me	2 Tim 4:18
d-ed to the saints	Jude 3

DELIVERANCE *salvation*

by a great **d**	Gen 45:7
given this great **d**	Judg 15:8

with songs of **d**	Ps 32:7
a God of **d-s**	Ps 68:20
d through...prayers	Phil 1:19

DELIVERER *savior*

the LORD raised up a **d**	Judg 3:9
give them **d-s**	Neh 9:27
my fortress and my **d**	Ps 18:2
d-s...ascend Mount	Obad 21
D...come from Zion	Rom 11:26

DELUDE *lead astray*

they have **d-d** you	Is 47:10
no one may **d** you	Col 2:4
who **d** themselves	James 1:22

DEMAND *order, require*

husband may **d** of him	Ex 21:22
but I **d** one thing	2 Sam 3:13
captors **d-ed** of us	Ps 137:3
do not **d** it back	Luke 6:30
d-ing of Him a sign	Luke 11:16

DEMETRIUS

1 *Ephesian smith*	Acts 19:24,38
2 *a Christian*	3 John 12

DEMOLISH *destroy*

d all...high places	Num 33:52
he **d-ed** its stones	2 Kin 23:15
to **d** its strongholds	Is 23:11

DEMON *devil*

sacrificed to **d-s**	Deut 32:17
daughters to the **d-s**	Ps 106:37
after the **d** was cast	Matt 9:33
sacrifice to **d-s**	1 Cor 10:20
d-s also believe	James 2:19
not to worship **d-s**	Rev 9:20

DEMONIACS *possessed ones*

d, epileptics	Matt 4:24
the *incident* of the **d**	Matt 8:33

DEMON-POSSESSED

many who were **d**	Matt 8:16
a dumb man, **d**	Matt 9:32
to the **d** man	Mark 5:16
sayings of one **d**	John 10:21

DEMONSTRATE *show*

God **d-s** His own love	Rom 5:8

DEMONSTRATION *a showing*

for the **d**, *I say*   Rom 3:26
in **d** of the Spirit   1 Cor 2:4

to **d** His wrath   Rom 9:22
d-d yourselves to be   2 Cor 7:11
d His patience   1 Tim 1:16

DEN *abode*

remains in its **d**   Job 37:8
From the **d-s** of lions   Song 4:8
the viper's **d**   Is 11:8
cast into the lions' **d**   Dan 6:7
it a robbers' **d**   Mark 11:17

DENARIUS

Roman silver coin   Matt 20:2,9
a day's wage   Luke 20:24
Denarii *(pl)*   John 6:7;12:5

DENOUNCE *accuse, slander*

And come, **d** Israel   Num 23:7
the LORD has not **d-d**   Num 23:8
let us **d** him   Jer 20:10

DENY *conceal, refuse*

Sarah **d-ied** *it*   Gen 18:15
lest you **d** your God   Josh 24:27
not **d-ied** the words   Job 6:10
and **d-ing** the LORD   Is 59:13
whoever shall **d** Me   Matt 10:33
has **d-ied** the faith   1 Tim 5:8
deeds they **d** *Him*   Titus 1:16
us to **d** ungodliness   Titus 2:12
d-ies the Son   1 John 2:23

DEPART *leave*

scepter shall not **d**   Gen 49:10
sword...never **d**   2 Sam 12:10
to **d** from evil is   Job 28:28
His spirit **d-s**   Ps 146:4
his folly will not **d**   Prov 27:22
turned aside and **d-ed**   Jer 5:23
I never knew you; **d**   Matt 7:23
d from Me, all you   Luke 13:27
D from your country   Acts 7:3
d and be with Christ   Phil 1:23

DEPARTURE *death or leaving*

after their **d** from   Ex 16:1
speaking of His **d**   Luke 9:31
time of my **d** has   2 Tim 4:6
any time after my **d**   2 Pet 1:15

DEPEND *rely, rest*

d-ed on the weapons   Is 22:8
you did not **d** on Him   Is 22:11
d the whole Law   Matt 22:40

DEPORTATION *exile*

after the **d** to   Matt 1:12
to the **d** to Babylon   Matt 1:17

DEPORTED *exiled*

d...to Babylon   Ezra 5:12
d...entire population   Amos 1:6

DEPOSE *release*

d you from your office   Is 22:19
d-d from his royal   Dan 5:20

DEPOSIT (n) *security*

in regard to a **d**   Lev 6:2
d which was entrusted   Lev 6:4

DEPOSIT (v) *place, put*

d them in the tent   Num 17:4
d *it* in your town   Deut 14:28
d...in the temple   Ezra 5:15
had **d-ed** the scroll   Jer 36:20

DEPRAVED *degenerate*

over to a **d** mind   Rom 1:28
men of **d** mind   2 Tim 3:8

DEPRIVE *take away*

d the needy of justice   Is 10:2
d-d of...my years   Is 38:10
d-ing one another   1 Cor 7:5
d-d of the truth   1 Tim 6:5

DEPTH *abyss, deep*

d-s boil like a pot   Job 41:31
hand are the **d-s**   Ps 95:4
went down to the **d-s**   Ps 107:26
sins Into the **d-s**   Mic 7:19
drowned in the **d**   Matt 18:6
it had no **d** of soil   Mark 4:5
nor height, nor **d**   Rom 8:39
the **d** of the riches   Rom 11:33
even the **d-s** of God   1 Cor 2:10

DEPUTY *proconsul*

he was the only **d**   1 Kin 4:19
Solomon's...**d-ies**   1 Kin 5:16
a **d** was king   1 Kin 22:47

DERISION *laughingstock*

d among...enemies   Ex 32:25
d to those around us   Ps 44:13
reproach and d all   Jer 20:8
d to the rest of the   Ezek 36:4

DESCEND *go down*

angels of God...d-ing   Gen 28:12
His glory will not d   Ps 49:17
breath of...d-s   Eccl 3:21
shall d to Hades   Matt 11:23
Spirit d-ing...dove   John 1:32
d into the abyss   Rom 10:7
who d-ed...ascended   Eph 4:10

DESCENDANT *seed, offspring*

your d-s I will give   Gen 12:7
will raise up your d   2 Sam 7:12
His d-s shall endure   Ps 89:36
So shall your d-s be   Rom 4:18
to the d of Abraham   Heb 2:16

DESCENT *hill or heritage*

of Median d   Dan 9:1
the d of the Mount   Luke 19:37
were of high-priestly d   Acts 4:6

DESCRIBE *explain*

you shall d the land   Josh 18:6
man, d the temple   Ezek 43:10
who had seen it d-d   Mark 5:16

DESECRATE *defile*

d the sanctuary   Dan 11:31
tried to d the temple   Acts 24:6

DESERT (n) *wilderness*

d plains of Jericho   Josh 5:10
grieved Him in the d   Ps 78:40
better to live in a d   Prov 21:19
in the d a highway   Is 40:3
Rivers in the d   Is 43:19
like a bush in the d   Jer 17:6
he lived in the d-s   Luke 1:80

DESERT (v) *abandon, forsake*

d-ed to the king   2 Kin 25:11
who had d-ed them   Acts 15:38
so quickly d-ing Him   Gal 1:6
but all d-ed me   2 Tim 4:16
I will never d you   Heb 13:5

DESERTERS *changers of loyalty*

d who had deserted   2 Kin 25:11

d who had gone over   Jer 39:9

DESERVE *earn, merit*

with him as he d-ed   Judg 9:16
done this d-s to die   2 Sam 12:5
He is d-ing of death   Matt 26:66
receiving what we d   Luke 23:41

DESIGN *creation, plan*

d-s for work in gold   Ex 31:4
makers of d-s   Ex 35:35
execute any d which   2 Chr 2:14
All their deadly d-s   Jer 18:23

DESIGNATE *appoint*

if he d-s her for   Ex 21:9
one whom I d to   1 Sam 16:3
were d-d by name   1 Chr 16:41
being d-d by God   Heb 5:10

DESIRABLE *attractive*

the tree was d   Gen 3:6
d in your eyes   1 Kin 20:6
more d than gold   Ps 19:10
What is d in a man   Prov 19:22
every kind of d object   Nah 2:9

DESIRE (n) *appetite, craving*

d...for your husband   Gen 3:16
poor from *their* d   Job 31:16
the d-s of your heart   Ps 37:4
d of the wicked will   Ps 112:10
d of the righteous   Prov 10:24
d of your eyes   Ezek 24:16
great man speaks the d   Mic 7:3
d and my prayer   Rom 10:1
d-s of the flesh   Eph 2:3
d to depart and be   Phil 1:23
evil d, and greed   Col 3:5

DESIRE (v) *crave, wish*

your heart d-s   Deut 14:26
as much as you d   1 Sam 2:16
I d to argue with God   Job 13:3
Thou dost d truth   Ps 51:6
not d his delicacies   Prov 23:3
all that my eyes d-d   Eccl 2:10
righteous men d-d   Matt 13:17
d the greater gifts   1 Cor 12:31
d...a good showing   Gal 6:12
d a better *country*   Heb 11:16

DESOLATE *lonely, waste*

your sanctuaries d   Lev 26:31

sons of the **d** one	Is 54:1
high places will be **d**	Ezek 6:6
d wilderness behind	Joel 2:3
loaves in a **d** place	Matt 15:33
homestead be made **d**	Acts 1:20
children of the **d**	Gal 4:27

DESOLATION *ruin, waste*

a **d** and a curse	2 Kin 22:19
a heap forever, a **d**	Josh 8:28
D is left in the city	Is 24:12
d-s of many generations	Is 61:4
an everlasting **d**	Ezek 35:9
the abomination of **d**	Dan 11:31
day of...**d**	Zeph 1:15
her **d** is at hand	Luke 21:20

DESPAIR (n) *grief*

words of one in **d**	Job 6:26
my soul is in **d**	Ps 42:6
Why are you in **d**	Ps 43:5

DESPAIR (v) *grieve*

Saul then will **d**	1 Sam 27:1
I...**d**-ed of all	Eccl 2:20
we **d**-ed even of life	2 Cor 1:8
but not **d**-ing	2 Cor 4:8

DESPISE *reject, scorn*

d-d his birthright	Gen 25:34
those who **d** Me	1 Sam 2:30
d-d...in her heart	2 Sam 6:16
not **d** the discipline	Job 5:17
hate and **d** falsehood	Ps 119:163
Fools **d** wisdom and	Prov 1:7
wisdom...is **d**	Eccl 9:16
has **d**-d the day of	Zech 4:10
have we **d**-d Thy name	Mal 1:6
not **d** one of these	Matt 18:10
hold to one, and **d**	Luke 16:13
do you **d**...church	1 Cor 11:22

DESPOIL *injure, lay waste*

d-ed all the cities	2 Chr 14:14
the wicked who **d** me	Ps 17:9
plundered and **d**-ed	Is 42:22

DESTINE *appoint*

is **d**-d for the sword	Job 15:22
d you for the sword	Is 65:12
things **d**-d to perish	Col 2:22
not **d**-d us for wrath	1 Thess 5:9

DESTITUTE *deprived, in need*

prayer of the **d**	Ps 102:17

the land is **d**	Ezek 32:15
being **d**, afflicted	Heb 11:37

DESTROY *abolish, ruin, waste*

to **d** all flesh	Gen 6:17
lest I **d** you	1 Sam 15:6
wouldst Thou **d** me	Job 10:8
seek my life to **d** it	Ps 40:14
the wicked, He will **d**	Ps 145:20
that which **d**-s kings	Prov 31:3
one sinner **d**-s much	Eccl 9:18
stronghold is **d**-ed	Is 23:14
shepherds...are **d**-ing	Jer 23:1
He will **d** mighty men	Matt 8:24
moth and rust **d**	Matt 6:19
who is able to **d**	Matt 10:28
You come to **d** us	Mark 1:24
seeking...to **d** Him	Mark 11:18
d the temple and	Mark 15:29
flood...**d**-ed them	Luke 17:27
D this temple, and	John 2:19
not for **d**-ing you	2 Cor 10:8
to save and to **d**	James 4:12
heavens will be **d**-ed	2 Pet 3:12
d the works of the	1 John 3:8

DESTROYER *devastator*

d of our country	Judg 16:24
of the **d**-s prosper	Job 12:6
d comes upon him	Job 15:21
d-s and devastators	Is 49:17
I shall set apart **d**-s	Jer 22:7

DESTRUCTION *calamity, ruin*

the **d** of my kindred	Esth 8:6
God apportion **d**	Job 21:17
Your tongue devises **d**	Ps 52:2
Pride *goes* before **d**	Prov 16:18
foolish son is **d** to	Prov 19:13
called the City of **D**	Is 19:18
d of the daughter of	Lam 2:11
broad that leads to **d**	Matt 7:13
whose end is **d**	Phil 3:19
d will come	1 Thess 5:3
penalty of eternal **d**	2 Thess 1:9
bringing swift **d** upon	2 Pet 2:1

DETERMINE *decide*

to **d** whether he laid	Ex 22:8
his days are **d**-d	Job 14:5
d-d *their* appointed	Acts 17:26
but rather **d** this	Rom 14:13
d-d to know nothing	1 Cor 2:2

65

DETEST *despise, loathe*

carcasses you shall **d**   Lev 11:11
not **d** an Egyptian   Deut 23:7
I **d** his citadels   Amos 6:8

DETESTABLE *abominable*

not eat any **d** thing   Deut 14:3
who is **d** and corrupt   Job 15:16
swine's flesh, **d**   Is 66:17
their **d** idols   Jer 16:18
remove all its **d**   Ezek 11:18
d...sight of God   Luke 16:15

DEVASTATE *destroy, lay waste*

d-**d** the nations   2 Kin 19:17
Until cities are **d**-**d**   Is 6:11
the LORD...**d**-s it   Is 24:1
my tents are **d**-**d**   Jer 4:20
d...pride of Egypt   Ezek 32:12

DEVASTATION *destruction*

d of the afflicted   Ps 12:5
Nor **d** or destruction   Is 60:18
raise up the former **d**-s   Is 61:4
d in their citadels   Amos 3:10

DEVICE *plan, scheme*

By their own **d**-s   Ps 5:10
not promote his *evil* **d**   Ps 140:8
a man of evil **d**-s   Prov 14:17
in their **d**-s you walk   Mic 6:16

DEVIL *demon, Satan*

tempted by the **d**   Matt 4:1
one of you is a **d**   John 6:70
you son of the **d**   Acts 13:10
firm against...the **d**   Eph 6:11
render powerless...**d**   Heb 2:14
serpent...the **d**   Rev 12:9
d...into the lake   Rev 20:10

DEVISE *design, scheme, plot*

d-**d** against the Jews   Esth 9:25
d-ing a vain thing   Ps 2:1
d-s mischief by decree   Ps 94:20
d-s evil continually   Prov 6:14
man who **d**-s evil   Prov 12:2
He **d**-s wicked schemes   Is 32:7
do not **d** evil in   Zech 7:10
d futile things   Acts 4:25

DEVOTE *commit, dedicate*

shall **d** to the LORD   Ex 13:12

d...to the law   2 Chr 31:4
d-ing...to prayer   Acts 1:14
d-**d** to one another   Rom 12:10
D yourselves to prayer   Col 4:2

DEVOTED *set apart (to God)*

d to destruction   Lev 27:28
Every **d** thing in   Num 18:14
d to destruction   1 Sam 15:21
d thing in Israel   Ezek 44:29

DEVOTION *consecration*

his deeds of **d**   2 Chr 32:32
excessive **d** *to books*   Eccl 12:12
the **d** of your youth   Jer 2:2

DEVOUR *consume, swallow*

wild beast **d**-ed him   Gen 37:20
the sword **d** forever   2 Sam 2:26
is **d**-ed by disease   Job 18:13
fire from...**d**-ed   Ps 18:8
love all words that **d**   Ps 52:4
To **d** the afflicted   Prov 30:14
has **d**-ed your prophets   Jer 2:30
caterpillar was **d**-ing   Amos 4:9
d widows' houses   Mark 12:40
bite...**d** one another   Gal 5:15

DEVOUT *God-fearing*

d men are taken away   Is 57:1
was righteous and **d**   Luke 2:25
d men, from every   Acts 2:5
the **d** women   Acts 13:50

DEW *drops of moisture*

God give...the **d**   Gen 27:28
d fell on the camp   Num 11:9
d on the fleece only   Judg 6:37
on him as the **d**   2 Sam 17:12
neither **d** nor rain   1 Kin 17:1
skies drip with **d**   Prov 3:20
the **d** of Hermon   Ps 133:3
Like a cloud of **d**   Is 18:4
drenched with the **d**   Dan 4:15
sky has withheld its **d**   Hag 1:10

DIALECT *language*

in the Hebrew **d**   Acts 21:40
the Hebrew **d**   Acts 22:2

DIAMOND *jewel*

a sapphire and a **d**   Ex 28:18
With a **d** point   Jer 17:1

DICTATION *spoken words*

at the **d** of Jeremiah	Jer 36:4
written at the **d** of	Jer 36:27
book at Jeremiah's **d**	Jer 45:1

DIE *decease, expire*

you shall surely **d**	Gen 2:17
not eat...which **d-s**	Deut 14:21
Where you **d**, I will **d**	Ruth 1:17
Curse God and **d**	Job 2:9
even wise men **d**	Ps 49:10
fools **d** for lack of	Prov 10:21
and the fool alike **d**	Eccl 2:16
soul who sins will **d**	Ezek 18:4
to **d** with You	Matt 26:35
child has not **d-d**	Mark 5:39
live even if he **d-s**	John 11:25
grain of wheat...**d-s**	John 12:24
she fell sick and **d-d**	Acts 9:37
d-d for the ungodly	Rom 5:6
we who **d-d** to sin	Rom 6:2
for whom Christ **d-d**	Rom 14:15
I **d** daily	1 Cor 15:31
I **d-d** to the Law	Gal 2:19
to **d** is gain	Phil 1:21
Jesus **d-d** and rose	1 Thess 4:14
to **d** once and after	Heb 9:27
these **d-d** in faith	Heb 11:13
who **d** in the Lord	Rev 14:13

DIFFICULT *hard*

too **d** for the LORD	Gen 18:14
test Solomon with **d**	2 Chr 9:1
anything too **d** for Me	Jer 32:27
speech or **d** language	Ezek 3:5
solving of **d** problems	Dan 5:12
last days **d** times	2 Tim 3:1

DIG *excavate, till*

opens a pit, or **d-s**	Ex 21:33
you can **d** copper	Deut 8:9
they **d** into houses	Job 24:16
He has **dug** a pit	Ps 7:15
dug through the wall	Ezek 8:8
dug a wine press	Matt 21:33
until I **d** around it	Luke 13:8

DIGNITY *majesty*

Preeminent in **d**	Gen 49:3
What honor or **d** has	Esth 6:3
all godliness and **d**	1 Tim 2:2
must be men of **d**	1 Tim 3:8

DILIGENCE *effort*

carried out with all **d**	Ezra 6:12
Watch...with all **d**	Prov 4:23
lagging behind in **d**	Rom 12:11
show the same **d**	Heb 6:11

DILIGENT *persistent*

hand of the **d** makes	Prov 10:4
plans of the **d** *lead*	Prov 21:5
d to present	2 Tim 2:15
I will also be **d**	2 Pet 1:15
d to enter that rest	Heb 4:11

DIM *cloudy, dark*

eye was not **d**	Deut 34:7
eyesight...to grow **d**	1 Sam 3:2
d because of grief	Job 17:7
windows grow **d**	Eccl 12:3

DIMINISH *dwindle, reduce*

you shall **d** its price	Lev 25:16
d their inheritance	Num 26:54
are **d-ed** and bowed	Ps 107:39

DINAH

daughter of Jacob	Gen 34:1,3
raped by Shechem	Gen 34:2,5

DINE *eat*

men are to **d** with	Gen 43:16
to **d** with a ruler	Prov 23:1
came and were **d-ing**	Matt 9:10

DINNER *meal*

I have prepared...**d**	Matt 22:4
because of...**d** guests	Mark 6:26
was giving a big **d**	Luke 14:16

DIP *plunge*

d-ped the tunic in	Gen 37:31
priest shall **d** his	Lev 4:6
d your piece of bread	Ruth 2:14
d-ped...seven times	2 Kin 5:14
d-ped...with Me	Matt 26:23
who **d-s** with Me	Mark 14:20
robe **d-ped** in blood	Rev 19:13

DIRECT *arrange, guide, order*

LORD **d-s** his steps	Prov 16:9
d your heart in the	Prov 23:19
had **d-ed** the Spirit	Is 40:13
walks to **d** his steps	Jer 10:23
I **d-ed** the churches	1 Cor 16:1
d their entire body	James 3:3

DIRECTION *path or order*

which turned every **d**   Gen 3:24
And it changes **d**   Job 37:12
d of the daughter   Jer 4:11
of their four **d-s**   Ezek 1:17

DIRGE *lament*

for you as a **d**   Amos 5:1
we sang a **d**   Luke 7:32

DISAPPEAR *vanish*

For the faithful **d**   Ps 12:1
When the grass **d-s**   Prov 27:25
old is ready to **d**   Heb 8:13

DISAPPOINT *frustrate*

and were not **d-ed**   Ps 22:5
hope does not **d**   Rom 5:5

DISASTER *calamity*

d was close to them   Judg 20:34
d on this people   Jer 6:19
because of all its **d-s**   Jer 19:8
In the day of their **d**   Obad 13

DISBELIEVE *doubt*

Jews who **d-d** stirred   Acts 14:2
for those who **d**   1 Pet 2:7

DISCERN *understand, recognize*

would **d**...future   Deut 32:29
king to **d** good   2 Sam 14:17
not **d** its appearance   Job 4:16
d-ed...the youths   Prov 7:7
O fools, **d** wisdom   Prov 8:5
d the...sky   Matt 16:3

DISCERNMENT *judgment*

blessed be your **d**   1 Sam 25:33
asked for yourself **d**   1 Kin 3:11
not a people of **d**   Is 27:11
knowledge and all **d**   Phil 1:9

DISCHARGE *emission*

a **d** from his body   Lev 15:2
leper or who has a **d**   Lev 22:4
everyone having a **d**   Num 5:2
d, or who is a leper   2 Sam 3:29
the **d** of your blood   Ezek 32:6

DISCIPLE *student, learner*

to listen as a **d**   Is 50:4
His twelve **d-s**   Matt 10:1
d is not above his   Matt 10:24

d-s rebuked them   Matt 19:13
d-s left Him...fled   Matt 26:56
make **d-s** of all   Matt 28:19
Your **d-s** do not fast   Mark 2:18
Passover...My **d-s**   Mark 14:14
gaze on His **d-s**   Luke 6:20
he cannot be My **d**   Luke 14:26
d-s believed in Him   John 2:11
His **d-s** withdrew   John 6:66
wash the **d-s** feet   John 13:5
d whom He loved   John 19:26
d-s were first called   Acts 11:26

DISCIPLINE (n) *chastisement*

the **d** of the LORD   Deut 11:2
d of the Almighty   Job 5:17
The rod of **d**   Prov 22:15
to see your good **d**   Col 2:5
d...of little profit   1 Tim 4:8

DISCIPLINE (v) *chastise*

as a man **d-s** his son   Deut 8:5
d-d you with whips   1 Kin 12:11
D your son while   Prov 19:18
d-d by the Lord   1 Cor 11:32
father does not **d**   Heb 12:7

DISCLOSE *reveal*

without **d-ing** it to   1 Sam 20:2
Esther had **d-d** what   Esth 8:1
will **d** Myself to him   John 14:21
d the motives of   1 Cor 4:5
secrets...are **d-d**   1 Cor 14:25

DISCOURAGE *dishearten*

d-ing the sons of   Num 32:7
people of the land **d-d**   Ezra 4:4
d-d with the work   Neh 6:9

DISCOVER *find, uncover*

strength was not **d-ed**   Judg 16:9
d the depths of God   Job 11:7
man may not **d**   Eccl 7:14
shamed...he is **d-ed**   Jer 2:26

DISCRETION *understanding*

LORD give you **d**   1 Chr 22:12
sound wisdom and **d**   Prov 3:21
woman who lacks **d**   Prov 11:22
Daniel replied with **d**   Dan 2:14

DISCUSS *converse, reason*

d matters of justice   Jer 12:1

d among themselves   Matt 16:7
What were you **d-ing**   Mark 9:33
d-ed together what   Luke 6:11

DISEASE *sickness*

none of the **d-s** on you   Ex 15:26
harmful **d-s** of Egypt   Deut 7:15
d-d in his feet   2 Chr 16:12
d-d...not healed   Ezek 34:4
heals all your **d-s**   Ps 103:3
various **d-s** and pains   Matt 4:24
power...to heal **d-s**   Luke 9:1

DISGRACE *reproach, shame*

a d to us   Gen 34:14
nakedness, it is a d   Lev 20:17
sin is a d to   Prov 14:34
not d the throne   Jer 14:21
and bear your d   Ezek 16:52

DISGRACEFUL *shameful*

d thing in Israel   Gen 34:7
shameful and d son   Prov 19:26
d for a woman to   1 Cor 11:6

DISGUISE *pretend*

d-d his sanity   1 Sam 21:13
Arise now, and d   1 Kin 14:2
king of Israel **d-d**   1 Kin 22:30
he **d-s** his face   Job 24:15
d-ing...as apostles   2 Cor 11:13

DISH *bowl, plate*

prepare a savory d   Gen 27:7
was one silver d   Num 7:43
as one wipes a d   2 Kin 21:13
30 gold **d-es**   Ezra 1:9

DISHEARTENED *discouraged*

not be d or crushed   Is 42:4
you d the righteous   Ezek 13:22

DISHONEST *untruthful*

those who hate d gain   Ex 18:21
order to get d gain   Ezek 22:27
cheat with d scales   Amos 8:5

DISHONOR (n) *disgrace, shame*

to· see the king's d   Ezra 4:14
Fill their faces with d   Ps 83:16
man conceals d   Prov 12:16

DISHONOR (v) *disgrace, shame*

who **d-s** his father   Deut 27:16

be ashamed and **d-ed**   Ps 35:4
and you d Me   John 8:49
bodies might be **d-ed**   Rom 1:24
do you d God   Rom 2:23

DISMAY *be troubled, fear*

d-ed at his presence   Gen 45:3
not tremble or be **d-ed**   Josh 1:9
d-ed and...afraid   1 Sam 17:11
lest I d you   Jer 1:17
are **d-ed** and caught   Jer 8:9
mighty men...be **d-ed**   Obad 9

DISMISS *release, send away*

d-ed the people   Josh 24:28
Solomon **d-ed**   1 Kin 2:27
priest did not d *any*   2 Chr 23:8
he **d-ed** the assembly   Acts 19:41

DISOBEDIENCE *rebellion*

the one man's d   Rom 5:19
in the sons of d   Eph 2:2
d received a just   Heb 2:2
same example of d   Heb 4:11

DISOBEDIENT *rebellious*

d and rebelled   Neh 9:26
hardened and d   Acts 19:9
d to parents   Rom 1:30
d...obstinate people   Rom 10:21

DISPERSE *spread*

d them in Jacob   Gen 49:7
d-d...the peoples   Esth 3:8
d them among the   Ezek 20:23
who are **d-d** abroad   James 1:1

DISPLAY *declare, show*

to d her beauty   Esth 1:11
d-d Thy splendor   Ps 8:1
d their sin like   Is 3:9
works of God...**d-ed**   John 9:3

DISPLEASE *annoy, trouble*

if it is **d-ing** to you   Num 22:34
d-ing in the sight   1 Sam 8:6
may not d the lords   1 Sam 29:7
d-ing in His sight   Is 59:15
it greatly **d-d** Jonah   Jon 4:1

DISPOSSESS *remove*

d-ed the Amorites   Num 21:32
Esau **d-ed** them   Deut 2:12
He will assuredly d   Josh 3:10

d-ing the nations   Acts 7:45

DISPUTE (n) *controversy*

When they have a d   Ex 18:16
bring the d-s to God   Ex 18:19
d in your courts   Deut 17:8
a great d among   Acts 28:29

DISPUTE (v) *contend, debate*

wished to d with Him   Job 9:3
with Israel he will d   Mic 6:2
without...d-ing   Phil 2:14
he d-d with the devil   Jude 9

DISSENSION *division*

great d and debate   Acts 15:2
d between the   Acts 23:7
those who cause d-s   Rom 16:17
without wrath and d   1 Tim 2:8

DISSIPATION *intemperance*

weighted...with d   Luke 21:34
wine, for that is d   Eph 5:18
not accused of d   Titus 1:6

DISSOLVE *melt*

dost d me in a storm   Job 30:22
I d my couch with   Ps 6:6
d-d in tears   Is 15:3
And the hills d   Nah 1:5

DISTANCE *far away*

sister stood at a d   Ex 2:4
some d from the   Judg 18:22
following...at a d   Matt 26:58
welcomed...from a d   Heb 11:13

DISTINCTION *difference*

the LORD makes a d   Ex 11:7
d between the holy   Lev 10:10
have made no d   Ezek 22:26
he made no d   Acts 15:9
for there is no d   Rom 3:22
d-s among yourselves   James 2:4

DISTINGUISH *discern*

I d between good   2 Sam 19:35
not d the sound   Ezra 3:13
d...the righteous   Mal 3:18
d-ing of spirits   1 Cor 12:10

DISTINGUISHING

became your d mark   Ezek 27:7
this is a d mark   2 Thess 3:17

DISTORT *pervert*

who d-s the justice   Deut 27:19
my garment is d-ed   Job 30:18
they d my words   Ps 56:5
d the gospel of Christ   Gal 1:7

DISTRESS *adversity, trouble*

day of my d   Gen 35:3
When you are in d   Deut 4:30
deliver me...d   1 Sam 26:24
I am in great d   2 Sam 24:14
cry to Thee in our d   2 Chr 20:9
refuge in the day of d   Jer 16:19
I am in d   Lam 1:20
d upon the land   Luke 21:23
d for every soul   Rom 2:9
assisted those in d   1 Tim 5:10
widows in their d   James 1:27

DISTRIBUTE *apportion*

d-d by lot in Shiloh   Josh 19:51
to d their kinsmen   Neh 13:13
d it to the poor   Luke 18:22
d-ing to each one   1 Cor 12:11

DISTRICT *area, province*

the d of Jerusalem   Neh 3:12
d around the Jordan   Matt 3:5
d of Galilee   Mark 1:28
the d-s of Libya   Acts 2:10

DISTURB *annoy, bother*

Why...d-ed me   1 Sam 28:15
no one d his bones   2 Kin 23:18
d them and destroy   Esth 9:24
being greatly d-ed   Acts 4:2
one who is d-ing you   Gal 5:10

DISTURBANCE *turmoil*

to cause a d in it   Neh 4:8
hear of wars and d-s   Luke 21:9
d among the soldiers   Acts 12:18
arrogance, d-s   2 Cor 12:20

DIVIDE *apportion, separate*

that d-s the hoof   Deut 14:6
D the living child   1 Kin 3:25
d my garments among   Ps 22:18
He will d the booty   Is 53:12
d-d up his garments   Matt 27:35
d-d his wealth   Luke 15:12

DIVINATION *witchcraft*

nor practice d or   Lev 19:26
witchcraft, used d   2 Chr 33:6
false vision, d.   Jer 14:14
falsehood and lying d Ezek 13:6
a spirit of d met us Acts 16:16

DIVINE (adj) *pertaining to deity*

in whom...d spirit   Gen 41:38
I see a d being   1 Sam 28:13
D Nature...gold   Acts 17:29
power and d nature Rom 1:20
is the d response   Rom 11:4

DIVINE (v) *practice divination*

d-d that the LORD   Gen 30:27
they d lies for you Ezek 21:29
d-ing lies for them Ezek 22:28
prophets d for money Mic 3:11

DIVINER *seer*

called for the...d-s 1 Sam 6:2
The d and the elder   Is 3:2
your d-s deceive you Jer 29:8
d-s will be embarrassed Mic 3:7
d-s see lying visions Zech 10:2

DIVISION *dissention, segment*

d between My people Ex 8:23
divided...into d-s 1 Sam 23:6
d in the multitude John 7:43
no d-s among you 1 Cor 1:10
d of soul and spirit Heb 4:12

DIVORCE (n) *separation*

a certificate of d   Deut 24:1
given her a writ of d   Jer 3:8
For I hate d   Mal 2:16

DIVORCE (v) *separate*

he cannot d her   Deut 22:19
husband d-s his wife   Jer 3:1
man to d his wife Matt 19:3
Whoever d-s his   Mark 10:11

DIVORCED *separated*

woman d from her   Lev 21:7
or of a d woman   Num 30:9
marries a d woman Matt 5:32
marries...who is d Luke 16:18

DOCTRINE *teaching*

Teaching as d the   Matt 15:9

every wind of d   Eph 4:14
to teach strange d-s 1 Tim 1:3
to exhort in sound d Titus 1:9

DOCUMENT *manuscript*

the d which you sent Ezra 4:18
And on the sealed d Neh 9:38
Darius signed the d   Dan 6:9

DOER *workman*

recompenses the...d Ps 31:23
d-s of the Law will Rom 2:13
d-s of the word   James 1:22
not a d of the law James 4:11

DOG *animal, scavenger*

Am I a d   1 Sam 17:43
d-s have surrounded Ps 22:16
they howl like a d   Ps 59:6
live d is better than Eccl 9:4
Beware of the d-s   Phil 3:2
d-s and the sorcerers Rev 22:15

DOMAIN *estate*

give You all this d   Luke 4:6
the d of darkness   Col 1:13
keep their own d   Jude 6

DOMINION *authority, rule*

Thine is the d   1 Chr 29:11
places of His d   Ps 103:22
d will be from sea Zech 9:10
and power and d   Eph 1:21
thrones or d-s or   Col 1:16
glory and the d forever Rev 1:6

DONKEY *ass*

a wild d of a man Gen 16:12
Balaam...to the d Num 22:29
the foal of a d   Zech 9:9
you will find a d Matt 21:2
and mounted on a d Matt 21:5
a dumb d, speaking 2 Pet 2:16

DOOR *entrance, opening*

crouching at the d   Gen 4:7
set the d of the ark Gen 6:16
Uriah slept at the d 2 Sam 11:9
over the d of my lips Ps 141:3
d turns on its   Prov 26:14
each had a double d Ezek 41:23
shut your d, pray   Matt 6:6
I am the d   John 10:9

DOOR

right at the d   James 5:9
before you an open d   Rev 3:8
I stand at the d   Rev 3:20

DOORKEEPER *guard*

d-s have gathered   2 Kin 22:4
the Levites, the d-s   2 Chr 34:9
eunuchs who were d-s   Esth 6:2
commanded the d   Mark 13:34
To him the d opens   John 10:3

DOORPOST

put it on the two d-s   Ex 12:7
write them on the d-s   Deut 6:9
on the seat by the d   1 Sam 1:9
Waiting at my d-s   Prov 8:34

DOORWAY *entrance, opening*

the d of the tent   Judg 4:20
d-s and doorposts   1 Kin 7:5
at my neighbor's d   Job 31:9
chamber with its d   Ezek 40:38

DORCAS

Tabitha, a Joppa Christian
     Acts 9:36-43

DOUBT (n) *unbelief*

life shall hang in d   Deut 28:66
why do d-s arise   Luke 24:38

DOUBT (v) *disbelieve*

why did you d   Matt 14:31
not d in his heart   Mark 11:23
d-s is condemned   Rom 14:23
who d-s is like the   James 1:6

DOUGH *flour mixture*

people took their d   Ex 12:34
the first of your d   Num 15:20
knead d to make cakes   Jer 7:18
took d, kneaded *it*   2 Sam 13:8

DOVE *bird*

he sent out a d   Gen 8:8
had wings like a d   Ps 55:6
eyes are *like* d-s   Song 1:15
descending as a d   Matt 3:16
descending as a d   John 1:32
selling the d-s   John 2:16

DOWNFALL *collapse*

became the d of   2 Chr 28:23
noise of their d   Jer 49:21

DOWNPOUR *rain*

the d and the rain   Job 37:6
d of waters swept   Hab 3:10

DOWRY *bequest*

must pay a d for her   Ex 22:16
to the d for virgins   Ex 22:17
d to his daughter   1 Kin 9:16

DRACHMA

Greek silver coin   Neh 7:70-72
     Matt 17:24

DRAG *draw, pull*

grasshopper d-s   Eccl 12:5
D them off like sheep   Jer 12:3
the dogs to d off   Jer 15:3
Paul and d-ged   Acts 14:19
d you into court   James 2:6

DRAGON *monster, serpent*

d who *lives* in the sea   Is 27:1
Who pierced the d   Is 51:9
d stood before the   Rev 12:4
he laid hold of the d   Rev 20:2

DRAIN *empty*

blood is to be d-ed   Lev 1:15
he d-ed the dew   Judg 6:38
must *and* drink down   Ps 75:8
drink it and d it   Ezek 23:34

DRAW *haul, pull*

out to d water   Gen 24:13
drew him out of the   Ex 2:10
but are d-n away   Deut 30:17
he d-s up the drops   Job 36:27
d near to my soul   Ps 69:18
They are d-ing back   Jer 46:5
redemption is d-ing   Luke 21:28
d all men to Myself   John 12:32
D near to God   James 4:8

DRAWERS *servant*

wood and d of water   Josh 9:21

DREAD (n) *fear*

in d...of Israel   Ex 1:12
in d night and day   Deut 28:66
d of the Jews   Esth 8:17
d comes like a storm   Prov 1:27
they are in great d   Ps 14:5

DREAD (v) *fear*

what I d befalls me   Job 3:25

Whom shall I **d**   Ps 27:1
whose two kings you **d**   Is 7:16
are **d-ed** and feared   Hab 1:7

DREAM (n) *vision*

had a **d**, and behold   Gen 28:12
man was relating a **d**   Judg 7:13
flies away like a **d**   Job 20:8
like a **d**, a vision   Is 29:7
visions and **d-s**   Dan 1:7
to Joseph in a **d**   Matt 2:13

DREAM (v) *see a vision*

asleep and **d-ed**   Gen 41:5
like those who **d**   Ps 126:1
when a hungry man **d-s** Is 29:8
Your old men will **d**   Joel 2:28

DREAMER *visionary*

Here comes this **d**   Gen 37:19
If a prophet or a **d**   Deut 13:1
your diviners, your **d-s** Jer 27:9

DRENCH *soak, wet*

d you with my tears   Is 16:9
head is **d-ed** with dew   Song 5:2
d-ed with the dew   Dan 4:33

DRESS (n) *clothing*

have taken off my **d**   Song 5:3
d was of fine linen   Ezek 16:3
or putting on **d-es**   1 Pet 3:3

DRESS (v) *array, clothe*

d-ed in his military   2 Sam 20:8
D-ed as a harlot   Prov 7:10
you **d** in scarlet   Jer 4:30
d-ed Him...purple   Mark 15:17

DRINK (n) *refreshment*

gave the lad a **d**   Gen 21:19
or wine, or strong **d** Deut 14:26
to desire strong **d**   Prov 31:4
thirsty...gave me **d**   Matt 25:35
My blood is true **d**   John 6:55
thirsty, give him a **d**   Rom 12:20

DRINK (v)

he **drank** of the wine   Gen 9:21
Do not **d** wine   Lev 10:9
d from the brook   1 Kin 17:6
they all **drank** from   Mark 14:23
after **d-ing** old *wine*   Luke 5:39
who eats and **d-s**   1 Cor 11:29

ground that **d-s** the   Heb 6:7

DRIP *drop*

clouds...They **d**   Job 36:28
lips...**d** honey   Song 4:11
d-ped with myrrh   Song 5:5
D down, O heavens   Is 45:8

DRIVE *chase, defeat*

Thou hast **d-n** me   Gen 4:14
and **drove** them away   Ex 2:17
angel...**d-ing** *them* on   Ps 35:5
d hard all your workers   Is 58:3
drove *them* all out   John 2:15
to **d** the ship   Acts 27:39

DROP (n) *drip*

the **d-s** of water   Job 36:27
a **d** from a bucket   Is 40:15
like **d-s** of blood   Luke 22:44

DROP (v) *fall*

olives shall **d** off   Deut 28:40
his bonds **d-ped**   Judg 15:14
d off his unripe grape   Job 15:33
d-ped their wings   Ezek 1:24

DROSS *metallic waste*

of the earth *like* **d**   Ps 119:119
Take away the **d**   Prov 25:4
silver has become **d**   Is 1:22
Israel has become **d**   Ezek 22:18

DROUGHT *dryness*

Like heat in **d**   Is 25:5
in regard to the **d**   Jer 14:1
I called for a **d**   Hag 1:11

DROWNED *sank*

d in the Red Sea   Ex 15:4
he be **d** in the depth   Matt 18:6
were **d** in the sea   Mark 5:13

DRUNK *intoxicated*

arrows **d** with blood   Deut 32:42
d, but not with wine   Is 29:9
made...**d** in My wrath   Is 63:6
not get **d** with wine   Eph 5:18
I saw the woman **d**   Rev 17:6

DRUNKARD *intoxicated person*

a glutton and a **d**   Deut 21:20
song of the **d-s**   Ps 69:12

DRUNKARD

Awake, **d-s**, and weep Joel 1:5
a reviler, or a **d** 1 Cor 5:11

DRUNKEN *intoxicated*

stagger like a **d** man Job 12:25
become like a **d** man Jer 23:9

DRUNKENNESS *intoxicated*

and not for **d** Eccl 10:17
weighted down...**d** Luke 21:34
in carousing and **d** Rom 13:13
envying, **d**, carousings Gal 5:21

DRY (adj) *parched, scorched*

let the **d** land appear Gen 1:9
In a **d** and weary land Ps 63:1
Better is a **d** morsel Prov 17:1
O **d** bones, hear Ezek 37:4

DRY (v) *scorch, wither*

My strength is **dried** Ps 22:15
d up...streams Ps 74:15
I **d** up the sea Is 50:2
new wine **dries** up Joel 1:10
dries up...rivers Nah 1:4

DUE (adj) *proper, right*

In **d** time their foot Deut 32:35
food in **d** season Ps 104:27
d penalty of their Rom 1:27

DUE (n) *what is owed*

as *their* **d** forever Lev 7:34
be the priests' **d** Deut 18:3
Indeed it is Thy **d** Jer 10:7

DULL *heavy, stupid*

eyes are **d** from wine Gen 49:12
Their ears **d** Is 6:10
people...become **d** Matt 13:15
become **d** of hearing Heb 5:11

DUMB *silent*

who makes *him* **d** Ex 4:11
I was **d** and silent Ps 39:2
behold, a **d** man Matt 9:32
and the **d** to speak Mark 7:37
astray to the **d** idols 1 Cor 12:2

DUNG *waste*

sweeps away **d** 1 Kin 14:10
dove's **d** for five 2 Kin 6:25
give you cow's **d** Ezek 4:15
their flesh like **d** Zeph 1:17

DUNGEON *prison*

put me into the **d** Gen 40:15
captive...in the **d** Ex 12:29
prisoners from the **d** Is 42:7
Jeremiah...into the **d** Jer 37:16

DUST *dirt, earth*

God formed man of **d** Gen 2:7
And **d** shall you eat Gen 3:14
the poor from the **d** 1 Sam 2:8
repent in **d** and ashes Job 42:6
d before the wind Ps 18:42
Will the **d** praise Thee Ps 30:9
You who lie in the **d** Is 26:19
shake off the **d** of Matt 10:14
the **d** of your city Luke 10:11
d on their heads Rev 18:19

DUTY *responsibility*

perform your **d** Gen 38:8
charged with any **d** Deut 24:5
the **d** of a husband's Deut 25:7
his **d** to his wife 1 Cor 7:3

DWELL *abide, live*

father of those who **d** Gen 4:20
Behold, I am **d-ing** 1 Chr 17:1
No evil **d-s** with Thee Ps 5:4
d on Thy holy hill Ps 15:1
I will **d** in the house Ps 23:6
d among the wise Prov 15:31
have **d-t** in Jerusalem Jer 35:11
flesh, and **d-t** among John 1:14
of God **d-s** in you 1 Cor 3:16
Christ may **d** in your Eph 3:17
mind **d** on these things Phil 4:8

DWELLING *habitation*

earth shall be your **d** Gen 27:39
name there for His **d** Deut 12:5
place for Thy **d** 1 Kin 8:13
into the eternal **d-s** Luke 16:9
might find a **d** place Acts 7:46

DYED *colored*

rams' skins **d** red Ex 25:5
A spoil of **d** work Judg 5:30

E

EAGLE *bird*

bore you on e-s' wings Ex 19:4
the e swoops down Deut 28:49
swifter than e-s 2 Sam 1:23
with wings like e-s Is 40:31
the face of an e Ezek 1:10
was like a flying e Rev 4:7

EAR *hearing*

heard with our e-s 2 Sam 7:22
the e test words Job 12:11
And His e-s are *open* Ps 34:15
and incline your e Ps 45:10
He whose e listens Prov 15:31
e of the wise seeks Prov 18:15
e has not been open Is 48:8
let your e receive Jer 9:20
He who has e-s to Matt 11:15
and cut off his e Matt 26:51
fingers into his e-s Mark 7:33
if the e should say 1 Cor 12:16
their e-s tickled 2 Tim 4:3
He who has an e Rev 2:7

EARLY *beforetime, soon*

they arose e and Gen 26:31
Let us rise e Song 7:12
dew which goes away e Hos 6:4
e on the first day Mark 16:2
at the tomb e Luke 24:22
the e and late rains James 5:7

EARNINGS *gain, wages*

her e she plants Prov 31:16
the e of a harlot Mic 1:7

EARRING *ornament*

brought...e-s Ex 35:22
e-s and necklaces Num 31:50
Like an e of gold Prov 25:12
her e-s and jewelry Hos 2:13

EARTH *land, world*

God created the...e Gen 1:1
Judge of all the e Gen 18:25
the e is the LORD'S Ex 9:29
way of all the e Josh 23:14
His stand on the e Job 19:25
foundation of the e Job 38:4
saints...in the e Ps 16:3

the shields of the e Ps 47:9
give birth to the e Ps 90:2
He established the e Ps 104:5
wisdom founded...e Prov 3:19
the e remains forever Eccl 1:4
made the e tremble Is 14:16
the vault of the e Is 40:22
the ends of the e Is 45:22
the e is My footstool Is 66:1
e shone with His Ezek 43:2
make the e dark Amos 8:9
e will be devoured Zeph 3:8
shall inherit the e Matt 5:5
you shall bind on e Matt 16:19
on e peace among Luke 2:14
glorified...on the e John 17:4
man is from the e 1 Cor 15:47
heavens and a new e 2 Pet 3:13
e and heaven fled Rev 20:11

EARTHENWARE *pottery*

bird in an e vessel Lev 14:5
holy water in an e Num 5:17
shatter them like e Ps 2:9
buy a potter's e jar Jer 19:1
vessels of...e 2 Tim 2:20

EARTHQUAKE *temblor*

LORD *was* not in...e 1 Kin 19:11
punished with...e Is 29:6
be famines and e-s Matt 24:7
will be great e-s Luke 21:11
there was a great e Rev 6:12
killed in the e Rev 11:13

EARTHY *mortal*

man is...e 1 Cor 15:47
those who are e 1 Cor 15:48

EASE *free from difficulty, pain*

He who is at e Job 12:5
at e and satisfied Job 21:23
women who are at e Is 32:9
Woe to those...at e Amos 6:1
nations who are at e Zech 1:15

EAST *direction of compass*

spread out...to the e Gen 28:14
directed an e wind Ex 10:13
sons of the e were Judg 7:12
men of the e Job 1:3
With the e wind Thou Ps 48:7
offspring from the e Is 43:5

faces toward the **e**   Ezek 8:16
Jerusalem on the **e**   Zech 14:4
saw His star in the **e**   Matt 2:2
lightning...the **e**   Matt 24:27
kings from the **e**   Rev 16:12

EAST GATE *see*
  GATES OF JERUSALEM

EASY *without difficulty*

knowledge is **e** to him Prov 14:6
My yoke is **e**, and   Matt 11:30

EAT *consume, dine, feast*

shall not **e** from it   Gen 3:17
they **ate** every plant   Ex 10:15
not **e**...blood   Lev 19:26
that we may **e** him 2 Kin 6:28
e and be satisfied   Ps 22:26
not **e** the bread of   Prov 31:27
will **e** curds and honey   Is 7:15
words...I **ate** them   Jer 15:16
e this scroll   Ezek 3:1
e-ing grass like cattle   Dan 4:33
what you shall **e**   Matt 6:25
e with unwashed   Matt 15:20
Take, **e**; this is My   Matt 26:26
sinners and **e**-s with   Luke 15:2
e...at My table   Luke 22:30
He took it and **ate**   Luke 24:43
e the flesh of...Son   John 6:53
Peter, kill and **ate**   Acts 10:13
kingdom...not **e**-ing   Rom 14:17
ate...spiritual food 1 Cor 10:3
e-s...judgment   1 Cor 11:29

EBAL

1 *son of Shobal*   Gen 36:23
2 *son of Joktan*   1 Chr 1:22
  also **Obal**   Gen 10:28
3 *mountain near Shechem*
    Deut 11:29

EBENEZER

a memorial stone   1 Sam 7:12

EBER

1 *line of Shem*   Gen 10:21-24
  progenitor of Jocktanide Arabs
    Gen 10:25-30
  progenitor of Hebrews
    Gen 11:16ff
2 *a Gadite*   1 Chr 5:13

3 *son of Elpaal*   1 Chr 8:12
4 *son of Shashak*   1 Chr 8:22
5 *priest*   Neh 12:20
  see also **HEBER**

EDEN

1 *garden of God*   Gen 2:15
    Is 51:3
2 *city area*   2 Kin 19:12
    Ezek 27:23
3 *son of Joah*   2 Chr 29:12

EDICT *decree*

the king's **e**-s   Ezra 8:36
a royal **e** be issued   Esth 1:19
king's command and **e** Esth 9:1
afraid of the king's **e** Heb 11:23

EDIFICATION *building up*

his good, to his **e**   Rom 15:2
speaks to men for **e** 1 Cor 14:3
all things...for **e** 1 Cor 14:26

EDIFY *build up*

but love **e**-ies   1 Cor 8:1
not all things **e** 1 Cor 10:23
man is not **e**-ied 1 Cor 14:7

EDOM

1 *name of Esau*   Gen 25:30
2 *Edomites* Num 20:18,20
3 *region or country* Gen 32:3
    Judg 11:17
  see also **SEIR**

EDUCATED *taught*

be **e** three years   Dan 1:5
Moses was **e** in all Acts 7:22
e under Gamaliel   Acts 22:3

EFFEMINATE *womanlike*

e, nor homosexuals 1 Cor 6:9

EGG

in the white of an **e**   Job 6:6
gathers abandoned **e**-s Is 10:14
hatch adders' **e**-s and   Is 59:5
is asked for an **e**   Luke 11:12

EGLON

1 *town in Judah* Josh 10:34-37
    Josh 15:39
2 *Moabite king* Judg 3:12-30

EGYPT

country in NE Africa Gen 12:10
Gen 37:25
on the Nile Ex 4:19;7:5
conflict with Moses Ex 7:8ff
scene of Passover Ex 12:1-36
source of food Gen 42:1,2

EHUD

1 *left-handed Benjamite*
judge of Israel Judg 3:15,21
2 *son of Bilhan* 1 Chr 7:10
3 *progenitor of clan* 1 Chr 8:6

EKRON

Philistine city Josh 13:3
1 Sam 5:10; Jer 25:20

ELAH

1 *Edomite* Gen 36:41
2 *valley SW of Jerusalem*
1 Sam 17:2
3 *king of Israel* 1 Kin 16:8-10
4 *father of Hoshea* 2 Kin 15:30
5 *son of Caleb* 1 Chr 4:15
6 *son of Uzzi* 1 Chr 9:8
7 *father of Shimei* 1 Kin 4:18

ELAM

1 *son of Shem* Gen 10:22
2 *son of Shashak* 1 Chr 8:24
3 *Korahite Levite* 1 Chr 26:3
4 *head of restoration family*
Ezra 2:7;Neh 7:12
5 *head of restoration family*
Ezra 2:31;Neh 7:34
6 *chief of people* Neh 10:14
7 *priest* Neh 12:42
8 *region E of Babylonia*
Is 21:2; Dan 8:2

ELATH/ELOTH *city*

at Gulf of Aqabah 2 Kin 14:22
near Ezion-geber

EL-BETHEL

altar Gen 35:7

ELDER *aged, older*

words of her e son Gen 27:42
the e-s of Israel Ex 17:6
sits among the e-s Prov 31:23
Assemble the e-s Joel 2:16

tradition of the e-s Matt 15:2
chief priests and e-s Matt 27:12
scribes...e-s came Mark 11:27
Council of e-s of Luke 22:66
e-s of the church Acts 20:17
I saw twenty-four e Rev 4:4

ELEAZAR

1 *son of Aaron* Ex 6:23
high priest Num 20:25-28
2 *son of Abinadab* 1 Sam 7:1
3 *son of Dodo* 2 Sam 23:9
4 *a Levite* 1 Chr 23:22
5 *son of Phinehas* Ezra 8:33
6 *son of Parosh* Ezra 10:18-25
7 *priest* Neh 12:27
8 *ancestor of Jesus* Matt 1:15

ELECT *chosen*

sake of the e Matt 24:22
to lead the e astray Mark 13:22
justice for His e Luke 18:7
against God's e Rom 8:33

ELEMENTARY *basic*

e principles of the Col 2:8
e principles of the Heb 5:12
e teaching about the Heb 6:1

ELEMENTS *physical matter*

e will be destroyed 2 Pet 3:10
the e will melt with 2 Pet 3:12

ELI

high priest 1 Sam 1:9;2:12
1 Sam 3:6;4:18

ELIAKIM

1 *son of Hilkiah* 2 Kin 18:18
2 Kin 19:2
2 *son of Josiah* 2 Kin 23:34
3 *priest* Neh 12:41
4 *ancestor of Jesus* Matt 1:13
5 *ancestor of Jesus* Luke 3:30,31

ELIEZER

1*Abraham's servant* Gen 15:2
2 *son of Moses* 1 Chr 23:15
3 *son of Becher* 1 Chr 7:8
4 *priest* 1 Chr 15:24
5 *son of Zichri* 1 Chr 27:16
6 *a prophet* 2 Chr 20:37

7 *served under Ezra* Ezra 8:16
8 *son of Jeshua* Ezra 10:18
9 *Levite* Ezra 10:10,23
10 *son of Harim* Ezra 10:10,31
11 *ancestor of Jesus* Luke 3:29

ELIHU

1 *son of Tohu* 1 Sam 1:1
2 *Manassite captain* 1 Chr 12:20
3 *temple gatekeeper* 1 Chr 26:1
4 *officer of Judah* 1 Chr 27:18
5 *one of Job's friends* Job 32-37

ELIJAH

1 *prophet* 1 Kin 17:1
  aided by widow 1 Kin 17:8ff
  revived child 1 Kin 17:23
  defeats prophets 1 Kin 18:20ff
  flees Jezebel 1 Kin 19:4-8
  chooses Elisha 1 Kin 19:19-21
  taken up 2 Kin 2:1-11
2 *Benjamite* 1 Chr 8:27
3 *son of Harim* Ezra 10:21
4 *son of Elam* Ezra 10:26

ELIMINATE *remove*

e *harmful beasts* Lev 26:6
I *am going to* e Jer 16:9
stomach, and is **e-d** Mark 7:19

ELIPHAZ

1 *son of Esau* Gen 36:4
2 *one of Job's friends* Job 2:11
  Job 4:1;42:7,9

ELISHA

prophet 2 Kin 6:12
called 1 Kin 19:19-21
Elijah's successor 2 Kin 2:1ff
miracle of oil 2 Kin 4:1-7
revived child 2 Kin 4:8-37
death 2 Kin 13:20

ELIZABETH

mother of John the Baptist
  Luke 1:7,13,41,57

ELOQUENT *persuasive*

I *have never been* e Ex 4:10
Apollos...an e *man* Acts 18:24

ELUL

sixth month of Hebrew
  calendar Neh 6:15

ELYMAS

magician Acts 13:8
also **Bar-Jesus**

EMBALM *preserve*

to e *his father* Gen 50:2
he was **e-ed** *and* Gen 50:26

EMBARRASSED *ashamed*

e *to lift up my face* Ezra 9:6
e *at the gardens* Is 1:29
diviners will be e Mic 3:7

EMBITTERED *resentful*

the people were e 1 Sam 30:6
e *them against the* Acts 14:2

EMBRACE *clasp, hug*

Esau ran...and **e-d** Gen 33:4
e...*a foreigner* Prov 5:20
A time to e Eccl 3:5
ran and e *him* Luke 15:20

EMBROIDERED *woven*

spoil of dyed work e Judg 5:30
be led...in e *work* Ps 45:14
silk, and **e-ed** *cloth* Ezek 16:13
purple, **e-ed** *work* Ezek 27:16

EMERALD *precious stone*

ruby, topaz and e Ex 28:17
throne, like an e Rev 4:3

EMINENT *renowned*

nor anything e Ezek 7:11
the most e *apostles* 2 Cor 11:5
*inferior to...*e 2 Cor 12:11

EMISSION *issuance*

man has a seminal e Lev 15:16
nocturnal e Deut 23:10

EMMAUS

village by Jerusalem Luke 24:13

EMPOWERED *authorized*

e *him to eat from* Eccl 5:19
God has not e *him* Eccl 6:2

EMPTY (adj) *containing nothing*

Now the pit was e Gen 37:24
did not return e 2 Sam 1:22
sent widows away e Job 22:9
deceive you with e Eph 5:6
*avoid...*e *chatter* 2 Tim 2:16

EMPTY (v) *remove contents*

e-ing their sacks	Gen 42:35
they e the house	Lev 14:36
I e-ied them out as	Ps 18:42
therefore e their net	Hab 1:17
e the golden oil	Zech 4:12
but e-ied Himself	Phil 2:7

ENCAMP *abide, lodge*

the tabernacle e-s	Num 1:51
and e-ed together	Josh 11:5
a host e against me	Ps 27:3
angel of the Lord e-s	Ps 34:7

ENCIRCLE *go around*

entirely e-ing the sea	2 Chr 4:3
he e-d the Ophel	2 Chr 33:14
cords...have e-d me	Ps 119:61
Who e yourselves with	Is 50:11

ENCOMPASS *surround*

waves of death e	2 Sam 22:5
e-ing the walls of	1 Kin 6:5
e-ed...with bitterness	Lam 3:5
Water e-ed me to the	Jon 2:5

ENCOURAGE *strengthen*

charge Joshua and e	Deut 3:28
e-d him in God	1 Sam 23:16
e them in the work	Ezra 6:22
Paul was e-ing them	Acts 27:33
e one another	1 Thess 5:11
e the young women	Titus 2:4

ENCOURAGEMENT *support*

I arose to be an e	Dan 11:1
God who gives...e	Rom 15:5
is any e in Christ	Phil 2:1
we may have strong e	Heb 6:18

END (n) *extremity, goal, result*

e of all flesh has	Gen 6:13
one e of the heavens	Deut 4:32
from beginning to e	1 Sam 3:12
what is my e	Job 6:11
very e-s of the earth	Ps 2:8
wicked come to an e	Ps 7:9
e is the way of death	Prov 14:12
no e to all his labor	Eccl 4:8
summer is e-ed	Jer 8:20
The e is coming	Ezek 7:2
who endures to...e	Matt 24:13
to the e of the age	Matt 28:20

kingdom...no e	Luke 1:33
He loved...to the e	John 13:1
Christ...e of the law	Rom 10:4
beginning and the e	Rev 21:6

END (v) *complete, stop*

border e-ed at the sea	Josh 15:4
words of Job are e-ed	Job 31:40
days there were e-ed	Acts 21:5
it e-s up being burned	Heb 6:8

ENDLESS *limitless*

writing...is e	Eccl 12:12
and e genealogies	1 Tim 1:4

ENDOW *provide a gift*

God has e-ed me	Gen 30:20
e-ed with discretion	2 Chr 2:12
To e those who love	Prov 8:21
e-ed with salvation	Zech 9:9

ENDURANCE *patience*

in much e, in	2 Cor 6:4
you have need of e	Heb 10:36
let us run with e	Heb 12:1
of the e of Job	James 5:11

ENDURE *persevere*

will be able to e	Ex 18:23
that I should e	Job 6:11
while the sun e-s	Ps 72:5
May his name e	Ps 72:17
and your name will e	Is 66:22
Can your heart e	Ezek 22:14
the one who has e-d	Matt 10:22
who e-s to the end	Mark 13:13
e-s all things	1 Cor 13:7
discipline that you e	Heb 12:7
blessed who e-d	James 5:11

ENEMY *foe*

delivered your e-ies	Gen 14:20
Thine e-ies perish	Judg 5:31
a man finds his e	1 Sam 24:19
consider me Thine e	Job 13:24
make the e...cease	Ps 8:2
presence of my e-ies	Ps 23:5
e has persecuted my	Ps 143:3
If your e is hungry	Prov 25:21
kisses of an e	Prov 27:6
love your e-ies, and	Matt 5:44
e of all righteousness	Acts 13:10
e is hungry, feed	Rom 12:20
e...be abolished	1 Cor 15:26

an **e** of God   James 4:4

ENGAGE *be involved, betroth*

virgin who is not **e-d**   Ex 22:16
the girl who is **e-d**   Deut 22:25
e-d in their work   1 Chr 9:33
e-d to...Joseph   Luke 1:27
to **e** in good deeds   Titus 3:8

ENGEDI

spring and town near Dead Sea
1 Sam 23:29;24:1; Song 1:14

ENGRAVE *inscribe*

shall **e** the two stones   Ex 28:11
e-d on the tablets   Ex 32:16
e an inscription   Zech 3:9
letters **e-d** on stones   2 Cor 3:7

ENGRAVINGS *carvings*

like the **e** of a seal   Ex 28:36
the **e** of a signet   Ex 39:30
carved **e** of cherubim 1 Kin 6:29

ENGULF *overwhelm, swallow*

water...to **e** them   Deut 11:4
sea **e-ed** their enemies   Ps 78:53
She has been **e-ed**   Jer 51:42
great deep **e-ed** me   Jon 2:5

ENLARGE *extend, increase*

May God **e** Japheth   Gen 9:27
Thou wilt **e** my heart   Ps 119:32
Sheol has **e-d** its   Is 5:14
He **e-s** his appetite   Hab 2:5

ENLIGHTEN *illumine*

e-ing the eyes   Ps 19:8
eyes...may be **e-ed**   Eph 1:18
who have...been **e-ed**   Heb 6:4

ENMITY *hostility*

e Between you and   Gen 3:15
had everlasting **e**   Ezek 35:5
at **e** with each other   Luke 23:12
sorcery, **e-ies**, strife   Gal 5:20
abolishing...the **e**   Eph 2:15

ENOCH

1 *son of Cain*   Gen 4:17
2 *Methuselah's father*   Gen 5:22
  walked with God   Gen 5:24

ENRAGE *anger*

e-d and curse their   Is 8:21

jealousy **e-s** a man   Prov 6:34
he became very **e-d**   Matt 2:16
dragon was **e-d** with   Rev 12:17

ENRICH *make wealthy*

king will **e** the   1 Sam 17:25
Thou dost greatly **e**   Ps 65:9
You **e-ed** the kings   Ezek 27:33

ENROLLED *recorded*

were **e** by genealogy 1 Chr 7:9
people to be **e** by   Neh 7:5
e in heaven   Heb 12:23

ENSLAVE *subjugate*

you have been **e-d**   Is 14:3
e-d and mistreated   Acts 7:6
if he **e-s** you   2 Cor 11:20
e-d to various lusts   Titus 3:3

ENSNARE *catch*

An evil man is **e-d**   Prov 12:13
e him who adjudicates   Is 29:21

ENTANGLE *ensnare*

camel **e-ing** her ways   Jer 2:23
No soldier...**e-s**   2 Tim 2:4
sin which...**e-s** us   Heb 12:1

ENTER *go in*

you shall **e** the ark   Gen 6:18
He **e-s** into judgment   Job 22:4
E His gates with   Ps 100:4
E the rock and hide   Is 2:10
He **e-s** into peace   Is 57:2
Spirit **e-ed** me and   Ezek 2:2
not **e** the kingdom   Matt 5:20
E by the narrow gate Matt 7:13
to **e** life crippled   Matt 18:8
afraid as they **e-ed**   Luke 9:34
e into the kingdom   John 3:5
not **e** by the door   John 10:1
shall not **e** My rest   Heb 3:11

ENTHRONED *exalt, make king*

e *above* the cherubim 2 Sam 6:2
LORD who is **e** *above*   1 Chr 13:6
e upon the praises of   Ps 22:3
who sits **e** from of old Ps 55:19
Who is **e** on high   Ps 113:5

ENTICE *deceive, seduce*

E your husband   · Judg 14:15
Who will **e** Ahab   2 Chr 18:19

if sinners e you   Prov 1:10
e-d by his own lust   James 1:14
e-ing unstable souls   2 Pet 2:14

ENTRAILS *inner organs*

fat that covers the e   Ex 29:13
e and the lobe   Lev 8:16
also washed the e   Lev 9:14

ENTRANCE *doorway*

cloud...at the e   Ex 33:10
mark well the e of   Ezek 44:5
stone against the e   Matt 27:60
e into the eternal   2 Pet 1:11

ENTREAT *appeal, ask*

E the LORD that He   Ex 8:8
Moses e-ed the LORD   Ex 32:11
Please e the LORD   1 Kin 13:6
gain if we e Him   Job 21:15
centurion...e-ing Him   Matt 8:5
demons *began* to e   Matt 8:31
they were e-ing Him   Luke 8:31
I e-ed the Lord   2 Cor 12:8
e you to walk in a   Eph 4:1

ENTRUST *assign, commit*

security e-ed *to him*   Lev 6:2
He e-ed the vineyard   Song 8:11
to whom they e-ed   Luke 12:48
not e-ing Himself to   John 2:24

ENVIOUS *covetous*

e of the arrogant   Ps 73:3
not be e of evil men   Prov 24:1
is your eye e   Matt 20:15
And you are e   James 4:2

ENVIRONS *outskirts, suburbs*

the e of Jerusalem   Jer 32:44
devour all his e   Jer 50:32
Bethlehem...its e   Matt 2:16

ENVOY *agent, messenger*

e-s of the rulers   2 Chr 32:31
faithful e *brings*   Prov 13:17
sent your e-s a great   Is 57:9
his e-s to Egypt   Ezek 17:15

ENVY (n) *jealousy*

full of e, murder   Rom 1:29
preaching...from e   Phil 1:15
out of which arise e   1 Tim 6:4
life in malice and e   Titus 3:3

e and all slander   1 Pet 2:1

ENVY (v) *be discontent, jealous*

Philistines e-ied him   Gen 26:14
e a man of violence   Prov 3:31
not let your heart e   Prov 23:17
e-ing one another   Gal 5:26

EPAPHRAS

Colossian Christian   Col 1:7
    Col 4:12
colleague of Paul   Philem 23

EPAPHRODITUS

Philippian Christian   Phil 2:25
colleague of Paul   Phil 4:18

EPHAH

1 *bushel, measure of capacity*
    Lev 5:11; Num 5:15
2 *son of Midian*   Gen 25:4
    1 Chr 1:33
3 *Caleb's concubine* 1 Chr 2:46
4 *son of Jahdai*   1 Chr 2:47

EPHESUS

city of Asia Minor   Acts 18:19
    1 Cor 16:8; Rev 1:11;2:1

EPHOD

1 *priestly garment*   Ex 28:6
    1 Sam 23:9; 2 Sam 6:14
2 *father of Hanniel* Num 34:23

EPHRAIM

1 *son of Joseph* Gen 41:52;48:1?
2 *tribe*   Josh 16:5; Judg 7:24
3 *northern kingdom*   Is 7:2-17
    Hos 4:17;9:3-17
4 *city* 2 Sam 13:23; John 11:54

EPHRAIM GATE *see*
GATES OF JERUSALEM

EPHRATH(AH)

1 *Bethlehem*   Gen 35:19;48:7
    Ruth 4:11; Mic 5:2
2 *wife of Caleb*   1 Chr 2:19,50
3 *territory* 1 Chr 2:24; Ps 132:6

EPHRON

1 *a Hittite*   Gen 23:8;50:13
2 *mountain ridge*   Josh 15:9
3 *city*   2 Chr 13:19

EPICUREAN

a *Greek philosophy*   Acts 17:18

EPOCHS *ages, seasons*

the times and the e   Dan 2:21
to know times or e   Acts 1:7

EQUAL *same*

or glass cannot e it   Job 28:17
a man my e   Ps 55:13
That I should be *his* e   Is 40:25
have made them e   Matt 20:12
Himself e with God   John 5:18

EQUIP *furnish, provide*

e-ped for war   Josh 4:13
e-ped for...work   2 Tim 3:17
e you in every good   Heb 13:21

EQUIPMENT *implements*

the e for the service   Ex 39:40
e for his chariots   1 Sam 8:12
e of a foolish   Zech 11:15

EQUITY *equality, fairness*

eyes look with e   Ps 17:2
hast established e   Ps 99:4
justice and e   Prov 1:3
e *and* every good   Prov 2:9

ERASTUS

Corinthian Christian   Acts 19:22
Rom 16:23; 2 Tim 4:20

ERROR *mistake, sin*

can discern *his* e-s   Ps 19:12
like an e which goes   Eccl 10:5
e against the LORD   Is 32:6
e of unprincipled   2 Pet 3:17
the spirit of e   1 John 4:6
rushed...into the e   Jude 11

ESARHADDON

Assyrian king   2 Kin 19:37
Ezra 4:2; Is 37:38

ESAU

son of Isaac   Gen 25:25
twin of Jacob   Gen 25:26
skillful hunter   Gen 25:27
sold birthright   Gen 25:34
despised Jacob   Gen 27:41
reconciled with Jacob   Gen 33:4

ESCAPE (n) *deliverance, refuge*

there will be no e   Job 11:20
is no e for me   Ps 142:4
Let there be no e   Jer 50:29
provide...e   1 Cor 10:13

ESCAPE (v) *elude*

slave who has e-d   Deut 23:15
let no one e *or*   2 Kin 9:15
Our soul has e-d   Ps 124:7
tells lies will not e   Prov 19:5
how shall we e   Is 20:6
nothing at all e-s   Joel 2:3
had not e-d notice   Luke 8:47
how shall we e if   Heb 2:3
it e-s their notice   2 Pet 3:5

ESTABLISH *confirm, found*

I will e my covenant   Gen 17:19
how God e-es them   Job 37:15
dost e the mountains   Ps 65:6
my ways may be e-ed   Ps 119:5
e-ed in lovingkindness   Is 16:5
to e the heavens   Is 51:16
we e the Law   Rom 3:31
may e your hearts   1 Thess 3:13
e-ed in the truth   2 Pet 1:12

ESTATE *domain or standard*

restore your...e   Job 8:6
us in our low e   Ps 136:23
squandered his e   Luke 15:13

ESTEEM (n) *honor*

man of high e   Dan 10:11
held them in high e   Acts 5:13

ESTEEM (v) *have high regard*

I e right all *Thy*   Ps 119:128
e-d Him stricken   Is 53:4
e-d among men   Luke 16:15
e them...in love   1 Thess 5:13

ESTHER

Hadassah, Hebrew name
cousin of Mordecai   Esth 2:7
Persian queen   Esth 2:16-18

ESTRANGED *separated*

completely e from me   Job 19:13
e from my brothers   Ps 69:8

ETERNAL *everlasting*

e God is a dwelling   Deut 33:27

82

E Father, Prince of   Is 9:6
An e decree   Jer 5:22
cast into the e fire   Matt 18:8
guilty of an e sin   Mark 3:29
to inherit e life   Luke 10:25
He may give e life   John 17:2
gift of God is e life   Rom 6:23
e weight of glory   2 Cor 4:17
with the e purpose   Eph 3:11
Now to the King e   1 Tim 1:17
source of e salvation   Heb 5:9
through the e Spirit   Heb 9:14
kept us in e bonds   Jude 6
an e gospel to preach   Rev 14:6

ETERNITY *perpetuity*

set e in their heart   Eccl 3:11
from e I am He   Is 43:13
Jesus from all e   2 Tim 1:9
to the day of e   2 Pet 3:18

ETHIOPIA

NE African country   Esth 1:1
Ps 68:31; Nah 3:9; Zeph 3:10

EUNICE

mother of Timothy   2 Tim 1:5

EUNUCH *chamberlain, official*

seven e-s who served   Esth 1:10
Neither let the e say   Is 56:3
children, and *the* e-s   Jer 41:16
made e-s by men   Matt 19:12
an Ethiopian e   Acts 8:27

EUPHRATES

river of Mesopotamia   Gen 2:14
Jer 13:5; 46:10; Rev 9:14; 16:12

EVANGELIST *proclaimer*

house of Philip the e   Acts 21:8
and some *as* e-s   Eph 4:11
do the work of an e   2 Tim 4:5

EVE

first woman   Gen 2:22
wife of Adam   Gen 2:23
deceived by serpent   Gen 3:1-7
named by Adam   Gen 3:20

EVENING *dusk, darkness*

cloud...from e   Num 9:21
eats food before e   1 Sam 14:24
as the e offering   Ps 141:2
not be idle in the e   Eccl 11:6

when e had come   Matt 8:16

EVENT *happening*

the e-s of the war   2 Sam 11:18
e became sin to the   1 Kin 13:34
recorded these e-s   Esth 9:20
time for every e   Eccl 3:1

EVERLASTING *eternal*

e covenant between   Gen 9:16
the LORD, the E God   Gen 21:33
are the e arms   Deut 33:27
e to e, Thou art God   Ps 90:2
lovingkindness is e   Ps 106:1
From e I was   Prov 8:23
The E God, the LORD   Is 40:28
e name which will   Is 56:5
LORD for an e light   Is 60:20
loved you with an e   Jer 31:3

EVIDENCE *facts, testimony*

the e of witnesses   Num 35:30
on the e of two   Deut 19:15
not able to give e   Ezra 2:59
and giving e   Acts 17:3

EVIDENT *obvious, plain*

the tares became e   Matt 13:26
for God made it e   Rom 1:19
work will become e   1 Cor 3:13
Law before God is e   Gal 3:11
it is e that our Lord   Heb 7:14

EVIL *bad, wicked, wrong*

man's heart is e   Gen 8:21
keep...from every e   Deut 23:9
discern good and e   2 Sam 14:17
rebellious and e city   Ezra 4:12
I fear no e   Ps 23:4
repay me e for good   Ps 35:12
turn away from e   Prov 3:7
run rapidly to e   Prov 6:18
returns e for good   Prov 17:13
taken away from e   Is 57:1
committed two e-s   Jer 2:13
deliver us from e   Matt 6:13
what e has He   Matt 27:23
If you then, being e   Luke 11:13
who does e hates the   John 3:20
Never...e for e   Rom 12:17
love of money is...e   1 Tim 6:10
tongue...restless e   James 3:8

EVILDOER *wicked one*

LORD repay the e	2 Sam 3:39
e-s will be cut off	Ps 37:9
e listens to wicked	Prov 17:4
Offspring of e-s	Is 1:4
is godless and an e	Is 9:17
depart...you e-s	Luke 13:27
punishment of e-s	1 Pet 2:14

EVIL-MERODACH

king of Babylon	2 Kin 25:27
	Jer 52:31

EWE *female sheep*

seven e lambs	Gen 21:28
e lamb without	Lev 14:10
poor man's e lamb	2 Sam 12:4
e-s with suckling	Ps 78:71
like a flock of e-s	Song 6:6

EXACT (adj) *certain, correct*

e amount of money	Esth 4:7
e meaning of all this	Dan 7:16
know the e truth	Luke 1:4
a more e knowledge	Acts 24:22

EXACT (v) *collect*

let him e a fifth	Gen 41:34
he shall not e it	Deut 15:2
He e-ed the silver	2 Kin 23:25
You are e-ing usury	Neh 5:7
e a tribute of grain	Amos 5:11

EXALT *extol, honor, lift*

He is highly e-ed	Ex 15:1
e-ed be God	2 Sam 22:47
He is e-ed in power	Job 37:23
let us e His name	Ps 34:3
e-ed far above all gods	Ps 97:9
city is e-ed	Prov 11:11
my God; I will e Thee	Is 25:1
E that which is low	Ezek 21:26
humbles...be e-ed	Matt 23:12
e-ed to...right hand	Acts 2:33
be e-ed in my body	Phil 1:20
He will e you	James 4:10

EXAMINE *investigate, search*

Thou dost e him every	Job 7:18
E me, O LORD, and try	Ps 26:2
e my heart's *attitude*	Jer 12:3
e-ing the Scriptures	Acts 17:11

e-d by scourging	Acts 22:24
a man e himself	1 Cor 11:28

EXAMPLE *model, pattern*

the e of his father	2 Chr 17:3
I gave you an e	John 13:15
e of those who	1 Tim 4:12
e of disobedience	Heb 4:11
be e-s to the flock	1 Pet 5:3
made them an e	2 Pet 2:6

EXCEL *be superior*

e in...wickedness	Jer 5:28
wisdom e-s folly	Eccl 2:13
you may e...more	1 Thess 4:1

EXCELLENCE *perfection*

greatness of Thine e	Ex 15:7
are a woman of e	Ruth 3:11
if there is any e	Phil 4:8
proclaim the e-ies of	1 Pet 2:9

EXCELLENT *outstanding*

e wife is the crown	Prov 12:4
E speech is not	Prov 17:7
He has done e things	Is 12:5
e governor Felix	Acts 23:26
a still more e way	1 Cor 12:31
a more e name	Heb 1:4

EXCESS *too much*

he...had no e	Ex 16:18
are in e among them	Num 3:48
same e of dissipation	1 Pet 4:4

EXCHANGE *trade, transfer*

shall e *it* for money	Deut 14:25
they e-d their glory	Ps 106:20
shall not sell or e	Ezek 48:14
e-d the truth of God	Rom 1:25

EXCLUDE *refuse to admit*

e-d from...assembly	Ezra 10:8
e-d all foreigners	Neh 13:3
e you for My name's	Is 66:5
e-d from the life of	Eph 4:18

EXCUSE *justification*

began to make e-s	Luke 14:18
no e for their sin	John 15:22
they are without e	Rom 1:20

EXECUTE *carry out*

e-d the justice of   Deut 33:21
He has e-d judgment   Ps 9:16
e vengeance on the   Ps 149:7
Lord will e His word   Rom 9:28
e judgment upon all   Jude 15

EXERCISE *perform*

man has e-d authority   Eccl 8:9
e-s lovingkindness   Jer 9:24
e authority over   Matt 20:25
e-s self-control in all   1 Cor 9:25

EXHAUSTED *used up, wearied*

sound asleep and e   Judg 4:21
too e to follow   1 Sam 30:21
of flour was not e   1 Kin 17:16
Their strength is e   Jer 51:30

EXHORT *admonish, urge*

and kept on e-ing   Acts 2:40
e, with...patience   2 Tim 4:2
e in sound doctrine   Titus 1:9
e and reprove   Titus 2:15
e-ing and testifying   1 Pet 5:12

EXHORTATION *urging*

with many other e-s   Luke 3:18
given them much e   Acts 20:2
who exhorts, in his e   Rom 12:8
this word of e   Heb 13:22

EXILE *banishment* or *capture*

Israel away into e   2 Kin 17:6
people of the e were   Ezra 4:1
captivity of the e-s   Neh 7:6
into e from Jerusalem   Esth 2:6
e will soon be set free   Is 51:14
Israel went into e   Ezek 39:23

EXIST *be, live, occur*

they had never e-ed   Obad 16
Strife e-s and   Hab 1:3
live and move and e   Acts 17:28
authority...which e   Rom 13:1

EXODUS *departure*

e of...Israel   Heb 11:22

EXPANSE *firmament, vastness*

e of the heavens   Gen 1:20
e of the waters   Job 37:10
in His mighty e   Ps 150:1
from above the e   Ezek 1:25

EXPECT *await*

never e-ed to see   Gen 48:11
e-ed good, then evil   Job 30:26
which we did not e   Is 64:3
lend, e-ing nothing   Luke 6:35

EXPECTATION *anticipation*

to my earnest e   Phil 1:20
e of judgment   Heb 10:27
your e is false   Job 41:9
e of the wicked   Prov 10:28

EXPECTED *awaited*

Are You the E One   Matt 11:3
Are You the E One   Luke 7:20

EXPERIENCE *undergo*

all who had not e-d   Judg 3:1
Thy people e hardship   Ps 60:3
e-s Thy judgments   Is 26:9
e-d mockings and   Heb 11:36

EXPERT *very skillful*

an e in warfare   2 Sam 17:8
be like an e warrior   Jer 50:9
an e in all customs   Acts 26:3

EXPLAIN *make clear*

no one who could e   Gen 41:24
he did not e to her   2 Chr 9:2
e its interpretation   Dan 5:7
E the parable to us   Matt 15:15
e-ing the Scriptures   Luke 24:32
e-ed to him the way   Acts 18:26

EXPOSE *disclose, reveal*

shame...be e-d   Is 47:3
He will e your sins   Lam 4:22
deeds should be e-d   John 3:20
would e their infants   Acts 7:19
are e-d by the light   Eph 5:13

EXTEND *enlarge, stretch out*

God e-s...border   Deut 12:20
e-ed lovingkindness   Ezra 7:28
e-s her hand to the   Prov 31:20
I e peace to her   Is 66:12
boundary shall e   Ezek 47:17

EXTENT *amount* or *degree*

the e of my days   Ps 39:4
e that you did it to   Matt 25:40
such an e that Jesus   Mark 1:45

EXTERMINATE *destroy*

planned to e us	2 Sam 21:5
He will e its sinners	Is 13:9

EXTERNAL *outward*

not with e service	Col 3:22
adornment be...e	1 Pet 3:3

EXTINGUISH *put out*

they will e my coal	2 Sam 14:7
not e the lamp of	2 Sam 21:17
my days are e-ed	Job 17:1
when *I* e you	Ezek 32:7
e all the flaming	Eph 6:16

EXTOL *praise*

God, and I will e Him	Ex 15:2
I will e Thee, O LORD	Ps 30:1
I will e Thee, my God	Ps 145:1
We will e your love	Song 1:4

EXTORTION *stealing*

practicing...e	Jer 22:17
practiced e, robbed	Ezek 18:18

EXTRAORDINARY *exceptional*

will bring e plagues	Deut 28:59
His e work	Is 28:21
insight, and e wisdom	Dan 5:14
e miracles by	Acts 19:11
showed us e kindness	Acts 28:2

EXULT *rejoice*

heart e-s in the LORD	1 Sam 2:1
Let the field e	1 Chr 16:32
e-ed when evil befell	Job 31:29
let them e before God	Ps 68:3
I will e in the LORD	Hab 3:18
e in our tribulations	Rom 5:3

EXULTATION *jubilation*

e like the nations	Hos 9:1
joy or crown of e	1 Thess 2:19
may rejoice with e	1 Pet 4:13

EYE *sight*

e-s are dull from	Gen 49:12
e for e, tooth for	Ex 21:24
be as e-s for us	Num 10:31
his e was not dim	Deut 34:7
right in his own e-s	Judg 17:6
open his e-s that he	2 Kin 6:17
e-s of the LORD move	2 Chr 16:9

was e-s to the blind	Job 29:15
e-s...look to Thee	Ps 145:15
Haughty e-s, a lying	Prov 6:17
e...mocks a father	Prov 30:17
e is not satisfied	Eccl 1:8
To open blind e-s	Is 42:7
e-s will bitterly weep	Jer 13:17
have e-s to see but	Ezek 12:2
Thine e-s...too pure	Hab 1:13
e for an e, and a	Matt 5:38
e...you to stumble	Matt 18:9
lamp...is your e	Luke 11:34
the clay to his e-s	John 9:6
which e has not seen	1 Cor 2:9
e-s of your heart may	Eph 1:18
e-s full of adultery	2 Pet 2:14
the lust of the e-s	1 John 2:16
God, who has e-s like	Rev 2:18
His e-s *are* a flame	Rev 19:12

EYEWITNESSES *observers*

e...of the word	Luke 1:2
e of His majesty	2 Pet 1:16

EZEKIEL

Hebrew prophet	Ezek 1:1
called by God	Ezek 1:1,3
taken captive	Ezek 33:21
spoke to Israel	Ezek 14-24
spoke to false prophets	Ezek 34
spoke to nations	Ezek 35,38
restored temple	Ezek 40-46

EZION-GEBER

on gulf of Aqabah	1 Kin 9:26
	1 Kin 22:48
near Elath/Eloth	Deut 2:8
	2 Chr 8:17

EZRA

priest	Ezra 7:1-5
scribe	Ezra 7:6
sent by king	Ezra 7:14,21
brought exiles	Ezra 8:1-14
Nehemiah's colleague	Neh 8:2-6

F

FACE *countenance*

sweat of your f You	Gen 3:19

Abram fell on his f	Gen 17:3
speak to Moses f to f	Ex 33:11
skin of his f shone	Ex 34:30
make His f shine	Num 6:25
hide Thy f from me	Ps 13:1
Who seek Thy f	Ps 24:6
His f to shine upon us	Ps 67:1
f of Thine anointed	Ps 84:9
makes a cheerful f	Prov 15:13
set My f against you	Jer 44:11
had the f of an eagle	Ezek 1:10
Each...had four f-s	Ezek 10:21
fast...wash your f	Matt 6:17
they spat in His f	Matt 26:67
like the f of an angel	Acts 6:15
natural f in a mirror	James 1:23
His f was like the sun	Rev 1:16

FACT *truth*

f may be confirmed	Matt 18:16
are undeniable f-s	Acts 19:36
f is to be confirmed	2 Cor 13:1

FACTIONS *divisions*

be f among you	1 Cor 11:19
dissensions, f	Gal 5:20

FADE *wither*

it f-s, and withers	Ps 90:6
people...f away	Is 24:4
rich man...will f	James 1:11
will not f away	1 Pet 1:4

FAIL *be spent* or *fall short*

He will not f you	Deut 4:31
none of his words f	1 Sam 3:19
no man's heart f	1 Sam 17:32
not one word...f-ed	1 Kin 8:56
my strength f-s me	Ps 38:10
the olive should f	Hab 3:17
faith may not f	Luke 22:32
Love never f-s	1 Cor 13:8

FAINT *languish, swoon*

has made my heart f	Job 23:16
soul f-ed within	Ps 107:5
grow f before Me	Is 57:16
I was f-ing away	Jon 2:7
men f-ing from fear	Luke 21:26
f when...reproved	Heb 12:5

FAINTHEARTED *weak*

Do not be f	Deut 20:3
encourage the f	1 Thess 5:14

FAIR HAVENS

harbor in Crete	Acts 27:8

FAITH *believe, trust*

because you broke f	Deut 32:51
Will you have f	Job 39:12
Who keeps f forever	Ps 146:6
will live by his f	Hab 2:4
Jesus seeing their f	Matt 9:2
f as a mustard seed	Matt 17:20
Your f has saved you	Luke 7:50
Increase our f	Luke 17:5
your f may not fail	Luke 22:32
man full of f	Acts 6:5
of f to the Gentiles	Acts 14:27
sanctified by f in Me	Acts 26:18
justified by f	Rom 5:1
f...from hearing	Rom 10:17
if I have all f	1 Cor 13:2
your f also is vain	1 Cor 15:14
we walk by f	2 Cor 5:7
live by f in the Son	Gal 2:20
saved through f	Eph 2:8
one Lord, one f	Eph 4:5
joy in the f	Phil 1:25
stability of your f	Col 2:5
breastplate of f	1 Thess 5:8
for not all have f	2 Thess 3:2
fall away from the f	1 Tim 4:1
conduct, love, f	1 Tim 4:12
they upset the f	2 Tim 2:18
sound in the f	Titus 1:13
showing all good f	Titus 2:10
full assurance of f	Heb 10:22
By f Enoch was taken	Heb 11:5
perfecter of f	Heb 12:2
ask in f	James 1:6
prayer offered in f	James 5:15
power of God...f	1 Pet 1:5
the f of the saints	Rev 13:10

FAITHFUL *loyal, trustworthy*

the f God, who keeps	Deut 7:9
raise...a f priest	1 Sam 2:35
heart f before Thee	Neh 9:8
LORD preserves the f	Ps 31:23
commandments...f	Ps 119:86
f witness will not lie	Prov 14:5
the LORD who is f	Is 49:7
Well done...f	Matt 25:23
God is f	1 Cor 1:9
F is He who calls	1 Thess 5:24

FAITHFUL

He considered me f	1 Tim 1:12
entrust to f men	2 Tim 2:2
souls to a f Creator	1 Pet 4:19
He is f...to forgive	1 John 1:9
Be f until death	Rev 2:10
called F and True	Rev 19:11

FAITHFULNESS *loyalty*

kindness and f	Gen 47:29
A God of f	Deut 32:4
make known Thy f	Ps 89:1
f to all generations	Ps 100:5
and mercy and f	Matt 23:23
nullify the f of God	Rom 3:3
kindness, goodness, f	Gal 5:22

FAITHLESS *unbelieving*

what f Israel did	Jer 3:6
O f daughter	Jer 31:22
Their heart is f	Hos 10:2
If we are f	2 Tim 2:13

FALL *descend* or *fail*

deep sleep to f upon	Gen 2:21
devices let them f	Ps 5:10
I am ready to f	Ps 38:17
dread...had f-en	Ps 105:38
wicked will f	Prov 11:5
a righteous man f-s	Prov 24:16
whether a tree f-s	Eccl 11:3
Assyrian will f	Is 31:8
Babylon has f-en	Jer 51:8
f down and worship	Dan 3:5
will f into a pit	Matt 15:14
f-ing on his knees	Mark 1:40
all may f...I will	Mark 14:29
appointed for the f	Luke 2:34
watching Satan f	Luke 10:18
house *divided*...f-s	Luke 11:17
f-ing headlong	Acts 1:18
sinned and f short	Rom 3:23
have f-en asleep	1 Cor 15:6
f-en from grace	Gal 5:4
rich f into temptation	1 Tim 6:9
rocks, F on us	Rev 6:16

FALLOW *unproductive*

rest and lie f	Ex 23:11
f ground of the poor	Prov 13:23

FALSE *deceitful, dishonest*

not bear a f report	Ex 23:1
I hate every f way	Ps 119:104
But a f witness	Prov 12:17
f witness will not go	Prov 19:5
f scale is not good	Prov 20:23
F and foolish visions	Lam 2:14
And tell f dreams	Zech 10:2
not bear f witness	Matt 19:18
f Christs and f	Matt 24:24
men are f apostles	2 Cor 11:13
the f circumcision	Phil 3:2
and the f prophet	Rev 20:10

FALSEHOOD *deception*

lifted up his soul to f	Ps 24:4
delight in f	Ps 62:4
I hate and despise f	Ps 119:163
Bread obtained by f	Prov 20:17
trusted in f	Jer 13:25
prophesying f in My	Jer 14:14
laying aside f	Eph 4:25

FAME *greatness*

heard of Thy f	Num 14:15
Joshua, and his f	Josh 6:27
the f of Solomon	1 Kin 10:1
heard My f	Is 66:19
f in *the things of*	2 Cor 8:18

FAMILY *household, relatives*

f-ies from the ark	Gen 8:19
all the f-ies of	Gen 12:3
f may redeem him	Lev 25:49
f-ies of the Levites	Num 3:20
my f is the least	Judg 6:15
f-ies like a flock	Ps 107:41
God of all the f-ies	Jer 31:1
f-ies of the earth	Amos 3:2
every f in heaven	Eph 3:15
upsetting whole f-ies	Titus 1:11

FAMINE *shortage of food*

a f in the land	Gen 12:10
seven years of f	Gen 41:27
If there is f	2 Chr 6:28
In f He will redeem	Job 5:20
keep them alive in f	Ps 33:19
f and pestilence	Jer 14:12
f and wild beasts	Ezek 5:17
f-s and earthquakes	Matt 24:7
plagues and f-s	Luke 21:11
Now a f came	Acts 7:11
mourning and f	Rev 18:8

FAMISHED *hungry, parched*

for I am f	Gen 25:30
strength is f	Job 18:12
honorable men are f	Is 5:13

FAMOUS *well-known*

f in Bethlehem	Ruth 4:11
men of valor, f men	1 Chr 5:24

FAR *distant*

f from a false charge	Ex 23:7
come from a f country	Josh 9:6
Be not f from me	Ps 22:11
f above all gods	Ps 97:9
As f as the east	Ps 103:12
LORD is f from the	Prov 15:29
a God f off	Jer 23:23
heart is f away from	Matt 15:8
f from the kingdom	Mark 12:34
glory f beyond all	2 Cor 4:17
f above all rule	Eph 1:21

FARM *agricultural land*

consume the f land	Amos 7:4
one to his own f	Matt 22:5
or f-s, for My sake	Mark 10:29

FARMER *husbandman*

Does the f plow	Is 28:24
will be your f-s	Is 61:5
f-s...put to shame	Jer 14:4
the f to mourning	Amos 5:16

FASHION *create, form*

f-ed into a woman	Gen 2:22
f us in the womb	Job 31:15
He who f-s the hearts	Ps 33:15
f a graven image	Is 44:9
I am f-ing calamity	Jer 18:11

FAST (n) *food abstinence*

Proclaim a f	1 Kin 21:9
you call this a f	Is 58:5
Consecrate a f	Joel 1:14
f was already over	Acts 27:9

FAST (v) *abstain from food*

and David f-ed	2 Sam 12:16
maidens also will f	Esth 4:16
you f for contention	Is 58:4
had f-ed forty days	Matt 4:2
whenever you f	Matt 6:16
disciples do not f	Mark 2:18

I f twice a week	Luke 18:12
had f-ed and prayed	Acts 13:3

FASTING *food abstinence*

times of f	Esth 9:31
weak from f	Ps 109:24
be seen f by men	Matt 6:16
by prayer and f	Matt 17:21
Pharisees were f	Mark 2:18

FAT *animal fat or obese*

f of the land	Gen 45:18
shall not eat any f	Lev 7:23
Go, eat of the f	Neh 8:10
their body is f	Ps 73:4
Good news puts f	Prov 15:30

FATE *destiny*

appalled at his f	Job 18:20
one f befalls them	Eccl 2:14
f for the righteous	Eccl 9:2
one f for all men	Eccl 9:3

FATHER *God or parent*

leave his f...mother	Gen 2:24
f of a multitude	Gen 17:4
Honor your f	Ex 20:12
who strikes his f	Ex 21:15
iniquity of the f-s	Deut 5:9
Is not He your F	Deut 32:6
your f-'s instruction	Prov 1:8
son makes a f glad	Prov 10:1
Eternal F, Prince of	Is 9:6
all have one f	Mal 2:10
F who sees in secret	Matt 6:4
Our F who art in	Matt 6:9
does the will of My F	Matt 7:21
in My F-'s kingdom	Matt 26:29
in the glory of His F	Mark 8:38
be in My F-'s house	Luke 2:49
F, hallowed be Thy	Luke 11:2
F, forgive them	Luke 23:34
begotten from the F	John 1:14
my F-'s house a	John 2:16
F...bears witness	John 8:18
the f of lies	John 8:44
I and the F are one	John 10:30
In My F-'s house are	John 14:2
F is the vinedresser	John 15:1
ask the F for	John 16:23
I ascend to My F	John 20:17
one God and F of all	Eph 4:6

FATHER-IN-LAW

she sent to her f	Gen 38:25
returned to Jethro his f	Ex 4:18
his f, the girl's	Judg 19:4
f of Caiaphas	John 18:13

FATHERLESS *orphan*

father of the f	Ps 68:5
He supports the f	Ps 146:9
fields of the f	Prov 23:10
f and the widow	Ezek 22:7

FATLING *young lamb or kid*

sacrificed...a f	2 Sam 6:13
f-s...in abundance	1 Kin 1:19
f-s of Bashan	Ezek 39:18

FATNESS *abundance*

f of the earth	Gen 27:28
Shall I leave my f	Judg 9:9
satisfied as with...f	Ps 63:5
eye bulges from f	Ps 73:7

FAULT *error, offense*

found no f in him	1 Sam 29:3
let no one find f	Hos 4:4
does He still find f	Rom 9:19
grumblers, finding f	Jude 16

FAVOR *kind regard*

Noah found f	Gen 6:8
I will grant...f	Ex 3:21
show no f to them	Deut 7:2
Why have I found f	Ruth 2:10
surround him with f	Ps 5:12
show f to Thy land	Ps 85:1
obtains f from the LORD	Prov 8:35
f is like a cloud	Prov 16:15
found f with God	Luke 1:30
in f with God and	Luke 2:52
seeking the f of men	Gal 1:10

FEAR (n) *awe, dread, reverence*

no f of God in	Gen 20:11
f of the LORD is clean	Ps 19:9
f...is the beginning	Ps 111:10
afraid of sudden f	Prov 3:25
f...prolongs life	Prov 10:27
f of man brings a	Prov 29:25
they cried out for f	Matt 14:26
guards shook for f	Matt 28:4
men fainting from f	Luke 21:26
for f of the Jews	John 7:13

no f of God before	Rom 3:18
in weakness and in f	1 Cor 2:3
knowing the f of the	2 Cor 5:11
with f and trembling	Eph 6:5
through f of death	Heb 2:15
love casts out f	1 John 4:18

FEAR (v) *be afraid, revere*

the midwives f-ed God	Ex 1:21
Moses said...Do not f	Ex 14:13
may learn to f Me	Deut 4:10
not f other gods	2 Kin 17:37
I f no evil	Ps 23:4
Whom shall I f	Ps 27:1
not f evil tidings	Ps 112:7
who f-s the LORD	Prov 31:30
Rather, f God	Eccl 5:7
Take courage, f not	Is 35:4
Do not f, for I am	Is 41:10
shall f and tremble	Jer 33:9
do not f them	Matt 10:26
f-ed the multitude	Matt 14:5
who did not f God	Luke 18:2
slavery leading to f	Rom 8:15
I f for you	Gal 4:11
let us f lest	Heb 4:1

FEARFUL *terrifying*

it is a f thing	Ex 34:10
were f and amazed	Luke 8:25
may be f of sinning	1 Tim 5:20

FEAST *celebration*

a f to the LORD	Ex 12:14
godless jesters at a f	Ps 35:16
hate...appointed f-s	Is 1:14
and cheerful f-s	Zech 8:19
refuse of your f-s	Mal 2:3
a wedding f	Matt 22:2
seeking Him at the f	John 7:11
celebrate the f	1 Cor 5:8
f with you without	Jude 12

FEASTS

1 **Feast of Booths**	Lev 23:24
	Deut 16:16; 2 Chr 8:13
also **Feast of Ingathering**	
2 **Feast of Dedication**	
	John 10:22
3 **Feast of Harvest**	Ex 23:16
also **Feast of Weeks**	
also **Feast of Pentecost**	
4 **Feast of Ingathering**	
	Ex 23:16

also **Feast of Booths**
5 **Feast of Passover**   Ex 34:25
                             Luke 2:41
6 **Feast of Unleavened Bread**
              Ex 23:15; Luke 22:1
7 **Feast of Weeks**   Ex 34:22
                          Deut 16:10,16
   also **Feast of Harvest**
   also **Feast of Pentecost**
8 **Feast of Pentecost**
        Acts 2:1;20:16; 1 Cor 16:8
   also **Feast of Harvest**
   also **Feast of Weeks**

FEEBLE *weak*

when the flock was f   Gen 30:42
What are these f Jews   Neh 4:2
strengthen the f   Is 35:3
knees that are f   Heb 12:12

FEED *eat, supply*

fed you with manna   Deut 8:3
f him sparingly   1 Kin 22:27
F me with the food   Prov 30:8
He f-s on ashes   Is 44:20
f you on knowledge   Jer 3:15
He fed me this scroll Ezek 3:2
I will f My flock   Ezek 34:15
dogs f on the   Matt 15:27
hungry, and f You   Matt 25:37
fed...the *crumbs*   Luke 16:21
enemy is hungry, f   Rom 12:20

FEEL *sense, touch*

I may f you, my son Gen 27:21
Isaac...felt him and Gen 27:22
Let me f the pillars Judg 16:26
He felt compassion   Matt 9:36
she felt...was healed Mark 5:29
Jesus felt a love for Mark 10:21
f-ing a sense of awe Acts 2:43
f sensual desires   1 Tim 5:11

FELIX

   Roman procurator   Acts 23:26
                        Acts 24:25;25:14

FELL *collapse, come upon*

wall f down flat   Josh 6:20
fire of the LORD f   1 Kin 18:38
the lot f on Jonah   Jon 1:7
seeds f beside the   Matt 13:4

He f asleep   Luke 8:23
he f to the ground   Acts 9:4
Holy Spirit f upon   Acts 10:44
star f from heaven   Rev 8:10

FELLOW *companion*

oil of joy above Thy f-s Ps 45:7
your f exiles   Ezek 11:15
beat his f slaves   Matt 24:49
f heirs with Christ   Rom 8:17
f citizens with the   Eph 2:19
Gentiles are f heirs   Eph 3:6
brother and f worker Phil 2:25
f worker in the   1 Thess 3:2
I am a f servant of   Rev 22:9

FELLOWSHIP *companionship*

had sweet f together   Ps 55:14
f...Holy Spirit   2 Cor 13:14
right hand of f   Gal 2:9
f of His sufferings   Phil 3:10
f is with the Father 1 John 1:3
f with one another   1 John 1:7

FEMALE *girl, woman*

and f He created   Gen 1:27
a f slave   Ex 21:7
f from the flock   Lev 5:6
likeness of male or f Deut 4:16
neither male nor f   Gal 3:28

FERTILE *productive*

a f land   Neh 9:25
the f valley   Is 28:4
in f soil   Ezek 17:5

FERVENT *ardent*

being f in Spirit   Acts 18:25
f in spirit, serving Rom 12:11
keep f in your love   1 Pet 4:8

FESTIVAL *celebration*

celebrate a great f   Neh 8:12
I reject your f-s   Amos 5:21
turn your f-s into   Amos 8:10
during the f, lest   Matt 26:5

FESTUS, PORCIUS

   Roman procurator of Judea
              Acts 25:14,23;26:25

FETTERS *chains*

your feet put in f   2 Sam 3:34

91

they are bound in f | Job 36:8
tear their f apart | Ps 2:3
with f of iron | Ps 149:8
he would burst his f | Luke 8:29

FEVER *inflammation*

bones burn with f | Job 30:30
in bed with a f | Matt 8:14
from a high f | Luke 4:38
He rebuked the f | Luke 4:39
the f left him | John 4:52

FIELD *productive land*

hail struck...the f | Ex 9:25
let me go to the f | Ruth 2:2
glean in another f | Ruth 2:8
f of the sluggard | Prov 24:30
Zion...plowed *as* a f | Jer 26:18
the lilies of the f | Matt 6:28
the f is the world | Matt 13:38
shepherds...in the f-s | Luke 2:8
Two men in the f | Luke 17:36
f-s...white for | John 4:35
F of Blood | Acts 1:19

FIERCE *violent*

anger, for it is f | Gen 49:7
Wrath is f | Prov 27:4
see a f people | Is 33:19
a f gale of wind | Mark 4:37
scorched with f heat | Rev 16:9
f wrath of God | Rev 19:15

FIERCENESS *intensity*

f of His anger | Josh 7:26
the f of battle | Is 42:25

FIERY *burning*

LORD sent f serpents | Num 21:6
with f heat | Deut 28:22
His arrows f shafts | Ps 7:13
f ordeal among you | 1 Pet 4:12

FIG *fruit*

they sewed f leaves | Gen 3:7
But the f tree said | Judg 9:11
a piece of f cake | 1 Sam 30:12
nor f-s from thistles | Matt 7:16
the f tree withered | Matt 21:19
f-s from thorns | Luke 6:44
under the f tree | John 1:48
Can a f tree | James 3:12

FIGHT *struggle*

Hebrews were f-ing | Ex 2:13
LORD will f for you | Ex 14:14
fought for Israel | Josh 10:14
stars fought from | Judg 5:20
and f our battles | 1 Sam 8:20
f for your brothers | Neh 4:14
f-ing against God | Acts 5:39
fought the good f | 2 Tim 4:7
so you f and quarrel | James 4:2

FIGURATIVE *metaphorical*

in f language | John 16:25

FIGURE *shape, type*

f-s resembling four | Ezek 1:5
f...of a man | Ezek 1:26
using a f of speech | John 16:29

FILIGREE *ornamental work*

f settings of gold | Ex 28:13
cords on the two f | Ex 28:25

FILL (n) *satisfaction*

eat your f | Lev 25:19
They drink their f | Ps 36:8
drink our f of love | Prov 7:18
its f of their blood | Jer 46:10

FILL (v) *make full*

and f the earth | Gen 1:28
f-ed with violence | Gen 6:11
Can you f his skin | Job 41:7
was f-ing with smoke | Is 6:4
I am f-ed with power | Mic 3:8
hall was f-ed | Matt 22:10
God of hope f you | Rom 15:13

FILTHY *offensive*

are full of f vomit | Is 28:8
like a f garment | Is 64:6
clothed...f garments | Zech 3:3
let the one who is f | Rev 22:11

FILTHINESS *disgustingly foul*

not washed...his f | Prov 30:12
your f is lewdness | Ezek 24:13
no f and silly talk | Eph 5:4
putting aside all f | James 1:21

FIND *discover, uncover*

not found a helper | Gen 2:20
But Noah found favor | Gen 6:8
sin will f you out | Num 32:23

that you may f rest   Ruth 1:9
he who f-s me f-s life   Prov 8:35
who f-s a wife f-s   Prov 18:22
f gladness and joy   Is 35:10
few...who f it   Matt 7:14
has **found** his life   Matt 10:39
f rest for your souls   Matt 11:29
f-ing one pearl   Matt 13:46
f a colt tied   Mark 11:2
found...sleeping   Mark 14:40
seek, and you shall f   Luke 11:9
found the Messiah   John 1:41
was **found** worthy   Rev 5:4

FINGER part of hand

the f of God   Ex 8:19
dip his f in the blood   Lev 4:6
six f-s on each   2 Sam 21:20
twenty-four f-s and   1 Chr 20:6
tip of his f in water   Luke 16:24
with His f wrote   John 8:6
Reach here your f   John 20:27

FINISH complete

Moses f-ed the work   Ex 40:33
Solomon f-ed the   2 Chr 7:11
It is f-ed   John 19:30
I may f my course   Acts 20:24
f doing it also   2 Cor 8:11
wrath of God is f-ed   Rev 15:1

FINS part of fish

that have f and scales   Lev 11:9
anything that has f   Deut 14:9

FIR tree, wood

instruments...of f   2 Sam 6:5
He plants a f   Is 44:14

FIRE burning or flame

the f and the knife   Gen 22:6
bush...burning with f   Ex 3:2
pillar of f by night   Ex 13:21
offered strange f   Num 3:4
f of the LORD fell   1 Kin 18:38
a chariot of f   2 Kin 2:11
jealousy burn like f   Ps 79:5
Israel will become a f   Is 10:17
Is not My word like f   Jer 23:29
the Holy Spirit and f   Matt 3:11
with unquenchable f   Matt 3:12
tongues as of f   Acts 2:3
lake that burns with f   Rev 21:8

FIREBRAND burning wood

who throws F-s   Prov 26:18
you were like a f   Amos 4:11

FIREPAN used in worship

a f full of coals   Lev 16:12
the f-s of pure gold   2 Chr 4:22

FIRM establish, steadfast

his bow remained f   Gen 49:24
stood f on dry ground   Josh 3:17
making my footsteps f   Ps 40:2
He made f the skies   Prov 8:28
stand f in the faith   1 Cor 16:13
f foundation of God   2 Tim 2:19
hope f until the end   Heb 3:6

FIRST number

f fruits of your labors   Ex 23:16
f of all your produce   Prov 3:9
seek f His kingdom   Matt 6:33
f take the log out   Matt 7:5
f will be last   Matt 19:30
f called Christians   Acts 11:26
to the Jew f   Rom 2:10
f fruits of the Spirit   Rom 8:23
He f loved us   1 John 4:19
I am the f and the   Rev 1:17
left your f love   Rev 2:4
f things have passed   Rev 21:4

FIRST-BORN oldest

Sidon, his f   Gen 10:15
the f bore a son   Gen 19:37
I am Esau your f   Gen 27:19
LORD killed every f   Ex 13:15
birth to her f son   Luke 2:7
church of the f   Heb 12:23
f of the dead   Rev 1:5

FIRST GATE see
  GATES OF JERUSALEM

FISH

rule over the f   Gen 1:26
Their f stink   Is 50:2
a great f to swallow   Jon 1:17
loaves and two f   Matt 14:17
snake instead of a f   Luke 11:11
net full of f   John 21:8

FISH GATE see
  GATES OF JERUSALEM

FISHERMEN *fishers*

f will lament	Is 19:8
for they were f	Matt 4:18
the f had gotten out	Luke 5:2

FISHERS *fishermen*

make you f of men	Matt 4:19
become f of men	Mark 1:17

FIT *be suitable, worthy*

f to remove His	Matt 3:11
f for the kingdom	Luke 9:62
f to be...apostle	1 Cor 15:9
body, being f-ted	Eph 4:16
f-ting in the Lord	Col 3:18

FIX *make firm, secure*

I will f your boundary	Ex 23:31
f-ed her hope on God	1 Tim 5:5
f-ing...eyes on Jesus	Heb 12:2
f your hope	1 Pet 1:13

FIXED *established*

the f festivals	1 Chr 23:31
f order of the moon	Jer 31:35
is a great chasm f	Luke 16:26

FLAME *fire*

ascended in the f	Judg 13:20
f...the wicked	Ps 106:18
f of the LORD	Song 8:6
his Holy One a f	Is 10:17
crackling of a f	Joel 2:5
f of a burning thorn	Acts 7:30
eyes *are* a f of fire	Rev 19:12

FLAMING *burning*

the f sword	Gen 3:24
f fire by night	Is 4:5
eyes were like f	Dan 10:6
angels in a f fire	2 Thess 1:7

FLASH *reflect, sparkle*

why do your eyes f	Job 15:12
lightning was f-ing	Ezek 1:13
Polished to f like	Ezek 21:10
He who f-es forth	Amos 5:9
light suddenly f-ed	Acts 22:6

FLASK *utensil*

take this f of oil	2 Kin 9:1
took oil in f-s	Matt 25:4

FLATTER

Nor f *any* man	Job 32:21
f with their tongue	Ps 5:9
adulteress who f-s	Prov 2:16
who f-s his neighbor	Prov 29:5

FLAX *plant*

the f was in bud	Ex 9:31
looks for wool and f	Prov 31:13
made from combed f	Is 19:9

FLEE *escape, run away*

arise, f to Haran	Gen 27:43
F *as* a bird	Ps 11:1
f from Thy presence	Ps 139:7
rulers have fled	Is 22:3
f to Egypt	Matt 2:13
left Him and fled	Matt 26:56
fled from the tomb	Mark 16:8
f from idolatry	1 Cor 10:14
f from youthful lusts	2 Tim 2:22
and heaven fled	Rev 20:11

FLEECE *wool*

put a f of wool	Judg 6:37
dry only on the f	Judg 6:39
warmed with the f	Job 31:20

FLEET *group of ships*

Solomon...built a f	1 Kin 9:26
sent...with the f	1 Kin 9:27

FLESH *body, meat*

f of my f	Gen 2:23
shall become one f	Gen 2:24
from my f I shall see	Job 19:26
heart and my f sing	Ps 84:2
All f is grass	Is 40:6
the f is weak	Matt 26:41
spirit...not have f	Luke 24:39
the Word became f	John 1:14
born of the f is f	John 3:6
who eats My f	John 6:56
children of the f	Rom 9:8
thorn in the f	2 Cor 12:7
desires of the f	Eph 2:3
polluted by the f	Jude 23
filled with their f	Rev 19:21

FLESHLY *carnal*

not in f wisdom	2 Cor 1:12
His f body	Col 1:22

abstain from f lusts   1 Pet 2:11

FLIES *insects*

sent...swarms of f	Ps 78:45
swarm of f and gnats	Ps 105:31
Dead f make a	Eccl 10:1

FLIGHT *departure*

F will perish from	Amos 2:14
f may not be in	Matt 24:20
foreign armies to f	Heb 11:34

FLINT *stone*

Zipporah took a f	Ex 4:25
f into a fountain	Ps 114:8
hoofs...seem like f	Is 5:28
emery harder than f	Ezek 3:9
hearts like f	Zech 7:12

FLOCK *goats, sheep*

a keeper of f-s	Gen 4:2
water their father's f	Ex 2:16
Thy people like a f	Ps 77:20
He will tend His f	Is 40:11
scattered My f	Jer 23:2
over their f by night	Luke 2:8
shall become one f	John 10:16
f of God among you	1 Pet 5:2

FLOOD *overflowing of water*

I am bringing the f	Gen 6:17
f came upon the earth	Gen 7:17
end...with a f	Dan 9:26
the f-s came	Matt 7:25
f...destroyed	Luke 17:27

FLOOR *ground*

threshing f of Atad	Gen 50:11
go down to the...f	Ruth 3:3
the f...with gold	1 Kin 6:30
f-s...full of grain	Joel 2:24
His threshing f	Matt 3:12
fell...from the third f	Acts 20:9

FLOUR *ground grain*

measures of fine f	Gen 18:6
only a handful of f	1 Kin 17:12
f...not exhausted	1 Kin 17:16

FLOURISH *blossom, thrive*

may the righteous f	Ps 72:7
who did iniquity f-ed	Ps 92:7
your bones shall f	Is 66:14

make the dry tree f   Ezek 17:24

FLOW *pour forth*

river f-ed out of Eden	Gen 2:10
f-ing with milk and	Ex 3:8
eyelids f with water	Jer 9:18
hills will f with milk	Joel 3:18
f of her blood	Mark 5:29
f...living waters	John 7:38

FLOWER *blossom*

As a f of the field	Ps 103:15
f-s have already	Song 2:12
to the fading f	Is 28:1
glory like the f	1 Pet 1:24

FLUTE *musical instrument*

tambourine, f, and	1 Sam 10:5
playing on f-s	1 Kin 1:40
the f or on the harp	1 Cor 14:7
musicians...f-players	Rev 18:22

FLY *soar*

let birds f above	Gen 1:20
a raven, and it flew	Gen 8:7
As sparks f upward	Job 5:7
f-ies away like a dream	Job 20:8
glory will f away	Hos 9:11
heard an eagle f-ing	Rev 8:13
the birds which f	Rev 19:17

FOAL *colt*

ties *his* f to the vine	Gen 49:11
f of a wild donkey	Job 11:12
f of a beast of burden	Matt 21:5

FODDER *animal food*

give his donkey f	Gen 42:27
eat salted f	Is 30:24

FOE *enemy*

before your f-s	1 Chr 21:12
A f and an enemy	Esth 7:6
iniquity of my f-s	Ps 49:5
the evil to my f-s	Ps 54:5
avenge...His f-s	Jer 46:10

FOLD *animal pen*

goats out of your f-s	Ps 50:9
the peaceful f-s	Jer 25:37
cut off from the f	Hab 3:17
not of this f	John 10:16

FOLLOW *imitate, pursue*

not f other gods	Deut 6:14

FOLLOW

turn back from f-ing   Ruth 1:16
f the LORD your God   1 Sam 12:14
who f...wickedness   Ps 119:150
bloodshed f-s   Hos 4:2
He said to them, F   Matt 4:19
left...and f-ed   Matt 4:20
his cross, and f Me   Matt 16:24
multitude was f-ing   Mark 5:24
allowed no one to f   Mark 5:37
and they f Me   John 10:27
Peter...f-ing Jesus   John 18:15
f-ing after...lusts   Jude 16
ones who f the Lamb   Rev 14:4

FOLLOWERS *disciples*

His f...*began* asking   Mark 4:10

FOLLY *foolishness*

this act of f   Judg 19:23
The naive inherit f   Prov 14:18
of fools spouts f   Prov 15:2
F is joy to him   Prov 15:21
devising of f is sin   Prov 24:9

FOOD *bread, meat*

shall be f for you   Gen 1:29
tree was good for f   Gen 3:6
in giving them f   Ruth 1:6
tears have been my f   Ps 42:3
it is deceptive f   Prov 23:3
his f was locusts   Matt 3:4
life more than f   Matt 6:25
f is to do the will   John 4:34
My flesh is true f   John 6:55
milk...not solid f   1 Cor 3:2

FOOL *unwise person*

The f has said in his   Ps 14:1
F-s despise wisdom   Prov 1:7
too high for a f   Prov 24:7
f multiplies words   Eccl 10:14
The prophet is a f   Hos 9:7
shall say, You f   Matt 5:22
f-s and blind men   Matt 23:17
wise, they became f-s   Rom 1:22
f-s for Christ's sake   1 Cor 4:10

FOOLISH *silly, unwise*

O f and unwise   Deut 32:6
a f son is a grief   Prov 10:1
False and f visions   Lam 2:14
Woe to the f   Ezek 13:3
f took their lamps   Matt 25:3

O f men and slow   Luke 24:25
let him become f   1 Cor 3:18
You f Galatians   Gal 3:1
do not be f   Eph 5:17

FOOLISHNESS *folly*

folly of fools is f   Prov 14:24
mouth is speaking f   Is 9:17
f of God is wiser   1 Cor 1:25
is f before God   1 Cor 3:19

FOOT *part of body*

she lay at his feet   Ruth 3:14
six toes on each f   2 Sam 21:20
pierced...my feet   Ps 22:16
the f of pride   Ps 36:11
lamp to my feet   Ps 119:105
their feet run to evil   Prov 1:16
signals with his feet   Prov 6:13
beautiful...your feet   Song 7:1
feet of the afflicted   Is 26:6
feet...polished bronze   Dan 10:6
dust of your feet   Matt 10:14
Bind...hand and f   Matt 22:13
f causes you to   Mark 9:45
kissing His feet   Luke 7:38
anointed the feet   John 12:3
the disciples' feet   John 13:5
beautiful...the feet   Rom 10:15
Satan under...feet   Rom 16:20
worship at the feet   Rev 22:8

FOOTSTEPS *path*

make His f into a way Ps 85:13
f of thine anointed   Ps 89:51
my f in Thy word   Ps 119:133

FOOTSTOOL *foot support*

the f of our God   1 Chr 28:2
worship at His f   Ps 99:5
Thine enemies a f   Ps 110:1
the earth is My f   Is 66:1
sit down by my f   James 2:3

FORBEARANCE *restraint*

By f...be persuaded Prov 25:15
in the f of God   Rom 3:25
showing f to one   Eph 4:2

FORBID *prohibit*

if her father should f   Num 30:5
f-ding to pay taxes   Luke 23:2
do not f to speak   1 Cor 14:39
men who f marriage 1 Tim 4:3

he f-s those who   3 John 10

FORCE (n) *power, strength*

with a heavy f   Num 20:20
captains of the f-s   2 Kin 25:23
use f against you   Neh 13:21
commanders of the f-s   Jer 43:5
with f and with   Ezek 34:4

FORCE (v) *compel*

are f-d into bondage   Neh 5:5
man f-d to labor   Job 7:1
f you to go one mile   Matt 5:41
not take...by f   Luke 3:14
f them to blaspheme   Acts 26:11
f-d to appeal to   Acts 28:19

FORCED LABOR *work as tax*

Canaanites to f   Josh 17:13
was over the f   2 Sam 20:24
will be put to f   Prov 12:24

FORCED LABORERS

Solomon levied f   1 Kin 5:13
Solomon raised as f   2 Chr 8:8
men will become f   Is 31:8

FORD *shallow place*

the f of the Jabbok   Gen 32:22
the f-s of the Jordan   Judg 12:5
f-s...been seized   Jer 51:32

FOREFATHER *ancestor*

iniquity of their f-s   Lev 26:40
Your first f sinned   Is 43:27
I swore to your f-s   Jer 11:5
Abraham, our f   Rom 4:1
the way my f-s did   2 Tim 1:3

FOREHEAD *brow*

on his bald f   Lev 13:42
stone...into his f   1 Sam 17:49
put a mark on the f-s   Ezek 9:4
seal of God on their f-s   Rev 9:4
upon her f a name   Rev 17:5

FOREIGN *alien, strange*

Put away the f gods   Gen 35:2
sojourner in a f land   Ex 2:22
sell her to a f people   Ex 21:8
drank f waters   2 Kin 19:24
married f women   Ezra 10:2
f armies to flight   Heb 11:34

FOREIGNER *alien, stranger*

no f is to eat of it   Ex 12:43
sell it to a f   Deut 14:21
charge...a f   Deut 23:20
since I am a f   Ruth 2:10
a f in their sight   Job 19:15
f-s entered his gate   Obad 11

FOREKNEW *know beforehand*

whom He f, He also   Rom 8:29
people whom He f   Rom 11:2
He was f-own before   1 Pet 1:20

FOREKNOWLEDGE

plan and f of God   Acts 2:23
f of God the Father   1 Pet 1:2

FOREMOST *first*

f commandment   Matt 22:38
among whom I am f   1 Tim 1:15

FORERUNNER *goes before*

Jesus...as a f for   Heb 6:20

FORESKIN

the flesh of your f   Gen 17:11
cut off her son's f   Ex 4:25
a hundred f-s   1 Sam 18:25
the f-s of your heart   Jer 4:4

FOREST *woods*

f devoured more   2 Sam 18:8
the f of Lebanon   1 Kin 7:2
f will sing for joy   1 Chr 16:33
every beast of the f   Ps 50:10
the glory of his f   Is 10:18
beasts in the f, Come   Is 56:9
a f is set aflame   James 3:5

FORETOLD *predicted*

the Holy Spirit f   Acts 1:16
just as Isaiah f   Rom 9:29

FOREVER *always, eternal*

eat, and live f   Gen 3:22
not strive with man f   Gen 6:3
throne shall be...f   1 Chr 17:14
the LORD abides f   Ps 9:7
LORD sits as King f   Ps 29:10
glorify Thy name f   Ps 86:12
riches are not f   Prov 27:24
One Who lives f   Is 57:15

FOREVER

Christ is to remain f   John 12:34
He...with you f   John 14:16
He is able to save f   Heb 7:25
Son, made perfect f   Heb 7:28
they shall reign f   Rev 22:5

FORFEIT *lose*

possessions...f-ed   Ezra 10:8
f-s his own life   Prov 20:2
f my head to the king   Dan 1:10
and f-s his soul   Matt 16:26

FORGET *forsake, neglect*

God has made me f   Gen 41:51
lest you f the LORD   Deut 6:12
f-got God who gave   Deut 32:18
God f-s...iniquity   Job 11:6
nations who f God   Ps 9:17
needy...be f-gotten   Ps 9:18
Do not f the afflicted   Ps 10:12
they f-got His deeds   Ps 78:11
do not f my teaching   Prov 3:1
you will f the shame   Is 54:4
My people f My name   Jer 23:27
f-ing what *lies* behind   Phil 3:13
f your work and   Heb 6:10

FORGIVE *pardon*

f the transgression   Gen 50:17
f their sin   Ex 32:32
f our sins   Ps 79:9
not f their iniquity   Jer 18:23
f us our debts   Matt 6:12
authority...to f sins   Matt 9:6
f-gave him the debt   Matt 18:27
can f sins but God   Mark 2:7
he who is f-n little   Luke 7:47
Father, f them   Luke 23:34
whom you f   2 Cor 2:10
f-ing each other   Eph 4:32
f-n us all our   Col 2:13
righteous to f us   1 John 1:9

FORGIVENESS *pardon*

a God of f   Neh 9:17
there is f with Thee   Ps 130:4
poured out...for f   Matt 26:28
repentance for f   Luke 24:47
receives f of sins   Acts 10:43
f of our trespasses   Eph 1:7
the f of sins   Col 1:14
there is no f   Heb 9:22

FORK *instrument*

a three-pronged f   1 Sam 2:13
His winnowing f   Matt 3:12

FORM (n) *appearance, shape*

beautiful of f and   Gen 29:17
the f of the LORD   Num 12:8
image in the f   Deut 4:23
like the f of a man   Is 44:13
in a different f   Mark 16:12
bodily f like a dove   Luke 3:22
f of corruptible man   Rom 1:23
existed in the f of God   Phil 2:6

FORM (v) *fashion, shape*

f-ed man of dust   Gen 2:7
f-ed the dry land   Ps 95:5
f my inward parts   Ps 139:13
One f-ing light   Is 45:7
who f-s mountains   Amos 4:13
f-s the spirit of man   Zech 12:1
plot was f-ed against   Acts 20:3
Christ is f-ed in you   Gal 4:19

FORMATION *rank*

in f against   1 Chr 19:17
battle f in the   2 Chr 14:10

FORMLESS *without form*

earth was f *and void*   Gen 1:2
behold, *it was* f   Jer 4:23

FORNICATION

f-s, thefts, false   Matt 15:19
were not born of f   John 8:41
strangled and from f   Acts 15:29

FORNICATORS

neither f, nor   1 Cor 6:9
f...God will judge   Heb 13:4

FORSAKE

Then he f-sook God   Deut 32:15
not fail you or f you   Josh 1:5
f-sook the law of the   2 Chr 12:1
f Him, He will f you   2 Chr 15:2
God has not f-n us   Ezra 9:9
why hast Thou f-n me   Ps 22:1
not f your mother's   Prov 1:8
wicked f his way   Is 55:7
Your sons have f-n Me   Jer 5:7
f the idols of Egypt   Ezek 20:8
hast Thou f-n Me   Matt 27:46

persecuted...not f-n 2 Cor 4:9
f-ing...assembling Heb 10:25
nor will I ever f you Heb 13:5

FORTIFICATIONS *stronghold*

the unassailable f Is 25:12
your f are fig trees Nah 3:12

FORTIFIED *walled*

live in the f cities Num 32:17
f with high walls Deut 3:5
strike every f city 2 Kin 3:19
f cities into Is 37:26

FORTRESS *stronghold*

God is my strong f 2 Sam 22:33
my rock and my f Ps 18:2
My refuge and my f Ps 91:2
wealth is his f Prov 10:15
f-es will be destroyed Hos 10:14

FORTUNE *one's lot*

and the f-s of Israel Jer 33:7
f-s of My people Hos 6:11
restore their f Zeph 2:7

FORTY *number*

f days and f nights Gen 7:4
flood...for f days Gen 7:17
ate the manna f years Ex 16:35
with the LORD f days Ex 34:28
fasted f days and f Matt 4:2
f days being tempted Mark 1:13

FOUL *putrid, rotten*

Nile will become f Ex 7:18
My wounds grow f Ps 38:5
f with your feet Ezek 34:19

FOUNDATION *establishment*

f-s of heaven were 2 Sam 22:8
I laid the f of the Job 38:4
the f of His throne Ps 97:2
the earth upon its f-s Ps 104:5
an everlasting f Prov 10:25
cornerstone *for the* f Is 28:16
a f upon the rock Luke 6:48
the firm f of God 2 Tim 2:19
didst lay the f Heb 1:10
a f of repentance Heb 6:1

FOUNDATION GATE *see*
GATES OF JERUSALEM

FOUNDED *established*

the day it was f Ex 9:18
f it upon the seas Ps 24:2
by wisdom f the earth Prov 3:19
f His vaulted dome Amos 9:6
f upon the rock Matt 7:25

FOUNTAIN *spring, well*

f-s of the great deep Gen 7:11
is the f of life Ps 36:9
The f of wisdom Prov 18:4
f of living waters Jer 2:13

FOUNTAIN GATE *see*
GATES OF JERUSALEM

FOWL *bird*

and fattened f 1 Kin 4:23
things and winged f Ps 148:10

FOX *small animal*

three hundred f-es Judg 15:4
f-s that are ruining Song 2:15
like f-es among ruins Ezek 13:4
The f-es have holes Matt 8:20
Go and tell that f Luke 13:32

FRAGMENTS *pieces*

forth His ice as f Ps 147:17
Gather up the...f John 6:12
twelve baskets with f John 6:13

FRAGRANCE *pleasant aroma*

oils have a pleasing f Song 1:3
given forth *their* f Song 2:13
f like *the* cedars Hos 14:6
we are a f of Christ 2 Cor 2:15

FRAME *structure*

f-s of the tabernacle Num 3:36
with *artistic* f-s 1 Kin 6:4
He...knows our f Ps 103:14
My f was not hidden Ps 139:15

FRANKINCENSE *spice*

spices with pure f Ex 30:34
f and the spices 1 Chr 9:29
trees of f Song 4:14
gold and f and myrrh Matt 2:11

FREE *at liberty*

she is not to go f Ex 21:7
be f from the oath Josh 2:20
let the oppressed go f Is 58:6

shall make you f — John 8:32
who has died is f-d — Rom 6:7
the f gift of God — Rom 6:23
f from the law — Rom 8:2
Christ set us f — Gal 5:1
whether slave or f — Eph 6:8

FREEDOM *liberty*

proclaim...f to — Is 61:1
f of the glory — Rom 8:21
you were called to f — Gal 5:13
do not use your f as — 1 Pet 2:16

FREEWILL OFFERINGS
see OFFERINGS

FRESH *new, recently prepared*

found a f jawbone — Judg 15:15
anointed with f oil — Ps 92:10
f water from your — Prov 5:15
new wine into f — Mark 2:22
f and bitter *water* — James 3:11

FRIEND *companion, comrade*

man speaks to his f — Ex 33:11
f-s are my scoffers — Job 16:20
loved ones and my f-s — Ps 38:11
my familiar f — Ps 55:13
A f loves at all — Prov 17:17
Wealth adds...f-s — Prov 19:4
who blesses his f — Prov 27:14
confidence in a f — Mic 7:5
f of tax-gatherers — Matt 11:19
F, your sins are — Luke 5:20
f of the bridegroom — John 3:29
his life for his f-s — John 15:13
You are My f-s, if — John 15:14

FRIENDSHIP

the f of God — Job 29:4
f with the world — James 4:4

FRIGHTEN *terrify*

to f *them* away — Deut 28:26
Thou dost f me — Job 7:14
I was f-ed and fell — Dan 8:17
Him and were f-ed — Mark 6:50
wars, do not be f-ed — Mark 13:7

FRINGE *edge*

the f-s of His ways — Job 26:14
touched the f of His — Matt 9:20

FROGS

smite...with f — Ex 8:2
f which destroyed — Ps 78:45
land swarmed with f — Ps 105:30
unclean spirits like f — Rev 16:13

FRONTALS *prayer bands*

they shall be as f — Deut 6:8
f on your forehead — Deut 11:18
see also PHYLACTERIES

FROST *freezing*

and the f by night — Gen 31:40
fine as the f — Ex 16:14
sycamore trees with f — Ps 78:47

FRUIT *growth, produce*

f trees bearing f — Gen 1:11
she took from its f — Gen 3:6
the f of the womb — Gen 30:2
offering of first f-s — Lev 2:12
its f in its season — Ps 1:3
yield f in old age — Ps 92:14
eat its choice f-s — Song 4:16
eaten the f of lies — Hos 10:13
know...by their f-s — Matt 7:16
bad tree bears bad f — Matt 7:17
f for eternal life — John 4:36
bear f of the Spirit — Gal 5:22
f in every good work — Col 1:10

FRUITFUL *productive*

be f and multiply — Gen 9:7
were f and increased — Ex 1:7
gather a f harvest — Ps 107:37
into the f land — Jer 2:7
f labor for me — Phil 1:22

FRUSTRATE *counteract*

to f their counsel — Ezra 4:5
He f-s the plotting — Job 5:12
plans are f-d — Prov 15:22

FUEL *that which burns*

people are like f — Is 9:19
You will be f — Ezek 21:32

FUGITIVE *one who flees*

do not betray the f — Is 16:3
Meet the f with bread — Is 21:14
gather the f-s — Jer 49:5

FULFILL *complete*

to f the word — 2 Chr 36:21

May the Lord **f** all   Ps 20:5
f-ing His word   Ps 148:8
to **f** the vision   Dan 11:14
the prophet was **f-ed**   Matt 2:17
to abolish, but to **f**   Matt 5:17
The time is **f-ed**   Mark 1:15
f-ed in the kingdom   Luke 22:16
Scripture..be **f-ed**   John 13:18
husband **f** his duty   1 Cor 7:3
f the law of Christ   Gal 6:2
f your ministry   2 Tim 4:5

FULFILLMENT *completion*

the **f** of every vision   Ezek 12:23
f of what had been   Luke 1:45
f of *the* law   Rom 13:10

FULL *complete, whole*

I went out **f**   Ruth 1:21
The earth is **f** of   Ps 33:5
until the **f** day   Prov 4:18
twelve **f** baskets   Matt 14:20
f of dead...bones   Matt 23:27
f of the Holy Spirit   Luke 4:1
also is **f** of light   Luke 11:34
f of grace and truth   John 1:14
f of the Spirit   Acts 6:3
f armor of God   Eph 6:11
f of compassion   James 5:11

FULLER *who bleaches cloth*

of the **f-**'s field   2 Kin 18:17
like **f-**'s soap   Mal 3:2

FULNESS *completeness*

Thy presence is **f** of   Ps 16:11
His **f** we...received   John 1:16
the **f** of the Gentiles   Rom 11:25
f of the time came   Gal 4:4
all the **f** of God   Eph 3:19
f to dwell in Him   Col 1:19
the **f** of Deity dwells   Col 2:9

FURIOUS *angry*

Pharaoh was **f**   Gen 41:10
became **f** and very   Neh 4:1
king became...**f**   Dan 2:12

FURNACE *oven*

As silver tried in a **f**   Ps 12:6
the **f** of affliction   Is 48:10
into the midst of a **f**   Dan 3:6
cast them into the **f**   Matt 13:42
to glow in a **f**   Rev 1:15

FURNISH *supply*

f-ed with silver bands   Ex 38:17
shall **f** him liberally   Deut 15:14
f-ing every kind   Ps 144:13
upper room **f-ed**   Mark 14:15

FURROW *trench*

its **f-s** weep together   Job 31:38
dost water its **f-s**   Ps 65:10
weeds in the **f-s**   Hos 10:4

FURY *anger*

brother's..**f** subsides   Gen 27:44
terrify them in His **f**   Ps 2:5
plucked up in **f**   Ezek 19:12
the **f** of a fire   Heb 10:27

FUTILE *useless, vain*

go after **f** things   1 Sam 12:21
devise **f** things   Acts 4:25
f in...speculations   Rom 1:21

FUTURE *that which is ahead*

discern their **f**   Deut 32:29
no **f** for the evil   Prov 24:20
is hope for your **f**   Jer 31:17
foundation for the **f**   1 Tim 6:19

G

GABRIEL

angel of high rank   Dan 8:16
    Dan 9:21; Luke 1:19,26

GAD

1 *son of Jacob* Gen 30:11;35:26
2 *tribe of*   Num 1:25;2:14
3 *seer, prophet* 2 Sam 24:11,18
4 *valley*   2 Sam 24:5

GAIETY *cheerfulness*

g...is banished   Is 24:11
an end to all her **g**   Hos 2:11

GAIN (n) *profit, increase*

hate dishonest **g**   Ex 18:21
Ill-gotten **g-s** do not   Prov 10:2
who rejects unjust **g**   Is 33:15
greedy for **g**   Jer 6:13
to die is **g**   Phil 1:21
fond of sordid **g**   1 Tim 3:8

GAIN (v) acquire

they might g insight   Neh 8:13
have **g-ed** the victory   Ps 98:1
he will g knowledge   Prov 19:25
will g ascendancy   Dan 11:5
g-s the whole world   Matt 16:26
that I may g Christ   Phil 3:8
may g the glory   2 Thess 2:14

GAIUS

1 *Macedonian*   Acts 19:29
2 *companion of Paul*   Acts 20:4
3 *Corinthian believer* 1 Cor 1:14
4 *addressee of 3 John*   3 John 1

GALATIA

Roman province in Asia Minor
1 Cor 16:1; 2 Tim 4:10

GALE *storm*

dust before a g   Is 17:13
a fierce g of wind   Mark 4:37

GALILEE

1 *district in N Palestine*
Josh 21:32; 1 Kin 9:11
Matt 2:22; Acts 10:37
2 *Sea of* Matt 4:18; Mark 7:31
also **Sea of Chinnereth**
also **Lake of Gennesaret**
also **Sea of Tiberias**

GALL *bitter herb, bitterness*

gave me g for my food Ps 69:21
drink...with g   Matt 27:34
the g of bitterness   Acts 8:23

GALLIO

governor of Achaia
Acts 18:12,17

GALLOWS *for hanging*

Have a g...made   Esth 5:14
hanged...on the g   Esth 7:10
his sons...on the g   Esth 9:25

GAMALIEL

1 *head of tribe* Num 2:20;7:54
2 *Pharisee*   Acts 5:34;22:3

GARDEN *planted area*

God walking in the g   Gen 3:8
from the g of Eden   Gen 3:23

Make my g breathe   Song 4:16
plant g-s, and eat   Jer 29:5
tabernacle like a g   Lam 2:6
in the g with Him   John 18:26
the g a new tomb   John 19:41

GARLAND *ornament*

a g instead of ashes   Is 61:3
brought...g-s to the   Acts 14:13

GARMENT *clothing, dress*

God made g-s of skin Gen 3:21
caught him by his g Gen 39:12
in g-s of fine linen   Gen 41:42
holy g-s for Aaron   Ex 28:2
divide my g-s among Ps 22:18
on g-s of vengeance   Is 59:17
g-s of glowing colors   Is 63:1
g of camel's hair   Matt 3:4
g as white as snow   Matt 28:3
I just touch His g-s   Mark 5:28
spread their g-s   Mark 11:8
dividing up His g-s Luke 23:34
put his outer g on   John 21:7
become old as a g   Heb 1:11
clothed in white g-s   Rev 3:5

GARRISON *defense*

g of the Philistines 1 Sam 13:4
the g...trembled   1 Sam 14:15
set g-s in the land   2 Chr 17:2

GATE *entry way*

is the g of heaven   Gen 28:17
oppressed in the g   Job 5:4
g-s with thanksgiving Ps 100:4
enter the g-s of Sheol Is 38:10
justice in the g   Amos 5:15
Enter...narrow g   Matt 7:13
g-s of Hades shall   Matt 16:18
did not open the g   Acts 12:14

GATEKEEPERS *guards*

g for the camp   1 Chr 9:18
divisions of the g 1 Chr 26:12
The sons of the g   Ezra 2:42
g, and the singers   Neh 10:39

GATES OF JERUSALEM

alternate names in italics

1 **Beautiful Gate**   Acts 3:10
East Gate

2 Benjamin Gate	Jer 20:2
	Zech 14:10
Sheep Gate	
Inspection Gate	
3 Corner Gate	2 Kin 14:13
	2 Chr 26:9
4 East Gate	Neh 3:29
	Ezek 10:19;44:1
Beautiful Gate	
5 Ephraim Gate	2 Kin 14:13
	Neh 8:16
Middle Gate	
Old Gate	
6 First Gate	Zech 14:10
7 Fish Gate	2 Chr 33:14
	Neh 3:3
8 Foundation Gate	2 Chr 23:5
Gate of Sur	
9 Fountain Gate	Neh 2:14
	Neh 12:37
"gate between two walls"	
	2 Kin 25:4; Jer 39:4
10 Guard, Gate of the	Neh 12:39
Inspection Gate	
11 Horse Gate	2 Chr 23:15
	Neh 3:28
12 Inspection Gate	Neh 3:31
Gate of the Guard	
Benjamin Gate	
13 Middle Gate	Jer 39:3
Ephraim Gate	
14 Old Gate	Neh 3:6
	Neh 12:39
Ephraim Gate	
15 Refuse Gate	Neh 2:13
	Neh 12:31
16 Sheep Gate	Neh 3:1
Benjamin Gate	
17 Sur, Gate of	2 Kin 11:6
Foundation Gate	
18 Valley Gate	2 Chr 26:9
	Neh 3:13
19 Water Gate	Neh 3:26
	Neh 8:1,3,16

GATEWAY *entrance*

the g of the court	Ex 40:8
the g of the peoples	Ezek 26:2

GATH

Philistine city Josh 11:22
1 Sam 17:23; 1 Chr 20:8

GATHER *assemble, collect*

g-ed to his people	Gen 25:8
g stubble for straw	Ex 5:12
He g-s the waters	Ps 33:7
G My godly ones	Ps 50:5
g all nations and	Is 66:18
hen g-s her chicks	Matt 23:37
elders...were g-ed	Matt 26:3
g...His elect	Mark 13:27
G up the leftover	John 6:12

GAZA

Philistine city Gen 10:19
Judg 16:1; Jer 47:5

GAZE (n) *view, glance*

Turn Thy g away from	Ps 39:13
let your g be fixed	Prov 4:25
I lifted my g and	Dan 8:3
turning His g on His	Luke 6:20

GAZE (v) *look, stare*

man...g-ing at her	Gen 24:21
and g after Moses	Ex 33:8
eye g-s on their	Job 17:2
LORD g-d upon the	Ps 102:19
g-ing...into the sky	Acts 1:10

GAZELLE *animal*

swift as the g-s	1 Chr 12:8
a g Or a young stag	Song 2:17
like a hunted g	Is 13:14

GEDERAH

1 *town of Judah* Josh 15:36
2 *town of Benjamin* 1 Chr 12:4

GEHAZI

servant of Elisha 2 Kin 4:12
2 Kin 5:20;8:4

GENEALOGY *family record*

found the book of...g	Neh 7:5
g of Jesus Christ	Matt 1:1
and endless g-ies	1 Tim 1:4
whose g is not traced	Heb 7:6

GENERATION *age, period*

this evil g	Deut 1:35
the righteous g	Ps 14:5
faithfulness to all g-s	Ps 100:5
salvation to all g-s	Is 51:8
this g seek for a sign	Mark 8:12

g-s...not made known   Eph 3:5
and perverse **g**   Phil 2:15

GENEROUS *bountiful*

g will be blessed   Prov 22:9
because I am **g**   Matt 20:15
g...ready to share   1 Tim 6:18

GENNESARET

1 *lake*   Luke 5:1
   also **Sea of Chinnereth**
   also **Sea of Galilee**
   also **Sea of Tiberius**
2 *land or district*   Matt 14:34
       Mark 6:53

GENTILES *foreigners, non-Jews*

Galilee of the **G**   Matt 4:15
deliver...to the **G**   Matt 20:19
revelation to the **G**   Luke 2:32
Why did the **G** rage   Acts 4:25
salvation...to the **G**   Rom 11:11
preach...among the **G**   3 John 7

GENTLE *compassionate, mild*

g answer turns away   Prov 15:1
I was like a **g** lamb   Jer 11:19
Blessed are the **g**   Matt 5:5
G, and mounted on   Matt 21:5
a **g** and quiet spirit   1 Pet 3:4

GENTLENESS *kindness*

and a spirit of **g**   1 Cor 4:21
and **g** of Christ   2 Cor 10:1
g, self-control   Gal 5:23
humility and **g**, with   Eph 4:2

GERAR

Philistine city   Gen 20:2;26:6

GERIZIM

mountain near Shechem
       Deut 11:29; Josh 8:33

GERSHOM

1 *son of Moses*   Ex 2:22;18:3
2 *son of Levi*   1 Chr 6:16,43
3 *line of Phinehas*   Ezra 8:2

GERSHON

son of Levi   Gen 46:11
       Ex 6:16

GETHSEMANE

garden on Mount of Olives
       Matt 26:36; Mark 14:32

GEZER

Canaanite city of Ephraim
       Josh 10:33; 1 Kin 9:17

GHOST *spirit*

resort to idols and **g-s**   Is 19:3
saying, It is a **g**   Matt 14:26
it was a **g**   Mark 6:49

GIANT

were born to the **g**   2 Sam 21:22
from the **g-s**   1 Chr 20:6

GIBEAH

1 *village in Judah*   Josh 15:57
2 *town of Benjamin*
   1 Sam 10:26;13:2; 2 Sam 23:29
3 *in Ephraim*   Josh 24:33

GIBEON

Canaanite city   Josh 9:3,17
       1 Kin 3:5; 1 Chr 8:29

GIDEON

son of Joash   Judg 6:11,36
judge   Judg 8:4-21

GIFT *present*

the sacred **g-s**   Num 18:32
children are a **g**   Ps 127:3
to Him **g-s**   Matt 2:11
g of the Holy Spirit   Acts 2:38
impart...spiritual **g**   Rom 1:11
g of God is eternal   Rom 6:23
desire...greater **g-s**   1 Cor 12:31
perfect **g** is from   James 1:17

GIHON

1 *river of Eden*   Gen 2:13
2 *spring*   2 Chr 32:30

GILBOA

mountain   2 Sam 1:6
where Saul died   2 Sam 21:12

GILEAD

1 *son of Machir*   Num 36:1
2 *descendant of Gad*   1 Chr 5:14
3 *father of Jephthah*   Judg 11:1
4 *land E of Jordan*   Num 32:29
5 *mountain*   Judg 7:3
6 *city*   Hos 6:8

GILGAL

1 *encampment in Jordan Valley*

Josh 5:9; 1 Sam 7:16

2 near Jericho   Josh 5:8,10
3 in N Judah   Josh 15:7
4 in Galilee   Josh 12:23
5 village near Bethel   2 Kin 2:1

GIRD *bind*

g him with the...band   Ex 29:5
g up your loins like   Job 38:3
g-ed me with gladness   Ps 30:11
g-s herself with   Prov 31:17
g-ed...with truth   Eph 6:14
g your minds for   1 Pet 1:13
g-ed across His breast   Rev 1:13

GIRDLE *belt, waistband*

man with a leather g   2 Kin 1:8
binds...with a g   Job 12:18
with a golden g   Rev 1:13

GIRGASHITE(S)

Canaanite tribe   Gen 10:16
   Deut 7:1; Josh 24:11; Neh 9:8

GIRL *maiden*

the g and consult   Gen 24:57
sold a g for wine   Joel 3:3
boys and g-s playing   Zech 8:5
the g has not died   Matt 9:24

GIVE *bestow, yield*

g light on the earth   Gen 1:17
g-n you every plant   Gen 1:29
gave me from...tree   Gen 3:12
in the land...God g-s   Ex 20:12
I will g you rest   Ex 33:14
g him to the LORD   1 Sam 1:11
G ear to my prayer   Ps 17:1
gave me vinegar   Ps 69:21
G me neither poverty   Prov 30:8
a son will be g-n   Is 9:6
gave birth to a Son   Matt 1:25
G us this day   Matt 6:11
g-ing thanks, He   Matt 15:36
g you the keys   Matt 16:19
authority...been g-n   Matt 28:18
what shall a man g   Mark 8:37
body which is g-n   Luke 22:19
gave His only...Son   John 3:16
not as the world g-s   John 14:27
gave up His spirit   John 19:30
what I do have I g   Acts 3:6
g-n among men   Acts 4:12

more blessed to g   Acts 20:35
was g-n me a thorn   2 Cor 12:7
always g-ing thanks   Eph 5:20
who gave Himself   1 Tim 2:6
g-s a greater grace   James 4:6
g-n us eternal life   1 John 5:11
to be g-n a mark   Rev 13:16

GLAD *pleased*

g in his heart   Ex 4:14
joy and a g heart   Deut 28:47
righteous see...are g   Job 22:19
Be g in the LORD   Ps 32:11
g when they said   Ps 122:1
son makes a father g   Prov 10:1
Rejoice, and be g   Matt 5:12
Be g in that day   Luke 6:23
who bring g tidings   Rom 10:15

GLADNESS *joy*

celebrate...with g   Neh 12:27
g...for the Jews   Esth 8:17
Serve the LORD with g   Ps 100:2
g and sincerity of   Acts 2:46
With the oil of g   Heb 1:9

GLASS *crystal*

or g cannot equal   Job 28:17
sea of g like crystal   Rev 4:6

GLEAM *brilliance*

awesome g of crystal   Ezek 1:22
g of a Tarshish stone   Ezek 10:9
g of polished bronze   Dan 10:6

GLEAN *gather, pick*

Nor shall you g   Lev 19:10
Do not go to g   Ruth 2:8
she g-ed in the field   Ruth 2:17
they g the vineyard   Job 24:6
g-ing ears of grain   Is 17:5

GLOOM *darkness*

cloud and thick g   Deut 4:11
The land of utter g   Job 10:22
darkness and g and   Heb 12:18
and your joy to g   James 4:9

GLORIFY *honor, worship*

g Thy name forever   Ps 86:12
Let the LORD be g-ied   Is 66:5
g your Father   Matt 5:16

105

shepherds...**g**-ing   Luke 2:20
Jesus...not yet **g-ied**   John 7:39
Father, g Thy name   John 12:28
God is **g-ied** in Him   John 13:31
were all **g**-ing God   Acts 4:21
Gentiles to g God   Rom 15:9
g God in your body   1 Cor 6:20
did not g Himself   Heb 5:5

GLORIOUS *exalted, great*

g name be blessed   Neh 9:5
G things are spoken   Ps 87:3
resting place will be g   Is 11:10
the law great and g   Is 42:21
g gospel of...God   1 Tim 1:11

GLORY (n) *honor, splendor*

show me Thy g   Ex 33:18
while My g is passing   Ex 33:22
Tell of His g   1 Chr 16:24
King of g may come   Ps 24:7
exchanged their g   Ps 106:20
earth is full of His g   Is 6:3
their g into shame   Hos 4:7
Solomon in all his g   Matt 6:29
g of the Lord shone   Luke 2:9
G...in the highest   Luke 2:14
He comes in His g   Luke 9:26
do not seek My g   John 8:50
short of the g of God   Rom 3:23
all to the g of God   1 Cor 10:31
eternal weight of g   2 Cor 4:17
body of His g   Phil 3:21
crowned Him with g   Heb 2:7
unfading crown of g   1 Pet 5:4

GLORY (v) *exalt*

and g in thy praise   1 Chr 16:35
G in His holy name   Ps 105:3
in Him they will g   Jer 4:2
I...have cause to g   Phil 2:16

GLUTTON *excessive eater*

g...come to poverty   Prov 23:21
a companion of **g-s**   Prov 28:7
evil beasts, lazy **g-s**   Titus 1:12

GNASH *grind*

They **g**-ed at me   Ps 35:16
He will g his teeth   Ps 112:10
They hiss and g   Lam 2:16
g-ing their teeth   Acts 7:54

GNAT *insect*

dust...became **g-s**   Ex 8:17
swarm of flies...**g-s**   Ps 105:31
strain out a g and   Matt 23:24

GO *move, proceed*

Let My people g   Ex 7:16
God who **g**-es before   Deut 1:30
where you g, I will g   Ruth 1:16
the way he should g   Prov 22:6
g one mile, g...two   Matt 5:41
G into all...world   Mark 16:15
I g to prepare a   John 14:2
night is almost **gone**   Rom 13:12

GOADS *inducements*

wise men are like g   Eccl 12:11
kick against the g   Acts 26:14

GOAL *end, object*

press on toward the g   Phil 3:14
g...is love   1 Tim 1:5

GOAT *animal*

curtains of **g-s'** hair   Ex 26:7
g for a sin offering   Num 15:27
quilt of **g-s'** hair   1 Sam 19:13
g *had* a...horn   Dan 8:5
shaggy g *represents*   Dan 8:21
sheep from the **g-s**   Matt 25:32
blood of **g-s**...bulls   Heb 9:13

GOD *Deity, Eternal One*

In the beginning G   Gen 1:1
G formed man of dust   Gen 2:7
G sent him out   Gen 3:23
G gave to Abraham   Gen 28:4
tablets were G-'s work   Ex 32:16
G is my...fortress   2 Sam 22:33
G of my salvation   Ps 18:46
In G...I put my trust   Ps 56:4
Search me, O G   Ps 139:23
word of G is tested   Prov 30:5
servant of the living G   Dan 6:20
I am G and not man   Hos 11:9
Will a man rob G   Mal 3:8
G descending...dove   Matt 3:16
they shall see G   Matt 5:8
What...G has joined   Matt 19:6
kingdom of G is at   Mark 1:15
My G, why hast   Mark 15:34
You the Son of G   Luke 22:70
the Word was G   John 1:1

No man has seen G John 1:18
the Lamb of G John 1:29
G so loved the world John 3:16
G is spirit John 4:24
voice of...Son of G John 5:25
obey G rather than Acts 5:29
judgment of G Rom 2:2
bear fruit for G Rom 7:4
we are children of G Rom 8:16
are a temple of G 1 Cor 3:16
full armor of G Eph 6:11
one G...one mediator 1 Tim 2:5
is inspired by G 2 Tim 3:16
word of G is...sharper Heb 4:12
impossible...G to lie Heb 6:18
G is love 1 John 4:8
great supper of G Rev 19:17

GODDESS *female deity*

Ashtoreth the g of 1 Kin 11:5
great g Artemis Acts 19:27
blasphemers of...g Acts 19:37

GODLESS *pagan, without God*

hope of the g will Job 8:13
joy of...g momentary Job 20:5
g man destroys his Prov 11:9
hands of g men Acts 2:23
become the of the g 1 Pet 4:18

GODLINESS *holiness*

in all g and dignity 1 Tim 2:2
the mystery of g 1 Tim 3:16
g is profitable 1 Tim 4:8
to a form of g 2 Tim 3:5
g, brotherly kindness 2 Pet 1:7

GODLY *holy*

keeps...His g ones 1 Sam 2:9
g man ceases to be Ps 12:1
not forsake His g ones Ps 37:28
and g sincerity 2 Cor 1:12
to live g in Christ 2 Tim 3:12
rescue the g from 2 Pet 2:9

GOD(S) *false deity, idols*

no other g-s before Me Ex 20:3
New g-s were chosen Judg 5:8
cast their g-s into Is 37:19
bowed...to other g-s Jer 22:9
no other g who is Dan 3:29
The voice of a g Acts 12:22

g-s...become like Acts 14:11
the g of this world 2 Cor 4:4

GOD, SON OF *see*
SON OF GOD

GOG

1 *a Reubenite* 1 Chr 5:4
2 *prince of Meshech and Tubal*
Ezek 38:2
3 *symbol of godless nations*
Rev 20:8

see also **MAGOG**

GOLAN

city of refuge Josh 21:27
a Levitical city 1 Chr 6:71

GOLD *precious metal*

g of that land is good Gen 2;12
mercy seat of pure g Ex 25:17
Almighty...be your g .Job 22:25
more desirable than g Ps 19:10
refine them like g Mal 3:3
to Him gifts of g Matt 2:11
Do not acquire g Matt 10:9
Divine Nature...g Acts 17:29
coveted no...g Acts 20:33
city was pure g Rev 21:18

GOLDSMITH *gold craftsman*

g-s and...merchants Neh 3:32
g, and he makes it Is 46:6

GOLGOTHA

hill of Crucifixion Matt 27:33
Mark 15:22; John 19:17

GOLIATH

Philistine giant 1 Sam 17:4,23
1 Sam 21:9; 1 Chr 20:5

GOMER

1 *son of Japheth* Gen 10:2
2 *peoples* Ezek 38:6
3 *wife of Hosea* Hos 1:3

GOMORRAH

city of Jordan plain Gen 10:19
Gen 14:10;19:24
probably S of Dead Sea
Is 13:19; 2 Pet 2:6

GOOD

GOOD complete, right

God saw that it was g   Gen 1:18
knowledge of g and   Gen 2:9
Proclaim g tidings   1 Chr 16:23
Do not withhold g   Prov 3:27
joyful heart is g   Prov 17:22
planted in g soil   Ezek 17:8
feed in...g pasture   Ezek 34:18
Seek g and not evil   Amos 5:14
how to give g gifts   Matt 7:11
Well done, g and   Matt 25:23
sown on the g soil   Mark 4:20
Salt is g   Mark 9:50
No one is g except   Luke 18:19
I am the g shepherd   John 10:11
men of g reputation   Acts 6:3
perseverance in...g   Rom 2:7
nothing g...in me   Rom 7:18
work together for g   Rom 8:28
overcome evil...g   Rom 12:21
is of g repute   Phil 4:8
g hope by grace   2 Thess 2:16
Fight the g fight   1 Tim 6:12
tasted the g word   Heb 6:5

GOODNESS excellence, value

My g pass before you   Ex 33:19
Surely g...will follow   Ps 23:6
How great is Thy g   Ps 31:19
kindness, g   Gal 5:22
every desire for g   2 Thess 1:11

GOODS possessions, supplies

the g for yourself   Gen 14:21
have acquired...g   Ezek 38:12

GORE stab

if an ox g-s a man   Ex 21:28
g the Arameans   1 Kin 22:11

GOSHEN

1 district of Egypt   Gen 45:10
   in Nile Delta   Gen 47:6,27
2 S Judah region   Josh 10:41
3 town in Judah   Josh 15:51

GOSPEL good news

proclaiming the g of   Matt 4:23
preach the g to all   Mark 16:15
not ashamed of the g   Rom 1:16
if our g is veiled   2 Cor 4:3
or a different g   2 Cor 11:4
distort the g of Christ   Gal 1:7

g of your salvation   Eph 1:13
g of peace   Eph 6:15
defense of the g   Phil 1:16
the hope of the g   Col 1:23
eternal g to preach   Rev 14:6

GOSSIP babbler

associate with a g   Prov 20:19
malice; they are g-s   Rom 1:29
g-s and busybodies   1 Tim 5:13

GOVERN rule

light to g the day   Gen 1:16
light to g the night   Gen 1:16
when the judges g-ed   Ruth 1:1

GOVERNMENT authority, rule

g...on His shoulders   Is 9:6
be no end to...His g   Is 9:7

GOVERNOR ruler

not offer it to your g   Mal 1:8
brought before g-s   Matt 10:18
g was quite amazed   Matt 27:14
Pilate was g of Judea   Luke 3:1
g over Egypt   Acts 7:10

GRACE benevolence, favor

G is poured upon Thy   Ps 45:2
g to the afflicted   Prov 3:34
g of God was upon   Luke 2:40
full of g and truth   John 1:14
g abounded...more   Rom 5:20
g of our Lord Jesus   Rom 16:20
My g is sufficient   2 Cor 12:9
by g you have been   Eph 2:8
justified by His g   Titus 3:7
to the throne of g   Heb 4:16
g to the humble   James 4:6

GRACIOUS kind

God be g to you   Gen 43:29
g to whom I will be   Ex 33:19
a g and...God   Neh 9:31
Be g to me, O LORD   Ps 6:2
and g, Slow to anger   Ps 86:15
g to a poor man   Prov 19:17
be g to...remnant   Amos 5:15

GRAFT insert, join

I might be g-ed in   Rom 11:19
God is able to g   Rom 11:23
g-ed into their own   Rom 11:24

GRAIN

Joseph stored up g	Gen 41:49
glean among the...g	Ruth 2:2
g...for your enemies	Is 62:8
then the mature g	Mark 4:28
g of wheat falls	John 12:24

GRAIN OFFERING see
OFFERINGS

GRANDCHILDREN

G are the crown of	Prov 17:6
widow has...or g	1 Tim 5:4

GRANDDAUGHTER

g-s, and all his	Gen 46:7
g of Omri king of	2 Kin 8:26

GRANDSON

g might fear the LORD	Deut 6:2
sons and thirty g-s	Judg 12:14
master's g shall eat	2 Sam 9:10

GRANT give, provide

g this people favor	Ex 3:21
hast g-ed me life	Job 10:12
g us Thy salvation	Ps 85:7
G that we may sit	Mark 10:37
He g-ed sight to	Luke 7:21
Father has g-ed Me	Luke 22:29
g repentance to	Acts 5:31
g-ing...deliverance	Acts 7:25

GRAPE fruit

nor eat...dried g-s	Num 6:3
of g-s you drank	Deut 32:14
when the g harvest is	Is 24:13
G-s are not gathered	Matt 7:16
g-s from a briar	Luke 6:44

GRASP hold, seize

hands g the spindle	Prov 31:19
He who g-s the bow	Amos 2:15
a thing to be g-ed	Phil 2:6

GRASS vegetation

g springs out	2 Sam 23:4
his days are like g	Ps 103:15
dry g collapses into	Is 5:24
g withers, the flower	Is 40:7
was given g to eat	Dan 5:21
if God so arrays...g	Matt 6:30

All flesh is like g	1 Pet 1:24
not hurt the g	Rev 9:4

GRASSHOPPER insect

the g in its kinds	Lev 11:22
we became like g-s	Num 13:33
inhabitants are like g-s	Is 40:22

GRATITUDE thankfulness

overflowing with g	Col 2:7
is received with g	1 Tim 4:4
let us show g	Heb 12:28

GRAVE sepulchre, tomb

pillar of Rachel's g	Gen 35:20
throat is an open g	Ps 5:9
I will open your g-s	Ezek 37:12
I will prepare your g	Nah 1:14
made the g secure	Matt 27:66

GRAVEN sculptured

make...a g image	Deut 4:23
ashamed who serve g	Ps 97:7
praise to g images	Is 42:8

GRAY color

g hair...in sorrow	Gen 42:38
with the man of g	Deut 32:25
Both the g-haired	Job 15:10
when I am old and g	Ps 71:18
g head is a crown	Prov 16:31

GRAZE feed

cattle...g-ing in	1 Chr 27:29
wolf...shall g	Is 65:25
he will g on Carmel	Jer 50:19

GREAT big, excellent, grand

made...two g lights	Gen 1:16
make you a g nation	Gen 12:2
lovingkindness is g	Ps 57:10
your iniquity is g	Jer 30:15
g day of the LORD	Zeph 1:14
rejoiced...with g joy	Matt 2:10
woman...faith is g	Matt 15:28
good news of a g joy	Luke 2:10
reward is g in	Luke 6:23
because of His g love	Eph 2:4
so g a salvation	Heb 2:3
we have a g...priest	Heb 4:14
so g a cloud of	Heb 12:1
g supper of God	Rev 19:17
a g white throne	Rev 20:11

GREATEST *most important*

who is the g among   Luke 22:26
g of these is love   1 Cor 13:13
least to the g   Heb 8:11

GREATNESS *magnitude*

Thine...is the g   1 Chr 29:11
g...lovingkindness   Neh 13:22
g of Thy compassion   Ps 51:1
the g of His strength   Is 63:1
amazed at the g of   Luke 9:43
surpassing g of His   Eph 1:19

GREECE

country in SE Europe   Dan 8:21
Dan 10:20;11:2; Zech 9:13
Acts 20:2

GREED *excessive desire*

caught by *their*...g   Prov 11:6
every form of g   Luke 12:15
wickedness, g, evil   Rom 1:29
a pretext for g   1 Thess 2:5
a heart trained in g   2 Pet 2:14

GREEDY *craving*

had g desires   Num 11:4
g man curses   Ps 10:3
Everyone is g for   Jer 6:13

GREEKS

people of Greece
Joel 3:6; Acts 16:1,3
Rom 1:16; 1 Cor 12:13

GREEN *fertile, fruitful*

every g plant for   Gen 1:30
lie down in g pastures   Ps 23:2
dry up the g tree   Ezek 17:24
nor any g thing   Rev 9:4

GREET *hail, welcome*

g no one on the way   Luke 10:4
G one another with   1 Pet 5:14

GRIEF *heartache, sorrow*

weeps because of g   Ps 119:28
foolish son is a g   Prov 17:25
acquainted with g   Is 53:3
our g-s He Himself   Is 53:4
joy and not with g   Heb 13:17

GRIEVE *distress, sorrow*

was g-d in his heart   Gen 6:6

Do not be g-d   Neh 8:10
g-d Him in the desert   Ps 78:40
g-d His Holy Spirit   Is 63:10
g-d at their hardness   Mark 3:5
Peter was g-d   John 21:17
not g the Holy Spirit   Eph 4:30

GRIND *crush, press*

my wife g for another   Job 31:10
g-ing...the poor   Is 3:15
millstones and g meal   Is 47:2
women...*be* g-ing   Matt 24:41
and g-s his teeth   Mark 9:18

GROAN *cry, moan*

From the city men g   Job 24:12
man rules, people g   Prov 29:2
wounded will g   Jer 51:52
whole creation g-s   Rom 8:22

GROANING *crying*

God heard their g   Ex 2:24
O Lord, Consider my g   Ps 5:1
g of the prisoner   Ps 79:11
g-s of a wounded   Ezek 30:24
g-s too deep for   Rom 8:26

GROPE *move about blindly*

you shall g at noon   Deut 28:29
They g in darkness   Job 12:25
g like...blind men   Is 59:10
g for Him and find   Acts 17:27

GROUND *earth, land, soil*

man of dust from...g   Gen 2:7
Cursed is the g   Gen 3:17
crossed on dry g   Josh 3:17
a spirit from the g   Is 29:4
talent in the g   Matt 25:25
finger wrote on the g   John 8:6
standing is holy g   Acts 7:33
g that drinks the rain   Heb 6:7

GROUNDED *established*

hope...is firmly g   2 Cor 1:7
rooted and g in love   Eph 3:17

GROW *develop, increase*

Moses had g-n up   Ex 2:11
You are g-n fat   Deut 32:15
my spirit g-s faint   Ps 77:3
youths g weary   Is 40:30
sun and moon g dark   Joel 3:15

lilies of the field g   Matt 6:28
love will g cold   Matt 24:12
Child continued to g   Luke 2:40
grew strong in faith   Rom 4:20
as your faith g-s   2 Cor 10:15
not g weary of   2 Thess 3:13
g in the grace   2 Pet 3:18

GROWTH *increase*

new g is seen   Prov 27:25
God who causes the g   1 Cor 3:7

GRUDGE *hostile feeling*

Esau bore a g   Gen 27:41
nor bear any g   Lev 19:18
Herodias had a g   Mark 6:19

GRUMBLE *complain*

they g-d against Moses   Ex 17:3
the congregation g   Num 14:36
g-d in their tents   Ps 106:25
scribes **began** to g   Luke 15:2
g among yourselves   John 6:43

GRUMBLING *complaint*

for He hears your g-s   Ex 16:7
g-s against Me   Num 17:10
Do all...without g   Phil 2:14

GUARD (n) *keeper*

dost set a g over me   Job 7:12
be a g for them   Ezek 38:7
g-s shook for fear   Matt 28:4
Him away under g   Mark 14:44

GUARD (v) *keep watch*

g the way to the tree   Gen 3:24
g-ed the threshold   2 Kin 12:9
G-ing...justice   Prov 2:8
Discretion will g you   Prov 2:11
soldier...was g-ing   Acts 28:16
shall g your hearts   Phil 4:7
g...from idols   1 John 5:21

GUARDHOUSE *prison*

the court of the g   Jer 37:21
the court of the g   Jer 38:28

GUARDIAN *overseer*

g-s of *the* children   2 Kin 10:1
under g-s and   Gal 4:2
G of your souls   1 Pet 2:25

GUEST *visitor*

Herod and his...g-s   Mark 6:22
Where...My g room   Mark 14:14
to the invited g-s   Luke 14:7
g of a...sinner   Luke 19:7

GUIDANCE *counsel*

no g, the people fall   Prov 11:14
make war by wise g   Prov 20:18

GUIDE (n) *advisor, director*

The righteous is a g   Prov 12:26
Woe to...blind g-s   Matt 23:16
You blind g-s, who   Matt 23:24
are a g to the blind   Rom 2:19

GUIDE (v) *direct, lead*

LORD alone g-d him   Deut 32:12
He g-s me in the paths   Ps 23:3
g us until death   Ps 48:14
my mind was g-ing *me*   Eccl 2:3
blind...g-s a blind   Matt 15:14
g you into...truth   John 16:13
unless someone g-s   Acts 8:31

GUILE *deceit*

in whom is no g   John 1:47
all malice and all g   1 Pet 2:1
lips from speaking g   1 Pet 3:10

GUILT *offence*

be free from g   Num 5:31
according to his g   Deut 25:2
charge me with a g   2 Sam 3:8
our g has grown   Ezra 9:6
land is full of g   Jer 51:5
must bear their g   Hos 10:2
I find no g in Him   John 18:38

GUILT OFFERING *see*
    OFFERINGS

GUILTY *charged* or *condemned*

he sins and becomes g   Lev 6:4
murderer...g of   Num 35:31
as one who is g   2 Sam 14:13
g by the blood   Ezek 22:4
g of an eternal sin   Mark 3:29
has become g of all   James 2:10

GUSHED *burst, flowed*

so that waters g out   Ps 78:20

111

the rock...water g   Is 48:21
all his bowels g out   Acts 1:18

H

HABAKKUK

prophet   Hab 1:1;3:1

HABITATION *abode, dwelling*

from Thy holy h   Deut 26:15
a rock of h   Ps 71:3
h-s of violence   Ps 74:20
live in a peaceful h   Is 32:18
holy and glorious h   Is 63:15
laid waste his h   Jer 10:25
a h of shepherds   Jer 33:12

HABOR

river in Mesopotamia
   2 Kin 17:6;18:11; 1 Chr 5:26

HADAD

1 *son of Ishmael*   Gen 25:25
   1 Chr 1:30
2 *son of Bedad*   Gen 36:35,36
   1 Chr 1:46,47
3 *a king of Edom*   Gen 36:39
4 *king of Edom*   1 Chr 1:50,51
5 *Edomite prince*   1 Kin 11:14ff

HADASSAH

Esther's Hebrew name   Esth 2:7

HADES *hell, place of dead*

shall descend to H   Matt 11:23
in H he lifted up   Luke 16:23
abandoned to H   Rev 1:18

HAGAR

Sarah's handmaiden   Gen 16:1
Abraham's slave wife   Gen 16:3
mother of Ishmael   Gen 16:15

HAGGAI

prophet   Ezra 5:1; Hag 1:1

HAGGITH

David's wife   2 Sam 3:4
mother of Adonijah   1 Kin 1:11

HAIL (n) *pieces of ice*

rained h on the land   Ex 9:23

storehouses of the h   Job 38:22
gave them h for rain   Ps 105:32
plague of the h   Rev 16:21

HAIL (v) *greeting*

H, Rabbi   Matt 26:49
H, King of...Jews   Matt 27:29

HAILSTONES *pieces of ice*

who died from the h   Josh 10:11
H and coals of fire   Ps 18:13
you, O h, will fall   Ezek 13:11
h...one hundred   Rev 16:21

HAIR

gray h...to Sheol   Gen 42:38
locks of his h and   Judg 16:14
h...bristled   Job 4:15
h...like pure wool   Dan 7:9
garment of camel's h   Matt 3:4
make one h white   Matt 5:36
h-s...all numbered   Matt 10:30
His feet with her h   John 11:2
not with braided h   1 Tim 2:9

HALL *corridor*

h of pillars   1 Kin 7:6
h of judgment   1 Kin 7:7
wedding h has   Matt 22:10

HALLELUJAH *praise Yahweh*

H! Salvation and   Rev 19:1
H! Her smoke rises   Rev 19:3
Amen. H   Rev 19:4
H! For the Lord our   Rev 19:6

HALLOWED *consecrated, holy*

H be Thy name   Matt 6:9

HAM

1 *son of Noah*   Gen 5:32;9:18
2 *city*   Gen 14:5
3 *poetic name for Egypt*
   Ps 105:27;106:22

HAMAN

Persian prime minister
son of Hammedatha   Esth 3:1

HAMATH

city in Aram   2 Kin 28:33;25:21

HAMMER *mallet, tool*

and seized a h   Judg 4:21
neither h nor axe   1 Kin 6:7
smash with...h-s   Ps 74:6
like a h which   Jer 23:29

HAMON-GOG

*valley where army of Gog
is defeated*   Ezek 39:11,15

HANANIAH

1 *son of Zerubbabel* 1 Chr 3:19
2 *son of Shishak*   1 Chr 8:24
3 *musician*   1 Chr 25:4,23
4 *in Uzziah's army* 2 Chr 26:11
5 *repaired wall*   Neh 3:30
6 *overseer of palace* Neh 7:2
7 *false prophet*   Jer 28:15
8 *Shadrach*   Dan 1:6,7
name of six other individuals

HAND *part of body*

cover you with My h   Ex 33:22
for tooth, h for h   Deut 19:21
sling was in his h   1 Sam 17:40
They pierced my h-s   Ps 22:16
buries his h   Prov 19:24
the hollow of His h   Is 40:12
clay in the potter's h Jer 18:6
not let your left h   Matt 6:3
laying His h-s upon   Mark 10:16
the right h of God   Mark 16:19
into the h-s of men   Luke 9:44
into Thy h-s I   Luke 23:46
reach here your h   John 20:27
not made with h-s   2 Cor 5:1
lifting up holy h-s   1 Tim 2:8
h-s of...God   Heb 10:31

HANDMAID *servant, slave*

save the son of Thy h Ps 86:16
the son of Thy h   Ps 116:16
her h-s are moaning   Nah 2:7

HANDSOME *attractive*

a choice and h *man* 1 Sam 9:2
ruddy, with a h   1 Sam 17:42

HANG *attach, suspend*

h you on a tree   Gen 40:19
h up the veil   Ex 40:8
h-ed is accursed of   Deut 21:23

h-ing in an oak   2 Sam 18:10
they h-ed Haman   Esth 7:10
he...h-ed himself   Matt 27:5
millstone were **hung** Luke 17:2
h-ing Him on a cross Acts 5:30
who h-s on a tree   Gal 3:13

HANNAH

mother of Samuel   1 Sam 2:21

HAPPINESS *joy*

give h to his wife   Deut 24:5
eat your bread in h   Eccl 9:7
I have forgotten h   Lam 3:17

HAPPY *blessed, joyful*

Leah said, **H** am I Gen 30:13
h...man whom God   Job 5:17
h...who keeps the   Prov 29:18

HARAN

1 *brother of Abraham* Gen 11:27
father of Lot   Gen 11:31
2 *Mesopotamian city* Gen 11:32
                      Gen 27:43
3 *Gershonite Levite* 1 Chr 23:9

HARD *difficult, firm*

bitter with h labor   Ex 1:14
case that is too h   Deut 1:17
made our yoke h   2 Chr 10:4
Water becomes h   Job 38:30
h for a rich man   Matt 19:23
h it is to enter   Mark 10:24
worked h all night   Luke 5:5

HARDEN *make hard, callous*

h Pharaoh's heart   Ex 7:3
dust h-s into a mass Job 38:38
who h-s *his* neck   Prov 29:1
h-s whom He   Rom 9:18
minds were h-ed   2 Cor 3:14
Do not h your hearts Heb 3:15

HARDNESS *callousness*

give them h of heart Lam 3:65
Because of your h   Matt 19:8
grieved at their h   Mark 3:5
unbelief and h of   Mark 16:14

HARDSHIP *difficulty*

H after h is with me Job 10:17
people experience h   Ps 60:3
afflictions, in h-s   2 Cor 6:4

our labor and h   1 Thess 2:9
Suffer h with *me*   2 Tim 2:3

HAREM *royal wives' quarters*

best place in the h   Esth 2:9
the court of the h   Esth 2:11
from the h to the   Esth 2:13
to the second h   Esth 2:14

HARLOT *prostitute*

thought she *was* a h   Gen 38:15
the hire of a h   Deut 23:18
h whose name was   Josh 2:1
Dressed as a h   Prov 7:10
city has become a h   Is 1:21
also played the h   Ezek 16:26
Traded a boy for a h   Joel 3:3
to a h is one body   1 Cor 6:16
Mother of H-s   Rev 17:5

HARLOTRY *prostitution*

with child by h   Gen 38:24
profaned by h   Lev 21:7
uncovered her h-ies Ezek 23:18
children of h   Hos 1:2
spirit of h   Hos 5:4

HARM (n) *evil, hurt*

pillar to me, for h   Gen 31:52
h to this people   Ex 5:22
keep *me* from h   1 Chr 4:10
Do not devise h   Prov 3:29
great h to yourselves   Jer 44:7
the fire without h   Dan 3:25
did me much h   2 Tim 4:14

HARM (v) *damage, hurt*

David seeks to h   1 Sam 24:9
planning to h me   Neh 6:2
have not h-ed me   Dan 6:22
in order to h you   Acts 18:10
is there to h you   1 Pet 3:13

HAR-MAGEDON

hill of Megiddo   Rev 16:16
see also **MEGIDDO**

HARMONY *agreement*

what h has Christ   2 Cor 6:15
live in h in the   Phil 4:2

HARP *musical instrument*

my h is turned to   Job 30:31

praises...with a h   Ps 33:2
Awake, h and lyre   Ps 57:8
gaiety of the h ceases   Is 24:8
having each one a h   Rev 5:8
holding h-s of God   Rev 15:2

HARSH *difficult, hard*

man was h and evil   1 Sam 25:3
h word stirs up anger Prov 15:1
A h vision   Is 21:2
under h servitude   Lam 3:1

HARVEST *reap and gather*

Seedtime and h   Gen 8:22
fruits of the wheat h   Ex 34:22
you reap your h   Deut 24:19
he who sleeps in h   Prov 10:5
snow...time of h   Prov 25:13
like rain in h   Prov 26:1
the gladness of h   Is 9:3
time of h will come   Jer 51:33
Lord of the h   Matt 9:38
h is the end of the   Matt 13:39
fields...white for h   John 4:35
h of the earth is   Rev 14:15

HARVEST, FEAST OF
see **FEASTS**

HASHUM

1 family of exiles   Ezra 2:19
2 was with Ezra   Neh 8:4

HASTEN *accelerate*

h-ed after deceit   Job 31:5
H to me, O God   Ps 70:5
they h to shed blood Prov 1:16
bird h-s to the snare Prov 7:23
eye h-s after wealth Prov 28:22
h-ing...day of God   2 Pet 3:12

HATE *despise, loathe*

you h discipline   Ps 50:17
who h the LORD   Ps 81:15
I h every false way Ps 119:104
fools h knowledge   Prov 1:22
spares his rod h-s   Prov 13:24
a time to h   Eccl 3:8
H evil, love good   Amos 5:15
For I h divorce   Mal 2:16
good to those who h Luke 6:27
you will be h-d   Luke 21:17

he who **h-s** his life   John 12:25
the very thing I **h**   Rom 7:15
Esau I **h-d**   Rom 9:13
h-ing one another   Titus 3:3
yet **h-s** his brother   1 John 2:9

HATERS *those who hate*

slanderers, **h** of God   Rom 1:30
brutal, **h** of good   2 Tim 3:3

HATRED *hate, ill will*

h for my love   Ps 109:5
H stirs up strife   Prov 10:12
who conceals **h** *has*   Prov 10:18

HAUGHTY *proud*

nor my eyes **h**   Ps 131:1
H eyes, a lying   Prov 6:17
h spirit before   Prov 16:18
Proud, **H,** Scoffer   Prov 21:24
wine betrays the **h**   Hab 2:5
do not be **h** in mind   Rom 12:16

HAVEN *harbor, shelter*

be a **h** for ships   Gen 49:13
to their desired **h**   Ps 107:30

HAVILAH

1 *region encompassed by one of
    Eden's rivers*   Gen 2:11
2 *area in W Arabia*   Gen 25:18
3 *second son of Cush*   Gen 10:7
4 *son of Joktan*   Gen 10:29
                             1 Chr 1:23

HAWK *bird*

sea gull, and the **h**   Deut 14:15
h-s shall be gathered   Is 34:15

HAZAEL

anointed by Elijah   1 Kin 19:15
killed Ben Hadad   2 Kin 8:15
Aramaic king   2 Kin 8:15;9:14
defeated Israel   2 Kin 10:32

HAZOR

1 *Canaanite city in N Palestine*
                             Josh 11:11
2 *town of the Negev*   Josh 15:23
3 *Benjamite city*   Neh 11:33
4 *desert kingdom*   Jer 49:33

HEAD *chief or part of body*

bruise you on the **h**   Gen 3:15

anointed my **h** with oil   Ps 23:5
h a garland of grace   Prov 4:9
gray **h** is a crown   Prov 16:31
coals on his **h**   Prov 25:22
h was made bald   Ezek 29:18
had four **h-s**   Dan 7:6
an oath by your **h**   Matt 5:36
nowhere to lay His **h**   Matt 8:20
h of John the Baptist   Matt 14:8
not a hair of your **h**   Luke 21:18
crown...on His **h**   John 19:2
God is the **h** of   1 Cor 11:3
husband is the **h**   Eph 5:23

HEADLONG *headfirst*

He rushes **h** at Him   Job 15:26
falling **h**, he burst   Acts 1:18
h into the error   Jude 11

HEAL *make well, restore*

will **h** their land   2 Chr 7:14
h-s the brokenhearted   Ps 147:3
a time to **h**   Eccl 3:3
H me, O LORD   Jer 17:14
will **h** their apostasy   Hos 14:4
h-ed all who were   Matt 8:16
H *the* sick, raise   Matt 10:8
h him on...Sabbath   Mark 3:2
Physician, **h** yourself   Luke 4:23
you may be **h-ed**   James 5:16
fatal wound was **h-ed**   Rev 13:3

HEALING *health, wholeness*

be **h** to your body   Prov 3:8
h to the bones   Prov 16:24
sorrow is beyond **h**   Jer 8:18
There is no **h** for   Jer 46:11
their leaves for **h**   Ezek 47:12
h every kind of   Matt 4:23
gifts of **h**   1 Cor 12:9
h of the nations   Rev 22:2

HEALTH *soundness, wholeness*

no **h** in my bones   Ps 38:3
restore you to **h**   Jer 30:17
and be in good **h**   3 John 2

HEAP (n) *mound, pile*

stones and made a **h**   Gen 31:46
waters stood...like a **h**   Ex 15:8
made a refuse **h**   Ezra 6:11
needy from the ash **h**   Ps 113:7

Jerusalem a **h** of ruins   Jer 9:11
altars are...**h-s**   Hos 12:11

HEAP (v) *pile up, place*

h misfortunes on   Deut 32:23
will **h** burning coals   Prov 25:22
H on the wood   Ezek 24:10
h up rubble to   Hab 1:10

HEAR *listen*

h-d the sound of   Gen 3:10
God **h-d** their groaning   Ex 2:24
H, O Israel   Deut 6:4
h the wisdom of   1 Kin 4:34
h Thou in heaven   1 Kin 8:30
Will God **h** his cry   Job 27:9
who dost **h** prayer   Ps 65:2
h Thy lovingkindness   Ps 143:8
poor **h-s** no rebuke   Prov 13:8
deaf shall **h** words   Is 29:18
bones, **h** the word   Ezek 37:4
ears to **h**, let him **h**   Matt 11:5
h of wars and   Mark 13:7
he who **h-s** My word   John 5:24
does not **h** sinners   John 9:31
sheep **h** My voice   John 10:27
we **h-d** of your faith   Col 1:4
anyone **h-s** My voice   Rev 3:20

HEARING *listening*

in the LORD's **h**   1 Sam 8:21
in the **h** of a fool   Prov 23:9
fulfilled in your **h**   Luke 4:21
I will give you a **h**   Acts 23:35
become dull of **h**   Heb 5:11

HEART *mind or seat of emotions*

intent of man's **h** is   Gen 8:21
I will harden his **h**   Ex 4:21
great searchings of **h**   Judg 5:16
LORD looks at the **h**   1 Sam 16:7
fool has said in his **h**   Ps 14:1
meditation of my **h**   Ps 19:14
My **h** is like wax   Ps 22:14
in me a clean **h**   Ps 51:10
and a contrite **h**   Ps 51:17
Thy word...in my **h**   Ps 119:11
Deceit is in the **h**   Prov 12:20
A joyful **h** is good   Prov 17:22
to a troubled **h**   Prov 25:20
bribe corrupts the **h**   Eccl 7:7
a new **h** and a new   Ezek 18:31

uncircumcised in **h**   Ezek 44:7
are the pure in **h**   Matt 5:8
adultery...in his **h**   Matt 5:28
and humble in **h**   Matt 11:29
h is far...from Me   Matt 15:8
pondering...in her **h**   Luke 2:19
pierced to the **h**   Acts 2:37
cleansing their **h-s**   Acts 15:9
who searches the **h-s**   Rom 8:27
tablets of human **h-s**   2 Cor 3:3
not lose **h** in doing   Gal 6:9
melody with your **h**   Eph 5:19
intentions of the **h**   Heb 4:12
deceives his *own* **h**   James 1:26

HEAT *hotness, warmth*

the **h** of the day   Gen 18:1
and **h** consume   Job 24:19
hidden from its **h**   Ps 19:6
a shade from the **h**   Is 25:4
burning **h** of famine   Lam 5:10
scorching **h** of the   Matt 20:12
with intense **h**   2 Pet 3:10
scorched with fierce **h**   Rev 16:9

HEAVE OFFERING
see **OFFERINGS**

HEAVEN *place of God or sky*

God created the **h-s**   Gen 1:1
rain bread from **h**   Ex 16:4
shut up the **h-s**   Deut 11:17
thunder in the **h-s**   1 Sam 2:10
fire came...from **h**   2 Kin 1:14
make windows in **h**   2 Kin 7:2
walks...vault of **h**   Job 22:14
I consider Thy **h-s**   Ps 8:3
h and earth praise   Ps 69:34
fixed patterns of **h**   Jer 33:25
lights in the **h-s**   Ezek 32:8
open...windows of **h**   Mal 3:10
kingdom of **h** is at   Matt 3:2
voice out of the **h-s**   Matt 3:17
reward in **h** is great   Matt 5:12
Father who art in **h**   Matt 6:9
shall be loosed in **h**   Matt 16:19
great signs from **h**   Luke 21:11
Him go into **h**   Acts 1:11
no...name under **h**   Acts 4:12
up to the third **h**   2 Cor 12:2
citizenship is in **h**   Phil 3:20
new **h** and a new   Rev 12:1

there was war in h Rev 12:7

HEAVENLY *related to God*

h Father is perfect Matt 5:48
h Father knows that Matt 6:32
h host praising God Luke 2:13
I tell you h things John 3:12
Him in the h *places* Eph 2:6
partakers of a h Heb 3:1
shadow of the h Heb 8:5

HEAVY *burdensome, hard to lift*

Moses' hands were h Ex 17:12
servitude was h on Neh 5:18
h drinkers of wine Prov 23:20
A stone is h Prov 27:3
Jerusalem a h stone Zech 12:3
eyes were very h Mark 14:40

HEBER

1 *son of Beriah* Gen 46:17
2 *husband of Jael* Judg 4:17
3 *son of Mered* 1 Chr 4:18
4 *son of Elpaal* 1 Chr 8:17
 see also **EBER**

HEBREW(S)

1 *people* Gen 14:13; Ex 1:15
 Ex 9:13; Jon 1:9
2 *language* John 19:17
 Acts 22:2;26:14
 see also **JUDEAN**
 see also **CANAAN**

HEBRON

1 *Judean town* Josh 11:21
 site of Sarah's death Gen 23:2
 visited by spies Num 13:22
 destroyed Josh 10:36
 city of refuge Josh 20:7
 residence of David 2 Sam 2:1
2 *son of Kohath* Ex 6:18
3 *son of Mareshah* 1 Chr 2:42

HEDGE *border or protection*

Thou not made a h Job 1:10
as a h of thorns Prov 15:19
along the h-s, and Luke 14:23

HEEL *back of foot*

bruise him on the h Gen 3:15
on to Esau's h Gen 25:26
his h against Me John 13:18

HEIFER *young cow*

unblemished red h Num 19:2
plowed with my h Judg 14:18
Egypt is a pretty h Jer 46:20
Like a stubborn h Hos 4:16

HEIGHT *elevation, heaven, sky*

in the h of heaven Job 22:12
from His holy h Ps 102:19
Praise Him in the h-s Ps 148:1
As the heavens for h Prov 25:3
ascend above the h-s Is 14:14
nor h, nor depth Rom 8:39

HEIR *person who inherits*

in my house is my h Gen 15:3
has he no h-s Jer 49:1
h-s also, h-s of God Rom 8:17
an h through God Gal 4:7
h-s of the kingdom James 2:5

HELIOPOLIS

ancient Egyptian city Jer 43:13
also **On**

HELL *place of dead*

go into the fiery h Matt 5:22
soul and body in h Matt 10:28
to be cast into h Mark 9:47
set on fire by h James 3:6
cast them into h 2 Pet 2:4
see also **HADES** and **SHEOL**

HELLENISTIC JEWS

Greek speaking Jews Acts 6:1
 Acts 9:29

HELMET *headpiece*

bronze h on his 1 Sam 17:5
h of salvation Is 59:17
take the h of Eph 6:17

HELP (n) *assistance, relief*

h is not within me Job 6:13
He is our h and our Ps 33:20
present h in trouble Ps 46:1
I cried for h Jon 2:2
gifts of...h-s 1 Cor 12:28

HELP (v) *aid, assist*

h-ing the Hebrew Ex 1:16
the LORD h-ed David 2 Sam 8:6
whence shall my h Ps 121:1
I will h you Is 41:13

Lord, **h** me | Matt 15:25
h my unbelief | Mark 9:24
must **h** the weak | Acts 20:35
Spirit also **h-s** our | Rom 8:26
earth **h-ed** the | Rev 12:16

HELPER *one who assists*

h of the orphan | Ps 10:14
O LORD, be Thou my **h** | Ps 30:10
Behold, God is my **h** | Ps 54:4
give you another **H** | John 14:16
H, the Holy Spirit | John 14:26

HELPLESS *weak*

the **h** has hope | Job 5:16
who considers the **h** | Ps 41:1
while we were still **h** | Rom 5:6

HEMAN

1 *sage of Solomon* | 1 Kin 4:31
2 *line of Samuel* | 1 Chr 15:19

HEMORRHAGE *bleeding*

suffering from a **h** | Matt 9:20
a **h** for twelve years | Mark 5:25
her **h** stopped | Luke 8:44

HEN *fowl*

h gathers her | Matt 23:27
as a **h** *gathers* her | Luke 13:34

HEPHZIBAH

Manasseh's mother | 2 Kin 21:1
Hezekiah's wife | 2 Kin 21:3

HERB *dried plant*

bread and bitter **h-s** | Ex 12:8
fade like the green **h** | Ps 37:2
h-s of...mountains | Prov 27:25
sweet-scented **h-s** | Song 5:13

HERD *cattle, flock*

first-born of your **h** | Deut 12:6
h, or flock taste a | Jon 3:7
h of many swine | Matt 8:30

HERDSMEN *keepers of flocks*

h of Abram's livestock | Gen 13:7
between my **h** and | Gen 13:8
the **h** ran away | Matt 8:33

HERITAGE *what is inherited*

the **h** decreed to him | Job 20:29
my **h** is beautiful | Ps 16:6
their land as a **h** | Ps 136:21

inherit the desolate **h-s** | Is 49:8
you who pillage My **h** | Jer 50:11

HERMES

1 *Greek god* | Acts 14:12
2 *Roman Christian* | Rom 16:14

HERMOGENES

*Asian Christian who failed
to support Paul* | 2 Tim 1:15

HERMON

mountain region in N Palestine
Josh 11:17; Ps 42:6;133:3
N boundary of Promised Land
Deut 3:8

HEROD

1 **Herod the Great**
king of Palestine | Matt 2:1
ruled during Jesus' birth
Matt 2:1ff
2 **Herod Archelaus**
son of Herod the Great
Matt 2:22
3 **Herod Antipas**
son of Herod the Great
Matt 14:1
tetrarch of Galilee | Luke 3:1
ruled at time of Jesus' ministry
Luke 13:31;23:7,8,11
executed John the Baptist
Matt 14:10; Mark 6:27
4 **Herod Philip I**
son of Herod the Great
Mark 6:17
brother of Herod Antipas
5 **Herod Philip II**
son of Herod the Great
Luke 3:1
6 **Herod Agrippa I**
grandson of Herod the Great
Acts 12:1
ruler of Judea and Samaria
persecuted the early church
Acts 12:2-23
7 **Herod Agrippa II**
son of Agrippa I | Acts 25:13
tetrarch of N Palestine
heard Paul's testimony
Acts 25:23ff;26:1ff

HERODIANS

influential Jews favoring Herod
Matt 22:16; Mark 3:6

HERODIAS

wife of Herod Antipas
          Matt 14:3; Mark 6:17
requested head of John the
   Baptist Matt 14:8; Mark 6:24

HETH

Hebrew eponym for Hittites
          Gen 10:15;23:10

HEW *chop, cut*

h down their Asherim Deut 7:5
h-n cisterns, vineyards Neh 9:25
h-n out in the rock Mark 15:46

HEZEKIAH

king of Judah	2 Kin 18:1
reformer	2 Kin 18:4
warrior	2 Kin 18:7,8
builder	2 Kin 20:20

HIDE *conceal, cover*

man and his wife **hid** Gen 3:8
I h from Abraham Gen 18:17
Moses **hid** his face Ex 3:6
h me in Sheol Job 14:13
h-ing my iniquity Job 31:33
H me in the shadow Ps 17:8
Do not h Thy face Ps 27:9
wrongs are not **h-den** Ps 69:5
sees evil *and* **h-s** Prov 27:12
hid your talent Matt 25:25
nothing is **h-den** Mark 4:22
Jesus **hid** himself John 8:59
h us from...Him Rev 6:16

HIDDEN (adj) *concealed*

Acquit me of h *faults* Ps 19:12
h wealth of secret Is 45:3
h snares for my feet Jer 18:22
profound and h Dan 2:22
some of the h manna Rev 2:17

HIDING PLACE

Clouds are a h Job 22:14
He lurks in a h Ps 10:9
Thou art my h Ps 32:7
uncovered his **h-s** Jer 49:10

HIEROPOLIS

city in Asia Minor Col 4:13

HIGH *elevated* or *heavenly*

it is still h day Gen 29:7

the h places of Baal Num 22:41
h above all nations Deut 26:19
h as the heavens Job 11:8
my advocate is on h Job 16:19
set him *securely* on h Ps 91:14
or h as heaven Is 7:11
to a very h mountain Matt 4:8
the h priest Matt 26:57
Son of the Most H Mark 5:7
from a h fever Luke 4:38
He ascended on h Eph 4:8

HIGH PLACE

worship place of God or idols
    Num 22:41; 1 Sam 9:12-14

HIGH PRIEST

first in hierarchy Ex 27:21
under Aaron Ex 28:1,2
enters Holy of Holies
    Ex 28:29,30; Heb 9:7
head of Sanhedrin
    Matt 26:57; Acts 5:21
Jesus as High Priest Heb 3:1
    Heb 5:5-9

HIGHWAY *road*

along the king's h Num 20:17
h from Egypt to Is 19:23
the H of Holiness Is 35:8
a h for our God Is 40:3
Go out into the **h-s** Luke 14:23

HILKIAH

1 *father of Eliakim* 2 Kin 18:18
2 *high priest* 2 Kin 22:4-14
3 *Merarite Levite* 1 Chr 6:45
4 *son of Hosah* 1 Chr 26:11
5 *was with Ezra* Neh 8:4
6 *returned from exile* Neh 12:7

HILL *mountain*

the everlasting **h-s** Gen 49:26
the h of God 1 Sam 10:5
dwell on Thy holy h Ps 15:1
to Thy holy h Ps 43:3
cattle...thousand **h-s** Ps 50:10
h-s, Fall on us Hos 10:8
city set on a h Matt 5:14
h...brought low Luke 3:5
the brow of the h Luke 4:29
h-s, Cover us Luke 23:30

HINDER *delay, impede, restrain*

h meditation before   Job 15:4
do not h them   Matt 19:14
do not h them   Luke 18:16
h-ed you from obeying Gal 5:7
prayers...not be **h-ed** 1 Pet 3:7

HINNOM

1 *valley SW of Jerusalem*
    Josh 15:8; Neh 11:30
2 *person for whom valley
    named* 2 Kin 23:10; Jer 7:31

HIP *part of body*

the sinew of the h   Gen 32:32
curves of your h-s are Song 7:1
h joints went slack   Dan 5:6

HIRAM/HURAM

1 *king of Tyre*   1 Kin 5:1ff
    2 Chr 2:3,11
2 *skilled craftsman*   1 Kin 7:14
    2 Chr 4:11

HIRE (n) *wages*

it came for its h   Ex 22:15
the h of a harlot   Deut 23:18

HIRE (v) *engage for labor*

h...for bread   1 Sam 2:5
and h the Arameans 2 Sam 10:6
to h...chariots   1 Chr 19:6
he who h-s a fool   Prov 26:10
to h laborers for   Matt 20:1

HIRED (adj) *employed*

as a h man, as if   Lev 25:40
oppress a h servant Deut 24:14
as one of your h   Luke 15:19

HIRELING *employee*

h...not a shepherd   John 10:12
because he is a h   John 10:13

HISS *to show dislike*

h him from his place Job 27:23
*object of...*h-ing   Jer 18:16
They h and shake   Lam 2:15
h *And* wave his hand Zeph 2:15

HITTITES

1 *people in Palestine in
    patriarchal age*   Gen 15:20
    Gen 49:29

2 *inhabitants of Aram during
    Israelite monarchy* 2 Kin 7:6
    2 Chr 8:7

HIVITES

*people dispossessed by
    the Israelites*   Ex 23:28
    Josh 3:10; 2 Sam 24:7

HOGLAH

daughter of Zelophehad
    Num 26:33;27:1; Josh 17:3

HOLD *grasp, retain*

Moses **held** his hand Ex 17:11
h fast to Him   Deut 11:22
h fast...evil purpose   Ps 64:5
heart h fast my words Prov 4:4
Take h of instruction Prov 4:13
h fast My covenant   Is 56:4
h to one and despise Matt 6:24
h to the tradition   Mark 7:8
h fast the word   1 Cor 15:2
h-ing to the mystery 1 Tim 3:9
h of the eternal   1 Tim 6:12
He **held** seven stars   Rev 1:16

HOLE *opening*

the h of the cobra   Is 11:8
a h in the wall   Ezek 8:7
a purse with h-s   Hag 1:6
foxes have h-s   Matt 8:20

HOLIDAY *period of leisure*

a feast and a h   Esth 8:17
a h for rejoicing   Esth 9:19
mourning into a h   Esth 9:22

HOLINESS *sacredness*

majestic in h   Ex 15:11
H befits Thy house   Ps 93:5
the Highway of H   Is 35:8
unblamable in h   1 Thess 3:13
we may share His h Heb 12:10

HOLLOW *empty space*

the h of a sling   1 Sam 25:29
in the h of His hand   Is 40:12

HOLY *sacred, sanctified*

standing is h ground   Ex 3:5
sabbath...keep it h   Ex 20:8
you are a h people   Deut 7:6
ten thousand h ones Deut 33:2

h like the LORD   1 Sam 2:2
Worship...h array   1 Chr 16:29
His h dwelling   2 Chr 30:27
Jerusalem, the h city   Neh 11:1
Zion, My h mountain   Ps 2:6
to His h land   Ps 78:54
bless His h name   Ps 145:21
H, H, H, is the LORD   Is 6:3
the H One of Israel   Is 30:15
what is h to dogs   Matt 7:6
righteous and h man   Mark 6:20
the H One of God   Luke 4:34
in the h Scriptures   Rom 1:2
and h sacrifice   Rom 12:1
with a h kiss   Rom 16:16
h both in body   1 Cor 7:34
lifting up h hands   1 Tim 2:8
with a h calling   2 Tim 1:9
I saw the h city   Rev 21:2

HOLY OF HOLIES

*most holy place in the
Tabernacle/Temple*
      Ex 26:33,34; 2 Chr 3:8

HOLY SPIRIT

Third Person of the Godhead
      Matt 28:19; 2 Cor 13:14
Helper   John 14:16,26
Giver of gifts   Rom 12:6-8
            1 Cor 12:8-11
fruit of the Spirit   Gal 5:22

HOMAGE *act of reverence*

my people shall do h   Gen 41:40
did h to the LORD   1 Chr 29:20
and paid h to Haman   Esth 3:2
did h to Daniel   Dan 2:46

HOME *place of dwelling*

free at h one year   Deut 24:5
God makes a h   Ps 68:6
man is not at h   Prov 7:19
to his eternal h   Eccl 12:5
Go h to your people   Mark 5:19
let him eat at h   1 Cor 11:34
at h in the body   2 Cor 5:6
at h with the Lord   2 Cor 5:8

HOMER *measure of capacity*

a h of barley   Lev 27:16
a h of seed   Is 5:10

from a h of wheat   Ezek 45:13

HOMESTEAD *family dwelling*

h forlorn and forsaken Is 27:10
guards his own h   Luke 11:21
h be made desolate   Acts 1:20

HOMOSEXUALS

effeminate, nor h   1 Cor 6:9
immoral men and h   1 Tim 1:10

HONEST *respectable, truthful*

we are h men   Gen 42:11
painful are h words   Job 6:25
an h and good heart   Luke 8:15

HONEY *sweetness*

with milk and h   Ex 3:8
swarm of bees and h Judg 14:8
is sweeter than h   Judg 14:18
sweet as h in my   Ezek 3:3
locusts and wild h   Matt 3:4

HONEYCOMB *honey storage*

drippings of the h   Ps 19:10
Pleasant words...a h Prov 16:24

HONOR (n) *glory, great respect*

both riches and h   1 Kin 3:13
stripped my h from   Job 19:9
wise will inherit h   Prov 3:35
is not without h   Matt 13:57
glory and h and   Rom 2:10
marriage *be held* in h Heb 13:4
blessing and h and   Rev 5:13

HONOR (v) *show respect*

H your father   Ex 20:12
h the aged   Lev 19:32
who h Me I will h   1 Sam 2:30
am h-ed in the sight   Is 49:5
A son h-s *his* father   Mal 1:6
may be h-ed by men   Matt 6:2
h-s Me with...lips   Matt 15:8
does not h the Son   John 5:23
fear God, h the king   1 Pet 2:17

HONORABLE *respectable*

the elder and h man   Is 9:15
one vessel for h use   Rom 9:21
whatever is h   Phil 4:8

HOOF

HOOF *part of animal foot*

which divide the h	Lev 11:4
with horns and h-s	Ps 69:31
h-s of beasts shall	Ezek 32:13
tear off their h-s	Zech 11:16

HOOK *fastener*

into pruning h-s	Is 2:4
My h in your nose	Is 37:29
h-s into your jaws	Ezek 38:4

HOPE (n) *expectation*

Where now is my h	Job 17:15
h of the afflicted	Ps 9:18
My h is in Thee	Ps 39:7
Thou art my h	Ps 71:5
while there is h	Prov 19:18
the h of Israel	Jer 17:13
our h has perished	Ezek 37:11
on trial for the h	Acts 23:6
h does not disappoint	Rom 5:5
rejoicing in h	Rom 12:12
may the God of h	Rom 15:13
ought to plow in h	1 Cor 9:10
now abide faith, h	1 Cor 13:13
h of righteousness	Gal 5:5
the h of His calling	Eph 1:18
the h of the gospel	Col 1:23
the h of glory	Col 1:27
the h of salvation	1 Thess 5:8
h of eternal life	Titus 3:7
to a living h	1 Pet 1:3
h that is in you	1 Pet 3:15

HOPE (v) *expect with confidence*

I will h in Him	Job 13:15
For I h in Thee	Ps 38:15
We h for justice	Is 59:11
are h-ing for light	Jer 13:16
Gentiles will h	Matt 12:21
h-s all things	1 Cor 13:7
first to h in Christ	Eph 1:12
I h in the Lord Jesus	Phil 2:19
of *things* h-d for	Heb 11:1
I h to come to you	2 John 12

HOPHNI

son of Eli   1 Sam 1:3;4:11

HOPHRA *see* **PHARAOH**

HOR

mountain   Num 20:22,23

place of Aaron's death
   Num 20:28; Deut 32:50

HORDE *throng*

against Babylon A h	Jer 50:9
h-s of grasshoppers	Nah 3:17

HOREB

another name for Mount Sinai
   Ex 3:1; Deut 4:10; Ps 106:19

HORITES

inhabitants of Mount Se.
in Edom   Gen 14:6;36:29

HORN

caught...by his h-s	Gen 22:13
h-s of the altar	Ex 29:12
you shall sound a h	Lev 25:9
with the ram's h	Josh 6:5
h of my salvation	2 Sam 22:3
the h, flute, lyre	Dan 3:5
it had ten h-s	Dan 7:7

HORROR *terror*

h overwhelms me	Is 21:4
object of h	Jer 49:13
clothed with h	Ezek 7:27
cup of h	Ezek 23:33

HORSE *animal*

bites the h-'s heels	Gen 49:17
h-s and chariots of	2 Kin 6:17
A h is a false hope	Ps 33:17
whip is for the h	Prov 26:3
slaves *riding* on h-s	Eccl 10:7
behold, a black h	Rev 6:5

HORSE GATE *see*
   GATES OF JERUSALEM

HORSEMEN *cavalry, horse rider*

Pharaoh, his h and	Ex 14:9
chariots and h	1 Kin 10:26
h riding on	Ezek 23:12
H charging, Swords	Nah 3:3
armies of the h	Rev 9:16

HOSANNA *acclamation of praise*

H to the Son of	Matt 21:9
H in the highest	Mark 11:10
H! Blessed is He	John 12:13

HOSEA

prophet   Hos 1:1,2

HOSHEA

1 *name of Joshua* Num 13:8,16
2 *king of Israel* 2 Kin 15:30
                 2 Kin 17:6
3 *Ephraim's officer* 1 Chr 27:20
4 *signer of covenant* Neh 10:23

HOSPITABLE *friendly*

h, able to teach 1 Tim 3:2
h, loving what is Titus 1:8
h to one another 1 Pet 4:9

HOSPITALITY *open to guests*

practicing h Rom 12:13
show h to strangers Heb 13:2

HOST *army, multitude*

all the h of heaven Deut 4:19
captain...LORD's h Josh 5:15
LORD of h-s, He is Ps 24:10
of the heavenly h Luke 2:13

HOSTILE *antagonistic*

h to...Jesus Acts 26:9
set on the flesh is h Rom 8:7
h to all men 1 Thess 2:15

HOT *very warm, violent*

when the sun grew h Ex 16:21
and h displeasure Deut 9:19
My heart was h within Ps 39:3
man walk on h coals Prov 6:28
neither cold nor h Rev 3:15

HOUR *time*

healed that *very* h Matt 8:13
watch...for one h Matt 26:40
the h is at hand Matt 26:45
ninth h Jesus cried Mark 15:34
save Me from this h John 12:27
the h has come John 17:1
the h of testing Rev 3:10

HOUSE *home or temple*

born in my h is my Gen 15:3
passed over the h-s Ex 12:27
the h of slavery Ex 20:2
consecrates his h Lev 27:14
as for me and my h Josh 24:15
Set your h in order 2 Kin 20:1
h of God forsaken Neh 13:11
h like the spider's Job 27:18
Holiness befits Thy h Ps 93:5

LORD builds the h Ps 127:1
Wisdom...built her h Prov 9:1
in My h of prayer Is 56:7
O h of Israel Jer 18:6
his h upon the rock Matt 7:24
My h...a h of Matt 21:13
devour widow's h-s Mark 12:40
left h or wife or Luke 18:29
In My Father's h John 14:2
h not made...hands 2 Cor 5:1
h for a holy 1 Pet 2:5

HOUSE OF GOD/LORD
  see **TEMPLE**

HOUSE OF THE LORD
  see **TABERNACLE**

HOUSEHOLD *family, home*

herds and a great h Gen 26:14
stole the h idols Gen 31:19
each one with his h Ex 1:1
to the ways of her h Prov 31:27
like a head of a h Matt 13:52
area of God's h Eph 2:19
manages his own h 1 Tim 3:4
in the h of God 1 Tim 3:15

HOUSETOP *roof*

As grass on the h-s 2 Kin 19:26
lonely bird on a h Ps 102:7
upon the h-s Matt 10:27
Peter went...the h Acts 10:9

HULDAH
a Hebrew prophetess
  2 Kin 22:14; 2 Chr 34:22

HUMAN *mankind, person*

the life of any h Lev 24:17
guilt of h blood Prov 28:17
they had h form Ezek 1:5
tablets of h hearts 2 Cor 3:3

HUMBLE (adj) *gentle, modest*

Moses was very h Num 12:3
h will inherit Ps 37:11
with the h is wisdom Prov 11:2
H, and mounted on Zech 9:9
gentle and h in Matt 11:29
along with h means Phil 4:12
grace to the h James 4:6

HUMBLE (v) *modest*

refuse to h yourself	Ex 10:3
He might h you	Deut 8:2
h...and pray	2 Chr 7:14
h-s...as this child	Matt 18:4
H yourselves	1 Pet 5:6

HUMILIATE *embarrass*

h-d who seek my hurt	Ps 71:24
Neither feel h-d	Is 54:4
His opponents...h-d	Luke 13:17

HUMILIATION *embarrassment*

h has overwhelmed me	Ps 44:15
go away together in h	Is 45:16
let our h cover us	Jer 3:25
In h His judgment	Acts 8:33

HUMILITY *self-abasement*

before honor...h	Prov 15:33
with h of mind	Phil 2:3
clothe...with h	1 Pet 5:5

HUNDRED *number or many*

Adam had lived one h	Gen 5:3
h of you will chase	Lev 26:8
captains of h-s	Num 31:14
h pieces of money	Josh 24:32
went out by h-s	2 Sam 18:14
in companies of h-s	Mark 6:40

HUNGER (n) *craving, starvation*

in h, in thirst	Deut 28:48
lions...suffer h	Ps 34:10
man will suffer h	Prov 19:15
h is not satisfied	Is 29:8
faint because of h	Lam 2:19
sleeplessness, in h	2 Cor 6:5

HUNGER (v) *crave, need food*

the righteous to h	Prov 10:3
are those who h	Matt 5:6
to Me shall not h	John 6:35
They shall h no more	Rev 7:16

HUNGRY *empty, needing food*

let you be h	Deut 8:3
people are h and	2 Sam 17:29
h soul He has filled	Ps 107:9
If your enemy is h	Prov 25:21
when a h man dreams	Is 29:8
He then became h	Matt 4:2
disciples became h	Matt 12:1
For I was h	Matt 25:35

HUNT *pursue, seek*

to h for game	Gen 27:5
h-s a partridge	1 Sam 26:20
evil h the violent	Ps 140:11
H-ed me down like	Lam 3:52
companions h-ed for	Mark 1:36

HUNTER *seeker of game*

Nimrod a mighty h	Gen 10:9
became a skillful h	Gen 25:27

HUR

1 *helped Moses and Aaron*	
	Ex 17:12;24:14
2 *Bezalel's grandfather*	Ex 31:2
3 *king of Midian*	Num 31:8
4 *father of Rephaiah*	Neh 3:9

HURAM

a Benjamite	1 Chr 8:5
see also **HIRAM/HURAM**	

HURT (n) *damage, harm, wound*

Who delight in my h	Ps 70:2
hoarded...to his h	Eccl 5:13
your brother is h	Rom 14:15

HURT (v) *cause pain, wound*

not allow him to h	Gen 31:7
may be.h by them	Eccl 10:9
will not h or destroy	Is 11:9
their power to h men	Rev 9:10

HUSBAND *family head, spouse*

desire...your h	Gen 3:16
honor to their h-s	Esth 1:20
crown of her h	Prov 12:4
is loved by her h	Hos 3:1
divorces her h and	Mark 10:12
have had five h-s	John 4:18
if her h dies	Rom 7:2
have her own h	1 Cor 7:2
unbelieving h is	1 Cor 7:14
h is the head of	Eph 5:23
H-s, love your wives	Eph 5:25
h-s of...one wife	1 Tim 3:12
adorned for her h	Rev 21:2

HUSHAI

servant of David	2 Sam 15:32
	2 Sam 16:17

HYMENAEUS
heretical teacher at Ephesus
1 Tim 1:20; 2 Tim 2:17

HYMN *song of praise*
h-s of thanksgiving Neh 12:46
after singing a h Matt 26:30
singing h-s of praise Acts 16:25
psalms and h-s and Eph 5:19

HYPOCRISY *pretense*
full of h and Matt 23:28
love be without h Rom 12:9
without h James 3:17

HYPOCRITE *a pretender*
as the h-s do Matt 6:2
and Pharisees, h-s Matt 23:13
You h, first take Luke 6:42

HYSSOP *fragrant plant*
bunch of h and dip it Ex 12:22
scarlet string and h Lev 14:4
Purify me with h Ps 51:7
upon *a branch of* h John 19:29

I

I AM
related to name of God
in Hebrew
I WHO I Ex 3:14
I has sent me Ex 3:14
I the LORD Ex 6:2
I the LORD your God Lev 19:3
I the first Is 44:6
I the Son of God Matt 27:43
Jesus said, I Mark 14:62
believe that I *He* John 8:24
will know that I *He* John 8:28
before Abraham...I John 8:58
believe that I *He* John 13:19
I the Alpha and Rev 1:8
I the first and Rev 1:17

ICE *frost*
turbid because of i Job 6:16
womb has come...i Job 38:29
casts forth His i Ps 147:17

ICHABOD
1 son of Phinehas 1 Sam 4:19,20
grandson of Eli 1 Sam 14:3
2 name commemorates
departed glory from Israel
1 Sam 4:21,22

ICONIUM
city of Asia Minor Acts 14:1,19
Acts 16:2; 2 Tim 3:11

IDLE *unemployed, uninvolved*
i man will suffer Prov 19:15
been standing here i Matt 20:6
this i babbler Acts 17:18

IDOL *false deity, image*
not make...an i Ex 20:4
Do not turn to i-s Lev 19:4
who makes an i or Deut 27:15
the gods...are i-s Ps 96:5
who blesses an i Is 66:3
abstain from...i-s Acts 15:20
guard...from i-s 1 John 5:21

IDOLATOR *idol worshiper*
covetous, or an i 1 Cor 5:11
do not be i-s 1 Cor 10:7
sorcerers and i Rev 21:8

IDOLATRY *idol worship*
flee from i 1 Cor 10:14
i, sorcery, enmities Gal 5:20
and abominable i-ies 1 Pet 4:3

IGNORANCE *lack of knowledge*
you worship in i Acts 17:23
i that is in them Eph 4:18
silence the i of 1 Pet 2:15

IGNORANT *without knowledge*
I was senseless and i Ps 73:22
not i of his schemes 2 Cor 2:11
and i speculations 2 Tim 2:23

ILL *unhealthy, sick*
woman who is i Lev 15:33
became mortally i Is 38:1
lunatic, and is...i Matt 17:15
healed many...i Mark 1:34

ILLEGITIMATE

ILLEGITIMATE *bastard*

No one of i birth	Deut 23:2
borne i children	Hos 5:7
you are i children	Heb 12:8

ILLNESS *infirmity, sickness*

sick with the i	2 Kin 13:14
after his i and	Is 38:9
because of a bodily i	Gal 4:13

ILLUMINE *light up*

God i-s my darkness	Ps 18:28
fire to i by night	Ps 105:39
glory of God has i-d	Rev 21:23
God shall i them	Rev 22:5

IMAGE *copy, likeness*

make man in Our i	Gen 1:26
i of God He made	Gen 9:6
burn their graven i-s	Deut 7:5
worshiped a molten i	Ps 106:19
made an i of gold	Dan 3:1
i and glory of God	1 Cor 11:7
i of the invisible	Col 1:15
the i of the beast	Rev 13:15

IMITATORS *followers*

be i of me	1 Cor 4:16
be i of God	Eph 5:1
i of the churches	1 Thess 2:14

IMMANUEL

1 son born to a virgin	Is 7:14
a sign to King Ahaz	Is 8:8
2 title of Jesus	Matt 1:23

IMMORAL *lewd, unchaste*

with i people	1 Cor 5:9
the i man sins	1 Cor 6:18
i men...liars	1 Tim 1:10
i or godless person	Heb 12:16
and i persons	Rev 21:8

IMMORALITY *immoral acts*

no i in your midst	Lev 20:14
except for i	Matt 19:9
Flee i	1 Cor 6:18
abstain from...i	1 Thess 4:3
the wine of her i	Rev 17:2

IMMORTALITY *everlasting life*

must put on i	1 Cor 15:53
alone possesses i	1 Tim 6:16
life and i to light	2 Tim 1:10

IMPATIENT *restless*

the people became i	Num 21:4
should I not be i	Job 21:4
my soul was i with	Zech 11:8

IMPERISHABLE *indestructable*

wreath, but we an i	1 Cor 9:25
will be raised i	1 Cor 15:52
inheritance...is i	1 Pet 1:4

IMPLEMENTS *tools, utensils*

| forger of all i of | Gen 4:22 |
| the i of the oxen | 1 Kin 19:21 |

IMPLORE *ask, beseech*

I i you, give glory	Josh 7:19
i-d him to avert	Esth 8:3
i the compassion of	Job 8:5
I i You by God	Mark 5:7

IMPORTED *brought in*

| chariot was i from | 1 Kin 10:29 |
| horses were i | 2 Chr 1:16 |

IMPOSE *force upon*

i-d hard labor on us	Deut 26:6
whatever you i on	2 Kin 18:14
you i heavy rent	Amos 5:11
i-d until a time of	Heb 9:10

IMPOSSIBLE *cannot be done*

nothing...will be i	Gen 11:6
With men this is i	Matt 19:26
i for God to lie	Heb 6:18
without faith it is i	Heb 11:6

IMPRISON *jail, restrict*

i-ed him at Riblah	2 Kin 23:33
i his princes at will	Ps 105:22
not i their survivors	Obad 14
I used to i and beat	Acts 22:19

IMPRISONMENT *confinement*

in i-s, in tumults	2 Cor 6:5
Remember my i	Col 4:18
even to i as a	2 Tim 2:9

IMPURE *unclean*

her i discharge	Lev 15:25
eating...with i hands	Mark 7:2
no immoral or i person	Eph 5:5

IMPURITY uncleanness

menstrual i for seven Lev 15:19
i-ies of the sons of Lev 16:19
the i of the nations Ezra 6:21
as slaves to i Rom 6:19
of i with greediness Eph 4:19

INCENSE fragrant substance

burn fragrant i on Ex 30:7
i as an offering Lev 2:16
gold pans, full of i Num 7:86
My altar, to burn i 1 Sam 2:28
i on the high places 2 Kin 14:4
i before the LORD 1 Chr 23:13
golden altar of i Heb 9:4
the smoke of the i Rev 8:4

INCEST illicit sexual relations

they...committed i Lev 20:12

INCITE stir up

i-d David against 2 Sam 24:1
Jezebel...i-d him 1 Kin 21:25
I will i Egyptians Is 19:2
who i-s the people Luke 23:14

INCLINE bend, lean

i your hearts to Josh 24:23
I my heart to Thy Ps 119:36
i-s toward wickedness Is 32:6
I Thine ear, O LORD Is 37:17
have not i-d your ear Jer 35:15

INCOME wages

i of the wicked Prov 10:16
i with injustice Prov 16:8
abundance with its Eccl 5:10

INCORRUPTIBLE not impure

glory of the i God Rom 1:23
Christ with a love i Eph 6:24

INCREASE (n) multiplication

the i of your herd Deut 7:13
the i of your house 1 Sam 2:33
the LORD give you i Ps 115:14
i of His government Is 9:7

INCREASE (v) multiply

If riches i, do not Ps 62:10
the righteous i Prov 28:28
i-ing in wisdom Luke 2:52

INCURABLE fatal, without cure

i-ing in...knowledge Col 1:10
Lord cause...to i 1 Thess 3:12

INCURABLE fatal, without cure

with an i sickness 2 Chr 21:18
sickliness and i pain Is 17:11
Your wound is i Jer 30:12

INDIA

lower Indus valley in
S Asia Esth 1:1;8:9

INDIGNANT be angry

i toward His enemies Is 66:14
the ten became i Matt 20:24
Jesus...was i Mark 10:14
i because Jesus had Luke 13:14

INDIGNATION anger

God who has i Ps 7:11
Pour out Thine i Ps 69:24
lips are filled with i Is 30:27
didst fill me with i Jer 15:17
stand before His i Nah 1:6

INDWELLS inhabits

but sin which i me Rom 7:17
His Spirit who i you Rom 8:11

INFANT child

carries a nursing i Num 11:12
an i who lives Is 65:20
tongue of the i Lam 4:4
the mouth of i-s Matt 21:16

INFECTION disease

an i of leprosy Lev 13:2
with the scaly i Lev 13:31
against an i of Deut 24:8

INFERIOR lower in status

I am not i to you Job 12:3
i against the honorable Is 3:5
i to...apostles 2 Cor 12:11

INFINITE unlimited

His understanding is i Ps 147:5

INFLICT strike, impose

frogs...He had i-ed Ex 8:12
i all these curses Deut 30:7
i-s pain, and gives Job 5:18
i-ed many blows Acts 16:23

INGATHERING, FEAST OF
see FEASTS

INHABIT *dwell*

no one would i	Job 15:28
She shall be i-ed	Is 44:26
build houses and i	Is 65:22
those i-ing the desert	Jer 9:26
who i the coastlands	Ezek 39:6
but not i *them*	Zeph 1:13

INHABITANT *resident*

i-s of the cities	Gen 19:25
cities...without i	Is 6:11
ruins Without i	Jer 4:7
i-s of the seacoast	Zeph 2:5
i-s of Jerusalem	Zech 12:10

INHERIT *receive a legacy*

shall i *it* forever	Ex 32:13
humble will i the land	Ps 37:11
wise will i honor	Prov 3:35
The naive i folly	Prov 14:18
gentle...i the earth	Matt 5:5
do to i eternal life	Luke 10:25
not i the kingdom	1 Cor 6:9
might i a blessing	1 Pet 3:9
who overcomes shall i	Rev 21:7

INHERITANCE *bequest, legacy*

Levites for an i	Num 18:24
the LORD is his i	Deut 10:9
the nations as Thine i	Ps 2:8
will He forsake His i	Ps 94:14
man leaves an i	Prov 13:22
I...abandoned My i	Jer 12:7
Thine i a reproach	Joel 2:17
A man and his i	Mic 2:2
the i will be ours	Mark 12:7
we...obtained an i	Eph 1:11
the i of the saints	Col 1:12
i...imperishable	1 Pet 1:4

INIQUITY *injustice, wickedness*

bear...their i-ies	Lev 16:22
the i of the fathers	Deut 5:9
those who plow i	Job 4:8
O LORD, Pardon my i	Ps 25:11
my i I did not hide	Ps 32:5
blot out all my i-ies	Ps 51:9
sows i will reap	Prov 22:8
weighed down with i	Is 1:4

the workers of i	Is 31:2
die for his own i	Jer 31:30
Repent...so that i	Ezek 18:30
the bondage of i	Acts 8:23
the *very* world of i	James 3:6
remembered her i-ies	Rev 18:5

INJUNCTION *decree*

establish the i	Dan 6:8
that no i or statute	Dan 6:15

INJURE *harm, wrong*

who seek to i me	Ps 38:12
i-d your neighbors	Ezek 22:12
nothing shall i you	Luke 10:19
do you i one another	Acts 7:26

INJURY *wound*

there is no *further* i	Ex 21:22
because of my i	Jer 10:19
no i...was found	Dan 6:23

INJUSTICE *inequity, unfairness*

do no i in judgment	Lev 19:15
A God...without i	Deut 32:4
there i on my tongue	Job 6:30
They devise i-s	Ps 64:6
is no i with God	Rom 9:14

INK *writing liquid*

I wrote them with i	Jer 36:18
with pen and i	3 John 13

INN *lodge for travelers*

no room...in the i	Luke 2:7
brought him to...i	Luke 10:34

INNKEEPER *traveler's host*

gave them to the i	Luke 10:35

INNOCENCE *blamelessness*

wash my hands in i	Ps 26:6
be incapable of i	Hos 8:5

INNOCENT *blameless*

do not kill the i	Ex 23:7
the blood of the i	Deut 19:13
i before the LORD	2 Sam 3:28
the i mock them	Job 22:19
that shed i blood	Prov 6:17
and i as doves	Matt 10:16
betraying i blood	Matt 27:4
i of this Man's	Matt 27:24
holy, i, undefiled	Heb 7:26

INQUIRE *ask, seek*

to i of the LORD	Gen 25:22
I of God, please	Judg 18:5
David i-d of...LORD	1 Sam 23:2
you come to i of Me	Ezek 20:3
i...where the Christ	Matt 2:4
i-d of them the hour	John 4:52

INSANE *mad*

a demon and is i	John 10:20
I speak as if i	2 Cor 11:23

INSCRIBE *carve, write*

were i-d in a book	Job 19:23
i it on a scroll	Is 30:8
and i a city on it	Ezek 4:1
i *it* on tablets	Hab 2:2

INSCRIPTION *writing*

could not read the i	Dan 5:8
I will engrave an i	Zech 3:9
Pilate wrote an i	John 19:19
i, To An Unknown	Acts 17:23

INSECTS

swarms of i on you	Ex 8:21
all other winged i	Lev 11:23

INSIGHT *discernment*

a counselor with i	1 Chr 26:14
according to his i	Prov 12:8
i with understanding	Dan 9:22
not gained any i	Mark 6:52
In all wisdom and i	Eph 1:8

INSIGNIFICANT *unimportant*

was i in Thine eyes	2 Sam 7:19
your beginning was i	Job 8:7
citizen of no i city	Acts 21:39

INSOLENT *arrogant*

acts with i pride	Prov 21:24
haters of God, i	Rom 1:30

INSPECTION GATE *see*
GATES OF JERUSALEM

INSPIRED *stimulated*

the love we i in you	2 Cor 8:7
All Scripture is i	2 Tim 3:16

INSTINCT *natural tendency*

as creatures of i	2 Pet 2:12

they know by i	Jude 10

INSTRUCT *teach*

Thy good Spirit to i	Neh 9:20
I will i you	Ps 32:8
the wise is i-ed	Prov 21:11
i-ed out of the Law	Rom 2:18
just as you were i-ed	Col 2:7
may i certain men	1 Tim 1:3

INSTRUCTION *teaching*

will walk in My i	Ex 16:4
Get wisdom and i	Ps 23:23
Heed i and be wise	Prov 8:33
i-s to His twelve	Matt 11:1
written for our i	Rom 15:4
i of the Lord	Eph 6:4
goal of our i is love	1 Tim 1:5
i about washings	Heb 6:2

INSTRUMENT *object, vessel*

cut...with sharp i-s	1 Chr 20:3
and i-s of music	2 Chr 5:13
with stringed i-s	Ps 150:4
he is a chosen i	Acts 9:15
i-s of unrighteousness	Rom 6:13

INSULT (n) *affront, indignity*

i-s of the nations	Ezek 34:29
casting the same i	Matt 27:44
and cast i-s at you	Luke 6:22
evil, or i for i	1 Pet 3:9

INSULT (v) *treat with scorn*

and do not i her	Ruth 2:15
to i the LORD	2 Chr 32:17
times you have i-ed	Job 19:3
i-ed the Spirit of	Heb 10:29

INTEGRITY *honesty,*

In the i of my heart	Gen 20:5
dealt in truth and i	Judg 9:19
holds fast his i	Job 2:3
He who walks with i	Ps 15:2
have walked in my i	Ps 26:1
The i of the upright	Prov 11:3

INTELLIGENCE *mental ability*

He deprives of i	Job 12:24
gave them...i	Dan 1:17
Paulus, a man of i	Acts 13:7

INTELLIGENT *bright, smart*

was i and beautiful	1 Sam 25:3

mind of the i seeks Prov 15:14
from *the* wise and i Matt 11:25

INTEND *purpose*

Are you i-ing to kill Ex 2:14
I i to build a house 1 Kin 5:5
i to make My people Jer 23:27
i-ing to betray Him John 12:4
i-ing...to take Paul Acts 20:13

INTENTION *aim, goal*

the i-s of the heart 1 Chr 29:18
i of your heart Acts 8:22
kind i of His will Eph 1:5

INTERCEDE *plead, mediate*

i-d for the people Num 21:7
who can i for him 1 Sam 2:25
And i-d for the Is 53:12
do not i with Me Jer 7:16
Spirit Himself i-s Rom 8:26

INTERCOURSE *copulation*

not have i with Lev 18:20
not have i...animal Lev 18:23
husband has had i Num 5:20

INTEREST *concern or usury*

not charge him i Ex 22:25
not take usurious i Lev 25:36
i to a foreigner Deut 23:20
his money at i Ps 15:5
mind on God's i-s Matt 16:23
money...with i Matt 25:27
he has a morbid i 1 Tim 6:4

INTERMARRY

And i with us Gen 34:9
shall not i with Deut 7:3
i with the peoples Ezra 9:14

INTERPRET *explain, translate*

no one who could i Gen 41:8
one who i-s omens Deut 18:10
He i the message Is 28:9
unless he i-s 1 Cor 14:5
pray that he may i 1 Cor 14:13

INTERPRETATION *explain*

i-s belong to God Gen 40:8
the dream and its i Judg 7:15
make its i known Dan 5:16

the i of tongues 1 Cor 12:10
of one's own i 2 Pet 1:20

INTIMATE *close*

my i friends have Job 19:14
i with the upright Prov 3:32
separates i friends Prov 16:28

INVADE *attack*

king of Assyria i-d 2 Kin 17:5
nation had i-d my land Joel 1:6
Assyrian i-s our land Mic 5:5

INVALIDATE *nullify*

i-d the word of God Matt 15:6
i-ing the word of Mark 7:13
does not i a covenant Gal 3:17

INVESTIGATE *examine*

the judges shall i Deut 19:18
the plot was i-d Esth 2:23
i, and to seek wisdom Eccl 7:25
having i-d everything Luke 1:3

INVISIBLE *unseen*

His i attributes Rom 1:20
image of the i God Col 1:15
visible and i Col 1:16
eternal, immortal, i 1 Tim 1:17

INVITE *request*

i-d us to impoverish Judg 14:15
you shall i Jesse 1 Sam 16:3
i-d all the king's 2 Sam 13:23
I am i-d by her Esth 5:12
did not i Me in Matt 25:43
i *the* poor Luke 14:13

IRON *metal*

was an i bedstead Deut 3:11
whose stones are i Deut 8:9
had i chariots Judg 1:19
made the i float 2 Kin 6:6
break them...rod of i Ps 2:9
from the i furnace Jer 11:4
as strong as i Dan 2:40
rule...rod of i Rev 19:15

ISAAC

birth, son of Abraham Gen 21:3
offered for sacrifice Gen 22:2
took Rebekah as wife Gen 24
father of twins Gen 25:26

blessed Jacob   Gen 27:1-40

ISAIAH
prophet of Judah   Is 1:1
son of Amoz   1 Kin 19:2
called   Is 6
under four kings   Is 1:1

ISCARIOT
geographical identity of Judas
     Mark 3:19; John 12:4;13:26

ISH-BOSHETH
son of Saul   2 Sam 2:8;3:8;4:8

ISHMAEL
1 *son of Abraham*   Gen 16:11
     Gen 17:18;25:17
2 *son of Nethaniah*   2 Kin 25:23
3 *line of Jonathan*   1 Chr 8:38
     1 Chr 9:44
4 *Zebadiah's father*   2 Chr 19:11
5 *son of Jehohanan*   2 Chr 23:1
6 *son of Pashhur*   Ezra 10:22

ISLAND *surrounded by water*
the many i-s be glad   Ps 97:1
He lifts up the i-s   Is 40:15
i was called Malta   Acts 28:1
every i fled away   Rev 16:20

ISOLATE *set apart*
priest shall i *him*   Lev 13:4
i *him for seven days* Lev 13:21
fortified city is i-d   Is 27:10

ISRAEL
1 *Jacob*
     Gen 32:22-32;35:10;37:3
2 *line of Jacob*   Gen 34:7
  tribal nation   Ex 1:7;4:22
     Num 10:29
3 *united kingdom* 1 Sam 15:35
     1 Kin 4:1
4 *northern kingdom*1 Kin 14:19
     1 Kin 15:9; 2 Kin 10:29
5 *under Roman rule* Luke 2:32
     John 1:49; Rom 9:6

ISSACHAR
1 *son of Jacob* Gen 30:18;49:14
2 *tribe*   Num 1:29; Josh 21:28
     Rev 7:7
3 *Levite*   1 Chr 26:5

ISSUE (n) *outflow, out go*
first i *of the womb* Num 3:12
offspring and i   Is 22:24
like the i *of horses* Ezek 23:20
concerning this i   Acts 15:2

ISSUE (v) *go forth, put forth*
Moses i-d *a command* Ex 36:6
shall i *from you* 2 Kin 20:18
decree was i-d *in* Esth 3:15
i-d *a proclamation* Dan 5:29

ITALY
S European country Acts 18:2
     Acts 27:1,6; Heb 13:24

ITURAEA
region N of Palestine Luke 3:1
tetrarchy of Philip

IVORY *elephant tusk*
a great throne of i 1 Kin 10:18
silver, i *and apes* 2 Chr 9:21
Out of i *palaces*   Ps 45:8
every article of i   Rev 18:12

J

JABAL
son of Lamech   Gen 4:20
father of herders

JABBOK
tributary of Jordan Gen 32:22
     Num 21:24; Josh 12:2
     Judg 11:13,22

JABESH-GILEAD
town of Gilead   Judg 21:8ff
E of Jordan River 1 Sam 11:1,9
     2 Sam 2:4,5

JACINTH *precious stone*
a j, *an agate*   Ex 28:19
the eleventh, j   Rev 21:20

JACKALS *wild dogs*
j *in their...palaces* Is 13:22
ruins, A haunt of j Jer 9:11
a lament like the j Mic 1:8

JACOB

JACOB

1 *son of Isaac*   Gen 25:26
  brother of Esau   Gen 25:27
  obtained birthright Gen 25:33
  fled to Aram   Gen 28:5,6
  marriage   Gen 29:1ff
  wrestled angel   Gen 32:24ff
  name changed   Gen 35:9,10
  went down to Egypt Gen 46
  death and burial Gen 49:28ff
2 *father of Joseph* Matt 1:15,16

JAEL

wife of Heber   Judg 4:17
slayer of Sisera   Judg 4:21
described as blessed Judg 5:24

JAHAZIEL

1 *Benjamite warrior* 1 Chr 12:4
2 *priest*   1 Chr 16:6
3 *son of Hebron*   1 Chr 23:19
4 *son of Zechariah* 2 Chr 20:14

JAIL *place of confinement*

put him into the j   Gen 39:20
in j in the house   Jer 37:15
put them in...j   Acts 5:18

JAILER *warden*

sight of the chief j   Gen 39:21
chief j did not   Gen 39:23
the j to guard them Acts 16:23

JAIR

1 *judge of Israel*   Judg 10:3
2 *son of Segub*   1 Chr 2:22
3 *father of Elhanan* 1 Chr 20:5
4 *Mordecai's father* Esth 2:5

JAIRUS

ruler of synagogue Mark 5:22
    Luke 8:41

JAMES

1 *son of Zebedee*   Matt 4:21
  brother of John   Matt 10:2
  called as apostle Matt 10:2ff
  martyred   Acts 12:2
2 *son of Alphaeus* Matt 10:3
  called as apostle Matt 10:3ff
3 *brother of Jesus* Matt 13:55
    Mark 6:3
  church leader Acts 12:17;15:13
4 *Judas' father*   Luke 6:16

JAPHETH

son of Noah   Gen 7:13;9:23,27

JAPHIA

1 *king of Lachish*   Josh 10:3
2 *town of Zebulun* Josh 19:12
3 *son of David*   2 Sam 5:15

JAR *container, jug*

and a j of honey   1 Kin 14:3
Bring me a new j   2 Kin 2:20
potter's earthenware j Jer 19:1
j full of sour wine   John 19:29

JASHAR

book quoted in Bible Josh 10:13
    2 Sam 1:18

JASON

Christian of Thessalonica
    Acts 17:5-9; Rom 16:21

JASPER *precious stone*

fourth row...a j   Ex 28:20
the onyx, and the j Ezek 28:13
was like a j stone   Rev 4:3
of crystal-clear j   Rev 21:11

JAVAN

*Hebrew word for Greeks
or Greece*
    Gen 10:2,4; 1 Chr 1:5,7
    Is 66:19; Ezek 27:13,19

JAVELIN *spear*

Stretch out the j   Josh 8:18
j *slung* between his 1 Sam 17:6
flashing spear and j Job 39:23
seize *their*...j   Jer 50:42

JAW *part of face*

j-s of the wicked   Job 29:17
cleaves to my j-s   Ps 22:15
j teeth *like* knives Prov 30:14
hooks into your j-s Ezek 38:4

JAWBONE

j of a donkey   Judg 15:15
threw the j from   Judg 15:17

JEALOUS *envious, zealous*

brothers were j of   Gen 37:11
your God, am a j God Ex 20:5
whose name is J, is Ex 34:14

j with My jealousy Num 25:11
He is a j God Josh 24:19
j and avenging God Nah 1:2
j for Jerusalem Zech 1:14
Jews, becoming j Acts 17:5
I will make you j Rom 10:19
love is kind...not j 1 Cor 13:4

JEBUS

Jerusalem
Judg 19:10,11;1 Chr 11:4,5

JEBUSITES

clan or tribe Gen 10:16
inhabitants of Jebus Ex 3:8,17
Josh 15:63; 2 Sam 24:16,18
Ezra 9:1; Zech 9:7

JECONIAH

variant of Jehoiachin's name
1 Chr 3:16,17; Esth 2:6

JEHOAHAZ

1 *son of Jehu* 2 Kin 10:35
king of Israel 2 Kin 13:1ff
2 *son of Josiah* 2 Kin 23:30-34
king of Judah 2 Kin 23:30
also **Shallum** 1 Chr 3:15
3 *son of Jehoram* 2 Chr 21:17
also **Ahaziah** 2 Chr 22:1ff

JEHOASH

1 *king of Judah* 2 Kin 11:21
son of Ahaziah 2 Kin 12:1-18
2 *king of Israel* 2 Kin 13:10
son of Jehoahaz 2 Kin 13:25
2 Kin 14:13

JEHOIACHIN

son of Jehoiakim 2 Kin 24:6
king of Judah 2 Kin 24:8-15
2 Chr 36:8,9; Jer 52:31,33

JEHOIADA

1 *father of Benaiah* 2 Sam 8:18
priest 1 Chr 27:5
2 *son of Benaiah* 1 Chr 27:34
3 *high priest* 2 Kin 11:4,9
4 *priest* Jer 29:26

JEHOIAKIM

son of King Josiah 2 Kin 23:34
2 Chr 36:4
king of Judah 2 Kin 23:36

2 Chr 36:5; Jer 22:18; Dan 1:2
father of Jehoiachin 2 Kin 24:6

JEHORAM

1 *son of Ahab* 2 Kin 3:1
king of Israel 2 Kin 3:6
2 *priest* 2 Chr 17:8
3 *Jehoshaphat's son* 2 Kin 8:16
king of Judah 2 Kin 8:25,29
see also **JORAM**

JEHOSHAPHAT

1 *son of Ahilud* 2 Sam 8:16
2 *son of Paruah* 1 Kin 4:17
3 *son of Asa* 1 Kin 15:24
king of Judah 1 Kin 22:2-51
2 Chr 17:1-12
4 *father of Jehu* 2 Kin 9:2,14
5 *wadi E of Jerusalem*
Joel 3:2,12

JEHU

1 *prophet, son of Hanani*
1 Kin 16:1,7,12; 2 Chr 19:2
2 *king of Israel* 1 Kin 19:16
2 Kin 9:14,30; 2 Chr 22:7
3 *Benjamite* 1 Chr 12:3
4 *man of Judah* 1 Chr 2:38
5 *Simeonite* 1 Chr 4:35

JEMIMAH

daughter of Job Job 42:14

JEPHTHAH

a Gileadite Judg 11:1
judge of Israel Judg 11:2-40

JEREMIAH

1 *lived in Libnah* 2 Kin 23:31
2 *man of Manasseh* 1 Chr 5:24
3 *three individuals who joined*
David 1 Chr 12:4,10,13
4 *prophet* Jer 1:1
called Jer 1:2-10
put in stocks Jer 20:2,3
life threatened Jer 26
put in prison Jer 32:2;37:13ff
taken to Egypt Jer 43:1-6
5 *son of Habazziniah* Jer 35:3
6 *priest* Neh 10:2
7 *priest from Babylon* Neh 12:1

JERICHO

city in Jordan Valley Josh 3:16

N of Dead Sea   Josh 6:1
    1 Kin 16:34; Luke 18:35

JEROBOAM

1 *Solomon's warrior* 1 Kin 11:28
  first king of N Kingdom
    1 Kin 12:26,27; 2 Chr 10:13
  made gold calves 1 Kin 12:28
2 *son of Joash*   2 Kin 14:27
  king of Israel 2 Kin 14:28,29

JERUBBAAL

name of Gideon   Judg 6:32
judge of Israel   Judg 7:1

JERUSALEM

city called Salem   Gen 14:18
city called Jebus   Judg 1:21
    Judg 19:10
David's capital   2 Sam 5:5,6
capital of united kingdom
    1 Kin 2:36;11:42
site of temple 1 Kin 6:2;8:6,12
destroyed by Babylonians
    Jer 52:12-14
rebuilt by remnant
    Neh 2:11-20;12:27
city of Roman period
Matt 2:1,3;21:1,10; Luke 13:34
    Acts 11:2,22
new Jerusalem Rev 3:12;21:2,10

JESHUA

1 *line of Aaron*   1 Chr 24:11
2 *under Hezekiah* 2 Chr 31:15
3 *high priest*   Ezra 2:2
    Neh 7:7
4 *of Pahath-moab*   Ezra 2:6
    Neh 7:11
5 *part of remnant*   Ezra 2:40
    Neh 7:43
6 *aided Ezra*   Neh 8:7
7 *village in Judah* Neh 11:26

JESHURUN

poetic name for Israel
    Deut 32:15;33:5,26; Is 44:2

JESSE

father of David   1 Sam 16:1,8
    2 Sam 20:1; 1 Kin 12:16
    1 Chr 2:12,13

JEST *joke, mock*

appeared...be j-ing Gen 19:14
Against whom do you j Is 57:4

JESUS

1 *name of the Lord* Matt 1:21
    Luke 1:31
  birth in Bethlehem
    Matt 1:18-25; Luke 2:1-7
  youth in Nazareth Matt 2:19ff
  baptized   Matt 3:13ff
    Mark 1:9ff; Luke 3:21
    John 1:31ff
  tempted   Matt 4:1-11
    Mark 1:12; Luke 4:1ff
  called disciples
    Matt 4:18ff; Mark 1:16ff
    Luke 5:1ff
  transfigured   Matt 17:1ff
    Mark 9:2ff; Luke 9:28ff
  triumphal entry to Jerusalem
    Matt 21:1ff; Mark 11:1ff
    Luke 19:29ff
  crucified   Matt 27:31ff
    Mark 15:20ff; Luke 23:26ff
    John 19:16ff
  resurrected Christ
    Matt 28:9ff; Mark 16:9ff
    Luke 24:13ff; John 20:11ff
  ascended to the Father
    Luke 24:50ff; Mark 16:19
    Acts 1:9ff
2 *Jewish Christian called Justus*
    Col 4:11

JETHRO

priest of Midian   Ex 3:1
Moses' father-in-law   Ex 4:18
    Ex 18:1-12

JEW(S)

originally an inhabitant of
 Judah, a Judean   2 Kin 16:6
Judean shortened to Jew
 during exile   2 Kin 25:25
synonym for Hebrew
    Ezra 4:12,23; Neh 4:1,2
    Esth 4:3,7; Jer 34:9
later term for all Israelites
 in Palestine and Disaspora
    Matt 27:11; Mark 7:3
    Luke 23:51; John 4:9

Acts 22:3; Rom 3:1
Gal 3:28; Rev 2:9

JEWEL *precious stone*

precious than j-s   Prov 3:15
better than j-s   Prov 8:11
adorns...her j-s   Is 61:10
the J of *his* kingdom   Dan 11:20

JEWISH

pertaining to Jews   Neh 5:1
Esth 6:13; John 2:6; Acts 13:6

JEZEBEL

1 *wife of Ahab*   1 Kin 21:5ff
                          2 Kin 9:7ff
2 *woman at Thyatira*   Rev 2:20

JEZREEL

1 *valley and plain*   Josh 17:16
                    Judg 6:33; Hos 1:5
2 *fortified town*   Josh 19:18
         1 Kin 18:45; 2 Kin 8:29;9:30
3 *descendant of Etam* 1 Chr 4:3
4 *son of Hosea*   Hos 1:4

JOAB

1 *son of Zeruiah*   2 Sam 8:16
  David's nephew   2 Sam 17:25
  David's commander
        1 Chr 11:6; 2 Sam 20:23
2 *son of Seraiah*   1 Chr 4:14
3 *father of those returning
  from captivity* Ezra 2:6;8:9
                          Neh 7:11

JOANNA

wife of Chuza   Luke 8:3
ministered to Jesus   Luke 24:10

JOASH

1 *father of Gideon* Judg 6:11,31
2 *son of Ahab*   1 Kin 22:26
                         2 Chr 18:25
3 *son of Ahaziah*   2 Kin 11:2
  king of Judah   2 Chr 24:1-4
4 *son of Jehoahaz*   2 Kin 13:9
  king of Israel   2 Kin 13:25
5 *line of Shelah*   1 Chr 4:22
6 *a Benjamite*   1 Chr 12:3
7 *son of Becher*   1 Chr 7:8
8 *official of David* 1 Chr 27:28

JOB

pious man from Uz   Job 1:1
experienced tragedy   Job 2:7,8
showed great endurance
              Job 2:9,10; James 5:11

JOB *occupation*

workmen...j to j   2 Chr 34:13

JOCHEBED

mother of Moses   Ex 6:20
                         Num 26:59

JOEL

1 *son of Samuel*   1 Sam 8:2
2 *ancestor of Samuel* 1 Chr 6:36
3 *line of Simeon*   1 Chr 4:35
4 *line of Reuben*   1 Chr 5:4
5 *chief of Gadites*   1 Chr 5:12
6 *son of Izrahiah*   1 Chr 7:3
7 *brother of Nathan* 1 Chr 11:38
8 *Gershonite Levite* 1 Chr 15:7
                        1 Chr 26:22
9 *son of Pedaiah*   1 Chr 27:20
10 *Kohathite Levite* 1 Chr 29:12
11 *son of Nebo*   Ezra 10:43
12 *son of Zichri*   Neh 11:9
13 *prophet*   Joel 1:1; Acts 2:16

JOHN

1 *father of Peter*   John 1:42
2 *the Baptist*   Matt 3:1
  birth foretold   Luke 1:13
  son of Zacharias   Luke 1:57ff
  preached   John 1:15
  baptized Matt 3:13; Mark 1:9
  praised by Jesus   Matt 11:11
                         Luke 7:28
  beheaded   Matt 14:10
                         Mark 6:25
3 *the apostle*   Matt 10:2
  called by Jesus   Matt 4:21
  Sons of Thunder   Mark 3:17
  inner circle   Matt 17:1
  request refused   Mark 10:35
  assigned the care of Mary
                    John 19:26,27
  with Peter   Acts 3:1,3
4 *Jewish leader*   Acts 4:6
5 *Mark, evangelist*
                    Acts 12:12,25

JOIN *bring together, couple*

do not **j** your hand	Ex 23:1
j field to field	Is 5:8
j...in hypocrisy	Dan 11:34
God...**j-ed** together	Matt 19:6
j-ed him...believed	Acts 17:34
j...*me* in suffering	2 Tim 1:8

JOINT *juncture*

bones are out of **j**	Ps 22:14
together by the **j-s**	Col 2:19
both **j-s** and marrow	Heb 4:12

JOKTAN

person and tribe descended	
from Shem	Gen 10:25,26
Gen 10:29; 1 Chr 1:19,20,23	

JONAH

prophet of Israel	Jon 1:1
son of Amittai	2 Kin 14:25
disobedient	Jon 1:3
preached to Nineveh	Jon 3:4

JONATHAN

1 *son of Gershom*	Judg 18:30
2 *son of King Saul*	1 Sam 13:16
	1 Sam 14:49
friend of David	1 Sam 18:1
3 *son of Abiathar*	2 Sam 15:36
4 *son of Shimei*	2 Sam 21:21
5 *son of Jada*	1 Chr 2:32
6 *son of Shagee*	1 Chr 11:34
7 *official of David*	1 Chr 27:25
8 *David's uncle*	1 Chr 27:32

JOPPA

seaport W of Jerusalem	
2 Chr 2:16; Ezra 3:7; Jon 1:3	
	Acts 9:36

JORAM

1 *son of Toi*	2 Sam 8:10
2 *son of Ahab*	2 Kin 8:16
king of Israel	2 Kin 8:25
3 *line of Eliezer*	1 Chr 26:25
4 *son of Jehoshaphat*	Matt 1:8
king of Judah	
see also **JEHORAM**	

JORDAN

1 *river in Palestine*	Gen 32:10
	Josh 3:17; Judg 8:4

	2 Kin 5:10; Matt 3:6
2 *valley*	Gen 13:10,11

JOSEPH

1 *son of Jacob*	Gen 30:23,24
sold by brothers	Gen 37:28
put in prison	Gen 40:3
prime minister	Gen 41:41
revealed himself	Gen 45:4
death	Gen 50:26
2 *father of spy*	Num 13:7
3 *son of Asaph*	1 Chr 25:9
4 *son of Binnui*	Ezra 10:42
5 *son of Shebaniah*	Neh 12:14
6 *husband of Mary*	
	Matt 1:18;2:13
	Luke 2:16; John 6:42
7 *brother of Jesus*	Matt 13:55
also **Joses**	
8 *brother of James the Less*	
	Matt 27:56
also **Joses**	
9 *of Arimathea*	Matt 27:57
in Sanhedrin	Mark 15:43
disciple of Jesus	John 19:38
provided tomb	Matt 27:57
10 *ancestor of Jesus*	Luke 3:24
11 *ancestor of Jesus*	Luke 3:30
12 *surname Barsabbas*	Acts 1:23
13 *Barnabas*	Acts 4:36

JOSES

1 *brother of James the Less*	
	Mark 15:40
also **Joseph**	
2 *brother of Jesus*	Mark 6:3
also **Joseph**	

JOSHUA

1 *Moses' successor*	Deut 31:23
attended Moses	Num 11:28
chosen by God	Num 27:18
encouraged by God	Josh 1:1-9
charged Israel	Josh 23:1ff
death	Josh 24:29
2 *of Beth-shemesh*	1 Sam 6:14
3 *governor*	2 Kin 23:8
4 *high priest*	Hag 1:1,12
	Zech 3:1ff
also **Jeshua**	

JOSIAH

1 *son of Amon*	2 Kin 21:24

king of Judah　　2 Kin 21:26
removed false worship
　　2 Kin 23:19,24; 2 Chr 34:33
responded to the Law
　　　　　　　2 Chr 34:15-28
2 *son of Zephaniah*　Zech 6:10

JOTHAM

1 *son of Gideon*　　Judg 9:5ff
2 *king of Judah*　　2 Kin 15:5
　son of Uzziah　　2 Chr 27:6
3 *line of Caleb*　　1 Chr 2:47

JOURNEY *traveling, trip*

Let us take our j　　Gen 33:12
day's j on the other　Num 11:31
seek...a safe j　　Ezra 8:21
a bag for *your* j　　Matt 10:10
nothing for *your* j　　Luke 9:3
Sabbath day's j away　Acts 1:12
on frequent j-s　　2 Cor 11:26

JOURNEYED *traveled*

about as they j east　Gen 11:2
Jacob j to Succoth　Gen 33:17
the sons of Israel j　Num 22:1
j from the river　　Ezra 8:31

JOY *delight, happiness*

raise sounds of j　　1 Chr 15:16
shouted aloud for j　Ezra 3:12
see His face with j　　Job 33:26
Restore to me the j　Ps 51:12
j at Thy name　　Ps 89:12
godly ones sing for j　Ps 132:9
Everlasting j will be　Is 61:7
their mourning into j　Jer 31:13
with great j　　Matt 2:10
enter into the j　　Matt 25:21
j in heaven over one　Luke 15:7
j in the Holy Spirit　Rom 14:17
love, j, peace　　Gal 5:22
make my j complete　Phil 2:2

JOYFUL *feeling gladness*

be altogether j　　Deut 16:15
j with gladness　　Ps 21:6
shall reap with j　　Ps 126:5
j heart is good　　Prov 17:22

JOYFULLY *full of joy, happy*

go j with the king　　Esth 5:14

Shout j to God, all　　Ps 66:1
They shout j together　Is 52:8
to praise God j　　Luke 19:37

JUBAL

inventor of harp and organ
　　　　　　　　Gen 4:21

JUBILANT *elated*

no...j shouting　　Is 16:10
Is this your j *city*　　Is 23:7
because you are j　　Jer 50:11
they may become j　Jer 51:39

JUBILEE, YEAR OF

return of ancestral possessions
　every fiftieth year
year of liberty　　Lev 25:8ff

JUDAH

1 *son of Jacob*　　Gen 29:35
　　Gen 37:26;44:14;49:8,10
2 *tribe*　　Num 1:27; Judg 1:8
　　　　2 Sam 2:4; 1 Kin 12:20
3 *border city*　　Josh 19:34
4 *S kingdom*　　1 Kin 14:21
　　1 Chr 9:1; Ps 60:7; Jer 20:4
5 *ancestor of Kadmiel* Ezra 3:9
6 *urged by Ezra to put away*
　foreign wife　　Ezra 10:23
7 *Benjamite*　　Neh 11:9
8 *Levite who returned from*
　captivity　　Neh 12:8
9 *participant in wall*
　dedication　　Neh 12:34
10 *musician*　　Neh 12:36

JUDAISM *Jewish way of life*

manner of life in J　　Gal 1:13
advancing in J　　Gal 1:14

JUDAS

1 *Iscariot*　　Matt 10:4
　son of Simon　　John 6:71
　used by Satan　　Luke 22:3
　treasurer　　John 13:29
　betrayed Jesus　　Matt 27:3
　　　　　　　　John 18:2
2 *Jesus' brother*　　Matt 13:55
　　　　　　　　Mark 6:3
3 *apostle*　　Luke 6:16
　　　　　　　　Acts 1:13

4 *Judas of Galilee*   Acts 5:37
5 *of Damascus*   Acts 9:11
6 *Barsabbas*   Acts 15:22,27

JUDE

brother of James   Jude 1
brother of Jesus   Matt 13:55
    Mark 6:3

JUDEA

*Roman province of Palestine
based on earlier Judah*
    Matt 2:1; Mark 1:5
    Luke 2:4; John 11:7

JUDEAN

language (Hebrew)
    2 Kin 18:26,28; Is 36:11,13
see also CANAAN
see also HEBREW

JUDGE (n) *leader*

J of all the earth   Gen 18:25
prince or a j over us   Ex 2:14
LORD was with the j   Judg 2:18
For God Himself is j   Ps 50:6
unrighteous j said   Luke 18:6
one Lawgiver and J   James 4:12

JUDGE (v) *pass judgment*

LORD j between you   Gen 16:5
Moses sat to j the   Ex 18:13
LORD will j...earth   1 Sam 2:10
coming to j the earth   Ps 98:9
He will j the poor   Is 11:4
not j lest you be j-d   Matt 7:1
Son...world to j   John 3:17
Law...not j a man   John 7:51
not come to j the   John 12:47
able to j...thoughts   Heb 4:12
adulterers God will j   Heb 13:4

JUDGMENT *condemnation*

I will execute j-s   Ex 12:12
partiality in j   Deut 1:17
let j be executed   Ezra 7:26
will not stand in the j   Ps 1:5
in the day of j   Matt 10:15
j, that the light   John 3:19
resurrection of j   John 5:29
My j is just   John 5:30
after this *comes* j   Heb 9:27
incur a stricter j   James 3:1
not fall under j   James 5:12

kept for the day of j   2 Pet 3:7
j of the great day   Jude 6
to execute j upon all   Jude 15
His j-s are true   Rev 19:2

JUMP *leap*

legs with which to j   Lev 11:21
if a fox should j   Neh 4:3
j-ed up, and came   Mark 10:50

JUNIPER *tree*

slept under a j tree   1 Kin 19:5
The j, the box tree   Is 60:13
like a j in the   Jer 48:6

JUST *fair, right*

shall have j balances   Lev 19:36
a man be j with God   Job 25:4
Hear a j cause, O LORD   Ps 17:1
He is j and endowed   Zech 9:9
My judgment is j   John 5:30
the j *for the* unjust   1 Pet 3:18

JUSTICE *fairness, righteousness*

shall not distort j   Deut 16:19
Does God pervert j   Job 8:3
j to the afflicted   Job 36:6
Righteousness and j   Ps 89:14
do not understand j   Prov 28:5
j is turned back   Is 59:14
let j roll down   Amos 5:24
j and mercy and   Matt 23:23
acknowledged...j   Luke 7:29
grant to your slaves j   Col 4:1

JUSTIFICATION *vindication*

because of our j   Rom 4:25
j of life to all men   Rom 5:18

JUSTIFY *declare guiltless*

how...j ourselves   Gen 44:16
they j the righteous   Deut 25:1
he j-ied himself   Job 32:2
wishing to j himself   Luke 10:29
these He also j-ied   Rom 8:30
God...j-ies   Rom 8:33
seeking to be j-ied   Gal 2:17

JUSTUS

1 *Joseph, apostolic candidate*
    Acts 1:23
2 *Titus, Corinthian disciple*
    Acts 18:7

3 *Jewish Christian*   Col 4:11

JUTTAH

Levitical city in Judah
                    Josh 15:55;21:16

K

KADESH/KADESH-BARNEA
desert oasis in S Palestine
                    Gen 14:7
Israelite encampment
                    Num 13:26;33:37

KEDAR

1 *son of Ishmael*   Gen 25:13
2 *tribal descendants*   Is 42:11

KEDEMAH

1 *son of Ishmael*   Gen 25:15
2 *tribal descendants* 1 Chr 1:31

KEDESH

1 *city in S Judah*   Josh 15:23
2 *city of Issachar*   1Chr 6:72
3 *city of Naphtali*   Josh 12:22
  city of refuge   Josh 20:7

KEEP *hold, guide, preserve*

k the way of the LORD Gen 18:19
love Me and k My   Ex 20:6
shall k your sabbath   Lev 23:32
LORD bless you, and k Num 6:24
to k the Passover   Matt 26:18
if anyone k-s My   John 8:51
he will k My word   John 14:23
k-ing faith and a   1 Tim 1:19
k yourself free from   1 Tim 5:22

KEEPER *guard, protector*

Am I my brother's k   Gen 4:9
been k-s of livestock Gen 46:32
The LORD is your k   Ps 121:5
I, the LORD, am its k Is 27:3

KEILAH

1 *town of Judah*   Josh 15:44
           1 Sam 23:1ff; Neh 3:17,18
2 *line of Caleb*   1 Chr 4:19

KENAZ

1 *Esau's grandson* Gen 36:10,11

2 *father of Othniel*   Josh 15:17
3 *line of Caleb*   1 Chr 4:15

KENITE(S)

Canaanite tribe   Gen 15:19
                    Num 24:21
tribe of metal-workers
              Judg 4:11; 1 Sam 15:6

KENIZZITE

*Canaanite tribe in S Palestine
  and Edom*   Gen 15:19
            Num 32:12; Josh 14:14

KEREN-HAPPUCH

daughter of Job   Job 42:14

KERIOTH

1 *town of Judah*   Josh 15:25
2 *town in Moab*   Jer 48:41
                       Amos 2:2

KETURAH

second wife of Abraham
              Gen 25:1,4; 1 Chr 1:32,33

KEY *unlocking tool*

k-s of the kingdom   Matt 16:19
the k of knowledge   Luke 11:52
k-s of death and of   Rev 1:18
k of the bottomless pit Rev 9:1

KEZIAH

daughter of Job   Job 42:14

KID *young goat*

a k from the flock   Gen 38:17
not boil a k...milk   Ex 34:26
prepare a k for you   Judg 13:15
never given me a k   Luke 15:29

KIDNEYS *innards*

two k and the fat   Ex 29:13
remove with the k   Lev 3:15
He splits my k open   Job 16:13

KIDRON

*brook and valley between Jeru-
  salem and Mount of Olives*
              2 Sam 15:23; 2 Kin 23:6
              2 Chr 29:16; John 18:1

KILL *take life*

for Cain k-ed him   Gen 4:25

k-ed every first-born   Ex 13:15
who k-s a man shall   Lev 24:21
LORD k-s and makes   1 Sam 2:6
Am I God, to k   2 Kin 5:7
anger k-s the simple   Job 5:2
he k-s the innocent   Ps 10:8
A time to k   Eccl 3:3
unable to k the   Matt 10:28
k-ed, and be raised   Luke 9:22
do you seek to k Me   John 7:19
Arise, Peter, k and   Acts 10:13
the letter k-s, but   2 Cor 3:6
who k their fathers   1 Tim 1:9
k a third of mankind   Rev 9:15

KIND (adj) *good, tender*

be k to this people   2 Chr 10:7
He Himself is k   Luke 6:35
love is k   1 Cor 13:4
be k to one another   Eph 4:32

KIND (n) *group, variety*

fruit after their k   Gen 1:11
plant all k-s of trees   Lev 19:23
all k-s of evil   Matt 5:11
k-s of tongues   1 Cor 12:28
every k of impurity   Eph 4:19

KINDLE *cause to burn*

anger...was k-d   Num 11:10
His breath k-s coals   Job 41:21
man to k strife   Prov 26:21
all you who k a fire   Is 50:11
k-d a fire in Zion   Lam 4:11

KINDNESS *tenderness*

teaching of k is on   Prov 31:26
to love k, And to   Mic 6:8
with deeds of k   Acts 9:36
k and...of God   Rom 11:22
joy, peace, patience, k   Gal 5:22
compassion, k   Col 3:12
tasted the k of the   1 Pet 2:3
godliness, brotherly k   2 Pet 1:7

KINDRED *relatives*

her people or her k   Esth 2:10
destruction of my k   Esth 8:6
no one...of k spirit   Phil 2:20

KING *monarch, regent*

the k-'s highway   Num 20:17
no k in Israel   Judg 17:6

appoint a k for us   1 Sam 8:5
annointed David k   2 Sam 5:3
my K and my God   Ps 5:2
The LORD is K forever   Ps 10:16
Who is the k of glory   Ps 24:8
will shatter k-s   Ps 110:5
By me k-s reign   Prov 8:15
He will...before k-s   Prov 22:29
The Creator your K   Is 43:15
O K of the nations   Jer 10:7
born K of the Jews   Matt 2:2
Are You the K of   Matt 27:11
your K is coming   John 12:15
no k but Caesar   John 19:15
K of k-s and Lord   1 Tim 6:15
God, honor the   1 Pet 2:17

KINGDOM *domain, monarchy*

his k was Babel   Gen 10:10
to Me a k of priests   Ex 19:6
tear the k from   1 Kin 11:11
will establish his k   1 Chr 28:7
the k is the LORD'S   Ps 22:28
Sing to God, O k-s   Ps 68:32
an everlasting k   Ps 145:13
k against k   Is 19:2
k of heaven is at   Matt 3:2
showed Him...k-s   Matt 4:8
Thy k come   Matt 6:10
sons of the k   Matt 13:38
keys of the k   Matt 16:19
in My Father's k   Matt 26:29
enter the k of God   Mark 10:24
to give you the k   Luke 12:32
cannot see the k   John 3:3
preaching the k   Acts 28:31
k of His beloved Son   Col 1:13
to His heavenly k   2 Tim 4:18
faith conquered k-s   Heb 11:33
heirs of the k   James 2:5

KINSMAN *relative*

of my master's k   Gen 24:48
he took his k-men   Gen 31:23
a man has no k   Lev 25:26
Naomi had a k of her   Ruth 2:1
k-men stand afar off   Ps 38:11
Herodion, my k   Rom 16:11

KIRIATHAIM

1 *Levitical city*   1 Chr 6:76
2 *Reubenite city*   Num 32:37
                        Josh 13:19

KIRIATH-ARBA

old name of Hebron Gen 23:2
Josh 14:15; 15:13,54; Judg 1:10
city of Refuge Josh 20:7

KIRIATH-JEARIM

Gibeonite town Josh 9:17
Judg 18:12; Jer 26:20
location of ark of covenant
1 Sam 6:21; 7:1,2; 2 Chr 1:4

KISH

1 *father of Saul* 1 Sam 9:3
1 Sam 10:21
2 *son of Jeiel* 1 Chr 8:30
3 *son of Mahli* 1 Chr 23:21
4 *son of Abdi* 2 Chr 29:12
5 *a Benjamite* Esth 2:5

KISHON

battle scene Judg 4:7
river Judg 4:13; 5:21
priests of Baal slain on
its bank 1 Kin 18:40

KISS (n) *expression of affection*

threw a k from my Job 31:27
the k-es of his mouth Song 1:2
You gave Me no k Luke 7:45
betraying...with a k Luke 22:48
with a holy k Rom 16:16
with a k of love 1 Pet 5:14

KISS (v) *expression of affection*

come close and k Gen 27:26
let me k my father 1 Kin 19:20
I would k you Song 8:1
Whomever I...k Mark 14:44
not...to k my feet Luke 7:45

KITTIM

1 *grandson of Japheth* Gen 10:4
1 Chr 1:7
2 *island of Cyprus* Num 24:24
Jer. 2:10; Dan 11:30

KNEAD *work dough, clay*

took flour, k-ed it 1 Sam 28:24
the women k dough Jer 7:18

KNEE *part of body*

strengthened feeble k-s Job 4:4

k-s began knocking Dan 5:6
every k shall bow Rom 14:11
every k should bow Phil 2:10

KNEEL *bend, rest on knee*

made the camels k Gen 24:11
people k-ed to drink Judg 7:6
k before the LORD Ps 95:6
k-ed...before Him Matt 27:29
man ran...knelt Mark 10:17
He knelt down Luke 22:41

KNIFE *cutting instrument*

k to slay his son Gen 22:10
jaw teeth *like* k-ves Prov 30:14
with a scribes k Jer 36:23

KNIT *joined together*

Jonathan was k to 1 Sam 18:1
k me together with Job 10:11
his thighs are k Job 40:17
His hand they are k Lam 1:14
k together in love Col 2:2

KNOCK *smite, strike*

his knees began k-ing Dan 5:6
k, and it shall be Matt 7:7
stand outside and k Luke 13:25
he k-ed at the door Acts 12:13
at the door and k Rev 3:20

KNOW *experience, understand*

like one of Us, k-ing Gen 3:22
make k-n the statutes Ex 18:16
k that my Redeemer Job 19:25
Make me k Thy ways Ps 25:4
He k-s the secrets Ps 44:21
k that I am God Ps 46:10
made k-n His salvation Ps 98:2
Try me and k my Ps 139:23
Thou k-est me, O LORD Jer 12:3
left hand k what Matt 6:3
k...by their fruits Matt 7:20
I never knew you Matt 7:23
God k-s your heart Luke 16:15
you shall k the truth John 8:32
I k My own John 10:14
k-ing that His hour John 13:1
k that I love You John 21:15
and k all mysteries 1 Cor 13:2
who knew no sin 2 Cor 5:21
k the love of Christ Eph 3:19

value of k-ing Christ   Phil 3:8
k...I have believed   2 Tim 1:12
k...eternal life   1 John 5:13
I k your deeds   Rev 2:2

KNOWLEDGE *information*

tree of the k of good   Gen 2:9
LORD is a God of k   1 Sam 2:3
anyone teach God k   Job 21:22
k is too wonderful   Ps 139:6
the beginning of k   Prov 1:7
fools hate k   Prov 1:22
Wise...store up k   Prov 10:14
k increases power   Prov 24:5
would He teach k   Is 28:9
in accordance with k   Rom 10:2
K make arrogant   1 Cor 8:1
k, it will be done   1 Cor 13:8
have no k of God   1 Cor 15:34
love...surpasses k   Eph 3:19
treasures of k   Col 2:3
grow in grace and k   2 Pet 3:18

KOHATH

son of Levi   Gen 46:11
    Num 3:17; Josh 21:5

KOHATHITES

line of Kohath   Num 3:30;4:34
    Josh 21:4

KOR *measure of capacity*

k-s of fine flour   1 Kin 4:22
20,000 k-s of barley   2 Chr 2:10
100 k-s of wheat   Ezra 7:22
a bath from *each* k   Ezek 45:14

KORAH

1 *son of Esau*   Gen 36:5
2 *opposed Moses*   Num 16:8,16
3 *son of Hebron*   1 Chr 2:43
4 *a Kohathite*   1 Chr 6:37

L

LABAN

1 *Abraham's kinsman* Gen 24:29
    Rachel's father   Gen 29:10,16
2 *place in the desert*   Deut 1:1

LABOR (n) *work* or *childbirth*

fruits of your l-s   Ex 23:16
their l to the locust   Ps 78:46
bread of painful l-s   Ps 127:2
return for their l   Eccl 4:9
like a woman in l   Is 42:14
in l and hardship   2 Cor 11:27
fruitful l for me   Phil 1:22
faith and l of love   1 Thess 1:3
cried out, being in l   Rev 12:2

LABOR (v) *toil, work*

Six days you shall l   Ex 20:9
l in vain who build   Ps 127:1
for whom am I l-ing   Eccl 4:8
l-ed over you in vain   Gal 4:11

LABORER *workman*

l-s for his vineyard   Matt 20:1
Call the l-s and pay   Matt 20:8
l-s into His harvest   Luke 10:2
l is worthy of his   Luke 10:7

LACHISH

city in Judah   Josh 10:3
    2 Kin 14:19; 2 Chr 32:9

LACK (n) *deficiency, need*

where there is no l   Judg 18:10
for l of instruction   Prov 5:23
for l of a shepherd   Ezek 34:5
l of self-control   1 Cor 7:5

LACK (v) *be deficient, need*

shall not l anything   Deut 8:9
l-ing in counsel   Deut 32:28
man l-ing sense   Prov 7:7
am I still l-ing   Matt 19:20
One thing you l   Mark 10:21
not l-ing in any gift   1 Cor 1:7
if any...l-s wisdom   James 1:5

LAD *boy*

God heard the l   Gen 21:17
the l is not *with us*   Gen 44:31
the l was dead   2 Kin 4:32
a l here who has five   John 6:9

LADDER *steps*

l...set on the earth   Gen 28:12

LADY *woman*

Thy noble l-ies   Ps 45:9
elder to the chosen l   2 John 1

LAISH

1 *a Benjamite*   1 Sam 25:44
    2 Sam 3:15

2 *place in N Palestine later
    called Dan*   Judg 18:27,29

LAKE *pool, water*

standing by the l   Luke 5:1
wind...upon the l   Luke 8:23
into the l, and were   Luke 8:33
into the l of fire   Rev 20:10

LAMB *young sheep*

l for the burnt   Gen 22:7
shall redeem with a l   Ex 34:20
l without defect   Lev 14:10
will dwell with the l   Is 11:6
l...led to slaughter   Is 53:7
wolf and the l shall   Is 65:25
send you out as l-s   Luke 10:3
Behold, the L of God   John 1:29
Tend My l-s   John 21:15
l before its shearer   Acts 8:32
Worthy is the L   Rev 5:12
blood of the L   Rev 12:11

LAME *crippled, disabled*

was l in both feet   2 Sam 9:13
feet to the l   Job 29:15
Then the l will leap   Is 35:6
the l walk   Matt 11:5
l from his mother's   Acts 14:8

LAMECH

1 *in linage of Cain* Gen 4:17,18
2 *father of Noah*   Gen 5:28,29

LAMENT (n) *dirge, wail*

this l over Saul   2 Sam 1:17
chanted a l   2 Chr 35:25
l must make a l   Mic 1:8

LAMENT (v) *mourn, wail*

house of Israel l-ed   1 Sam 7:2
her gates will l   Is 3:26
fishermen will l   Is 19:8
And l over you   Ezek 27:32
weep and l over her   Rev 18:9

LAMENTATION *weeping*

great...sorrowful l   Gen 50:10

in Ramah, **L** *and*   Jer 31:15
your sons into l   Amos 8:10
made loud l over him Acts 8:2

LAMP *light*

Thou art my l   1 Sam 22:29
l-s of pure gold   2 Chr 4:20
his l goes out   Job 18:6
Thy word is a l   Ps 119:105
commandment is a l   Prov 6:23
l of the body is the   Matt 6:22
l-s are going out   Matt 25:8
l-s in the upper room Acts 20:8
l shining in a dark   2 Pet 1:19
seven l-s of fire   Rev 4:5

LAMPSTAND *candlestick*

l of pure gold   Ex 25:31
and a chair and a l   2 Kin 4:10
puts it on a l   Luke 8:16
will remove your l   Rev 2:5

LAND *country, earth*

let the dry l appear   Gen 1:9
famine in the l   Gen 12:10
I have given this l   Gen 15:18
out of the l of Egypt   Ex 6:13
l flowing with milk   Deut 6:3
in to possess the l   Josh 1:11
l of their captivity   2 Chr 6:38
will heal their l   2 Chr 7:14
the l of the living   Job 28:13
will inherit the l   Ps 37:11
in a dry and weary l   Ps 63:1
l be born in one day   Is 66:8
again to this l   Jer 24:6
l is filled with blood Ezek 9:9
smite the l with a   Mal 4:6
darkness...all the l   Matt 27:45
owned a tract of l   Acts 4:37

LANDOWNER *landlord*

slaves of the l   Matt 13:27
kingdom...like a l   Matt 20:1
l who planted a   Matt 21:33

LANGUAGE *speech, word*

according to his l   Gen 10:5
earth used the same l Gen 11:1
speech or difficult l   Ezek 3:5
in figurative l   John 16:25
speak in his own l   Acts 2:6
many kinds of l-s   1 Cor 14:10

LANGUAGE

LANGUISH *faint*

l-ed because of the   Gen 47:13
My soul l-es for   Ps 119:81
never l again   Jer 31:12
refresh...who l-es   Jer 31:25

LAODICEA

city in Asia Minor   Col 2:1
location of early church
    Col 4:15; Rev 1:11;3:14

LAODICEANS

people of Laodicea   Col 4:16

LAPIS LAZULI *precious stone*

polishing *was* like l   Lam 4:7
like l in appearance   Ezek 1:26
the jasper; The l   Ezek 28:13

LARGE *big, great, huge*

tears in l measure   Ps 80:5
a l upper room   Mark 14:15
a l multitude   Luke 7:11
what l letters   Gal 6:11

LAST *final, utmost*

breathed his l   Gen 25:8
In the l days   Is 2:2
first will be l   Matt 19:30
The l Adam   1 Cor 15:45
at the l trumpet   1 Cor 15:52
in these l days   Heb 1:2
it is the l hour   1 John 2:18
the first and the l   Rev 1:17

LATIN

language of the Roman Empire
one of three languages written
on Jesus' cross   John 19:20

LATTICE *trellis*

fell through the l   2 Kin 1:2
looked out...my l   Ps 7:6
peering through...l   Song 2:9

LAUGH *be amused, mock*

Why did Sarah l   Gen 18:13
will l at violence   Job 5:22
l at your calamity   Prov 1:26
weep, and a time to l   Eccl 3:4
began l-ing at Him   Matt 9:24

LAUGHINGSTOCK *derision*

l among the peoples   Ps 44:14
was not Israel a l   Jer 48:27
I have become a l   Lam 3:14

LAUGHTER *amusement*

God has made l for   Gen 21:6
Even in l the heart   Prov 14:13
Sorrow is better than l   Eccl 7:3

LAVER *wash basin*

make a l of bronze   Ex 30:18
set the l between   Ex 40:7
anoint the l   Ex 40:11

LAW *scripture, statute*

tablets with the l   Ex 24:12
Moses wrote this l   Deut 31:9
found the...l   2 Kin 22:8
walk in My l   2 Chr 6:16
l...is perfect   Ps 19:7
I delight in Thy l   Ps 119:70
abolish the L or the   Matt 5:17
Our L...not judge   John 7:51
by that l He ought   John 19:7
by a l of faith   Rom 3:27
L brings...wrath   Rom 4:15
not under l   Rom 6:14
Is the L sin   Rom 7:7
the L is holy   Rom 7:12
L...become our tutor   Gal 3:24
thus fulfill the l   Gal 6:2
L...nothing perfect   Heb 7:19

LAWFUL *legal, right*

not l for him to eat   Matt 12:4
Is it l to heal   Matt 12:10
l...man to divorce   Mark 10:2
All things are l   1 Cor 6:12

LAWGIVER *lawmaker*

The LORD is our l   Is 33:22
one L and Judge   James 4:12

LAWLESS *illegal, without law*

l one will be   2 Thess 2:8
are l and rebellious   1 Tim 1:9
from every l deed   Titus 2:14

LAWYER *interpreter of law*

a l, asked Him *a*   Matt 22:35
one of the l-s said   Luke 11:45
Woe to you l-s   Luke 11:52

LAY *place, put*

laid him on the altar	Gen 22:9
l My hand on Egypt	Ex 7:4
laid its cornerstone	Job 38:6
l my glory in the dust	Ps 7:5
he l-s up deceit	Prov 26:24
l up...treasures	Matt 6:20
laid Him in a tomb	Mark 15:46
l-s down His life	John 10:11
I l down My life	John 10:15
have you **laid** Him	John 11:34
I l in Zion a stone	Rom 9:33
l-ing aside falsehood	Eph 4:25
l-ing hold of...hope	Heb 6:18

LAYMAN *non-ecclesiastic*

l shall not eat *them*	Ex 29:33
married to a l	Lev 22:12
l who comes near	Num 3:10

LAZARUS

1 *beggar*	Luke 16:20-25
2 *brother of Mary and Martha*	
	John 11:1,2,5,11,43

LAZY *idle, slothful*

Because they are l	Ex 5:8
You are l, *very* l	Ex 5:17
You wicked, l slave	Matt 25:26
beasts, l gluttons	Titus 1:12

LEAD (n) *metal*

They sank like l	Ex 15:10
an iron stylus and l	Job 19:24
l is consumed by	Jer 6:29
l in the furnace	Ezek 22:18

LEAD (v) *direct, guide*

God **led** the people	Ex 13:18
cloud by day to l	Ex 13:21
l-s me beside quiet	Ps 23:2
L me in Thy truth	Ps 25:5
led captive *Thy*	Ps 68:18
little boy will l	Is 11:6
lamb that is **led** to	Is 53:7
not l us into	Matt 6:13
l the elect astray	Mark 13:22
led Him...crucify	Mark 15:20
and l-s them out	John 10:3
led by the Spirit	Rom 8:14
led captive a host	Eph 4:8
that l-s to salvation	2 Tim 3:15

LEADER *director, guide*

Let us appoint a l	Num 14:4
one l of every tribe	Num 34:18
l over My people	1 Kin 14:7
the l as the servant	Luke 22:26
Obey your l-s	Heb 13:17

LEADING (adj) *chief, noted*

gathered l men	Ezra 7:28
number...l women	Acts 17:4
l men of the Jews	Acts 28:17

LEAF *foliage*

sewed fig l-ves	Gen 3:7
sound of a driven l	Lev 26:36
its l does not wither	Ps 1:3
puts forth its l-ves	Matt 24:32

LEAH

wife of Jacob	Gen 29:23,30
mother of Reuben, Simeon,	
Levi and Judah	Gen 29:32-35

LEAN (adj) *thin*

seven l...ugly cows	Gen 41:20
my flesh has grown l	Ps 109:24
and the l sheep	Ezek 34:20

LEAN (v) *incline, rest*

may l against them	Judg 16:26
l...own understanding	Prov 3:5
l on the God of Israel	Is 48:2

LEAP *jump, spring*

l-ing and dancing	2 Sam 6:16
I can l over a wall	Ps 18:29
baby l-ed in her	Luke 1:41
and l *for joy*	Luke 6:23
l-ed up and *began*	Acts 14:10

LEARN *get knowledge*

l to fear the LORD	Deut 31:13
I may l Thy statutes	Ps 119:71
have I l-ed wisdom	Prov 30:3
will they l war	Is 2:4
l from Me	Matt 11:29
l-ed to be content	Phil 4:11
He l-ed obedience	Heb 5:8

LEARNING (n) *knowledge*

increase *his* l	Prov 9:9
l of the Egyptians	Acts 7:22
great l is driving	Acts 26:24

LEAST

LEAST *insignificant*

l of my master's	2 Kin 18:24
greatest to the l	2 Chr 34:30
l in the kingdom	Matt 5:19
he who is l...is	Matt 11:11
l of the apostles	1 Cor 15:9
very l of all saints	Eph 3:8

LEATHER *animal skin*

man with a l girdle	2 Kin 1:8
a l belt about his	Matt 3:4
and *wore* a l belt	Mark 1:6

LEAVE *abandon, depart, forsake*

shall l his father	Gen 2:24
arise, l this land	Gen 31:13
not l me defenseless	Ps 141:8
kindness and truth l	Prov 3:3
l the ninety-nine	Matt 18:12
Peace I l with you	John 14:27
I am l-ing...world	John 16:28

LEAVEN *yeast*

no l found in your	Ex 12:19
not be baked with l	Lev 6:17
seven days no l shall	Deut 16:4
heaven is like the	Matt 13:33
little l leavens the	1 Cor 5:6

LEAVENED *raised by yeast*

whoever eats what is l	Ex 12:19
with cakes of l bread	Lev 7:13
not eat l bread	Deut 16:3
until it was all l	Matt 13:33

LEBANON

mountain range N of Palestine
Josh 9:1; Judg 3:3; 1 Kin 5:6
showing God's greatness Ps 29:6
symbol of prosperity Ps 92:12

LEGAL *lawful*

has a l matter	Ex 24:14
Give me l protection	Luke 18:3

LEGION *division, group*

twelve l-s of angels	Matt 26:53
My name is L	Mark 5:9
man who had...l	Mark 5:15
L; for many demons	Luke 8:30

LEG *part of body*

l-s are pillars of	Song 5:15
Uncover the l	Is 47:2

not break His l-s   John 19:33

LEMUEL

royal author of section of
Proverbs   Prov 31:1,4

LEND *loan*

l-ing them money	Neh 5:10
l-s...on interest	Ezek 18:13
l, expecting nothing	Luke 6:35
l me three loaves	Luke 11:5

LENDER *loaner*

becomes the l-'s slave	Prov 22:7
l like the borrower	Is 24:2

LENGTH

the l of the ark	Gen 6:15
l of days and years	Prov 3:2
breadth and l and	Eph 3:18
l and width...equal	Rev 21:16

LEOPARD *animal*

l will lie down with	Is 11:6
Or the l his spots	Jer 13:23
Like a l I will lie	Hos 13:7
beast...was like a l	Rev 13:2

LEPER *one having leprosy*

As for the l	Lev 13:45
King Uzziah...a l	2 Chr 26:21
a l came to Him	Matt 8:2
cleanse *the* l-s	Matt 10:8
home of Simon the l	Mark 14:3

LEPROSY *infectious disease*

of l on the skin	Lev 13:2
mark of l on a	Lev 14:34
an infection of l	Deut 24:8
cure him of his l	2 Kin 5:3
his l was cleansed	Matt 8:3

LEPROUS *having leprosy*

hand was l like snow	Ex 4:6
is a l malignancy	Lev 13:51
ten l...met Him	Luke 17:12

LET *allow, permit*

L there be light	Gen 1:3
L My people go	Ex 5:1
L the children alone	Matt 19:14
l this cup pass from	Matt 26:39
L not your heart be	John 14:1

LETTER *epistle or symbol*

a l sent to Solomon   2 Chr 2:11
smallest l or stroke   Matt 5:18
You are our l   2 Cor 3:2
l caused you sorrow   2 Cor 7:8
large l-s I am writing   Gal 6:11

LEVEL *flat, plain*

lead me in a l path   Ps 27:11
path of the righteous l   Is 26:7
stood on a l place   Luke 6:17

LEVI

1 *son of Jacob*   Gen 34:25
2 *tribe*   Num 1:49; Rev 7:7
3 *two ancestors of Jesus*
     Luke 3:24,29
4 *apostle*   Mark 2:14
     Luke 5:27,29

LEVIATHAN

symbolic monster of the deep
   Job 3:8; Ps 104:26; Is 27:1

LEVITES

descendants of Levi   Ex 6:19,25
charged with the care of
the sanctuary   Num 1:50;3:41

LEVY (n) *payment, tax*

the LORD's l   Num 31:38
l *fixed by* Moses   2 Chr 24:6

LEVY (v) *impose a tax*

l a tax for the LORD   Num 31:28
l-ied forced laborers   1 Kin 9:21

LEWDNESS *lascivious, lust*

land...full of l   Lev 19:29
not commit this l   Ezek 16:43
I will uncover her l   Hos 2:10

LIAR *one telling lies*

who...prove me a l   Job 24:25
a poor man than a l   Prov 19:22
I shall be a l like   John 8:55
hypocrisy of l-s   1 Tim 4:2
we make Him a l   1 John 1:10

LIBATION *see* **OFFERINGS**

LIBERTY *freedom*

I will walk at l   Ps 119:45

proclaim l to captives   Is 61:1
spy out our l   Gal 2:4
the *law* of l   James 1:25

LIBNAH

1 *place in wilderness*
     Num 33:21
2 *Canaanite city*   Josh 10:29
     2 Kin 23:31
   a Levitical city   1 Chr 6:57

LIBYA

country in N Africa   Ezek 30:5
     Acts 2:10

LICK *lap up*

dogs shall l up your l   1 Kin 21:19
his enemies l the dust   Ps 72:9
dogs were...l-ing   Luke 16:21

LIE (n) *false statement*

speak l-s go astray   Ps 58:3
tells l-s will perish   Prov 19:9
prophesy a l to you   Jer 27:10
the father of l-s   John 8:44
truth of God for a l   Rom 1:25
no l is of the truth   1 John 2:21

LIE (v) *make false statement*

nor l to one another   Lev 19:11
l-d to Him with their   Ps 78:36
l-d about the LORD   Jer 5:12
l to the Holy Spirit   Acts 5:3
not l to one another   Col 3:9
impossible...God to l   Heb 6:18

LIE (v) *recline*

when you l down   Deut 11:19
she lay at his feet   Ruth 3:14
Saul lay sleeping   1 Sam 26:7
makes me l down   Ps 23:2
lying in a manger   Luke 2:12

LIFE *living or salvation*

the breath of l   Gen 2:7
l for l   Ex 21:23
l...is in the blood   Lev 17:11
Our l for yours   Josh 2:14
my l is *but* breath   Job 7:7
Who redeems your l   Ps 103:4
the springs of l   Prov 4:23
way of l and...death   Jer 21:8
to everlasting l   Dan 12:2
take my l from me   Jon 4:3

anxious for your l | Matt 6:25
loses his l for My | Matt 16:25
His l a ransom for | Matt 20:28
to inherit eternal l | Mark 10:17
l is more than food | Luke 12:23
but have eternal l | John 3:16
out of death into l | John 5:24
I am the bread of l | John 6:35
lays down his l | John 10:11
resurrection and...l | John 11:25
truth, and the l | John 14:6
lay down his l for | John 15:13
walk in newness of l | Rom 6:4
the Spirit gives l | 2 Cor 3:6
Christ, who is our l | Col 3:4
an undisciplined l | 2 Thess 3:11
receive...crown of l | James 1:12
lay down our l-ves | 1 John 3:16
book of l of the Lamb | Rev 13:8

LIFEBLOOD

I will require your l | Gen 9:5
poured out their l | Is 63:6
l of the innocent | Jer 2:34

LIFETIME *length of life*

Throughout his l | 2 Chr 34:33
His favor is for a l | Ps 30:5
my l of futility | Eccl 7:15
as the l of a tree | Is 65:22

LIFT *exalt, raise*

l up your eyes and | Gen 13:14
l up your staff and | Ex 14:16
l up your voice | Job 38:34
One who l-s my head | Ps 3:3
I Will l up my eyes | Ps 121:1
will not l up sword | Is 2:4
Spirit l-ed me up | Ezek 3:14
Son of Man be l-ed | John 3:14
He was l-ed up | Acts 1:9
l-ing up holy hands | 1 Tim 2:8

LIGHT *brightness, lamp*

Let there be l | Gen 1:3
Israel had l in | Ex 10:23
l of the wicked | Job 18:5
LORD is my l | Ps 27:1
And a l to my path | Ps 119:105
like the l of dawn | Prov 4:18
walk in the l of the | Is 2:5
your l has come | Is 60:1
stars for l by night | Jer 31:35

the l of the world | Matt 5:14
body will be full of l | Matt 6:22
l of revelation to | Luke 2:32
There was the true l | John 1:9
I am the l | John 8:12
while you have...l | John 12:35
l of the gospel | 2 Cor 4:4
walk as children of l | Eph 5:8
Father of l-s | James 1:17
if we walk in the l | 1 John 1:7

LIGHTNING *flash of light in sky*

thunder and l flashes | Ex 19:16
He spreads His l | Job 36:30
makes l for the rain | Jer 10:13
l...from the east | Matt 24:27
appearance...like l | Matt 28:3

LIKENESS *similarity*

according to Our l | Gen 1:26
an idol, or any l | Ex 20:4
the l of sinful flesh | Rom 8:3
made in the l of men | Phil 2:7

LILY *flower*

The l of the valleys | Song 2:1
blossom like the l | Hos 14:5
l-ies of the field | Matt 6:28

LIMIT *end, extent*

there is no l | 1 Chr 22:16
no l to windy words | Job 16:3
set a l for the rain | Job 28:26
no l to the treasure | Nah 2:9

LINE *boundary or cord*

draw your *border* l | Num 34:7
ran from...battle l | 1 Sam 4:12
a l into the Nile | Is 19:8
plumb l in the hand | Zech 4:10

LINEN *type of cloth*

makes l garments | Prov 31:24
buy...a l waistband | Jer 13:1
left the l sheet | Mark 14:52
wrapped Him...l | Mark 15:46
saw the l wrappings | John 20:5
clothed in fine l | Rev 19:14

LINTEL *horizontal crosspiece*

blood on the l | Ex 12:23
l *and* five-sided | 1 Kin 6:31

LION *wild animal*

Judah is a l-'s whelp   Gen 49:9
a l or a bear   1 Sam 17:34
hunt me like a l   Job 10:16
tear my soul like a l   Ps 7:2
are bold as a l   Prov 28:1
cast into the l-s'   Dan 6:16
like a roaring l   1 Pet 5:8

LIPS *part of mouth*

My l will praise   Ps 63:3
With her flattering l   Prov 7:21
Your l, *my bride*   Song 4:11
a man of unclean l   Is 6:5
honors Me with...l   Matt 15:8

LIQUOR *alcoholic drink*

concerning wine and l   Mic 2:11
drink no wine or l   Luke 1:15

LISTEN *hear, heed*

Paraoh will not l   Ex 7:4
l to His voice   Deut 4:30
l...commandments   Deut 11:27
scoffer does not l   Prov 13:1
L to your father   Prov 23:22
draw near to l   Eccl 5:1
L to Me, O Jacob   Is 48:12
L...another parable   Matt 21:33
care what you l to   Mark 4:24
l-ing to the word   Luke 5:1
My Son...l to Him   Luke 9:35

LITERATURE *writings*

teach them the l   Dan 1:4
every *branch of* l   Dan 1:17

LITTLE *small quantity*

a l lower than God   Ps 8:5
a l boy will lead   Is 11:6
O men of l faith   Matt 6:30
forgiven l, loves l   Luke 7:47
a l leaven leavens   1 Cor 5:6
l children, abide   1 John 2:28

LIVE (v) *reside or be alive*

eat, and l forever   Gen 3:22
does not l by bread   Deut 8:3
my Redeemer l-s   Job 19:25
Let my soul l   Ps 119:175
Listen, that you may l   Is 55:3
can these bones l   Ezek 37:3
righteous will l by   Hab 2:4

not l on bread alone   Matt 4:4
l even if he dies   John 11:25
because I l   John 14:19
shall l by faith   Rom 1:17
Christ died and l-d   Rom 14:9
no longer I who l   Gal 2:20
to l is Christ   Phil 1:21
worship Him who l-s   Rev 4:10

LIVER *internal organ*

the lobe of the l   Ex 29:13
l of the sin offering   Lev 9:10
pierces through his l   Prov 7:23
he looks at the l   Ezek 21:21

LIVESTOCK *domestic animals*

was very rich in l   Gen 13:2
their l to Joseph   Gen 47:17
l of Egypt died   Ex 9:6
large number of l   Num 32:1

LIVING (adj) *alive*

man became a l being   Gen 2:7
voice of the l god   Deut 5:26
Divide the l child   1 Kin 3:25
Son of the l God   Matt 16:16
given you l water   John 4:10
I am the l bread   John 6:51
l and holy sacrifice   Rom 12:1
became a soul   1 Cor 15:45
temple of the l God   2 Cor 6:16
word of God is l   Heb 4:12

LIVING (n) *what is alive*

mother of all *the* l   Gen 3:20
land of the l   Job 28:13
that the l may know   Dan 4:17
God...of the l   Matt 22:32
judge the l and the   1 Pet 4:5

LOAD *burden*

in all their l-s   Num 4:27
l alone bear the l   Deut 1:12
My l is light   Matt 11:30

LOAF *portion of bread*

gave him a l of bread   Jer 37:21
shall ask him for a l   Matt 7:9
five l-ves and two   Matt 14:17

LO-AMMI

second son of Hosea   Hos 1:9

LOAN

LOAN *something lent*

your neighbor a l	Deut 24:10
rich with l-s	Hab 2:6

LOATHE *despise, detest*

I l-d *that* generation	Ps 95:10
sated man l-s money	Prov 27:7
I l the arrogance of	Amos 6:8

LOATHSOME *detestable*

l to the Egyptians	Gen 46:34
like l food to me	Job 6:7
l and malignant sore	Rev 16:2

LOCK (n) *tuft of hair*

seven l-s of my hair	Judg 16:13
flowing l-s of your	Song 7:5
a l of my head	Ezek 8:3

LOCK (v) *secure, shut*

l the door behind	2 Sam 13:17
l-ed quite securely	Acts 5:23
l up...the saints	Acts 26:10

LOCUST *grasshopper*

wind brought the l-s	Ex 10:13
you may eat: the l	Lev 11:22
come in like l-s	Judg 6:5
leap like the l	Job 39:20
l-s have no king	Prov 30:27
like the swarming l	Nah 3:17
food was l-s and wild	Matt 3:4

LOD/LYDDA

town of Benjamin SE of coastal Jaffa
1 Chr 8:12
Neh 11:35; Acts 9:32-38

LODGE *dwell, spend the night*

where you l, I will l	Ruth 1:16
drank and l-d there	Job 19:4
In his neck l-s	Job 41:22
l in the wilderness	Ps 55:7

LODGING (adj) *dwelling*

fodder at the l place	Gen 42:27
A wayfarers' l place	Jer 9:2
prepare for me a l	Philem 22

LOFTINESS *elevated, haughty*

l of man will be	Is 2:11
l of your dwelling	Obad 3

LOFTY *grand, high*

built Thee a l house	1 Kin 8:13
high and l mountain	Is 57:7

LOG *beam, wood*

he who splits l-s	Eccl 10:9
l out of your own eye	Matt 7:5

LOINS *lower back*

with your l girded	Ex 12:11
Gird up your l	2 Kin 4:29
l are full of anguish	Is 21:3
having girded your l	Eph 6:14

LOIS

grandmother of Timothy
2 Tim 1:5

LONELY *alone, isolated*

I am l and afflicted	Ps 25:16
makes a home for the l	Ps 68:6
How l sits the city	Lam 1:1
to a l place and rest	Mark 6:31

LONG (adj) *extended*

there was a l war	2 Sam 3:1
L life is in her	Prov 3:16
you make l prayers	Matt 23:14
if a man has l hair	1 Cor 11:14

LONG (v) *desire, want*

Who l for death	Job 3:21
my soul l-s for Thee	Is 26:9
l-ing to be fed	Luke 16:21
I l to see you	Rom 1:11
angels l to look	1 Pet 1:12
l for the pure milk	1 Pet 2:2

LOOK *see, stare*

Do not l behind you	Gen 19:17
afraid to l at God	Ex 3:6
LORD l-s at the heart	1 Sam 16:7
L upon my affliction	Ps 25:18
The sea l-ed and fled	Ps 114:3
not l on the wine	Prov 23:31
l eagerly for Him	Is 8:17
l to the Holy One	Is 17:7
l on Me...pierced	Zech 12:10
L at the birds of	Matt 6:26
l-ing up...heaven	Matt 14:19
plow and l-ing back	Luke 9:62
l on the fields	John 4:35
l on Him...pierced	John 19:37

150

l-ing for the blessed Titus 2:13
l-ing for...heavens 2 Pet 3:13

LOOSE *release*

l the cords of Orion Job 38:31
hast l-d my bonds Ps 116:16
l on earth shall be Matt 16:19
you l on earth Matt 18:18

LORD *personal name of God*

Old Testament
Different Hebrew words
are translated as Lord

LORD *(Yahweh)* Gen 4:1
Ex 3:2,15; Ps 23:1; Is 40:31
Ezek 11:23
Lord GOD *(Adonai Yahweh)*
Gen 15:2; 2 Sam 7:18,19
Is 1:24; Ezek 28:6; Hab 3:19
LORD God *(Yahweh Elohim)*
Gen 2:4; Ps 59:5;68:18
Jer 15:16; Jon 1:9
Lord *(Adonai)* Gen 18:27
Ex 4:10; Josh 3:11; Ps 68:19
Mic 4:13
LORD GOD *(Yah Yahweh)*
Is 12:2

New Testament
Different Greek words
are translated as Lord
Lord *(Kyrios, refers to either*
the Father or the Son)
Matt 1:20; John 11:2; Acts 5:19
2 Cor 5:6; 1 Thess 4:16
Lord *(Despotes)* Luke 2:29
Acts 4:24; Rev 6:10
Lord God *(Kyrios Theos, refers*
to either the Father or
the Son) Luke 1:32
Rev 1:8;11:17;16:7;18:8
Lord Jesus *(Kyrios Iesous)*
Mark 16:19; Luke 24:3
Acts 4:33;7:59
Lord Jesus Christ *(Kyrios Iesous*
Christos)
Acts 15:26; Rom 1:7;5:1
1 Cor 1:10; Eph 1:2,3
1 Thess 5:9; James 2:1

LORD *human master, ruler*

Hear us, my l Gen 23:6
not my l be angry Gen 31:35
Moses, my l Num 11:28
l-s of...Philistines Judg 16:27
counsel of my l Ezra 10:3
l-s of the nations Is 16:8
his l commanded Matt 18:25
write to my l Acts 25:26

LO-RUHAMAH

daughter of Hosea Hos 1:6,8

LOSE *mislay, suffer loss*

do not l courage 2 Chr 15:7
lost their confidence Neh 6:16
stars l their Joel 2:10
his life shall l it Matt 10:39
that which was lost Matt 18:11
not l his reward Mark 9:41
whoever l-s his life Luke 9:24

LOSS *damage, what is lost*

might not suffer l Dan 6:2
damage and great l Acts 27:10
might not suffer l 2 Cor 7:9
all things to be l Phil 3:8

LOST (adj) *missing, ruined*

like a l sheep Ps 119:176
have become l sheep Jer 50:6
l sheep...of Israel Matt 10:6
the wine is l Mark 2:22

LOST (n) *without God*

I will seek the l Ezek 34:16
sent only to the l Matt 15:24

LOT

nephew of Abraham Gen 12:5
Gen 19:15,36

LOT *portion or decision process*

one l for the LORD Lev 16:8
clothing they cast l-s Ps 22:18
your l with us Prov 1:14
let us cast l-s Jon 1:7
tear it, but cast l-s John 19:24
l fell to Matthias Acts 1:26

LOUD *great, noisy*

very l trumpet sound Ex 19:16
with a l shout Ezra 3:13

Jesus cried...l voice   Matt 27:50
heard...a l voice   Rev 1:10

LOVE (n) *compassion, devotion*

l covers all   Prov 10:12
in unchanging l   Mic 7:18
l will grow cold   Matt 24:12
abide in My l   John 15:10
Greater l has no one   John 15:13
demonstrates His...l   Rom 5:8
separate us from...l   Rom 8:39
l edifies   1 Cor 8:1
l is kind   1 Cor 13:4
Pursue l   1 Cor 14:1
l of Christ controls   2 Cor 5:14
through l serve one   Gal 5:13
fruit...is l   Gal 5:22
speaking...truth in l   Eph 4:15
l of money is a root   1 Tim 6:10
for l is from God   1 John 4:7
God is l   1 John 4:16
l casts out fear   1 John 4:18
have left your first l   Rev 2:4

LOVE (v)

who l Me and keep My   Ex 20:6
l your neighbor as   Lev 19:18
l the LORD your God   Deut 6:5
the LORD l-d Israel   1 Kin 10:9
I l Thy testimonies   Ps 119:119
LORD l-s He reproves   Prov 3:12
friend l-s at all   Prov 17:17
Do not l sleep   Prov 20:13
A time to l   Eccl 3:8
Hate evil, l good   Amos 5:15
do not l perjury   Zech 8:17
l your enemies   Matt 5:44
l to stand and pray   Matt 6:5
God so l-d the world   John 3:16
you l one another   John 13:34
l-s a cheerful giver   2 Cor 9:7
Husbands, l...wives   Eph 5:25
Do not l the world   1 John 2:15
whom I l, I reprove   Rev 3:19

LOVERS *one who desires, loves*

l have been crushed   Jer 22:20
I called to my l   Lam 1:19
the hands of your l   Ezek 16:39
I will go after my l   Hos 2:5
l of pleasure...l of   2 Tim 3:4

LOVINGKINDNESS *compassion*

His l is upon Israel   Ezra 3:11
abundant and in the l   Ps 86:15
sing of the l of the   Ps 89:1
By l and truth   Prov 16:6
with everlasting l   Is 54:8

LOWLAND *low hills*

country and in the l   Deut 1:7
the Negev and the l   Josh 10:40
sycamores in the l   2 Chr 1:15
the cities of the l   Jer 32:44
see also **SHEPHELAH**

LOWLY *humble, little*

He sets on high...l   Job 5:11
He regards the l   Ps 138:6
associate with the l   Rom 12:16

LOYALTY *faithfulness*

Is this your l   2 Sam 16:17
proclaims his own l   Prov 20:6
l delight in l   Hos 6:6

LUKE

associate of Paul
                            2 Tim 4:11; Philem 1:24
author of Luke and Acts
                            Luke 1:1; Acts 1:1
physician   Col 4:14

LUKEWARM *tepid*

because you are l   Rev 3:16

LUST *sexual desire*

looks...woman to l   Matt 5:28
from youthful l-s   2 Tim 2:22
You l and do not   James 4:2
l of the eyes   1 John 2:16

LUXURIANT *lush, productive*

beneath...l tree   1 Kin 14:23
Israel is a l vine   Hos 10:1

LUXURY *extravagance*

L is not fitting for   Prov 19:10
clothed and live in l   Luke 7:25

LUZ

1 *ancient name of Bethel*
                            Gen 28:19;48:3
2 *town in Aram*   Judg 1:26

LYCAONIA
Roman province in Asia Minor
Acts 14:6

LYDDA *see* **LOD**

LYDIA
1 *seller of purple dyes and goods*
Acts 16:14,40
2 *region on the W coast of*
Asia Minor Jer 46:9

LYING (adj) *false*
with a l tongue Ps 109:2
hatred *has* l lips Prov 10:18
l pen of the scribes Jer 8:8
and l divination Ezek 13:6

LYRE *stringed instrument*
play the l and pipe Gen 4:21
prophesy with l-s 1 Chr 25:1
Awake, harp and l Ps 57:8

LYSTRA
a Lycaonian town Acts 14:6
Acts 16:1,2

M

MACEDONIA
Roman province Acts 16:9,12
Phil 4:15;1 Tim 1:3
visited by Paul Acts 16:10
2 Cor 2:13

MACHIR
1 *grandson of Joseph* Josh 17:1
2 *son of Ammiel* 2 Sam 9:4,5

MACHPELAH
cave near Hebron Gen 23:17,19
Sarah's burial place Gen 23:19
Abraham buried there Gen 25:9
burial place of Jacob, Isaac,
Rebekah, and Leah
Gen 49:29ff;50:13

MAD *insane*
makes a wise man m Eccl 7:7
nations are going m Jer 51:7

MADMAN *insane person*
behaving as a m 1 Sam 21:14
m who prophesies Jer 29:26

MADNESS *lunacy*
laughter, It is m Eccl 2:2
consider...m and folly Eccl 2:12

MAGDAN
village on the Sea of Galilee
Matt 15:39

MAGDALENE
Mary Matt 27:56,61
from village of Magdala
Mark 15:40,47; John 20:1,18

MAGI
wise men from Persia who
visited Jesus, Mary, and Joseph
Matt 2:1,7,16

MAGIC *sorcery*
practicing m Acts 8:9
who practiced m Acts 19:19

MAGICIAN *sorcerer, wizard*
called for...m-s Gen 41:8
the m-s of Egypt Ex 7:11
of any m, conjurer or Dan 2:10
found a certain m Acts 13:6

MAGISTRATE
appear before the m Luke 12:58
to the chief m-s Acts 16:20

MAGNIFY *extol, praise*
name...be m-ied 2 Sam 7:26
Thou dost m him Job 7:17
O m the LORD with me Ps 34:3
hast m-ied Thy word Ps 138:2
Jesus was...m-ied Acts 19:17
I m my ministry Rom 11:13

MAGOG
1 *son of Japheth* 1 Chr 1:2,5
2 *region in Asia Minor or further*
N ruled by Gog Ezek 38:2
see also **GOG** Ezek 39:6

MAHANAIM
city in N Trans-Jordan
Josh 13:26,30

153

MAHANAIM

city of refuge   Josh 21:38
Levitical city   1 Chr. 6:80

MAHER-SHALAL-HASH-BAZ

*symbolic name of one of
  Isaiah's sons*   Is 8:3

MAHLAH

1 daughter of Zelophehad
   Num 26:33;27:1; Josh 17:3
2 a Manassite   1 Chr 7:18

MAHLON

husband of Ruth Ruth 1:5;4:10

MAID

Hagar, Sarai's m   Gen 16:8
gave my m to my   Gen 30:18
I am Ruth your m   Ruth 3:9
way of a man...a m   Prov 30:19

MAIDEN *young woman*

at the Nile...her m-s   Ex 2:5
m-s...tambourines   Ps 68:25

MAIDSERVANT *female slave*

do...to your m   Deut 15:17
give Thy m a son   1 Sam 1:11
Let your m speak   2 Sam 14:12
while your m slept   1 Kin 3:20

MAJESTIC *dignified, grand*

Who is like Thee, m   Ex 15:11
with His m voice   Job 37:4
How m is Thy name   Ps 8:1
They are the m ones   Ps 16:3
m is His work   Ps 111:3
by the M Glory   2 Pet 1:17

MAJESTY *grandeur*

Around God is...m   Job 37:22
He is clothed with m   Ps 93:1
The m of our God   Is 35:2
right hand of the M   Heb 1:3
revile angelic m-ies   Jude 8

MAKE *cause, create, do*

Let Us make man in   Gen 1:26
not m for...an idol   Ex 20:4
M me know Thy ways   Ps 25:4
M ready the way of   Matt 3:3
m you fishers of men   Matt 4:19

MAKER *creator*

Where is God my M   Job 35:10

154

---

kneel before...our M   Ps 95:6
M of heaven and   Ps 115:15
I, the LORD, am the m   Is 44:24

MAKKEDAH

Canaanite city in Judah
   Josh 10:21;15:41

MALACHI

prophet   Mal 1:1

MALCHUS

*servant whose ear was cut
  off by Peter*   John 18:10

MALE

m and female He   Gen 1:27
lamb...unblemished m   Ex 12:5
likeness of m or   Deut 4:16
slew...m children   Matt 2:16
made...m and female   Matt 19:4
neither m nor female   Gal 3:28

MALICE *evil, mischief*

perceived their m   Matt 22:18
leaven of m and   1 Cor 5:8
wrath, m, slander   Col 3:8
putting aside all m   1 Pet 2:1

MALICIOUS *harmful, spiteful*

to be a m witness   Ex 23:1
m gossips, without   2 Tim 3:3

MALTA

*island S of Sicily where Paul
  was shipwrecked*   Acts 28:1

MAMMON *wealth*

serve God and m   Matt 6:24
m of unrighteousness   Luke 16:9

MAMRE

*1 Abraham's dwelling place
  near Hebron*   Gen 13:18
2 Amorite chieftain   Gen 14:24

MAN *male*

make m in Our image   Gen 1:26
God formed m of dust   Gen 2:7
Elisha the m of God   2 Kin 5:8
m is born for trouble   Job 5:7
blessed is the m   Ps 1:1
m is a mere breath   Ps 39:11
righteous m hates   Prov 13:5
Will a m rob God   Mal 3:8

light...before **men**   Matt 5:16
fishers of **men**   Mark 1:17
Sabbath...for **m**   Mark 2:27
rich **m** to enter   Mark 10:25
what is a **m** profited Luke 9:25
a **m**, sent from God   John 1:6
How can a **m** be born John 3:4
a...**m** of Macedonia   Acts 16:9

through one **m** sin   Rom 5:12
as is common to **m** 1 Cor 10:13
when I became a **m** 1 Cor 13:11
m...leave his father   Eph 5:31

MAN, SON OF

see SON OF MAN

MANASSEH

1 *son of Joseph* Gen 41:51;46:20
2 *tribe and area*   Num 13:11
     Josh 17:1
3 *king of Judah*   2 Kin 21:1,11
4 *son of Hashum*   Ezra 10:33
5 *Pahath-moab's son* Ezra 10:30

MANDRAKES *love plant*

found **m** in the field Gen 30:14
m...fragrance   Song 7:13

MANGER

spend...at your **m**   Job 39:9
the **m** is clean   Prov 14:4
laid Him in a **m**   Luke 2:7

MANIFEST *reveal*

I **m**-ed Thy name   John 17:6
became **m** to those Rom 10:20
made **m** to God   2 Cor 5:11
m-ed to His saints   Col 1:26

MANIFOLD *many and varied*

the **m** wisdom of God Eph 3:10
stewards...**m** grace 1 Pet 4:10

MANKIND *the human race*

God...dwell with **m** 2 Chr 6:18
All **m** is stupid   Jer 51:17
Authority over all **m** John 17:2
His love for **m**   Titus 3:4
kill a third of **m**   Rev 9:15

MANNA *food of the desert*

Israel named it **m**   Ex 16:31
m was like coriander Num 11:7
m ceased on the day Josh 5:12

He rained down **m**   Ps 78:24
Our fathers ate the **m** John 6:31

MANNER *way*

Thy **m** with those   Ps 119:132
spoke in such a **m**   Acts 14:1
m worthy of...saints Rom 16:2
walk in a **m** worthy   Eph 4:1

MANOAH

father of Samson   Judg 13:2ff

MANSLAYER

for the **m** to flee to   Num 35:6
m might flee there   Deut 4:42
the **m** who kills any Josh 20:3

MANTLE *cloak, garment*

threw his **m** on him 1 Kin 19:19
the **m** of Elijah   2 Kin 2:13
as a **m** Thou wilt roll Heb 1:12

MARAH

spring of bitter water Ex 15:23

MARCH *pace, walk*

m around...seven times Josh 6:4
m everyone in his path Joel 2:8

MARDUK

chief Babylonian god   Jer 50:2

MARESHAH

1 *father of Hebron* 1 Chr 2:42
2 *son of Laadah*   1 Chr 4:21
3 *town in Judah*   2 Chr 11:5-8

MARK *sign, spot*

make any tattoo **m**-s Lev 19:28
m on the foreheads Ezek 9:4
m on his forehead   Rev 14:9
m of the beast   Rev 19:20

MARK, JOHN

author of Gospel of Mark
cousin of Barnabas   Col 4:10
accompanied Paul and Barnabas
     Acts 13:5;15:37

MARKET *selling or trading place*

was the **m** of nations   Is 23:3
coastlands were...**m** Ezek 27:15
idle in the **m** place   Matt 20:3
sold in the meat **m** 1 Cor 10:25

MARRIAGE

MARRIAGE *wedlock*

a m alliance with   1 Kin 3:1
nor are given in m   Matt 22:30
m *be held* in honor   Heb 13:4
m supper of the Lamb Rev 19:9

MARRY *join in wedlock*

m-ied foreign wives Ezra 10:10
m-ies a divorced   Matt 5:32
better not to m   Matt 19:10
neither m, nor are Mark 12:25
m-ied woman is bound Rom 7:2
better to m than to 1 Cor 7:9

MARTHA

sister of Lazarus and Mary
              John 11:1,5

MARVEL *be amazed, wonder*

Jesus heard...He m-ed Matt 8:10
the multitude m-ed Matt 15:31
do not m that I said John 3:7
m at the sight   Acts 7:31

MARVELOUS *extraordinary*

and see this m sight   Ex 3:3
It is m in our eyes Ps 118:23
into His m light   1 Pet 2:9
m are Thy works   Rev 15:3

MARY

1 *mother of Jesus*   Matt 1:16
2 *Mary Magdalene* Matt 27:56
              Mark 15:40
3 *mother of James and Joseph*
    Matt 27:56; Mark 16:1
4 *sister of Martha and Lazarus*
              John 11:1
5 *mother of Mark* Acts 12:12
6 *wife of Clopas* John 19:25
7 *Roman believer* Rom 16:6

MASTER *lord, ruler*

God of...m Abraham Gen 24:12
m shall pierce his ear Ex 21:6
can serve two m-s Matt 6:24
death no longer is m Rom 6:9
sin shall not be m Rom 6:14
obedient to...your m-s Eph 6:5
a M in heaven   Col 4:1

MATTHEW

tax-gatherer   Matt 9:9;10:3

apostle   Matt 10:3
     Luke 6:15; Acts 1:13

MATTHIAS

replaced Judas Acts 1:23,26

MATURE *full grown* or *stable*

then the m grain Mark 4:28
those who are m 1 Cor 2:6
your thinking be m 1 Cor 14:20
food is for the m Heb 5:14

MATURITY *ripeness, adulthood*

bring no fruit to m Luke 8:14
let us press on to m Heb 6:1

MEAL *prepared food*

a m for enjoyment Eccl 10:19
not even eat a m Mark 3:20
washed before...m Luke 11:38
m-s together with Acts 2:46
for a *single* m   Heb 12:16

MEAL OFFERING
see OFFERINGS

MEANINGLESS *senseless*

with m arguments   Is 29:21
not use m repetition Matt 6:7

MEASURE (n) *amount*

a full and just m Deut 25:15
good m, pressed Luke 6:38
to each a m of faith Rom 12:3
m of Christ's gift   Eph 4:7

MEASURE (v) *determine extent*

he stopped m-ing *it* Gen 41:49
m their former work Is 65:7
he m-ed the gate Ezek 40:13
shall be m-ed to you Mark 4:24
rod to m the city Rev 21:15

MEASURING *standard*

justice the m line Is 28:17
was given me a m rod Rev 11:1

MEAT *flesh, food*

Who will give us m Num 11:4
LORD will give you m Num 11:18
you may eat m Deut 12:20
rained m upon them Ps 78:27
from m sacrificed Acts 21:25
good not to eat m Rom 14:21

I will never eat m 1 Cor 8:13
m sacrificed...idols 1 Cor 10:28

MEDE(S)
ancient Indo-Europeans of
NW Iran Dan 5:31;11:1

MEDEBA
Moabite town E of Jordan
Josh 13:9; 1 Chr 19:7

MEDIA
country of the Medes Ezra 6:2
Esth 1:18;Is 21:2

MEDIATOR *intermediary*
by the agency of a m Gal 3:19
one m...between God 1 Tim 2:5
Jesus...m of a new Heb 12:24

MEDITATE *ponder*
Isaac went out to m Gen 24:63
His law he m-s day Ps 1:2
M in your heart Ps 4:4
I m on Thee in the Ps 63:6

MEDITATION *deep reflection*
m...Be acceptable Ps 19:14
m be pleasing to Him Ps 104:34
my m all the day Ps 119:97

MEDIUM *summons spirits*
not turn to m-s or Lev 19:31
m...be put to death Lev 20:27
a m, or a spiritist Deut 18:11
woman who is a m 1 Sam 28:7
will resort to...m-s Is 19:3

MEEKNESS *gentleness*
cause of truth and m Ps 45:4
m and...of Christ 2 Cor 10:1

MEET *encounter*
Esau ran to m him Gen 33:4
people out...to m God Ex 19:17
God...will m me Ps 59:10
Prepare to m...God Amos 4:12
to m the bridegroom Matt 25:1
m-s his accusers Acts 25:16
m...in the air 1 Thess 4:17

MEETING *assembly*
house of m for all Job 30:23
midst of Thy m place Ps 74:4

MEETING, TENT OF
see **TABERNACLE**

MEGIDDO
strategic city in N Palestine
Josh 12:21; 2 Kin 9:27
plain in Jezreel Valley
2 Chr 35:22; Zech 12:11
see also **HAR-MAGEDON**

MELCHIZEDEK
1 *king of Salem* Gen 14:18,19
priest Ps 110:4
2 *type of undying priesthood*
Heb 5:6,10;6:20;7:1ff

MELODY *tune*
lyre...the sound of m Ps 98:5
singing...making m Eph 5:19

MELT *dissolve*
people m with fear Josh 14:8
His voice...earth m-ed Ps 46:6
mountains m-ed like Ps 97:5
As silver is m-ed Ezek 22:22

MEMBER *part of the whole*
m-s of...household Matt 10:25
m-s one of another Rom 12:5
if one m suffers 1 Cor 12:26
m-s of His body Eph 5:30

MEMORIAL *commemoration*
this is My m-name Ex 3:15
in a book as a m Ex 17:14
stones...become a m Josh 4:7
ascended as a m Acts 10:4

MEMORY *remembrance*
M of him perishes Job 18:17
cut off their m Ps 109:15
m of the righteous Prov 10:7
spoken of in m of Mark 14:9

MEMPHIS
city in Egypt Is 19:13
Jer 46:19;Ezek 30:13

MENAHEM
king of Israel 2 Kin 15:14,17

MENSTRUAL
m impurity for seven Lev 15:19

a woman during...m   Ezek 18:6

MENSTRUATION

in the days of her m   Lev 12:2
like her bed at m   Lev 15:26

MEPHIBOSHETH

1 *son of Jonathan*   2 Sam 4:4
   also **Merib-baal**   1 Chr 8:34
2 *son of Saul*   2 Sam 21:8

MERAB

Saul's daughter   1 Sam 18:17,19

MERARI

son of Levi   Gen 46:11
head of a Levitical family
   Ex 6:19; 2 Chr 34:12

MERCHANDISE

and your m   Ezek 27:33
a house of m   John 2:16

MERCHANT *buyer/seller*

m-s procured *them*   1 Kin 10:28
m of the peoples   Ezek 27:3
A m, in whose hands   Hos 12:7
m seeking...pearls   Matt 13:45
m-s of the earth   Rev 18:3

MERCIFUL *compassionate*

God m and gracious   Ps 86:15
the Lord is...and m   Ps 145:8
The m man...good   Prov 11:17
Blessed are the m   Matt 5:7
as your Father is m   Luke 6:36
m to me, the sinner   Luke 18:13

MERCY *compassion*

Great are Thy m-ies   Ps 119:156
in His m He redeemed   Is 63:9
m to *the* poor   Dan 4:27
the orphan finds m   Hos 14:3
they shall receive m   Matt 5:7
tender m of our God   Luke 1:78
m on whom I have m   Rom 9:15
by the m-ies of God   Rom 12:1
God, being rich in m   Eph 2:4

MERCY SEAT *covering over ark*

a m of pure gold   Ex 25:17
put the m on the ark   Ex 26:34
in front of the m   Ex 30:6
sprinkle it on the m   Lev 16:15

overshadowing the m   Heb 9:5

MERIBAH

1 *fountain of Rephidim*   Ex 17:7
2 *fountain of Kadesh-Barnea*
   Num 27:14

MERODACH-BALADAN

king of Babylon   Is 39:1
also **Berodach-Baladan**

MERRY *joyful, lively*

David...making m   1 Chr 15:29
wine makes life m   Eccl 10:19
eat, drink *and* be m   Luke 12:19
m with my friends   Luke 15:29

MESHA

1 *territorial boundary in Arabia*
   Gen 10:30
2 *Moabite king*   2 Kin 3:4
3 *man of Judah*   1 Chr 2:42
4 *a Benjamite*   1 Chr 8:9

MESHACH

*one of three Jews thrown into
   furnace*   Dan 3:19ff
also **Mishael**   Dan 1:7

MESHECH

1 *son of Japheth*   Gen 10:2
2 *descendants and nation*
   Is 66:19; Ezek 27:13

MESOPOTAMIA

*land of Tigris and Euphrates
   Rivers*   Deut 23:4
   Judg 3:8; 1 Chr 19:6; Acts 7:2

MESSAGE *communication*

m from God for you   Judg 3:20
m...with authority   Luke 4:32
m and my preaching   1 Cor 2:4
the m of truth   Eph 1:13
m we have heard   1 John 1:5

MESSENGER *one sent*

My m whom I send   Is 42:19
m of the Lord of hosts   Mal 2:7
I send My m before   Matt 11:10
m-s of the churches   2 Cor 8:23
m of Satan   2 Cor 12:7

MESSIAH

anointed one Dan 9:25,26
       John 1:41;4:25
Greek: Christ

METAL

like glowing m   Ezek 1:4
their m images   Dan 11:8

METHUSELAH

son of Enoch   Gen 5:21
grandfather of Noah Gen 5:25ff

MICAH

1 *an Ephraimite* Judg 17:1
2 *line of Reuben* 1 Chr 5:5
3 *father of Abdon* 2 Chr 34:20
4 *prophet* Jer 26:18; Mic 1:1
name of several other people

MICAIAH

1 *prophet*   1 Kin 22:8-26
2 *father of Achbor* 2 Kin 22:12
3 *wife of Rehoboam* 2 Chr 13:2
4 *under Jehoshaphat* 2 Chr 17:7
5 *line of Asaph* Neh 12:35
6 *under Nehemiah* Neh 12:41
7 *son of Gemariah* Jer 36:11

MICHAEL

1 *an archangel* Dan 10:21;12:1
      Jude 9; Rev 12:7
2 *Jehoshaphat's son* 2 Chr 21:2
 prince of Judah
3 *army captain* 1 Chr 12:20
4 *line of Gershom* 1 Chr 6:40
name of seven other people

MICHAL

daughter of Saul 1 Sam 18:20
David's wife 1 Sam 19:11

MIDDLE *midst*

the m of the garden Gen 3:3
sun stopped in the m Josh 10:13
m of the lampstands Rev 1:13

MIDDLE GATE
see **GATES OF JERUSALEM**

MIDHEAVEN *directly overhead*

eagle flying in m Rev 8:13
angel flying in m Rev 14:6
birds which fly in m Rev 19:17

MIDIAN

1 *a son of Abraham* Gen 25:1,2
2 *land SE of Canaan in desert*
 Ex 2:15; Num 31:8; Judg 8:28

MIDIANITES

people of Midian Gen 37:36
    Num 31:2; Judg 7:7

MIDST *middle, within*

God is in the m Ps 46:5
in the m of the fire Dan 3:25
Holy One in your m Hos 11:9
I am in their m Matt 18:20

MIDWIFE *aids childbirth*

m...tied a scarlet Gen 38:28
before the m can get Ex 1:19

MIGDOL

1 *Israelite camp near Red Sea*
    Ex 14:2; Num 33:7
2 *town in Egypt* Jer 44:1

MIGHT *strength*

my first-born; My m Gen 49:3
and with all your m Deut 6:5
With Him are...m Job 12:13
Not by m nor by Zech 4:6
strength of His m Eph 1:19

MIGHTY *powerful*

a m hunter before Gen 10:9
m...awesome God Deut 10:17
m men of valor 1 Chr 12:8
The LORD m in battle Ps 24:8
a m king will rule Is 19:4
m in the Scriptures Acts 18:24
the m hand of God 1 Pet 5:6

MILCAH

1 *daughter of Haran* Gen 11:29
2 *daughter of Zelophehad*
 Num 26:33;27:1; Josh 17:3

MILCOM

god of Ammonites 1 Kin 11:5,33
   2 Kin 23:13; Zeph 1:5
also Molech

MILE *distance, measurement*

one m, go with him Matt 5:41
m-s from Jerusalem Luke 24:13

MILETUS

town in Asia Minor
    Acts 20:15,17; 2 Tim 4:20

MILK

land flowing with m   Ex 3:8
pour me out like m   Job 10:10
m produces butter   Prov 30:33
m to drink, not   1 Cor 3:2
pure m of the word   1 Pet 2:2

MILL *grinding stones*

sound of the...m   Eccl 12:4
at the grinding m   Lam 5:13
women...at the m   Matt 24:41

MILLO

1 *fort near Shechem*
  Beth-millo   Judg 9:6,20
2 *fortress in Jerusalem*
    2 Sam 5:9; 1 Kin 9:15,24
    1 Chr 11:8; 2 Chr 32:5

MILLSTONE *grinding stone*

upper m in pledge   Deut 24:6
woman threw...m   Judg 9:53
m be hung around   Matt 18:6
stone like a great m   Rev 18:21

MINA

measure of gold or silver coin
    1 Kin 10:17; Ezra 2:69
    Neh 7:71; Luke 19:13ff

MIND *memory, thought*

God tries the...m-s   Ps 7:9
Recall it to m   Is 46:8
I test the m   Jer 17:10
Let his m be changed   Dan 4:16
He opened...m-s   Luke 24:45
with one m in the   Acts 2:46
to a depraved m   Rom 1:28
m set on the flesh   Rom 8:7
the m of Christ   1 Cor 2:16
m-s were hardened   2 Cor 3:14
with humility of m   Phil 2:3

MINDFUL *aware*

Lord be m of me   Ps 40:17
He is m that we are   Ps 103:14
LORD has been m   Ps 115:12
m of the...faith   2 Tim 1:5

MINISTER (n) *one who serves*

m-s before the ark   1 Chr 16:4

spoken of as m-s   Is 61:6
a m and a witness   Acts 26:16
a m of Christ Jesus   Rom 15:16
is Christ then a m   Gal 2:17
I was made a m   Eph 3:7
faithful m in the   Eph 6:21
His m-s a flame of   Heb 1:7
a m in the sanctuary   Heb 8:2

MINISTER (v) *give help, serve*

to m as priest to Me   Ex 28:1
the boy m-ed to   1 Sam 2:11
not stand to m   1 Kin 8:11
to the LORD, To m   Is 56:6
angels were m-ing   Mark 1:13
follow Him and m   Mark 15:41

MINISTRY *service*

He began His m   Luke 3:23
to the m of the word   Acts 6:4
m of the Spirit   2 Cor 3:8
m of reconciliation   2 Cor 5:18
fulfill your m   2 Tim 4:5
a more excellent m   Heb 8:6

MIRACLE *supernatural event*

Work a m   Ex 7:9
I will perform m-s   Ex 34:10
m-s had occurred   Matt 11:21
He could do no m   Mark 6:5
perform a m in My   Mark 9:39
this m of healing   Acts 4:22
works m-s among you   Gal 3:5
wonders and...m-s   Heb 2:4

MIRE *mud*

cast me into the m   Job 30:19
Deliver me from the m   Ps 69:14
wallowing in the m   2 Pet 2:22

MIRIAM

1 *sister of Moses and Aaron*
    Ex 15:20; Num 12:4,10;20:1
2 *line of Ezrah*   1 Chr 4:17

MIRROR *image reflector*

see in a m dimly   1 Cor 13:12
natural face in a m   James 1:23

MISCARRIAGE *aborted fetus*

so that she has a m   Ex 21:22
m-s of a woman   Ps 58:8

MISERABLE *unhappy*

loathe this m food   Num 21:5
m and chronic   Deut 28:59
Be m and mourn   James 4:9
m and poor and blind Rev 3:17

MISERY *sorrow, suffering*

conscious of my m   Job 10:15
Destruction and m   Rom 3:16

MISFORTUNE *adversity*

M will not come   Jer 5:12
m which He has   Jer 26:13
The day of his m   Obad 12

MISHAEL

1 *of family of Kohath*
    Ex 6:22; Lev 10:4
2 *associate of Ezra*   Neh 8:4
3 *Daniel's friend*   Dan 1:6
    Dan 1:7,11,19;2:17
also **Meshach**

MISLEAD *lead astray*

m-s a blind *person* Deut 27:18
m-led My people   Ezek 13:10
that no one m-s you Mark 13:5
m-ing our nation   Luke 23:2

MISSILES *what is thrown or shot*

m of the evil *one*   Eph 6:16

MISTREAT *treat badly, wrong*

not m...the stranger   Jer 22:3
slaves...m-ed them   Matt 22:6
pray for...who m   Luke 6:28
mocked and m-ed   Luke 18:32
m and to stone them Acts 14:5

MISTRESS *woman in charge*

her m was despised   Gen 16:4
m of the house   1 Kin 17:17
the maid like her m   Is 24:2
the m of sorceries   Nah 3:4

MIZPAH/MIZPEH

1 *heap of stones*   Gen 31:49
2 *town in Gilead*   Judg 10:17
3 *near Mt. Hermon*   Josh 11:3
4 *village in Judah*   Josh 15:38
5 *Benjamite town*   Josh 18:26
6 *Moabite town*   1 Sam 22:3

MIZRAIM

1 *son of Ham*   Gen 10:6
    father of nations   Gen 10:13
2 *Heb. for Egypt* 1 Chr 1:8,11

MOAB

1 *son of Lot*   Gen 19:37
2 *country E of the Dead Sea*
    Ex 15:15; Josh 24:9; Ruth 1:2
    2 Kin 3:7; Ps 60:8; Jer 48:1

MOCK *ridicule, scorn*

lads...m-ed him   2 Kin 2:23
Fools m at sin   Prov 14:9
who m-s the poor   Prov 17:5
soldiers also m-ed   Luke 23:36
God is not m-ed   Gal 6:7

MOCKERY *object of ridicule*

a m of the Egyptians   Ex 10:2
made a m of me   Num 22:29
a m of justice   Prov 19:28
m *and* insinuations   Hab 2:6

MOLECH

god of the Ammonites
Lev 18:21; 1 Kin 11:7; Jer 32:35
also **Milcom**

MOLTEN *cast metal*

made it into a m calf   Ex 32:4
make...no m gods   Ex 34:17
destroy...m images Num 33:52
capitals of bronze 1 Kin 7:16
his m images are   Jer 10:14

MONEY *currency*

take double *the* m   Gen 43:12
not sell her for m   Deut 21:14
time to receive m   2 Kin 5:26
loves m will not be   Eccl 5:10
no m in their belt   Mark 6:8
m in the bank   Luke 19:23
love of m is a root 1 Tim 6:10

MONEYCHANGERS

the tables of the m Matt 21:12
coins of the m   John 2:15

MONSTER *enormous animal*

created...sea m-s   Gen 1:21
sea, or the sea m   Job 7:12
sea m-s in the waters Ps 74:13

belly of the sea m   Matt 12:40

MOON

m and...were bowing   Gen 37:9
the m stopped   Josh 10:13
m and stars to rule   Ps 136:9
beautiful as...m   Song 6:10
the m into blood   Joel 2:31
m will not...light   Matt 24:29
signs in...and m   Luke 21:25

MORALS *principles*

Bad...good m   1 Cor 15:33

MORDECAI

1 *returned from exile with
Zerubbabel*   Ezra 2:2
2 *Esther's cousin*   Esth 2:7
Esth 3:2;9:20;10:3

MORIAH

*land/mountain where Abraham
offered Isaac*   Gen 22:2
*threshing floor of
Araunah (Ornan)*   2 Sam 24:18
site of Temple   2 Chr 3:1

MORNING *dawn*

was m, a fifth day   Gen 1:23
Rise early in the m   Ex 8:20
the m stars sang   Job 38:7
m or evening sowing   Eccl 11:6
the bright m star   Rev 22:16

MORSEL *piece of bread*

have eaten my m   Job 31:17
Better is a dry m   Prov 17:1
after the m, Satan   John 13:27

MORTAL *what eventually dies*

not trust...In m man   Ps 146:3
life to your m bodies   Rom 8:11
m...immortality   1 Cor 15:53
in our m flesh   2 Cor 4:11

MOSES

birth   Ex 2:1-3
in Pharaoh's care   Ex 2:5-10
killed an Egyptian   Ex 2:11,12
exiled   Ex 2:15
called by God   Ex 3:1-22
opposed Pharaoh   Ex 5-11

crossed Red Sea   Ex 14
*Ten Commandments*Ex 20:1-18
saw Canaan   Deut 3:23ff;34:1ff
death   Deut 31:14;34:5

MOTH *insect*

crushed before the m   Job 4:19
The m will eat them   Is 50:9
like a m to Ephraim   Hos 5:12
m and rust destroy   Matt 6:19

MOTHER

leave...and his m   Gen 2:24
m of all *the* living   Gen 3:20
Honor...and your m   Ex 20:12
a grief to his m   Prov 10:1
Contend with your m   Hos 2:2
When His m Mary   Matt 1:18
take...and His m   Matt 2:13
Who is My m   Matt 12:48
Honor your...m   Matt 19:19
Behold, your m   John 19:27

MOTHER-IN-LAW

who lies with his m   Deut 27:23
Orpah kissed her m   Ruth 1:14
lying sick in bed   Matt 8:14

MOTIVES *attitudes, intentions*

LORD weighs the m   Prov 16:2
disclose the m of   1 Cor 4:5
than from pure m   Phil 1:17
judges with evil m   James 2:4
ask with wrong m   James 4:3

MOUND *bank of earth, hill*

throw up a m   2 Kin 19:32
cities...on their m-s   Josh 11:13
against the seige m-s   Jer 33:4

MOUNT (n) *hill, mountain*

In the m of the LORD   Gen 22:14
Moses on M Sinai   Num 3:1
Israel at M Carmel   1 Kin 18:19
M Zion which He   Ps 78:68
M of Olives...split   Zech 14:4

MOUNT (v) *climb up*

to m his chariot   2 Chr 10:18
m up *with* wings   Is 40:31
My fury will m up   Ezek 28:18
m-ed on a donkey   Zech 9:9
m-ed on a donkey   Matt 21:5

MOUNT OF OLIVES
  see **OLIVES, MOUNT OF**

MOUNT ZION
  see **ZION, MOUNT**

MOUNTAIN

sacrifice on the **m**	Gen 31:54
from His holy **m**	Ps 3:4
lift up...to the **m-s**	Ps 121:1
lovely on the **m-s**	Is 52:7
eat at the **m** shrines	Ezek 18:6
m-s will melt	Mic 1:4
the **m** will move	Zech 14:4
m-s, Fall on us	Luke 23:30
withdrew...to the **m**	John 6:15
faith...remove **m-s**	1 Cor 13:2

MOURN *grieve, lament*

m her father and	Deut 21:13
David **m-ed**...son	2 Sam 13:37
A time to **m**	Eccl 3:4
earth **m-s** *and* withers	Is 24:4
comfort all who **m**	Is 61:2
Blessed...who **m**	Matt 5:4
shall **m** and weep	Luke 6:25
Be miserable and **m**	James 4:9

MOUSE *rodent*

the mole, and the **m**	Lev 11:29
five golden **mice**	1 Sam 6:4
mice that ravage	1 Sam 6:5

MOUTH

has made man's **m**	Ex 4:11
m condemns you	Job 15:6
From the **m** of infants	Ps 8:2
Let the words of my **m**	Ps 19:14
fool's **m** is his ruin	Prov 18:7
your **m** is lovely	Song 4:3
out of the **m** of God	Matt 4:4
confess with your **m**	Rom 10:9

MOVE *change position, stir*

Spirit of God...**m-ing**	Gen 1:2
pillar of cloud **m-d**	Ex 14:19
I shall not be **m-d**	Ps 10:6
all the hills **m-d**	Jer 4:24
m-d with compassion	Mark 1:41
m-ing of the waters	John 5:3
in Him we live...**m**	Acts 17:28
m-d by the...Spirit	2 Pet 1:21

MULE *animal*

mounted his **m**	2 Sam 13:29
Absalom...on *his* **m**	2 Sam 18:9
ride on the king's **m**	1 Kin 1:44
war horses and **m-s**	Ezek 27:14

MULTIPLY *increase*

Be fruitful and **m**	Gen 1:22
the fool **m-ies** words	Eccl 10:14
He **m-ies** lies and	Hos 12:1
and peace be **m-ied**	2 Pet 1:2

MULTITUDE *crowd*

father of a **m** of	Gen 17:4
send the **m-s** away	Matt 14:15
He summoned the **m**	Mark 8:34
Him a great **m**	Luke 23:27
cover a **m** of sins	James 5:20
love covers a **m** of	1 Pet 4:8

MURDER *premeditated killing*

You shall not **m**	Ex 20:13
Whoever commits **m**	Matt 5:21
m-ed the prophets	Matt 23:31
full of envy, **m**	Rom 1:29

MURDERER *killer*

m shall be put to	Num 35:30
m from...beginning	John 8:44
this man is a **m**	Acts 28:4
no **m** has eternal	1 John 3:15

MUSIC *harmony, melody*

instruments of **m**	1 Chr 15:16
m to the LORD	2 Chr 7:6
m upon the lyre	Ps 92:3
heard **m** and	Luke 15:25

MUSICIAN *skilled in music*

m, a mighty man	1 Sam 16:18
the **m-s** after *them*	Ps 68:25
harpists and **m-s**	Rev 18:22

MUSTARD *type of plant*

kingdom...like a **m**	Matt 13:31
faith as a **m** seed	Matt 17:20
It is like a **m** seed	Luke 13:19

MUZZLE *gag*

shall not **m** the ox	Deut 25:4
guard...as with a **m**	Ps 39:1

MYRIADS *countless*

chariots...are **m**	Ps 68:17
m of angels	Heb 12:22

number...was m   Rev 5:11

MYRRH *spice*

aromatic gum...m   Gen 43:11
Dripping with...m   Song 5:13
frankincense and m   Matt 2:11
mixture of m and   John 19:39

MYRTLE *type of plant*

the m, and the olive   Is 41:19
among the m trees   Zech 1:11

MYSTERY *hidden truth, secret*

no m baffles you   Dan 4:9
God's wisdom in a m 1 Cor 2:7
know all m-ies   1 Cor 13:2
into the m of Christ   Eph 3:4
the m of the gospel   Eph 6:19
the m of the faith   1 Tim 3:9

MYTHS *fables*

to pay attention to m 1 Tim 1:4
will turn aside to m 2 Tim 4:4
attention to Jewish m Titus 1:14

N

NAAMAH

1 *daughter of Lamech* Gen 4:22
2 *wife of Solomon* 1 Kin 14:21
3 *town in Judah*   Josh 15:41

NAAMAN

1 *son of Benjamin*   Gen 46:21
2 *Ben-hadad's commander*
            2 Kin 5:1ff

NABAL

husband of Abigail 1 Sam 25:3ff
refused to help David

NABOTH

*owner of a vineyard taken
   by Ahab*   1 Kin 21:1-19

NADAB

1 *son of Aaron*   Ex 6:23
2 *king of Israel*   1 Kin 14:20
3 *son of Shammai* 1 Chr 2:28
4 *son of Jehiel*   1 Chr 8:29,30

NAHOR

1 *Abram's grandfather*
            Gen 11:24ff
2 *brother of Abram* Gen 11:27
            Gen 22:23
3 *city in N Mesopotamia*
            Gen 24:10

NAHUM

1 *prophet*   Nah 1:1
2 *ancestor of Christ* Luke 3:25

NAILED (v) *attached, pinned*

you n to a cross   Acts 2:23
n it to the cross   Col 2:14

NAILS (n) *finger ends or pins*

and trim her n   Deut 21:12
fasten it with n   Jer 10:4
imprint of the n   John 20:25

NAIVE *simple, not suspicious*

prudence to the n   Prov 1:4
n believes everything Prov 14:15
the n becomes wise Prov 21:11
goes astray or is n Ezek 45:20

NAKED *unclothed*

n and...not ashamed Gen 2:25
n I shall return there Job 1:21
n...you clothed Me Matt 25:36

NAKEDNESS *unclothed*

the n of his father   Gen 9:22
n of...father's sister Lev 18:12
Your n...be uncovered Is 47:3
shame of your n   Rev 3:18

NAME *designation, title*

man gave n-s to all Gen 2:20
takes His n in vain   Ex 20:7
blot out his n   Deut 29:20
How majestic is Thy n Ps 8:1
sing praises to Thy n Ps 18:49
good n...desired   Prov 22:1
LORD, that is My n   Is 42:8
Hallowed be Thy n Matt 6:9
n-s of the twelve   Matt 10:2
such child in My n Matt 18:5
n-s are recorded Luke 10:20
will come in My n Luke 21:8
baptized in the n   Acts 2:38
of faith in His n   Acts 3:16
other n under heaven Acts 4:12

n-s are in the book   Phil 4:3

NAOMI

woman of Bethlehem Ruth 1:1
Ruth's mother-in-law Ruth 1:4,6

NAPHTALI

1 *son of Jacob*   Gen 30:8
2 *tribe/district*   Num 13:14
                        1 Chr 2:2; Rev 7:6

NARD *fragrant ointment*

henna with n plants   Song 4:13
perfume of pure n   John 12:3

NARROW *limited*

stood in a n path   Num 22:24
Enter by the n gate   Matt 7:13
the way is n   Matt 7:14

NATHAN

1 *a son of David*   2 Sam 5:14
                       Luke 3:31
2 *prophet*   2 Sam 7:2;12:1ff
3 *son of Attai*   1 Chr 2:36
4 *helped Ezra*   Ezra 8:16,17
several other individuals

NATHANAEL

disciple of Jesus   John 1:49

NATION *government, people*

make you a great n   Gen 12:2
priests and a holy n Ex 19:6
scatter...the n-s   Lev 26:33
the n-s in an uproar Ps 2:1
n-s...fear the name   Ps 102:15
N will not lift up sword Is 2:4
sprinkle many n-s   Is 52:15
glory among the n-s   Is 66:19
n...rise against n   Matt 24:7
n should not perish   John 11:50
men, from every n   Acts 2:5
tongue...people and n Rev 5:9

NATIVE *indigenous*

or a n of the land   Ex 12:19
Or see his n land   Jer 22:10
the n-s showed us   Acts 28:2
n-s saw the creature Acts 28:4

NATURAL *normal*

died a n death   Ezek 44:31
n man...not accept   1 Cor 2:14

is sown a n body   1 Cor 15:44

NATURE *essence*

of the same n as you Acts 14:15
n itself teach you   1 Cor 11:14
We *are* Jews by n   Gal 2:15
of *the* divine n   2 Pet 1:4

NAZARENE

1 *of Nazareth*   John 18:7
2 *follower of Jesus* Acts 24:5

NAZARETH

town of Galilee   Matt 2:23
home of Joseph, Mary,
and Jesus Luke 4:16;John 1:45

NAZIRITE

1 *one consecrated to God*
                    Num 6:2,19,20
2 *religious vow*   Judg 13:5,7
                      Amos 2:11,12

NEBO

1 *Moabite town*   Num 32:38
2 *mountain where Moses*
   viewed promised land
                    Deut 32:49;34:1
3 *Babylonian god*   Is 46:1
4 *town W of Jordan* Ezra 2:29
                      Neh 7:33
5 *Jew whose sons married*
   foreign wives   Ezra 10:43

NEBUCHADNEZZAR

king of Babylon   2 Kin 24:1,10
captured Judah   1 Chr 6:15
                      Ezra 2:1

NEBUZARADAN

Babylonian commander
responsible for destruction of
Jerusalem and the Temple
             2 Kin 25:8ff;Jer 39:9,10

NECK *part of body*

you shall break its n Ex 13:13
yoke on your n   Deut 28:48
stiffened their n-s   Jer 17:23
risked their own n-s Rom 16:4

NECKLACE *neck ornament*

n around his neck   Gen 41:42

earrings and n-s   Num 31:50
pride is their n   Ps 73:6

NECO *see* PHARAOH

NEED *necessity, obligation*

sufficient for his n   Deut 15:8
ministered to...n-s   Acts 20:34
n-s of the saints   2 Cor 9:12
supply all your n-s   Phil 4:19

NEEDLE

the eye of a n   Matt 19:24
n than for a rich   Mark 10:25

NEEDY *destitute, poor*

to your n and poor   Deut 15:11
a father to the n   Job 29:16
n will not always be   Ps 9:18
the LORD hears the n   Ps 69:33
n will lie down in   Is 14:30

NEGEV

desert in S Palestine   Gen 12:9
    Judg 1:9; Jer 32:44; Zech 7:7

NEGLECT *disregard, ignore*

You n-ed the Rock   Deut 32:18
who n-s discipline   Prov 15:32
n so great a salvation   Heb 2:3
n to show hospitality   Heb 13:2
do not n doing good   Heb 13:16

NEHEMIAH

1 *Jewish exile* Ezra 2:2; Neh 7:7
2 *son of Azbuk*   Neh 3:16
3 *son of Hacaliah*   Neh 1:1
    rebuilt walls   Neh 3:1ff
    governor of Jerusalem
        Neh 8:9

NEIGHBOR *one living nearby*

not covet...n-'s wife   Ex 20:17
shall love your n   Lev 19:18
make your n-s drink   Hab 2:15
love your n, and   Matt 5:43
And who is my n   Luke 10:29
love your n as   Gal 5:14

NEPHEW

and Lot his n   Gen 12:5
Lot, Abram's n   Gen 14:12

NEPHILIM

people of great stature
        Gen 6:4; Num 13:33

NEST

n is set in the cliff   Num 24:21
n among the stars   Obad 4
birds...*have* n-s   Matt 8:20

NET *snare*

a n for my steps   Ps 57:6
an antelope in a n   Is 51:20
casting a n into   Matt 4:18
left the n-s and   Mark 1:18
n *full* of fish   John 21:8

NETHINIM

temple servants   Ezra 7:24

NEW *fresh, recent*

nothing n under the   Eccl 1:9
Will gain n strength   Is 40:31
a n spirit within   Ezek 11:19
n wine into old   Mark 2:22
A n commandment   John 13:34
he is a n creature   2 Cor 5:17
a n and living way   Heb 10:20
making all things n   Rev 21:5

NEWBORN *just born*

like n babes, long   1 Pet 2:2

NEWNESS *freshness*

walk in n of life   Rom 6:4
in n of the Spirit   Rom 7:6

NEWS *report, tidings*

a day of good n   2 Kin 7:9
Good n puts fat on   Prov 15:30
the n about Jesus   Matt 14:1
n about Him went   Mark 1:28
n of a great joy   Luke 2:10
n of your faith   1 Thess 3:6

NICODEMUS

Pharisee   John 3:1,4,9
in Sanhedrin   John 7:50;19:39

NICOLAITANS

sect in Ephesian and
    Pergamum church   Rev 2:6,15

NICOLAS

proselyte from Antioch Acts 6:5
deacon

NIGHT darkness

darkness He called n   Gen 1:5
pillar of fire by n   Ex 13:21
meditate...day and n   Josh 1:8
make n into day   Job 17:12
The terror by n   Ps 91:5
At n my soul longs   Is 26:9
over their flock by n   Luke 2:8
a thief in the n   1 Thess 5:2
tormented day and n   Rev 20:10

NILE

river of Egypt   Gen 41:1
   Ex 1:22;7:20; Is 23:10

NIMROD

son of Cush   Gen 10:8
a mighty hunter   Gen 10:9
ruler of Shinar   Gen 10:10

NINEVAH

capital of Assyria   2 Kin 19:36
visited by Jonah   Jon 1:1ff

NISAN

*first month of the Hebrew
   calendar*   Neh 2:1; Esth 3:7

NOAH

1 *son of Lamech*   Gen 5:28,29
   *father of Shem, Ham,
     Japheth*   Gen 5:32
   built an ark   Gen 6:14-22
   saved from Flood   Gen 6:9
     Gen 7:15;8:1;8:13
   promised by God   Gen 9:9-17
2 *daughter of Zelophedad*
     Num 26:33;27:1;36:11

NO-AMON

Egyptian city of Thebes
     Nah 3:8

NOBLE lofty, renown

king's most n princes   Esth 6:9
speak n things   Prov 8:6
all the n-s of Judah   Jer 39:6

NOBLEMAN of high rank

the house of a n   Job 21:28
a certain n went to   Luke 19:12

NOISE loud sound

You who were full of n   Is 22:2

Egypt *is but* a big n   Jer 46:17
from heaven a n   Acts 2:2

NOMADS desert wanderers

n of the desert bow   Ps 72:9

NONSENSE foolishness

a fool speaks n   Is 32:6
appeared...as n   Luke 24:11

NORTH direction of compass

stretches out the n   Job 26:7
Zion *in* the far n   Ps 48:2
king of the N will   Dan 11:13
three gates on the n   Rev 21:13

NOSE part of face

the ring on her n   Gen 24:47
n-s...cannot smell   Ps 115:6
My hook in your n   Is 37:29

NOSTRILS nose

breathed into his n   Gen 2:7
breath of His n   2 Sam 22:16
breath of God...my n   Job 27:3

NOTICE attention

take n of me   Ruth 2:10
not n the log   Matt 7:3
deeds to be n-d by   Matt 23:5

NOURISH feed, sustain

n-s and cherishes it   Eph 5:29
constantly n-ed on   1 Tim 4:6
she might be n-ed   Rev 12:6

NULLIFY annul, make void

LORD n-ies the counsel   Ps 33:10
unbelief will not n   Rom 3:3
the promise is n-ied   Rom 4:14
n the grace of God   Gal 2:21

NUMBER (n) group, total

their n according to   Num 29:21
the n of the stars   Ps 147:4
increasing in n daily   Acts 16:5
his n is six hundred   Rev 13:18

NUMBER (v) count, enumerate

n...by their armies   Num 1:3
Thou dost n my steps   Job 14:16
hairs...all n-ed   Matt 10:30

NUN

father of Joshua   Ex 33:11
           Num 14:6;Josh 1:1

NURSE (n) *attendant*

Deborah, Rebekah's n   Gen 35:8
and call a n for you   Ex 2:7
n carries a nursing   Num 11:12
n in the bedroom   2 Kin 11:2

NURSE (v) *suckle an infant*

Sarah...n children   Gen 21:7
the child and n-d him   Ex 2:9
morning to n my son   1 Kin 3:21
who n babes in   Mark 13:17
breasts...never n   Luke 23:29

O

OAK *type of tree*

by the o-s of Mamre   Gen 13:18
the diviners' o   Judg 9:37
o-s of righteousness   Is 61:3
strong as the o-s   Amos 2:9

OAR *pole used in rowing*

no boat with o-s shall   Is 33:21
all who handle...o   Ezek 27:29
straining at the o-s   Mark 6:48

OATH *declaration, vow*

confirm the o which   Deut 9:5
free from the o   Josh 2:20
make no o at all   Matt 5:34
priests without an o   Heb 7:21

OBADIAH

1 *in Ahab's court*   1 Kin 18:3ff
2 *Gadite warrior*   1 Chr 12:8,9
3 *Levite, of Merari*   2 Chr 34:12
4 *son of Jekhiel*   Ezra 8:9
5 *signer of covenant*   Neh 10:1,5
6 *prophet*   Obad 1
7 *sent to teach*   2 Chr 17:7
name of five other Old
   Testament people

OBED

1 *son of Ruth/Boaz*   Ruth 4:17
   ancestor of Jesus   Matt 1:5
             Luke 3:32
2 *son of Ephlal*   1 Chr 2:37

3 *warrior*   1 Chr 11:26,47
4 *temple gatekeeper*   1 Chr 26:1
5 *father of Azariah*   2 Chr 23:1

OBED-EDOM

1 *a Gittite*   2 Sam 6:10-12
2 *temple gatekeeper* 1 Chr 15:21
3 *in charge of Temple vessels*
             2 Chr 25:24

OBEDIENCE *submission*

the o of the peoples   Gen 49:10
pretend o to me   2 Sam 22:45
the o of the One   Rom 5:19
leading to o *of faith* Rom 16:26
in o to the truth   1 Pet 1:22

OBEDIENT *willing to obey*

we will be o   Ex 24:7
o from the heart   Rom 6:17
o to the...death   Phil 2:8
Children, be o to   Col 3:20

OBEY *follow commands, orders*

have o-ed My voice Gen 22:18
o My voice and keep   Ex 19:5
o the LORD your God Deut 27:10
to o is better than   1 Sam 15:22
O-ing...His word   Ps 103:20
and the sea o Him   Matt 8:27
o God rather than   Acts 5:29
o your parents   Eph 6:1
O your leaders   Heb 13:17
may o Jesus Christ   1 Pet 1:2

OBJECT

struck...an iron o   Num 35:16
an o of loathing to   Ps 88:8
o like a great sheet Acts 10:11
god or o of worship 2 Thess 2:4

OBLIGATION *duty*

o toward the LORD   Num 32:22
for his daily o-s   2 Chr 31:16
under o, not to the   Rom 8:12
o to keep the...Law   Gal 5:3

OBSERVE *keep or notice*

surely o My sabbaths   Ex 31:13
o all My statutes   Lev 19:37
you may o discretion   Prov 5:2
the ant...O her ways   Prov 6:6
O how the lilies   Matt 6:28
o-ing the traditions   Mark 7:3
the word...o it   Luke 11:28

o days and months   Gal 4:10

OBSTACLE *hindrance*

Remove *every* o out of Is 57:14
an o or stumbling   Rom 14:13

OBSTINATE

you are an o people   Ex 33:3
made his heart o   Deut 2:30
Israel is...o   Ezek 3:7
disobedient and o   Rom 10:21

OBTAIN *get possession of*

o children through   Gen 16:2
finds a wife...o-s   Prov 18:22
may o eternal life   Matt 19:16
o the gift of God   Acts 8:20
o-ed an inheritance   Eph 1:11
for o-ing salvation 1 Thess 5:9

OCCUR *happen, take place*

this sign shall o   Ex 8:23
will o at the final   Dan 8:19
lest a riot o   Matt 26:5
predestined to o   Acts 4:28

ODED

1 *father of Azariah* 2 Chr 15:1,8
2 *prophet*   2 Chr 28:9

ODIOUS *offensive*

o in Pharaoh's sight   Ex 5:21
o to the Philistines 1 Sam 13:4

OFFEND *insult or violate*

I will not o *anymore* Job 34:31
A brother o-ed *is*   Prov 18:19
Pharisees were o-ed Matt 15:12

OFFENSE *anger or transgression*

of my *own* o-s   Gen 41:9
they took o at Him Matt 13:57
of the o of Adam   Rom 5:14
and a rock of o   1 Pet 2:8

OFFER (v) *give, present*

o him...as a burnt   Gen 22:2
O to God a sacrifice   Ps 50:14
my mouth o-s praises   Ps 63:5
o both gifts and   Heb 5:1
o-ed Himself   Heb 9:14
prayer o-ed in faith James 5:15
o...spiritual sacrifices 1 Pet 2:5

OFFERING (n) *contribution*

freewill o to the LORD Ex 35:29
o of first fruits   Lev 2:12
your worthless o-s   Is 1:13
presenting your o   Matt 5:23
any o for sin   Heb 10:18

OFFERINGS

1 **Burnt Offering**   Gen 22:13
    Lev 1:17
2 **Drink Offering**   Phil 2:17
    2 Tim 4:6
  also **Libation**
3 **Freewill Offering**   Ex 35:29
    Lev 7:16
4 **Grain Offering**   Lev 9:4
    Josh 22:29
  also **Meal Offering**
5 **Guilt Offering**   Lev 5:6
    Num 6:12
6 **Heave Offering** Ex 29:27,28
7 **Libation Offering**
    Num 6:15,17;28:9,10
  also **Drink Offering**
8 **Meal Offering**   2 Kin 16:15
    Ps 40:6
  also **Grain Offering**
9 **Ordination Offering** Lev 8:28
    Lev 8:31
10 **Peace Offering**   Lev 4:31
    Num 6:14
11 **Sin Offering**   Ex 29:14
    Ezek 46:20
12 **Thank Offering** 2 Chr 33:16
    Jer 33:11
13 **Votive Offering**   Deut 12:26
    Deut 23:18
14 **Wave Offering**   Lev 14:12
    Num 18:18

OFFICE *function or position*

wield the staff of o   Judg 5:14
priests in their o-s 2 Chr 35:2
sitting in the tax o   Luke 5:27
to the o of overseer 1 Tim 3:1

OFFICIAL *one in authority*

o-s in the palace 2 Kin 20:18
o of the synagogue   Luke 8:41

OFFSPRING *descendants*

o in place of Abel   Gen 4:25

bring forth o from   Is 65:9
Being...the o of God Acts 17:29
you are Abraham's o   Gal 3:29
and the o of David   Rev 22:16

OG

Amorite King   Num 21:33
     Deut 3:4; Josh 12:4

OHOLAH

symbolic for Samaria Ezek 23:4

OHOLIBAH

symbolic for Jerusalem
     Ezek 23:4

OHOLIBAMAH

1 *wife of Esau*   Gen 36:2-25
2 *descendant of Esau* Gen 36:41

OIL

o for lighting   Ex 25:6
anointed my head...o   Ps 23:5
the o of joy   Ps 45:7
words...softer than o   Ps 55:21
prudent took o in   Matt 25:4
not anoint...with o   Luke 7:46

OINTMENT *salve*

a jar of o   Job 41:31
anointed...with o   John 11:2

OLD *aged, obsolete*

buried at a...o age   Gen 15:15
too o to have a   Ruth 1:12
honor of o men   Prov 20:29
o men will dream   Joel 2:28
wine into o wineskins Matt 9:17
be born when he is o   John 3:4
o self was crucified   Rom 6:6
o things passed away 2 Cor 5:17
men of o gained   Heb 11:2
serpent of o...devil   Rev 12:9

OLD GATE *see* **GATES OF JERUSALEM**

OLIVE *tree or fruit*

freshly picked o leaf   Gen 8:11
land of o oil and   Deut 8:8
cherubim of o wood 1 Kin 6:23
children like o plants Ps 128:3

OLIVES, MOUNT OF

mountain E of Jerusalem
     2 Sam 15:30; Zech 14:4
     Matt 24:3; Mark 11:1
place where Jesus prayed
     Matt 26:30; Luke 22:39-41

OMEGA

last letter of Gr. alphabet
     Rev 1:8
title of Jesus Christ   Rev 21:6
expresses eternalness of God
     Rev 22:13

OMEN *foretells a future event*

who interprets o-s   Deut 18:10
took this as an o   1 Kin 20:33

OMER *dry measure*

take an o apiece   Ex 16:16
o is a tenth of an   Ex 16:36

OMRI

1 *king of Israel*   1 Kin 16:22ff
2 *a Benjamite*   1 Chr 7:8
3 *line of Perez*   1 Chr 9:4
4 *son of Michael*   1 Chr 27:18

ON

1 *Egyptian city*   Gen 41:45,50
     Gen 46:20
2 *son of Peleth*   Num 16:1
   also **Heliopolis**

ONE *single unit*

shall become o flesh   Gen 2:24
God, the LORD is o   Deut 6:4
Holy O of Israel   Ps 71:22
His chosen o-s   Ps 105:6
Are You the...O   Matt 11:3
joy...over o sinner   Luke 15:7
I...Father are o   John 10:30
they may all be o   John 17:21
o body in Christ   Rom 12:5
o died for all   2 Cor 5:14
o Lord, o faith   Eph 4:5
o God...o mediator   1 Tim 2:5
husband of o wife   1 Tim 3:2

ONESIMUS

Christian slave of Philemon
     Col 4:9; Philem 10

ONESIPHORUS

Ephesian Christian 2 Tim 1:16
2 Tim 4:19

ONYX *precious stone*

bdellium and the o Gen 2:12
o, and the jasper Ezek 28:13

OPEN (adj) *not shut, exposed*

throat is an o grave Ps 5:9
Better is o rebuke Prov 27:5
before you an o door Rev 3:8

OPEN (v) *expose, free, unfasten*

eyes will be o-ed Gen 3:5
Ezra o-ed the book Neh 8:5
He o-s their ear Job 36:10
O LORD, o my lips Ps 51:15
O my eyes, that I Ps 119:18
To o blind eyes Is 42:7
o...windows of heaven Mal 3:10
knock...shall be o-ed Matt 7:7
o-ed a door of faith Acts 14:27
and o-s the door Rev 3:20
worthy to o the book Rev 5:2

OPHEL

*citadel on the S part of
Jerusalem* 2 Chr 27:3;33:14
Neh 3:27
*home of temple servants
(Nethinim)* Neh 3:26;11:21

OPHIR

1 *son of Joktan* Gen 10:29
2 *gold producing region of SW
Arabia* 1 Kin 10:11; Job 22:24

OPPONENT *adversary*

friends...with your o Matt 5:25
protection from my o Luke 18:3

OPPORTUNITY *occasion*

o to betray Him Matt 26:16
o for your testimony Luke 21:13
an o for the flesh Gal 5:13
not give...devil an o Eph 4:27

OPPOSE *contend, resist*

o the Prince of Dan 8:25
o-d the ordinance of Rom 13:2
men also o the truth 2 Tim 3:8

God is o-d to the James 4:6

OPPOSITION *hostility*

you...know My o Num 14:34
these are in o Gal 5:17
gospel...much o 1 Thess 2:2

OPPRESS (v) *trouble, tyrannize*

enslaved and o-ed Gen 15:13
Egyptians are o-ing Ex 3:9
not o your neighbor Lev 19:13
woman o-ed in 1 Sam 1:15
do not o the widow Zech 7:10
healing all...o-ed Acts 10:38
the rich who o you James 2:6

OPPRESSED (n) *afflicted*

stronghold for the o Ps 9:9
justice for the o Ps 146:7
let the o go free Is 58:6
devour...o in secret Hab 3:14
vengeance for the o Acts 7:24

OPPRESSION *affliction*

Do not trust in o Ps 62:10
o makes a...man mad Eccl 7:7
and water of o Is 30:20
o of My people Acts 7:34

OPPRESSOR *one who afflicts*

And crush the o Ps 72:4
a great o lacks Prov 28:16
punish all their o-s Jer 30:20

ORACLE *revelation*

The o of Balaam Num 24:3
o concerning Babylon Is 13:1
the o of the LORD Jer 23:33
and misleading o-s Lam 2:14
entrusted with the o-s Rom 3:2

ORDAIN *invest, set apart*

anoint...and o them Ex 28:41
o Aaron and his sons Ex 29:9
o-ed His covenant Ps 111:19
law as o-ed by angels Acts 7:53

ORDEAL *difficulty, trial*

great o of affliction 2 Cor 8:2
at the fiery o 1 Pet 4:12

ORDER (n) *arrangement*

Set your house in o 2 Kin 20:1

fixed o of the moon   Jer 31:35
the o of Melchizedek   Heb 5:6

ORDER (v) *command or request*

I will o *my prayer*   Ps 5:3
o-ed him to tell no   Luke 5:14
confidence...to o you   Philem 8

ORDINANCE *statute*

o of the Passover   Ex 12:43
they rejected My o-s   Lev 26:43
o-s of the heavens   Job 38:33
opposed the o of God   Rom 13:2

ORDINATION

Aaron's ram of o   Ex 29:26
and the o offering   Lev 7:37
period of your o   Lev 8:33

ORDINATION OFFERING
see OFFERINGS

ORIGIN *beginning, source*

of Jewish o   Esth 6:13
o is from antiquity   Is 23:7
Your o and your   Ezek 16:3

ORIGINATE *bring into being*

not o from woman   1 Cor 11:8
all things o...God   1 Cor 11:12

ORION

constellation of stars   Job 9:9
   Job 38:31; Amos 5:8

ORNAMENT *decoration*

put off your o-s   Ex 33:5
o of fine gold   Prov 25:12
beauty of His o-s   Ezek 7:20

ORNAN

*Jebusite owner of threshing
floor on Mount Moriah*
   1 Chr 21:15,18
*sells threshing floor to David
for altar and temple*
   1 Chr 21:25,28
also Araunah

ORPAH

daughter-in-law of Naomi
   Ruth 1:4,14

ORPHAN *fatherless child*

not afflict any...o   Ex 22:22

justice for the o   Deut 10:18
helper of the o   Ps 10:14
may plunder the o-s   Is 10:2
Leave...o-s behind   Jer 49:11
visit o-s and widows   James 1:27

OSTRICH *bird*

the o and the owl   Lev 11:16
a companion of o-es   Job 30:29
cruel Like o-es   Lam 4:3
mourning like the o-es   Mic 1:8

OTHNIEL

son of Kenaz   Josh 15:17
brother or nephew of Caleb
   Judg 1:13;3:11

OUTBURST *sudden release*

great o of anger   Deut 29:24
o of anger I hid My   Is 54:8
jealousy, o-s of anger   Gal 5:20

OUTCAST *rejected*

the o-s of Israel   Ps 147:2
Hide the o-s   Is 16:3
called you an o   Jer 30:17
o-s from...synagogue   John 16:2

OUTCRY *strong cry or protest*

no o in our streets   Ps 144:14
o is heard among the   Jer 50:46
a *single* o arose   Acts 19:34

OUTSIDER *stranger*

o may not come near   Num 18:4
toward o-s   1 Thess 4:12

OUTSTRETCHED *extended*

redeem...with an o arm   Ex 6:6
war...with an o hand   Jer 21:5

OUTWARD *external*

at the o appearance   1 Sam 16:7
is o in the flesh   Rom 2:28

OVEN *baking, cooking vessel*

appeared a...o   Gen 15:17
make them as a fiery o   Ps 21:9

OVERCOME *conquer, master*

a man o with wine   Jer 23:9
I have o the world   John 16:33
but o evil with good   Rom 12:21
have o the evil one   1 John 2:13

who **o-s** shall inherit　Rev 21:7

OVERFLOW *flood, inundate*

My cup **o-s**　Ps 23:5
waters shall **o** the　Is 28:17
I am **o-ing** with joy　2 Cor 7:4
o-ing with gratitude　Col 2:7

OVERLAID *decorate, spread*

o...with gold　1 Kin 6:28
vessel **o** with silver　Prov 26:23
o with gold...silver　Hab 2:19

OVERLOOK *ignore or view*

o a transgression　Prov 19:11
widows were...**o-ed**　Acts 6:1

OVERPOWER *subdue*

deceive you and **o** you　Obad 7
Hades shall not **o**　Matt 16:18
attacks him and **o-s**　Luke 11:22

OVERSEER *director, leader*

o in the house of　Jer 29:26
the **o-s** and deacons　Phil 1:1
the office of **o**　1 Tim 3:1
o...above reproach　Titus 1:7

OVERSHADOW *engulf, obscure*

Most High...**o** you　Luke 1:35
o-ing the mercy seat　Heb 9:5

OVERSIGHT *supervision*

o of the house of　2 Kin 12:11
having **o** at...gates　Ezek 44:11
exercising **o** not　1 Pet 5:2

OVERWHELM *crush, overcome*

humiliation has **o-ed**　Ps 44:15
darkness will **o** me　Ps 139:11
my spirit was **o-ed**　Ps 142:4
o-ed by...sorrow　2 Cor 2:7

OWE *be indebted*

Pay...what you **o**　Matt 18:28
O nothing to anyone　Rom 13:8
that you **o** to me　Philem 19

OWL *bird*

the **o**, the sea gull　Deut 14:15
o of the waste places　Ps 102:6
houses...full of **o-s**　Is 13:21

OWN (adj) *belonging to*

man in His **o** image　Gen 1:27

led...His **o** people　Ps 78:52
calls his **o** sheep　John 10:3
in his **o** language　Acts 2:6

OWN (n) *belonging to*

He came to His **o**　John 1:11
provide for his **o**　1 Tim 5:8

OWNER *possessor*

restitution to its **o**　Ex 22:12
when the **o**...comes　Matt 21:40
who were **o-s** of land　Acts 4:34

OX *bull used as draft animal*

oxen and donkeys　Gen 12:16
servant or his **o**　Ex 20:17
horns of the wild **oxen**　Ps 22:21
An **o** knows its owner　Is 1:3
not muzzle the **o**　1 Tim 5:8

P

PACE *step, stride*

the **p** of the cattle　Gen 33:14
not slow down the **p**　2 Kin 4:24

PACT *agreement*

Sheol we...made a **p**　Is 28:15
p with Sheol shall　Is 28:18

PADDAN-ARAM

upper Mesopotamia　Gen 25:20
home of Laban　Gen 28:5
*birthplace of most of
　Jacob's sons*　Gen 35:22-26

PAHATH-MOAB

1 *head of Jewish clan*　Ezra 2:6
2 *Jewish clan*　Neh 3:11

PAIN *discomfort, hurt*

multiply Your **p**　Gen 3:16
p-s came upon her　1 Sam 4:19
rejoice in unsparing **p**　Job 6:10
rest from your **p**　Is 14:3
Your **p** is incurable　Jer 30:15
bring **p** to my soul　Lam 3:51
suffering great **p**　Matt 8:6
no longer be...**p**　Rev 21:4

PAINFUL *hurting*

p are honest words　Job 6:25

the bread of **p** labors   Ps 127:2

PALACE *royal residence*

build...royal **p**	2 Chr 2:12
to the king's **p**	Esth 2:8
Out of ivory **p-s**	Ps 45:8
A **p** of strangers	Is 25:2
luxury...royal **p-s**	Luke 7:25

PALLET *bed, mat*

they let down the **p**	Mark 2:4
take up your **p** and	Mark 2:9

PALM *type of tree*

the city of **p** trees	Deut 34:3
flourish like the **p**	Ps 92:12
branches of the **p**	John 12:13

PALTI

1 *son of Raphu*	Num 13:9
spy for Israel	Num 13:2
2 *Michal's husband*	1 Sam 25:44

PAMPHYLIA

Roman province in Asia Minor
     Acts 2:10;13:13;14:24

PANGS *sudden pains*

beginning of birth **p**	Mark 13:8
like birth **p**	1 Thess 5:3

PANIC *fear*

P seized them there	Ps 48:6
P and pitfall have	Lam 3:47
great **p**...will fall	Zech 14:13

PANT *breathe rapidly*

deer **p-s** for the water	Ps 42:1
my soul **p-s** for Thee	Ps 42:1
I will both gasp and **p**	Is 42:14
beasts...**p** for Thee	Joel 1:20

PAPHOS

city on Cyprus   Acts 13:6,13

PAPYRUS *water plant*

p...without marsh	Job 8:11
Even in **p** vessels	Is 18:2

PARABLE *story for illustration*

speak a **p** to	Ezek 17:2
p of the sower	Matt 13:18
heard His **p-s**	Matt 21:45
p from the fig tree	Mark 13:28
spoke by way of a **p**	Luke 8:4

PARADISE

abode of the righteous dead
Luke 23:43; 2 Cor 12:4; Rev 2:7
see also **ABRAHAM'S BOSOM**

PARALYTIC

said to the **p**—Rise	Matt 9:6
p, carried by four	Mark 2:3

PARAN

wilderness area in Sinai
     Gen 21:21; Num 13:3
place of Israelite wanderings
  and encampments Num 12:16
mountain in Sinai   Deut 33:2

PARDON *forgive, release*

he will not **p** your	Ex 23:21
May the...LORD **p**	2 Chr 30:18
O LORD, **P** my iniquity	Ps 25:11
He will abundantly **p**	Is 55:7
p, and you will be	Luke 6:37

PARENTS *father and mother*

rise up against **p**	Matt 10:21
left house or...**p**	Luke 18:29
evil, disobedient to **p**	Rom 1:30
children, obey your **p**	Eph 6:1
disobedient to **p**	2 Tim 3:2

PART *portion*

God...have no **p** in	2 Chr 19:7
form my inward **p-s**	Ps 139:13
have no **p** with Me	John 13:8
no **p** or portion in	Acts 8:21
prophesy in **p**	1 Cor 13:9
now I know in **p**	1 Cor 13:12
tongue is a small **p**	James 3:5

PARTAKERS *participators*

do not be **p** with	Eph 5:7
become **p** of Christ	Heb 3:14
p of the Holy Spirit	Heb 6:4
p of *the* divine nature	2 Pet 1:4

PARTIAL *favoring*

not be **p** to the poor	Lev 19:15
you shall not be **p**	Deut 16:19
now be **p** to no one	Job 32:21
You are not **p**	Matt 22:16

PARTIALITY *favoritism*

show **p** in judgment Deut 1:17

p is not good | Prov 28:21
God shows no p | Gal 2:6

PARTICIPATE *take part*

not p...deeds of | Eph 5:11
p-s in his evil deeds | 2 John 11
may not p in her sins | Rev 18:4

PARTNER *comrade*

is a p with a thief | Prov 29:24
been p-s with them | Matt 23:30
regard me as a p | Philem 17

PASS *proceed*

LORD will p over the | Ex 12:23
My glory is p-ing by | Ex 33:22
heaven and earth p | Matt 5:18
words shall not p | Matt 24:35
this cup p from Me | Matt 26:39
p-ed out of death | John 5:24
old things p-ed away | 2 Cor 5:17
first earth p-ed away | Rev 21:1

PASSION *desire, lust*

p is rottenness to | Prov 14:30
over to degrading p-s | Rom 1:26
flesh with its p-s | Gal 5:24
dead to...p | Col 3:5
not in lustful p | 1 Thess 4:5

PASSOVER

*Israel's firstborn protected from
the plague of death prior to the
exodus from Egypt* Ex 12:1-30
*Feast commemorating Israelite
exodus and protection from
death* Ex 12:42,43; Lev 23:5
Num 9:2,12,14; Matt 26:2,18
John 19:14; Acts 12:4

see also FEASTS

PASTORS *shepherds of people*

and some *as* p | Eph 4:11

PASTURE (n) *grazing field*

lie down in green p-s | Ps 23:2
sheep of Thy p | Ps 79:13

PASTURE (v) *feed, graze*

Moses...p-ing the flock | Ex 3:1
They will p on it | Zeph 2:7
So I p-d the flock | Zech 11:7

PATCH *mending cloth*

p of unshrunk cloth | Matt 9:16
p pulls away from it | Mark 2:21

PATH *way*

snake in the p | Gen 49:17
the p of life | Ps 16:11
a light to my p | Ps 119:105
p of the upright is | Prov 15:19
Make His p-s straight | Matt 3:3

PATHROS

upper Egypt | Is 11:11
Jer 44:1,15; Ezek 29:14;30:14

PATIENCE *endurance*

try the p of men | Is 7:13
in p, in kindness | 2 Cor 6:6
love, joy, peace, p | Gal 5:22
exhort, with great p | 2 Tim 4:2
endure it with p | 1 Pet 2:20

PATIENT *bearing, enduring*

Love is p, love is | 1 Cor 13:4
p when wronged | 2 Tim 2:24
Lord...is p toward | 2 Pet 3:9

PATMOS

*Aegean island, site of John's
exile* | Rev 1:9

PATRIARCH *father of clan*

regarding the p David | Acts 2:29
the twelve p-s | Acts 7:8
Abraham, the p, gave | Heb 7:4

PATTERN *model, plan*

fixed p-s of heaven | Jer 33:25
walk according to...p | Phil 3:17

PAUL

heritage Acts 21:39;22:3
Phil 3:5
persecuted believers Acts 7:58
Acts 8:1,3;9:1,2; 1 Cor 15:9
conversion and call Acts 9:1-19
name changed Acts 13:9
Jerusalem council Acts 15:2-6
missionary journeys Acts 13:1ff
Acts 15:36ff;18:23ff;21:14ff
apostolic defense Acts 11:5ff
Gal 1:13ff
arrest and imprisonment
Acts 21:33;22:24-28:31

defense   Acts 22:1ff;24:10 ff
    Acts 25:10,11;26:2ff
*final journey to Rome*Acts 27,28
see also SAUL

PAULUS, SERGIUS

proconsul of Cyprus   Acts 13:7

PAVEMENT *paved road*

on a p of stone   2 Kin 16:17
mosaic p of porphyry   Esth 1:6
place called The P   John 19:13

PAY *give what is due*

thief...p double   Ex 22:7
p Thee my vows   Ps 66:13
P back what you   Matt 18:28
never p back evil   Rom 12:17
p the penalty   2 Thess 1:9

PEACE *calmness, tranquility*

grant p in the land   Lev 26:6
made p with David   1 Chr 19:19
Seek p, and pursue   Ps 34:14
for the p of Jerusalem Ps 122:6
all her paths are p   Prov 3:17
a time for p   Eccl 3:8
Prince of P   Is 9:6
p...like a river   Is 66:12
have withdrawn My p   Jer 16:5
not come to bring p   Matt 10:34
on earth p among   Luke 2:14
P I leave with you   John 14:27
we have p with God   Rom 5:1
love, joy, p   Gal 5:22
He Himself is our p   Eph 2:14
gospel of p   Eph 6:15
p of God...surpasses   Phil 4:7
p through the blood   Col 1:20
take p from the earth   Rev 6:4

PEACEMAKERS

Blessed are the p   Matt 5:9

PEACE OFFERING
  see OFFERINGS

PEARL *precious gem*

wisdom is above...p-s Job 28:18
p-s before swine   Matt 7:6
one p of great value Matt 13:46

PECK-MEASURE *container*

lamp...under the p   Matt 5:15
not...put under a p   Mark 4:21

PEKAH

king of Israel   2 Kin 15:25ff

PEKAHIAH

king of Israel   2 Kin 15:22,23

PELEG

son of Eber   Gen 10:25
descendant of Shem Gen 11:18

PENALTY *punishment*

you will bear the p   Ezek 23:49
pay the p of eternal 2 Thess 1:9

PENIEL

where Jacob wrestled with God
    Gen 32:30

also Penuel

PENTECOST

Jewish feast held at end
  of Passover   Acts 20:16
    1 Cor 16:8
coming of the Holy Spirit
    Acts 2:1

see also FEASTS

PENUEL

1 *tower destroyed*   Judg 8:17
  rebuilt   1 Kin 12:25
  also Peniel
2 *father of Gedor*   1 Chr 4:4
3 *son of Shashak*   1 Chr 8:25

PEOPLE *group, nation*

they are one p   Gen 11:6
Let My p go   Ex 5:1
You are an obstinate p Ex 33:5
blessed above all p-s Deut 7:14
Forgive Thy p Israel Deut 21:8
LORD loves His p   2 Chr 2:11
p who are called by 2 Chr 7:14
restores His captive p Ps 14:7
We are His p   Ps 100:3
LORD will judge His p Ps 135:14
p are unrestrained Prov 29:18
p whom I formed   Is 43:21
do p say that I am Mark 8:27
they feared the p Luke 20:19
should die for the p John 11:50
not rejected His p Rom 11:2
every tribe and p   Rev 13:7

PEOR

1 *mountain in Moab* Num 23:28
2 *Moabite deity* Num 25:3

PERCEIVE *be aware, discern*

p-d all the wisdom 1 Kin 10:4
listening, but do not p Is 6:9
p-ing in Himself Mark 5:30
p with their heart John 12:40

PERDITION *damnation*

the son of p John 17:12

PEREZ

son of Judah Gen 38:29

PERFECT (adj) *flawless*

His work is p Deut 32:4
law of the LORD is p Ps 19:7
heavenly Father is p Matt 5:48
p bond of unity Col 3:14
be p and complete James 1:4
p love casts out 1 John 4:18

PERFECT (v) *complete*

is p-ed in weakness 2 Cor 12:9
love is p-ed with us 1 John 4:17

PERFORM *carry out*

I will p miracles Ex 34:10
p My judgments Lev 18:4
p-s righteous deeds Ps 103:6
p a miracle in My Mark 9:39
John p-ed no sign John 10:41
p-ing great wonders Acts 6:8

PERFUME *fragrant oil*

and p make the heart Prov 27:9
instead of sweet p Is 3:24
p upon My body Matt 26:12
anointed...with p Luke 7:46
prepared...p-s Luke 23:56

PERGA

city in Asia Minor Acts 13:13

PERGAMUM

city in Asia Minor Rev 1:11
early church Rev 2:12

PERISH *be destroyed*

we p, we are dying Num 17:12
weapons...p-ed 2 Sam 1:27
if I p, I p Esth 4:16

hope...will p Job 8:13
the wicked will p Ps 1:6
rod of his fury will p Prov 22:8
our hope has p-ed Ezek 37:11
little ones p Matt 18:14
p by the sword Matt 26:52
p, but have eternal John 3:16
for any to p 2 Pet 3:9

PERIZZITES

early Canaanite tribe Gen 34:30
Ex 23:23; Deut 7:1

PERMANENT *lasting*

it is a p ordinance Lev 6:18
p right of redemption Lev 25:32
use them as p slaves Lev 25:46
p home for the ark 1 Chr 28:2

PERMISSION *consent*

p they had from Cyrus Ezra 3:7
He gave them p Mark 5:13
he had given him p Acts 21:40

PERMIT *allow*

not p-ting...demons Mark 1:34
p the children Mark 10:14
Spirit...did not p Acts 16:7
if the Lord p-s 1 Cor 16:7

PERPETUAL *lasting*

p incense before the Ex 30:8
as a p covenant Ex 31:16
for a p priesthood Ex 40:15
may sleep a p sleep Jer 51:39

PERSECUTE *afflict, oppress*

Why do you p me Job 19:22
has p-d my soul Ps 143:3
pray for those who p Matt 5:44
p you in this city Matt 10:23
why are you p-ing Me Acts 9:4
used to p the church Gal 1:13

PERSECUTION *oppression*

p arises because of Mark 4:17
p arose against the Acts 8:1
a p against Paul Acts 13:50
distress, or p, or Rom 8:35

PERSEVERANCE *persistence*

by p in doing good Rom 2:7
tribulation brings...p Rom 5:3

for your p and faith 2 Thess 1:4
p of the saints   Rev 14:12

PERSIA

ancient near eastern empire
    2 Chr 36:20; Ezra 1:1; Esth 1:3
       Ezek 27:10; Dan 8:20

PERSON *human being*

If a p sins   Lev 4:2
hungry p unsatisfied   Is 32:6
p be in subjection   Rom 13:1
hidden p of the heart 1 Pet 3:4

PERSUADE *convince, prevail on*

a ruler may be p-d Prov 25:15
trying to p Jews and Acts 18:4
p-s men to worship Acts 18:13
you will p me   Acts 26:28

PERSUASIVE *convincing*

p words of wisdom   1 Cor 2:4
delude you with p   Col 2:4

PERVERSE *corrupt*

a p and crooked   Deut 32:5
A p heart shall depart Ps 101:4
mind will utter p   Prov 23:33
and p generation   Phil 2:15

PERVERT *distort, misdirect*

not p the justice   Ex 23:6
Does God p justice   Job 8:3
have p-ed their way   Jer 3:21

PESTILENCE *epidemic, plague*

LORD sent a p upon 2 Sam 24:15
sword, famine, and p Jer 27:13
p and mourning and Rev 18:8

PETER

heritage and occupation
      John 1:42,44; Matt 4:18
called by Jesus   Matt 1:17
      Mark 3:16; Luke 5:1ff
names: Cephas, Simon
      Matt 4:18; Mark 3:16
      John 1:42; Acts 15:14
walked on water Matt 14:28ff
confessed Jesus as Messiah
      Matt 16:16; Luke 9:20
on mount of Transfiguration
      Matt 17:1ff; Mark 9:2ff

denied Jesus   Matt 26:70
    Mark 14:70; Luke 22:58
at Pentecost   Acts 2
apostle of Christ   Gal 2:8
      1 Pet 1:1; 2 Pet 1:1

PETITION *request, supplication*

God...grant your p 1 Sam 1:17
p to any god or man Dan 6:7
p-s...be made   1 Tim 2:1

PHARAOH *title of Egyptian*
  kings

1 **Pharaoh,** *time of Abraham*
      Gen 12:15ff
2 **Pharaoh,** *time of Joseph*
      Gen 37:36;39:1-50:26
3 **Pharaoh** *during oppression*
      Ex 1:8-2:23
4 **Pharaoh** *during the Exodus*
      Ex 5:1-12:41
5 **Pharaoh** *father of Bithiah*
      1 Chr 4:17
6 **Pharaoh,** *time of David*
      1 Kin 11:14ff
7 **Pharaoh** *whose daughter*
  married Solomon 1 Kin 3:1
      1 Kin 7:8;9:16
8 **Shishak,** *time of Rehoboam*
      1 Kin 14:25,26
9 **So,** *time of Hoshea* 2 Kin 17:4
10 **Tirhakah,** *time of Hezekiah*
      2 Kin 19:9;Is 37:9
11 **Neco,** *slew Josiah*
      2 Kin 23:29,33,34
12 **Hophra,** *subject of prophecy*
      Jer 44:30

PHARISEES

Jewish religious party Matt 3:7
    Matt 23:13;Mark 2:18;7:3
      Luke 11:42;16:14
      John 3:1;11:47

PHARPAR

river of Damascus   2 Kin 5:12

PHILADELPHIA

city in Asia Minor   Rev 1:11
early church   Rev 3:7

PHILEMON

owner of Onesimus   Philem 1
friend of Paul

PHILIP

1 *Herod Philip I, son of Herod
the Great* Mark 6:17
see also **HEROD**
2 *Herod Philip II, son of Herod
the Great* Luke 3:1
see also **HEROD**
3 *Philip the apostle* Matt 10:3
Mark 3:18;Luke 6:14
John 1:43ff; Acts 1:13
4 *Philip the evangelist* Acts 6:5
Acts 8:5,29;21:8

PHILIPPI

Macedonian city Acts 16:12;20:6

PHILIPPIANS

people of Philippi Phil 4:15

PHILISTIA

coastal area of SW Palestine
Ex 15:14; Ps 60:8;83:7; Joel 3:4

PHILISTINES

people of Philistia Gen 10:14
Josh 13:2;Judg 13:1;1 Sam 4:2

PHINEHAS

1 *grandson of Aaron* Num 25:7
Num 31:6;Judg 20:28
2 *son of Eli* 1 Sam 1:3;4:4,11
3 *father of a priest* Ezra 8:33

PHOEBE

*Cenchrea (Corinth) deaconess
commended by Paul* Rom 16:1

PHOENICIA

coastal land N of Palestine
Acts 11:19;21:2
visited by Paul Acts 15:3

PHRYGIA

Asia Minor province Acts 2:10
visited by Paul Acts 16:6;18:23

PHYGELUS

Asian Christian, deserted Paul
2 Tim 1:15

PHYLACTERIES *prayer bands*

as **p** on your forehead Ex 13:16
they broaden their **p** Matt 23:5

see also **FRONTALS**

PHYSICIAN

all worthless **p-s** Job 13:4
healthy who need a **p** Matt 9:12
P, heal yourself Luke 4:23
Luke, the beloved **p** Col 4:14

PIECE *part, portion*

dip your **p** of bread Ruth 2:14
thirty **p-s** of silver Matt 27:3
gave Him a **p**...fish Luke 24:42
woven in one **p** John 19:23

PIERCE *penetrate*

master shall **p** his ear Ex 21:6
They **p-d** my hands Ps 22:16
He was **p-d** through Is 53:5
whom they have **p-d** Zech 12:10
sword will **p**...soul Luke 2:35
p-d His side John 19:34
p-d to the heart Acts 2:37

PIETY *reverence*

learn to practice **p** 1 Tim 5:4
because of His **p** Heb 5:7

PILATE, PONTIUS

Roman governor of Judah
Matt 27:2;Luke 3:1
presided at Jesus' trial
Matt 27:11ff;Mark 15:2ff
Luke 23:1ff;John 18:28-38
warned by his wife Matt 27:19
orders Jesus' crucifixion
Matt 27:24ff;Mark 15:15
Luke 23:24,25;John 19:15,16

PILLAR *column or memorial*

became a **p** of salt Gen 19:26
p of fire by night Ex 13:21
he set up...a **p** 2 Sam 18:18
hewn...her seven **p-s** Prov 9:1
feet like **p-s** of fire Rev 10:1

PILOT *steersman*

sailors, and your **p-s** Ezek 27:27
the **p** and...captain Acts 27:11
inclination of the **p** James 3:4

PINION *wing*

p and plumage of Job 39:13
cover you with His **p-s** Ps 91:4

PINNACLE *highest point*

had Him...on the **p** Matt 4:5

p of the temple   Luke 4:9

PISGAH

mountain height in Moab
    Num 21:20; Josh 13:20

PISHON

river of Eden   Gen 2:11

PISIDIA

district of Asia Minor
    Acts 13:14;14:24

PIT *deep hole, dungeon*

full of tar p-s   Gen 14:10
Joseph...not in the p Gen 37:29
redeems...from the p Ps 103:4
harlot is a deep p Prov 23:27
silenced me in the p Lam 3:53
to p-s of darkness 2 Pet 2:4
the bottomless p   Rev 9:1

PITCH (n) *tar*

inside and out with p Gen 6:14
covered it over...p   Ex 2:3

PITCH (v) *set up*

p-ed his tent in the Gen 31:25
he will p the tents Dan 11:45
tabernacle...Lord p-ed Heb 8:2

PITCHER *container*

torches inside the p-s Judg 7:16
Fill four p-s   1 Kin 18:33
carrying a p of   Mark 14:13

PITHOM

*Egyptian storage city built by
Hebrew slaves*   Ex 1:11

PITY (n) *sympathy*

shall not show p   Deut 19:21
I will not show p   Jer 13:14
no eye looked with p Ezek 16:5

PITY (v) *have compassion*

she had p on him   Ex 2:6
eye shall not p them Deut 7:16
P me, p me, O you Job 19:21
take p on us   Mark 9:22
most to be p-ied 1 Cor 15:19

PLACE *area, space*

waters...into one p Gen 1:9
he enters the holy p Ex 28:29

God is a dwelling p Deut 33:27
a p for My people 1 Chr 17:9
earth out of its p   Job 9:6
Thou art my hiding p Ps 32:7
love the p of honor Matt 23:6
a p called Golgotha Matt 27:33
I go to prepare a p John 14:2

PLAGUE *contagious disease*

no p will befall you Ex 12:13
Remove Thy p from Ps 39:10
p of the hail   Rev 16:21
the seven last p-s Rev 21:9

PLAIN *flat area*

p in...Shinar   Gen 11:2
desert p-s of Jericho Josh 4:13
the p of Megiddo 2 Chr 35:22
broad p of the earth Rev 20:9

PLAN *design, scheme*

tabernacle...its p Ex 26:30
P-s formed long ago Is 25:1
follow our own p-s Jer 18:12
p and foreknowledge Acts 2:23

PLANT (n) *growth from soil*

every p yielding seed Gen 1:29
eat the p-s of the Gen 3:18
hail...struck every p Ex 9:25
God appointed a p Jon 4:6

PLANT (v) *put into soil*

LORD God p-ed a garden Gen 2:8
p...trees for food Lev 19:23
shall p a vineyard Deut 28:30
A time to p   Eccl 3:2
her earnings she p-s Prov 31:16
p-ed a vineyard Mark 12:1
I p-ed, Apollos   1 Cor 3:6

PLATTER *shallow dish*

on a p the head of Matt 14:8
his head on a p   Mark 6:28

PLAY *take part*

who p the lyre   Gen 4:21
man who can p 1 Sam 16:17
p-ed the fool   1 Sam 26:21
P skillfully with a Ps 33:3
nursing child will p Is 11:8
not p the harlot   Hos 3:3
We p-ed the flute Matt 11:17

PLEAD *appeal, beseech*

p-ed with the LORD   Deut 3:23
man...p with God   Job 16:21
LORD will p their case   Prov 22:23
P for the widow   Is 1:17
Elijah...p-s with God   Rom 11:2

PLEASANT *pleasing*

despised the p land   Ps 106:24
P words are a   Prov 16:24
sleep...is p   Eccl 5:12
Speak to us p words   Is 30:10

PLEASE *satisfy*

it p Thee to bless   2 Sam 7:29
Thou art p-d with me   Ps 41:11
sacrifices...not p Him   Hos 9:4
how he may p his   1 Cor 7:33
p all men in all   1 Cor 10:33
striving to p men   Gal 1:10
to walk and p God   1 Thess 4:1
impossible to p   Heb 11:6

PLEASING *agreeable, gratifying*

tree that is p   Gen 2:9
meditation be p   Ps 104:34
not as p men but   1 Thess 2:4
p in His sight   1 John 3:22

PLEASURE *gratification*

old, shall I have p   Gen 18:12
p in His people   Ps 149:4
He who loves p will   Prov 21:17
work for *His* good p   Phil 2:13
lovers of p rather   2 Tim 3:4
passing p-s of sin   Heb 11:25

PLEDGE *promise*

cloak as a p   Ex 22:26
those who give p-s   Prov 22:26
the Spirit as a p   2 Cor 5:5
p of our inheritance   Eph 1:14

PLEIADES

constellation of stars   Job 9:9
    Job 38:31; Amos 5:8

PLENTIFUL *abundant*

shed abroad a p rain   Ps 68:9
harvest is p   Matt 9:37

PLOT *plan, scheme*

wicked p-s against   Ps 37:12

you have p-ted *evil*   Prov 30:32
Jews p-ted together   Acts 9:23

PLOW *dig the soil*

not p with an ox   Deut 22:10
those who p iniquity   Job 4:8
sluggard does not p   Prov 20:4
his hand to the p   Luke 9:62
ought to p in hope   1 Cor 9:10

PLOWSHARES *blade of plow*

their swords into p   Is 2:4
your p into swords   Joel 3:10

PLUMB LINE *vertical line*

the p of emptiness   Is 34:11
p In the midst of My   Amos 7:8
when they see the p   Zech 4:10

PLUNDER (n) *booty, loot*

took no p in silver   Judg 5:19
you will become p   Hab 2:7
wealth will become p   Zeph 1:13

PLUNDER (v) *rob*

will p the Egyptians   Ex 3:22
stouthearted were p-ed   Ps 76:5
he will p his house   Matt 12:29

POINT *particular time*

grieved, to the p of   Matt 26:38
obedient to the p of   Phil 2:8
to the p of shedding   Heb 12:4

POISON *lethal substance*

P...under their lips   Ps 140:3
given us p-ed water   Jer 8:14
turned justice into p   Amos 6:12

POLL-TAX *income and head tax*

collect customs or p   Matt 17:25
give a p to Caesar   Matt 22:17

POLLUTE *contaminate*

blood p-s the land   Num 35:33
earth is also p-d   Is 24:5

POMEGRANATE *fruit*

golden bell and a p   Ex 28:34
p-s of blue and purple   Ex 39:24
juice of my p-s   Song 8:2
the fig tree, the p   Hag 2:19

181

PONDER *think deeply*

' not p the path of life   Prov 5:6
Or p things...past   Is 43:18

PONTUS

region in N Asia Minor
    Acts 2:9; 1 Pet 1:1
homeland of Aquila   Acts 18:2

POOL *pond*

of the upper p   2 Kin 18:17
rock into a p   Ps 114:8
land will become a p   Is 35:7
in the p of Siloam   John 9:7

POOR *impoverished, needy*

p will never cease   Deut 15:11
raises the p from the   1 Sam 2:8
lest you become p   Prov 20:13
not rob the p   Prov 22:22
are the p in spirit   Matt 5:3
a p widow came   Mark 12:42
p you always have   Mark 14:7
sake He became p   2 Cor 8:9
not God choose the p   James 2:5

POPULATE *increase number*

P the earth abundantly   Gen 9:7
whole earth was p-d   Gen 9:19

POPULATION *people*

with all *his* great p   Is 16:14
deported an entire p   Amos 1:6

PORPOISE SKIN

covering of p-s above   Ex 26:14
put sandals of p on   Ezek 16:10

PORTICO *porch*

in the p of Solomon   John 10:23
one accord in...p   Acts 5:12

PORTION *part, share*

gather a day's p   Ex 16:4
LORD'S p is...people   Deut 32:9
double p of...spirit   2 Kin 2:9
The LORD is my p   Ps 119:57
joy over their p   Is 61:7

POSSESS *control, take*

give...this land to p   Gen 15:7
are to p their land   Lev 20:24
go in and p the land   Deut 1:8
dost p all the nations   Ps 82:8

p-ed by Beelzebul   Mark 3:22
sell all you p   Mark 10:21
p-ed with demons   Luke 8:27
do not p silver and   Acts 3:6

POSSESSION *ownership*

for an everlasting p   Gen 17:8
you shall be My own p   Ex 19:5
people for His own p   Deut 4:20
full of Thy p-s   Ps 104:24
charge of all his p-s   Matt 24:47
selling their...p-s   Acts 2:45

POSSIBLE *can be done*

all things are p   Matt 19:26
p with God   Luke 18:27

POSTERITY *descendants*

P will serve Him   Ps 22:30
p of the wicked   Ps 37:38

POT *container, vessel*

death in the p   2 Kin 4:40
refining p is for   Prov 17:3
I see a boiling p   Jer 1:13

POTIPHAR

*Egyptian official who purchased
Joseph*   Gen 39:1

POTIPHERA

Joseph's father-in-law
    Gen 41:45,50;46:20

POTSHERD *piece of pottery*

p to scrape himself   Job 2:8
is dried up like a p   Ps 22:15

POTTER *one who molds clay*

clay say to the p   Is 45:9
and Thou our p   Is 64:8
as it pleased the p   Jer 18:4
Throw it to the p   Zech 11:13

POTTER'S FIELD

Judas' burial place   Matt 27:3ff

POUR *cause to flow*

p me out like milk   Job 10:10
I p out my soul   Ps 42:4
P out your heart   Ps 62:8
I will p out My Spirit   Is 44:3
P out Thy wrath   Jer 10:25

p out...a blessing Mal 3:10
p-ed it upon His Matt 26:7
p forth of My Spirit Acts 2:17

POVERTY *destitution, want*

glutton...come to **p** Prov 23:21
neither **p** nor riches Prov 30:8
through His **p** might 2 Cor 8:9

POWER *authority, strength*

to show you My **p** Ex 9:16
from the **p** of Sheol Ps 49:15
the **p** of His works Ps 111:6
p of the tongue Prov 18:21
the **p** of the sword Jer 18:21
Not by might nor...**p** Zech 4:6
Thine is...the **p** Matt 6:13
the right hand of **p** Mark 14:62
clothed with **p** from Luke 24:49
you shall receive **p** Acts 1:8
gospel...**p** of God Rom 1:16
the **p** of our Lord 1 Cor 5:4
p of sin is the law 1 Cor 15:56
p of Christ...dwell 2 Cor 12:9
prince of the **p** of Eph 2:2
p of His resurrection Phil 3:10
timidity, but of **p** 2 Tim 1:7
by the word of His **p** Heb 1:3
quenched the **p** of Heb 11:34
p-s...been subjected 1 Pet 3:22

POWERLESS *without strength*

p before this great 2 Chr 20:12
He might render **p** Heb 2:14

PRACTICE (n) *custom, habit*

evil of their **p-s** Ps 28:4
disclosing their **p-s** Acts 19:18
laid aside...evil **p-s** Col 3:9

PRACTICE (v) *engage in*

keep...statutes and **p** Lev 20:8
He who **p-s** deceit Ps 101:7
Who **p** righteousness Ps 106:3
p-ing hospitality Rom 12:13
learn to **p** piety 1 Tim 5:4
the one who **p-s** sin 1 John 3:8

PRAETORIUM/PRAETORIAN

1 *Pontius Pilate's palace in
  Jerusalem* Matt 27:27
      Mark 15:16; John 18:28,33
2 *Herod's palace at Caesarea*
      Acts 23:35

3 *Imperial palace guards in
  Rome* Phil 1:13

PRAISE (n) *acclamation, honor*

offering of **p** Lev 19:24
sing **p-s** to Him 1 Chr 16:9
songs of **p**...hymns Neh 12:46
From Thee...my **p** Ps 22:25
sound His **p** abroad Ps 66:8
makes Jerusalem a **p** Is 62:7
his **p** is not from men Rom 2:29
anything worthy of **p** Phil 4:8
a sacrifice of **p** Heb 13:15
Give **p** to our God Rev 19:5

PRAISE (v) *extol, glorify*

I will **p** Him Ex 15:2
greatly to be **p-d** 1 Chr 16:25
Will the dust **p** Thee Ps 30:9
My lips will **p** Thee Ps 63:3
heavens will **p** Thy Ps 89:5
P Him, sun and moon Ps 148:3
P Him with trumpet Ps 150:3
Death cannot **p** Thee Is 38:18
I **p** Thee, O Father Matt 11:25
heavenly host **p-ing** Luke 2:13
disciples began to **p** Luke 19:37
leaping and **p-ing** God Acts 3:8

PRAY *ask, worship*

Abraham **p-ed** to Gen 20:17
For this boy I **p-ed** 1 Sam 1:27
found *courage* to **p** 1 Chr 17:25
For to Thee do I **p** Ps 5:2
P for...Jerusalem Ps 122:6
p to a god who cannot Is 45:20
We earnestly **p** Jon 1:14
p for...persecute Matt 5:44
by Himself to **p** Matt 14:23
p and ask, believe Mark 11:24
until I have **p-ed** Mark 14:32
Lord, teach us to **p** Luke 11:1
they ought to **p** Luke 18:1
I have **p-ed** for you Luke 22:32
p-ed with fasting Acts 14:23
if I **p** in a tongue 1 Cor 14:14
p without ceasing 1 Thess 5:17
p for one another James 5:16
p-ing in the...Spirit Jude 20

PRAYER

I have heard your **p** 2 Chr 7:12

And my **p** is pure — Job 16:17
LORD receives my **p** — Ps 6:9
Give ear to my **p** — Ps 55:1
p of the righteous — Prov 15:29
joyful in My house of **p** — Is 56:7
ask in **p**, believing — Matt 21:22
you make long **p-s** — Matt 23:14
whole night in **p** — Luke 6:12
My house...of **p** — Luke 19:46
devoting...to **p** — Acts 1:14
offering **p** with joy — Phil 1:4
but in everything by **p** — Phil 4:6
p-s...not be hindered — 1 Pet 3:7
p-s of the saints — Rev 5:8

PREACH *exhort, proclaim*

Jesus began to **p** — Matt 4:17
as you go, **p** — Matt 10:7
teach and **p** in their — Matt 11:1
p-ing...repentance — Mark 1:4
p the gospel to all — Mark 16:15
p the kingdom of — Luke 4:43
he **p-ed** Jesus to him — Acts 8:35
p...the good news — Acts 13:32
how shall they **p** — Rom 10:15
we **p** Christ crucified — 1 Cor 1:23
He...**p-ed** peace — Eph 2:17
p the word — 2 Tim 4:2

PREACHER *one who proclaims*

hear without a **p** — Rom 10:14
appointed a **p** and an — 1 Tim 2:7
Noah, a **p** of — 2 Pet 2:5

PRECEPTS *commandments*

All His **p** are sure — Ps 111:7
meditate on Thy **p** — Ps 119:15
as doctrines the **p** of — Matt 15:9

PRECIOUS *beloved or costly*

P in the sight of — Ps 116:15
like **p** oil upon the — Ps 133:2
more **p** than jewels — Prov 3:15
p things...no profit — Is 44:9
more **p** than gold — 1 Pet 1:7
with **p** blood — 1 Pet 1:19

PREDESTINED *foreordained*

purpose **p** to occur — Acts 4:28
foreknew, He also **p** — Rom 8:29
God **p** before the ages — 1 Cor 2:7
p us to adoption — Eph 1:5

p according to His — Eph 1:11

PREDETERMINED

p plan...of God — Acts 2:23

PREEMINENT *foremost*

P in dignity — Gen 49:3

PREFECTS *Persian officials*

shatter governors...**p** — Jer 51:23
the satraps, the **p** — Dan 3:3

PREGNANT *with child*

womb of...**p** woman — Eccl 11:5
And her womb ever **p** — Jer 20:17
ripped open...**p** — Amos 1:13
Elizabeth...became **p** — Luke 1:24

PREPARATION *readiness*

distracted with...**p-s** — Luke 10:40
Jewish day of **p** — John 19:42
making **p-s**, he fell — Acts 10:10
p of the gospel of — Eph 6:15

PREPARE *make ready*

p a savory dish — Gen 27:4
mind **p-s** deception — Job 15:35
p a table before me — Ps 23:5
P to meet your God — Amos 4:12
will **p** Your way — Matt 11:10
kingdom **p-d** for — Matt 25:34
to **p** Me for burial — Matt 26:12
p-d spices and — Luke 23:56
I go to **p** a place — John 14:2
worlds were **p-d** by — Heb 11:3

PRESENCE *appearance*

My **p** shall go *with* — Ex 33:14
in the **p** of my enemies — Ps 23:5
the light of Thy **p** — Ps 44:3
tremble at Thy **p** — Is 64:2
the **p** of His glory — Jude 24
the **p** of the Lamb — Rev 14:10

PRESENT (n) *gift*

a **p** for his brother — Gen 32:13
sent a **p** to the king — 2 Kin 16:8
and a **p** to Hezekiah — Is 39:1

PRESENT (v) *give, offer*

p you with a crown of — Prov 4:9
you **p** the blind for — Mal 1:8
p Him to the Lord — Luke 2:22
p yourselves to God — Rom 6:13

p your bodies a   Rom 12:1
p you before Him holy Col 1:22

PRESERVE *protect*

no son to **p** my   2 Sam 18:18
P me, O God   Ps 16:1
Do **p** my soul   Ps 86:2
LORD **p-s** the simple   Ps 116:6
p-d ones of Israel   Is 49:6
p the unity of the   Eph 4:3
be **p-d** complete   1 Thess 5:23

PRESS *compel, force*

measure, **p-ed** down Luke 6:38
I **p** on toward...goal Phil 3:14

PRETEND *deceive, feign*

p to be a mourner 2 Sam 14:2
p to be another   1 Kin 14:5
p-s to be poor   Prov 13:7
spies who **p-ed** to Luke 20:20

PREVAIL *exist or triumph*

water **p-ed**...increased Gen 7:18
not by might...man **p** 1 Sam 2:9
Iniquities **p** against me Ps 65:3
overcome me and **p-ed** Jer 20:7

PREY *what is hunted*

birds of **p** came   Gen 15:11
lion tearing the **p** Ezek 22:25
no longer be a **p** to Ezek 34:28

PRICE *cost, value*

shall increase its **p** Lev 25:16
their redemption **p** Num 18:16
p of the pardoning of Is 27:9
it is the **p** of blood Matt 27:6
p of his wickedness Acts 1:18
kept back *some*...**p** Acts 5:2
bought with a **p** 1 Cor 7:23

PRIDE *exaggerated self-esteem*

P goes before   Prov 16:18
you an everlasting **p** Is 60:15
p of Israel testifies Hos 5:5
envy, slander, **p** Mark 7:22
boastful **p** of life 1 John 2:16

PRIEST *intermediary*

a **p** of God Most Gen 14:18
a kingdom of **p-s** Ex 19:6
Aaron's sons, the **p-s** Lev 1:5
if the anointed **p** sins Lev 4:3

p...make atonement Lev 4:31
without a teaching **p** 2 Chr 15:3
Thou art a **p** forever Ps 110:4
all the chiefs **p-s** Matt 2:4
show yourself to the **p** Matt 8:4
faithful high **p** Heb 2:17
have a great high **p** Heb 4:14
Thou art a **p** forever Heb 5:6

PRIESTHOOD *office of priest*

for a perpetual **p** Ex 40:15
have defiled the **p** Neh 13:29
His **p** permanently Heb 7:24
royal **p**, a holy nation 1 Pet 2:9

PRIME *fully mature period*

die in the **p** of life 1 Sam 2:33
p of life...fleeting Eccl 11:10

PRINCE *ruler*

Who made you a **p** Ex 2:14
p-s of the tribes 1 Chr 29:6
contempt upon **p-s** Ps 107:40
Do not trust in **p-s** Ps 146:3
Father, **P** of Peace Is 9:6
p-s will rule justly Is 32:1
to death the **P** of life Acts 3:15
p of...the air   Eph 2:2

PRISCA/PRISCILLA

wife of Aquila   Rom 16:3
co-worker with Paul
Acts 18:2,18,26; 1 Cor 16:19

PRISON *jail*

Put this man in **p** 1 Kin 22:27
my soul out of **p** Ps 142:7
beheaded in the **p** Matt 14:10
I was in **p**, and Matt 25:36
opened...the **p** Acts 5:19
spirits *now* in **p** 1 Pet 3:19

PRISONER *one who is confined*

sets the **p-s** free Ps 146:7
a notorious **p** Matt 27:16
p of the law of sin Rom 7:23
Paul, a **p** of Christ Philem 1

PRIVATE *not public*

reprove him in **p** Matt 18:15
but I did so in **p** Gal 2:2

PRIZE *reward*

one receives the **p** 1 Cor 9:24

p of the upward call   Phil 3:14

PROCEED *go forth*

p from evil to evil   Jer 9:3
p-s out of the mouth   Matt 4:4
p-s from...Father   John 15:26

PROCLAIM *announce, declare*

p...name of the LORD   Ex 33:19
P good tidings   1 Chr 16:23
appointed...to p   Neh 6:7
p liberty to captives   Is 61:1
p justice to the   Matt 12:18
he *began* to p Jesus   Acts 9:20
first to p light   Acts 26:23
faith is being p-ed   Rom 1:8
p...eternal life   1 John 1:2

PROCLAMATION *declaration*

a p was circulated   Ex 36:6
made p to the spirits   1 Pet 3:19

PROCONSUL *Roman governor*

the p, Sergius Paulus Acts 13:7
p-s are *available*   Acts 19:38

PRODUCE (n) *yield of the soil*

land will yield its p   Lev 25:19
tithe all the p   Deut 14:22
earth has yielded its p   Ps 67:6
precious p of...soil   James 5:7

PRODUCE (v) *bring forth*

milk p-s butter   Prov 30:33
cannot p bad fruit   Matt 7:18
they p quarrels   2 Tim 2:23
faith p-s endurance   James 1:3

PROFANE *defile, desecrate*

p My holy name   Lev 20:3
is p-d by harlotry   Lev 21:7
and p-d My sabbaths Ezek 22:8
p-d your sanctuaries Ezek 28:18
to p the covenant   Mal 2:10

PROFESS *confess, declare*

P-ing to be wise   Rom 1:22
They p to know God Titus 1:16

PROFIT (n) *benefit, gain*

labor there is p,   Prov 14:23
no p for the charmer Eccl 10:11
not seeking my...p 1 Cor 10:33
business...make a p James 4:13

PROFIT (v) *reap an advantage*

p...my destruction   Job 30:13
what does it p a   Mark 8:36
the flesh p-s nothing John 6:63
it p-s me nothing   1 Cor 13:3

PROFITABLE *useful*

not all things are p 1 Cor 6:12
godliness is p   1 Tim 4:8
p for teaching   2 Tim 3:16

PROMINENT *well-known*

a p member of the Mark 15:43
of p Greek women   Acts 17:12
p men of the city   Acts 25:23

PROMISE (n) *agreement, pledge*

p of the Holy Spirit Acts 2:33
the p made by God   Acts 26:6
the p is nullified   Rom 4:14
children of the p   Rom 9:8
commandment...a p   Eph 6:2
heirs of the p   Heb 6:17
precious...p-s   2 Pet 1:4
the p of His coming 2 Pet 3:4

PROMISED *made an agreement*

land which He had Deut 9:28
p to keep Thy words Ps 119:57
p long ages ago   Titus 1:2
He who p is faithful Heb 10:23

PRONOUNCE *declare officially*

shall p him clean   Lev 13:23
I will p My judgments Jer 1:16
Pilate p-d sentence Luke 23:24
God...p-d judgment Rev 18:20

PROOF *evidence*

furnished p to all   Acts 17:31
p of your love   2 Cor 8:24
p of the Christ   2 Cor 13:3

PROPER *suitable*

fulfilled...p time   Luke 1:20
is it p for a woman 1 Cor 11:13
as is p among saints   Eph 5:3

PROPERTY *goods or land*

acquire p in it   Gen 34:10
p...too great   Gen 36:7
buys a slave as *his* p Lev 22:11
who owned much p Matt 19:22

selling their **p** and   Acts 2:45
things...common **p**   Acts 4:32

PROPHECY *proclamation*

seal up vision and **p**   Dan 9:24
p...fulfilled   Matt 13:14
have *the* gift of **p**   1 Cor 13:2
no **p**...of human will   2 Pet 1:21
the spirit of **p**   Rev 19:10

PROPHESY *predict, proclaim*

to **p** with lyres   1 Chr 25:1
he never **p**-ies good   2 Chr 18:7
p-ing...false vision   Jer 14:14
P over these bones   Ezek 37:4
sons and...will **p**   Joel 2:28
did we...**p** in Your   Matt 7:22
P to us...Christ   Matt 26:68
speaking...**p-ing**   Acts 19:6
who **p**-ies edifies   1 Cor 14:4

PROPHET *spokesman for God*

Aaron shall be your **p**   Ex 7:1
a **p** or a dreamer   Deut 13:1
I will raise up a **p**   Deut 18:18
p in your place   1 Kin 19:16
summon all...**p-s**   2 Kin 10:19
vision of...the **p**   2 Chr 32:32
Woe...foolish **p-s**   Ezek 13:3
written by the **p**   Matt 2:5
persecuted the **p-s**   Matt 5:12
Beware...false **p-s**   Matt 7:15
He...receives a **p**   Matt 10:41
the **p** Jesus   Matt 21:11
false **p-s**...arise   Mark 13:22
p of the Most High   Luke 1:76
great **p** has arisen   Luke 7:16
Are you the **P**   John 1:21
reading Isaiah the **p**   Acts 8:30
a Jewish false **p**   Acts 13:6
All are not **p-s**   1 Cor 12:29
and some *as* **p-s**   Eph 4:11
beast and...false **p**   Rev 20:10

PROPHETESS *speaker for God*

Miriam the **P**   Ex 15:20
Deborah, a **p**   Judg 4:4
there was a **p**, Anna   Luke 2:36
calls herself a **p**   Rev 2:20

PROPHETIC *predictive*

not...**p** utterances   1 Thess 5:20

p word...sure   2 Pet 1:19

PROPITIATION *atonement*

a **p** in His blood   Rom 3:25
p for the sins   Heb 2:17
He himself is the **p**   1 John 2:2
p for our sins   1 John 4:10

PROSELYTE *convert*

both Jews and **p-s**   Acts 2:10
a **p** from Antioch   Acts 6:5
God-fearing **p-s**   Acts 13:43

PROSPER *flourish, succeed*

I will surely **p** you   Gen 32:12
David was **p-ing**   1 Sam 18:14
they build and **p-ed**   2 Chr 14:7
His ways **p** at all   Ps 10:5
they **p** who love you   Ps 122:6

PROSPERITY *success, wealth*

my **p** has passed away   Job 30:15
soul will abide in **p**   Ps 25:13
saw the **p** of the wicked   Ps 73:3
know how to live in **p**   Phil 4:12

PROSPEROUS *successful*

exceedingly **p**   Gen 30:43
make your way **p**   Josh 1:8
generous man...be **p**   Prov 11:25

PROSTITUTE *harlot*

Where...temple **p**   Gen 38:21
male cult **p-s** in the   1 Kin 14:24
an adulterer and a **p**   Is 57:3

PROSTRATE *fall down flat*

p-d himself before   2 Sam 18:28
man dies and lies **p**   Job 14:10
falling down, **p-d**   Matt 18:26

PROTECT *guard, shield*

The LORD will **p** him   Ps 41:2
LORD **p-s** the strangers   Ps 146:9
LORD...**p** Jerusalem   Is 31:5
He will...**p** you   2 Thess 3:3
p-ed by the power of   1 Pet 1:5

PROTECTION *safe-keeping*

p has been removed   Num 14:9
For wisdom is **p**   Eccl 7:12
p from the storm   Is 4:6
let him rely on My **p**   Is 27:5

PROUD

PROUD *exaggerated self-esteem*

heart becomes **p**	Deut 8:14
recompense to the **p**	Ps 94:2
eyes and a **p** heart	Prov 21:4
daughters of Zion are **p**	Is 3:16
opposed to the **p**	James 4:6

PROVE *establish, test*

you be **p-d** a liar	Prov 30:6
shall **p** Myself holy	Ezek 20:41
p to be My disciples	John 15:8
p...the will of God	Rom 12:2
p yourselves doers	James 1:22

PROVERB *adage, short saying*

become...a **p**	Deut 28:37
spoke 3,000 **p-s**	1 Kin 4:32
Israel...become a **p**	1 Kin 9:7
To understand a **p**	Prov 1:6
quote this **p** to Me	Luke 4:23
to the true **p**	2 Pet 2:22

PROVIDE *furnish, supply*

p for Himself...lamb	Gen 22:8
p for...redemption	Lev 25:24
p bread from heaven	Neh 9:15
Who **p-s** rain for the	Ps 147:8
p...way of escape	1 Cor 10:13
not **p** for his own	1 Tim 5:8
God had **p-d**	Heb 11:40

PROVINCE *district or territory*

rulers of the **p-s**	2 Kin 20:17
holiday for the **p-s**	Esth 2:18
whole **p** of Babylon	Dan 2:48
arrived in the **p**	Acts 25:1

PROVISION *supply*

bread of their **p** was	Josh 9:5
bless her **p**	Ps 132:15
p-s of the law	Matt 23:23
no **p** for the flesh	Rom 13:14

PROVOKE *evoke, excite*

images to **p** Me	1 Kin 14:9
who **p** God are secure	Job 12:6
love...is not **p-d**	1 Cor 13:5
not **p** your children	Eph 6:4

PROWL *roam in search*

beasts...**p** about	Ps 104:20
devil, **p-s** about like	1 Pet 5:8

PRUDENT *careful, wise*

a **p** man conceals	Prov 12:16
p wife is from the	Prov 19:14
the **p** took oil in	Matt 25:4
you are **p** in Christ	1 Cor 4:10

PRUNING *cutting*

spears into **p** hooks	Is 2:4

PSALMS *sacred songs*

shout...with **p**	Ps 95:2
P must be fulfilled	Luke 24:44
speaking...in **p**	Eph 5:19

PUBLIC *open*

of his **p** appearance	Luke 1:80
beaten us in **p**	Acts 16:37
refuted...Jews in **p**	Acts 18:28
made a **p** display	Col 2:15
made a **p** spectacle	Heb 10:33

PUL

Tiglath Pileser III, king of
Assyria 2 Kin 15:19; 1 Chr 5:26

PUNISH *chastise, penalize*

p them for their sin	Ex 32:34
and are **p-ed** for it	Prov 22:3
p the world for its	Is 13:11
will **p** your iniquity	Lam 4:22
p Him and release	Luke 23:16
I **p-ed** them often	Acts 26:11
p all disobedience	2 Cor 10:6

PUNISHMENT *pen...*

My **p** is too great	Gen 4:13
p of the sword	Job 19:29
fear involves **p**	1 John 4:18
the **p** of eternal fire	Jude 7

PUPIL *student*

as the **p** of His eye	Deut 32:10
p is not above his	Luke 6:40

PURCHASE *buy*

p-d with His...blood	Acts 20:28
p for God with Thy	Rev 5:9

PURE *genuine, undefiled*

mercy seat of **p** gold	Ex 25:17
be **p** before his Maker	Job 4:17
My teaching is **p**	Job 11:4
commandment...is **p**	Ps 19:8
pleasant words are **p**	Prov 15:26

As **p** as the sun Song 6:10
hair...like **p** wool Dan 7:9
Blessed are the **p** in Matt 5:8
whatever is **p** Phil 4:8
love from a **p** heart 1 Tim 1:5
p milk of the word 1 Pet 2:2
the city was **p** gold Rev 21:18

PURGE remove

p...evil from among Deut 13:5
Many will be **p**-d Dan 12:10

PURIFICATION cleansing

Jewish custom of **p** John 2:6
He...made **p** of sins Heb 1:3

PURIFY make clean

p-ied these waters 2 Kin 2:21
P me with hyssop Ps 51:7
p...a people Titus 2:14
p your hearts James 4:8
p-ied your souls 1 Pet 1:22

PURIM

Jewish festival Esth 9:26ff

PURITY not corrupted

who loves **p** of heart Prov 22:11
love, faith and **p** 1 Tim 4:12
with **p** in doctrine Titus 2:7

PURPLE color

a veil of blue and **p** Ex 26:31
Those reared in **p** Lam 4:5
clothed Daniel with **p** Dan 5:29
dressed Him...**p** Mark 15:17
a seller of **p** fabrics Acts 16:14
clothed in **p** and Rev 17:4

PURPOSE intention, reason

p of shedding blood Ezek 22:9
rejected God's **p** Luke 7:30
for this **p** I have Acts 26:16
according to His **p** Rom 8:28

PURSE bag, pouch

gold from the **p** Is 46:6
Carry no **p**, no bag Luke 10:4
p-s...do not wear Luke 12:33

PURSUE chase, follow

p the manslayer Deut 19:6
They **p** my honor Job 30:15
the enemy **p** my soul Ps 7:5
Seek peace, and **p** it Ps 34:14

Adversity **p**-s sinners Prov 13:21
p-s righteousness Prov 21:21
may **p** strong drink Is 5:11
p righteousness 2 Tim 2:22
P peace with...men Heb 12:14

PUT place

p enmity Between Gen 3:15
He **p** a new song Ps 40:3
p on the Lord Jesus Rom 13:14
p on the new self Eph 4:24
P on the full armor Eph 6:11

PUT

1 son of Ham Gen 10:6
  1 Chr 1:8
2 African country Jer 46:9
  Ezek 27:10;30:5; Nah 3:9

Q

QUAIL type of bird

q-s came up and Ex 16:13
q from the sea Num 11:31

QUAKE shake, tremble

The mountains **q**-d Judg 5:5
made the land **q** Ps 60:2
The earth **q**-d Ps 68:8
q at Thy presence Is 64:1

QUALITY character

test the **q** of each 1 Cor 3:13
imperishable **q** of a 1 Pet 3:4

QUANTITY amount

large **q**-ies of cedar 1 Chr 22:4
a great **q** of fish Luke 5:6

QUARANTINE isolation

shall **q** the article Lev 13:50
q the house for Lev 14:38

QUARREL (n) altercation

if men have a **q** Ex 21:18
So abandon the **q** Prov 17:14
are **q**-s among you 1 Cor 1:11
the source of **q**-s James 4:1

QUARREL (v) contend, fight

did not **q** over it Gen 26:22
Why do you **q** with me Ex 17:2

any fool will q   Prov 20:3
those who q with you   Is 41:12

QUART *measure*

A q of wheat for a   Rev 6:6

QUEEN *female sovereign*

when the q of Sheba 1 Kin 10:1
king saw Esther the q   Esth 5:2
The q of kingdoms   Is 47:5
The Q of *the* South Matt 12:42
Candace, q of the   Acts 8:27

QUENCH *extinguish*

donkeys q their thirst   Ps 104:11
waters cannot q love   Song 8:7
not q the Spirit   1 Thess 5:19
q-d...power of fire   Heb 11:34

QUESTION (n) *inquiry, problem*

Was it not just a q 1 Sam 17:29
answered all her q-s 2 Chr 9:2
Jesus asked...a q   Matt 22:41
in controversial q-s   1 Tim 6:4

QUESTION (v) *ask*

q-ed the priests   2 Chr 31:9
Jeremiah and q-ed   Jer 38:27
He *began* to q them   Mark 9:33
to q Him closely on Luke 11:53
Q those who have   John 18:21

QUICK (adj) *rapid*

is q-tempered exalts   Prov 14:29
q to hear, slow to   James 1:19

QUICK (n) *deepest feelings*

cut to the q and   Acts 5:33
were cut to the q   Acts 7:54

QUIET (adj) *calm, still*

he knew no q within Job 20:20
me beside q waters   Ps 23:2
lead a...q life   1 Tim 2:2
gentle and q spirit   1 Pet 3:4

QUIET (v) *become calm, still*

God, do not remain q   Ps 83:1
and q-ed my soul   Ps 131:2
will be q in His love Zeph 3:17
Be q, and come out Mark 1:25

QUIRINIUS

Roman governor at time of
   Judean census   Luke 2:2

QUIVER *case for holding arrows*

your q and your bow Gen 27:3
man whose q is full   Ps 127:5
hidden Me in His q   Is 49:2
q is like an open grave Jer 5:16
fill the q-s   Jer 51:11

QUOTA *portion assigned*

complete your work q   Ex 5:13
deliver the q of bricks Ex 5:18

QUOTE *repeat a passage*

who q-s proverbs   Ezek 16:44
will q this proverb   Luke 4:23

R

RAAMSES/RAMESES

where Joseph settled Gen 47:11
Egyptian store-city built by
   Hebrew slaves   Ex 1:11
origin of exodus   Ex 12:37
            Num 33:3,5

RABBI/RABBONI

respectful form of address
   Matt 23:7;26:25; Mark 10:51
master, teacher John 1:49;6:25
         John 11:8;20:16

RAB-MAG

title of Babylonian official
            Jer 39:3,13

RAB-SARIS

title of Assyrian official
   2 Kin 18:17; Jer 39:3,13

RABSHAKEH

title of Assyrian official
   2 Kin 18:17ff; Is 36:2,4,11

RACA *worthless fool*

shall say...R   Matt 5:22

RACE (n) *nation, people*

r has intermingled   Ezra 9:2
mongrel r will dwell Zech 9:6
advantage of our r   Acts 7:19
you are a chosen r   1 Pet 2:9

RACE (n) *competition of speed*

r is not to...swift   Eccl 9:11
in a r all run, but   1 Cor 9:24
r...set before us   Heb 12:1

RACHEL

Jacob's wife   Gen 29:18,28
mother of Joseph and Benjamin
    Gen 30:25;35:24;46:19

RADIANCE *brightness*

a r around Him   Ezek 1:27
His r is like   Hab 3:4
r of His glory   Heb 1:3

RADIANT *shining brightly*

looked to Him...were r   Ps 34:5
you will see and be r   Is 60:5
His garments...r   Mark 9:3

RAFTS *boat*

r *to go* by sea   1 Kin 5:9
bring it to you on r   2 Chr 2:16

RAGE (n) *violent anger*

Haman was filled...r   Esth 3:5
with r as they heard   Luke 4:28

RAGE (v) *be very angry*

r-s against the LORD   Prov 19:3
foolish man...r-s   Prov 29:9
Why...Gentiles r   Acts 4:25

RAHAB

1 *harlot in Jericho*   Josh 2:1
    assisted spies   Josh 2:4-7
    family spared   Josh 2:13,14
    Josh 6:22,23
    ancestor of Jesus   Matt 1:5
    example of faith   Heb 11:31
    James 2:25
2 *symbolic for sea monster*
    Job 9:13;26:12; Ps 89:10
3 *symbolic for Egypt*
    Ps 87:4; Is 30:7

RAID *make a sudden attack*

a r on the land   1 Sam 23:27
a r on the camels   Job 1:17
Bandits r outside   Hos 7:1

RAIN (n)

God had not sent r   Gen 2:5

r fell upon the earth   Gen 7:12
I shall give you r-s   Lev 26:4
LORD sent...r   1 Sam 12:18
no r in the land   1 Kin 17:7
the mountain r-s   Job 24:8
shed...a plentiful r   Ps 68:9
r is over *and* gone   Song 2:11
anger a flooding r   Ezek 13:13
r on *the* righteous   Matt 5:45
ground...drinks the r   Heb 6:7

RAIN (v) *fall down, pour*

r bread from heaven   Ex 16:4
the LORD r-ed hail   Ex 9:23
it r-ed fire and   Luke 17:29
not r...for three   James 5:17

RAINBOW *colored arc in sky*

appearance of the r   Ezek 1:28
a r around the throne   Rev 4:3
r was upon his head   Rev 10:1

RAISE *elevate, lift*

will r up a prophet   Deut 18:18
LORD r-d up judges   Judg 2:16
r-s the poor from   1 Sam 2:8
eyelids are r-d in   Prov 30:13
r up shepherds over   Jer 23:4
He will r us up   Hos 6:2
Heal...r *the* dead   Matt 10:8
He will be r-d up   Matt 20:19
three days I will r   John 2:19
Jesus God r-d up   Acts 2:32
r-d a spiritual   1 Cor 15:44
r-d us up with Him   Eph 2:6
God is able to r men   Heb 11:19

RAISIN *dried grapes*

clusters of r-s   2 Sam 16:1
Sustain me with r   Song 2:5
and love r cakes   Hos 3:1

RAM *male sheep*

Abraham...took the r   Gen 22:13
a r without defect   Lev 5:15
the r of atonement   Num 5:8
r which had two horns   Dan 8:3

RAMAH

1 *city of Naphtali*   Josh 19:36
2 *town of Asher*   Josh 19:29
3 *town of Benjamin*   Josh 18:25
    Judg 4:5; 19:13

4 *town in the Negev* Josh 19:8
5 *town in Gilead* 2 Kin 8:28,29
2 Chr 22:5,6

RAMOTH

1 *city in Gilead*   Deut 4:43
Josh 20:8

see RAMOTH-GILEAD

2 *city in the Negev* 1 Sam 30:27
also **Ramah of the Negev**
3 *Gershonite city*   1 Chr 6:73

RAMOTH-GILEAD

Gadite city E of the Jordan
Deut 4:43
city of refuge   Josh 20:8
Ahab killed   1 Kin 22:29-37

RAMPART *bulwark, siege*

and r for security   Is 26:1
Whose r *was* the sea Nah 3:8
station myself on the r Hab 2:1

RANK *position*

men of r are a lie   Ps 62:9
He...has a higher r   Josh 1:15
a Man...higher r   John 1:30

RANSOM (n) *payment*

give a r for himself   Ex 30:12
not take r for   Num 35:31
wicked is a r for   Prov 21:18
His life a r for   Matt 20:28
gave Himself as a r   1 Tim 2:6

RANSOM (v) *redeem*

Thou hast r-ed me   Ps 31:5
R me because of my   Ps 69:18
LORD has r-ed Jacob   Jer 31:11
I will r them from   Hos 13:14

RAVAGE *devastate*

famine will r the   Gen 41:30
mice that r the land 1 Sam 6:5
r-ing the church   Acts 8:3

RAVEN *type of bird*

he sent out a r   Gen 8:7
young r-s which cry Ps 147:9
Consider the r-s   Luke 12:24

RAVENOUS *wildly hungry*

Benjamin is a r wolf Gen 49:27
inwardly are r wolves Matt 7:15

RAVINE *gorge*

settle on the steep r-s Is 7:19
smooth *stones* of the r Is 57:6
Every r shall be filled Luke 3:5

RAVISH *seize and take*

you may r them   Judg 19:24
And their wives r-ed Is 13:16
r-ed...women in Zion Lam 5:11

RAZOR *instrument for shaving*

no r shall pass over Num 6:5
no r shall come upon Judg 13:5
A r has never come Judg 16:17
Like a sharp r   Ps 52:2

READ

you shall r this   Deut 31:11
r from the scroll   Jer 36:6
who r-s it may run   Hab 2:2
r-ing...Isaiah   Acts 8:28
prophets...are **read** Acts 13:27
Moses is **read**   2 Cor 3:15
Blessed is he who r-s Rev 1:3

READY *equipped, prepared*

and r to forgive   Ps 86:5
Let Thy hand be r Ps 119:173
Make r the way   Matt 3:3
you be r too   Matt 24:44
be r in season   2 Tim 4:2
r to make a defense 1 Pet 3:15

REALIZE *achieve or understand*

Desire r-d is sweet Prov 13:19
r-d through Jesus   John 1:17
to r...assurance   Heb 6:11

REALM *area, kingdom*

ruler over the r of   Dan 4:17
kingdom is not...r John 18:36

REAP *cut, gather*

when you r...harvest Lev 19:9
iniquity will r vanity Prov 22:8
they r the whirlwind Hos 8:7
neither do they r   Matt 6:26
neither sow nor r Luke 12:24
sows...another r-s   John 4:37
r eternal life   Gal 6:8
your sickle and r   Rev 14:15

REAPER *harvester*

after the r-s	Ruth 2:3
will overtake the r	Amos 9:13
the r-s are angels	Matt 13:39

REASON (n) *explanation*

this r the Father	John 10:17
this r I found mercy	1 Tim 1:16
For this r, rejoice	Rev 12:12

REASON (v) *analyze, argue*

upright would r with	Job 23:7
let us r together	Is 1:18
Pharisees began to r	Luke 5:21
r-ing in...synagogue	Acts 17:17
as a child, r as a	1 Cor 13:11

REBEKAH

wife of Isaac   Gen 24:67;26:8
mother of Esau and Jacob
              Gen 25:21ff

REBEL (n) *rebellious one*

Your rulers are r-s	Is 1:23
called a r from birth	Is 48:8
their princes are r-s	Hos 9:15

REBEL (v) *revolt*

not r against the	Num 14:9
r-led against...words	Ps 107:11
r-led against Me	Ezek 20:21

REBELLION *insurrection*

he has counseled r	Deut 13:5
I know your r	Deut 31:27
r is as the sin of	1 Sam 15:23
my r and my sin	Job 13:23
children of r	Is 57:4

REBELLIOUS *defiant*

r against the LORD	Deut 9:7
r generation	Ps 78:8
A r man seeks only	Prov 17:11
stubborn and r heart	Jer 5:23
there are many r	Titus 1:10

REBUILD *restore*

r the house of the	Ezra 1:3
let us r the wall	Neh 2:17
r the ancient ruins	Is 58:12
r it in three days	Matt 26:61
r the tabernacle	Acts 15:16

REBUKE (n) *reprimand*

amazed at His r	Job 26:11
At Thy r they fled	Ps 104:7
the poor hears no r	Prov 13:8

REBUKE (v) *scold*

r me not in Thy wrath	Ps 38:1
r the arrogant	Ps 119:21
LORD r you, Satan	Zech 3:2
Jesus r-d the winds	Matt 8:26
He r-d the fever	Matt 17:18
Do not sharply r	Luke 4:39
reprove, r, exhort	1 Tim 5:1
	2 Tim 4:2

RECEIVE *encounter, take*

The LORD r-s my prayer	Ps 6:9
r me to glory	Ps 73:24
man r-s a bribe	Prov 17:23
freely you r-d	Matt 10:8
who r-s you, r-s Me	Matt 10:40
the blind r sight	Matt 11:5
ask...you shall r	Matt 21:22
r-d up into Heaven	Mark 16:19
This man r-s sinners	Luke 15:2
as many as r-d Him	John 1:12
r you to Myself	John 14:3
R the Holy Spirit	John 20:22
you shall r power	Acts 1:8
to give than to r	Acts 20:35
one r-s the prize	1 Cor 9:24
r the crown of life	James 1:12
whatever...ask we r	1 John 3:22
r-d the mark of	Rev 19:20

RECHABITES

line of Jonadah   Jer 35:6
strict life style   Jer 35:1-18

RECKONED *accounted for*

r it to him as	Gen 15:6
r among the nations	Num 23:9
his wage is not r	Rom 4:4
r...as righteousness	James 2:23

RECLINE *lean, lie down*

r on beds of ivory	Amos 6:4
r on the grass	Matt 14:19
r *at the table* in	Luke 13:29
r-ing on Jesus'	John 13:23

RECOGNIZE *be aware, know*

he did not r him	Gen 27:23

RECOGNIZE

Saul r-d David's — 1 Sam 26:17
r that He is near — Matt 24:33
I did not r Him — John 1:31

RECOMPENSE (n) *reward*

the r of the wicked — Ps 91:8
r to the proud — Ps 94:2
r of God will come — Is 35:4
received a just r — Heb 2:2

RECOMPENSE (v) *compensate*

the LORD has r-d me — 2 Sam 22:25
He will r the evil — Ps 54:5
But if you do r Me — Joel 3:4

RECONCILE *bring together*

r-d to your brother — Matt 5:24
be r-d to God — 2 Cor 5:20
r them both in one — Eph 2:16
r all...to Himself — Col 1:20

RECONCILIATION

now received the r — Rom 5:11
the r of the world — Rom 11:15
the ministry of r — 2 Cor 5:18
the word of r — 2 Cor 5:19

RECORD (n) *document, register*

the r-s are ancient — 1 Chr 4:22
r-s of the kings — 2 Chr 33:18
discover in...r books — Ezra 4:15
I found the...r — Neh 7:5

RECORD (v) *register, write*

r-ed their starting — Num 33:2
R the vision — Hab 2:2
are r-ed in heaven — Luke 10:20

RECOVER *reclaim, regain*

did you not r them — Judg 11:26
Will I r from this — 2 Kin 8:8
and they will r — Mark 16:18

RED *color*

first came forth r — Gen 25:25
water...r as blood — 2 Kin 3:22
they are r like crimson — Is 1:18
the sky is r — Matt 16:2
a great r dragon — Rev 12:3

RED SEA

Hebrew: Sea of Reeds — Ex 10:19
body of water between Egypt
and Sinai — Ex 13:18; Ps 106:9
— Jer 49:21; Heb 11:29

REDEEM *buy back*

I will also r you — Ex 6:6
family may r him — Lev 25:49
wish to r the field — Lev 27:19
I will r it — Ruth 4:4
God will r my soul — Ps 49:15
He will r Israel — Ps 130:8
Christ r-ed us — Gal 3:13
He might r those — Gal 4:5

REDEEMER *one who buys back*

left you without a r — Ruth 4:14
know that my R lives — Job 19:25
my rock and my R — Ps 19:14
your R is the Holy — Is 41:14
our Father, Our R — Is 63:16
Their R is strong — Jer 50:34

REDEMPTION *deliverance*

r of the land — Lev 25:24
have my right of r — Ruth 4:6
r of his soul is — Ps 49:8
r is drawing near — Luke 21:28
r...in Christ Jesus — Rom 3:24
r of our body — Rom 8:23
r through His blood — Eph 1:7
in whom we have r — Col 1:14
obtained eternal r — Heb 9:12

REED *tall marsh grass*

set *it* among the r-s — Ex 2:3
bruised r He will — Is 42:3
the r...to beat Him — Matt 27:30
and put it on a r — Matt 27:48

REEL *stagger, sway*

earth r-s to and fro — Is 24:20
r with strong drink — Is 28:7

REFINE *purify*

r-d seven times — Ps 12:6
in order to r — Dan 11:35
R them as silver — Zech 13:9
r them like gold — Mal 3:3
gold r-d by fire — Rev 3:18

REFRAIN *abstain*

not r from spitting — Job 30:10
to r from working — 1 Cor 9:6
R his tongue...evil — 1 Pet 3:10
r from judging — Rev 6:10

REFRESH *renew, replenish*

you may r yourselves — Gen 18:5

R me with apples   Song 2:5
times of r-ing may   Acts 3:19
r my heart in Christ Philem 20

REFUGE *protection, shelter*

in whom I take r   2 Sam 22:3
God is our r   Ps 46:1
r in the LORD   Ps 118:8
the r of lies   Is 28:17
r in...distress   Jer 16:19
who have fled for r   Heb 6:18

REFUGE, CITIES OF
  see **CITIES OF REFUGE**

REFUSE (n) *waste*

be made a r heap   Ezra 6:11
corpses lay like r   Is 5:25
its waters toss up r   Is 57:20
sell...r of the wheat   Amos 8:6

REFUSE (v) *decline*

r you his grave   Gen 23:6
r to let My people go   Ex 10:4
his hands r to work   Prov 21:25
they r to know Me   Jer 9:6
r-d to be comforted   Matt 2:18
can r the water   Acts 10:47
not r Him who is   Heb 12:25

REFUSE GATE *see* **GATES OF**
  JERUSALEM

REFUTE *confute*

R me if you can   Job 33:5
he...r-d the Jews   Acts 18:28
to r those who   Titus 1:9

REGAIN *recover*

r-ed their sight   Matt 20:34
want to r my sight   Mark 10:51
he might r his sight   Acts 9:12

REGARD (n) *respect*

LORD had r for Abel   Gen 4:4
r to the prayer   1 Kin 8:28
have r for his Maker   Is 17:7
r for the humble   Luke 1:48

REGARD (v) *esteem, respect*

If I r wickedness   Ps 66:18
Yet He r-s the lowly   Ps 138:6
who r-s reproof is   Prov 15:5

highly r-ed by him   Luke 7:2
you r one another   Phil 2:3
did not r equality   Phil 2:6

REGENERATION *renewal*

r when the Son   Matt 19:28
the washing of r   Titus 3:5

REGION *area*

r of the Jordan   Josh 22:10
the r-s of Galilee   Matt 2:22
to the r of Judea   Mark 10:1
same r...shepherds   Luke 2:8

REGISTER *enroll, record*

r...people of Israel   2 Sam 24:4
to r for the census   Luke 2:3

REHOBOAM

son of Solomon   1 Kin 11:43
king of Judah   1 Kin 12:16ff
              2 Chr 11:1ff

REIGN *rule*

LORD shall r forever   Ex 15:18
Shall Saul r over   1 Sam 11:12
David r-ed over all   2 Sam 8:15
The LORD r-s   Ps 93:1
By me kings r   Prov 8:15
will r righteously   Is 32:1
death r-ed...Adam   Rom 5:14
He must r until   1 Cor 15:25
also r with Him   2 Tim 2:12
He will r forever   Rev 11:15
will r with Him   Rev 20:6

REJECT *decline, refuse*

have r-ed the LORD   Num 11:20
will r you forever   1 Chr 28:9
not r the discipline   Prov 3:11
A fool r-s his   Prov 15:5
have r-ed this word   Is 30:12
He who r-s unjust gain   Is 33:15
r-ed My ordinances   Ezek 20:13
have r-ed knowledge   Hos 4:6
they r-ed the law   Amos 2:4
the builders r-ed   Matt 21:42
who r-s you r-s Me   Luke 10:16
He who r-s Me   John 12:48

REJOICE *be glad*

r before the LORD   Lev 23:40
R, O nations   Deut 32:43
I r in Thy salvation   1 Sam 2:1

195

let the earth r   1 Chr 16:31
my soul shall r   Ps 35:9
king will r in God   Ps 63:11
Let us r and be glad Ps 118:24
I r at Thy word   Ps 119:162
R, young man   Eccl 11:9
God will r over you   Is 62:5
r-d exceedingly   Matt 2:10
r at his birth   Luke 1:14
multitude was r-ing Luke 13:17
you would have r-d John 14:28
r-ing in hope   Rom 12:12
yet always r-ing   2 Cor 6:10

R in the Lord   Phil 4:4
I r in my sufferings Col 1:24
r, O heavens   Rev 12:12

REJOICING (n) *delight*

a holiday for r   Esth 9:19
hills gird...with r   Ps 65:12
Jerusalem for r   Is 65:18

RELATIONS *sexual intercourse*

r with his wife Eve   Gen 4:1
had no r with a man Judg 11:39
we may have r with Judg 19:22
had r with Hannah 1 Sam 1:19

RELATIVE *kinsman*

and to my r-s   Gen 24:4
The man is our r   Ruth 2:20
My r-s have failed   Job 19:14
among his *own* r-s   Mark 6:4
your r Elizabeth has Luke 1:36

RELEASE (n) *liberation*

a r through the land Lev 25:10
r for you the King   Mark 15:9
r to the captives   Luke 4:18

RELEASE (v) *set free*

he r-d Barabbas   Matt 27:26
wanting to r Jesus Luke 23:20
efforts to r Him   John 19:12
you r-d from a wife 1 Cor 7:27
r-d us from our Sin Rev 1:5
R the four angels   Rev 9:14

RELENT *yield*

I am tired of r-ing   Jer 15:6
r...the calamity   Jer 18:8
whether He will...r Joel 2:14
God may turn and r Jon 3:9

RELIEF *lessening of burden*

r and deliverance   Esth 4:14
my *prayer for* r   Lam 3:56
r of the brethren   Acts 11:29

RELIGION *system of belief*

about their own r   Acts 25:19
sect of our r   Acts 26:5
pure and undefiled r James 1:27

RELIGIOUS *devout, pious*

r in all respects   Acts 17:22
thinks...to be r   James 1:26

RELY *depend, trust*

r-ied on the LORD   2 Chr 16:8
who...r on horses   Is 31:1
r on his God   Is 50:10
You r on your sword Ezek 33:26
r upon the Law   Rom 2:17

REMAIN *abide, be left*

While the earth r-s Gen 8:22
R...in his place   Ex 16:29
ark...with us   1 Sam 5:7
r-s yet...youngest 1 Sam 16:11
flee to Egypt, and r Matt 2:13
dove...r-ed upon Him John 1:32
not r in darkness   John 12:46
not r on the cross John 19:31
let her r unmarried 1 Cor 7:11
gospel might r   Gal 2:5
He r-s faithful   2 Tim 2:13

REMEMBER *recall, recollect*

God r-ed Noah   Gen 8:1
I will r My covenant Gen 9:15
R the sabbath day Ex 20:8
not r the sins of my Ps 25:7
R also your Creator Eccl 12:1
O LORD, R me   Jer 15:15
sin I will r no more Jer 31:34
Peter r-ed the word Matt 26:75
R Lot's wife   Luke 17:32
r the words of   Acts 20:35
to r the poor   Gal 2:10

REMEMBRANCE *memory*

Thy r, O LORD   Ps 135:13
Put Me in r   Is 43:26
a book of r was   Mal 3:16
do this in r of Me Luke 22:19
in r of Me   1 Cor 11:25

REMNANT *remaining part*

preserve for you a r   Gen 45:7
prayer for the r   2 Kin 19:4
an escaped r   Ezra 9:8
A r will return   Is 10:21
the r of Israel   Jer 6:9
a r of the Spirit   Mal 2:15
r that will be saved   Rom 9:27

REMOVE *take away or off*

r your sandals   Ex 3:5
r-d all the idols   1 Kin 15:12
He r-d the high   2 Kin 18:4
r the heart of stone   Ezek 36:26
not fit to r His   Matt 3:11
r this cup from Me   Luke 22:42
R the stone   John 11:39
as to r mountains   1 Cor 13:2

REND *tear*

r the heavens   Is 64:1
r their garments   Jer 36:24
r your heart and not   Joel 2:13

RENDER *inflict, repay*

I will r vengeance   Deut 32:41
R recompense to the   Ps 94:2
r to Caesar the   Matt 22:21
R to all what is due   Rom 13:7

RENEW *make new, revive*

r a steadfast spirit   Ps 51:10
r-ed like the eagle   Ps 103:5
R our days as of old   Lam 5:21
inner man...r-ed   2 Cor 4:16

RENOWN *fame*

men of r   Gen 6:4
a people, for r   Jer 13:11
shame into...and r   Zeph 3:19

REPAIR *restore*

r the house of   1 Chr 26:27
r-ing...foundations   Ezra 4:12
r of the walls   Neh 4:7

REPAY *pay back*

you thus r the LORD   Deut 32:6
so God has **repaid**   Judg 1:7
LORD r the evildoer   2 Sam 3:39
repaid me evil for   Ps 109:5
r their iniquity   Jer 16:18
He will fully r   Jer 51:56
in secret will r   Matt 6:4

is Mine, I will r   Rom 12:19
no one r-s...evil   1 Thess 5:15

REPENT *change mind*

that He should r   Num 23:19
r in dust and ashes   Job 42:6
have refused to r   Jer 5:3
R, for the kingdom   Matt 3:2
r-ed long ago in   Matt 11:21
r and believe   Mark 1:15
one sinner who r-s   Luke 15:7
R,...be baptized   Acts 2:38
all...should r   Acts 17:30
r and turn to God   Acts 26:20

REPENTANCE *penitence*

with water for r   Matt 3:11
baptism of r   Mark 1:4
r for forgiveness   Luke 24:47
appropriate to r   Acts 26:20
r without regret   2 Cor 7:10
r from dead works   Heb 6:1
to come to r   2 Pet 3:9

REPHAIM

1 *pre-Israelite people of*
  Palestine   Gen 14:5; 15:20
  people of large stature
2 *valley near Jerusalem*
    Josh 15:8; 2 Sam 23:13

REPHIDIM

Israelite campsite in Sinai
    Ex 17:1,8; Num 33:14,15

REPORT *account, statement*

not bear a false r   Ex 23:1
r concerning Him   Luke 7:17
has believed our r   John 12:38

REPRESENTATION *likeness*

exact r of His nature   Heb 1:3

REPRESENTATIVE *substitute*

people's r before God   Ex 18:19
the king's r   Neh 11:24

REPROACH (n) *dishonor*

taken away my r   Gen 30:23
a r on all Israel   1 Sam 11:2
I have become a r   Ps 31:11
with dishonor...r   Prov 18:3
not fear the r of   Is 51:7
the r of Christ   Heb 11:26

REPROACH (v) accuse, rebuke

to r the living God	2 Kin 19:4
My heart does not r	Job 27:6
foolish man r-s Thee	Ps 74:22
enemies have r-ed me	Ps 102:8
He...to r the cities	Matt 11:20
He r-ed them for	Mark 16:14

REPROOF correction, rebuke

spurned all my r	Prov 1:30
regards r is prudent	Prov 15:5
who hates r will	Prov 15:10
and r give wisdom	Prov 29:15
for teaching, for r	2 Tim 3:16

REPROVE correct, rebuke

r your neighbor	Lev 19:17
LORD loves He r-s	Prov 3:12
Do not r a scoffer	Prov 9:8
R the ruthless	Is 1:17
r him in private	Matt 18:15
r, rebuke, exhort	2 Tim 4:2
whom I love, I r	Rev 3:19

REPTILE snake

and the sand r	Lev 11:30
r-s of the earth	Mic 7:17
r-s and creatures	James 3:7

REPUTATION character

seven men of good r	Acts 6:3
a r for good works	1 Tim 5:10

REQUEST desire, petition

my people as my r	Esth 7:3
the r of his lips	Ps 21:2
He gave them their r	Ps 106:15
r-s be made known to	Phil 4:6

REQUIRE demand, insist

r your lifeblood	Gen 9:5
God r from you	Deut 10:12
as each day r-d	Ezra 3:4
your soul is r-d	Luke 12:20
r-d of stewards	1 Cor 4:2

REQUIREMENT necessity

r-s of the Lord	Luke 1:6
r of the Law	Rom 8:4
law of physical r	Heb 7:16

RESCUE deliver, redeem

O LORD, r my soul	Ps 6:4
R the weak and needy	Ps 82:4

He delivers and r-s	Dan 6:27
r the godly from	2 Pet 2:9

RESERVE retain, store up

r-d a blessing for	Gen 27:36
darkness...in r	Job 20:26
lips may r knowledge	Prov 5:2
r-s wrath for	Nah 1:2
r-d in heaven	1 Pet 1:4
r-d for fire	2 Pet 3:7

RESIDE dwell, live

stranger who r-s	Lev 19:34
a son of man r in it	Jer 49:18
r-d in...Nazareth	Matt 2:23
those who r as aliens	1 Pet 1:1

RESIST oppose, withstand

not r him who is	Matt 5:39
none...able to r	Luke 21:15
r-ing the Holy Spirit	Acts 7:51
he who r-s authority	Rom 13:2
R the devil	James 4:7

RESPECT (n) regard

no r for the old	Deut 28:50
where is My r	Mal 1:6
please Him in...r-s	Col 1:10
to your masters...r	1 Pet 2:18

RESPECT (v) esteem

They will r my son	Matt 21:37
not fear God nor r	Luke 18:4
R what is right	Rom 12:17
wife...r her husband	Eph 5:33

RESPOND answer, reply

He will r to them	Is 19:22
r to the heavens	Hos 2:21
how you should r	Col 4:6
Peter r-d to her	Acts 5:8

REST (n) remainder

r turned and fled	Judg 20:45
the r of the exiles	Ezra 6:16
the r of your days	Prov 19:20
I will slay the r	Amos 9:1
to the r...parables	Luke 8:10

REST (n) tranquility

r from our work	Gen 5:29
sabbath of solemn r	Lev 16:31
God gives you r	Josh 1:13
the weary are at r	Job 3:17

Return to your r   Ps 116:7
whole earth is at r   Is 14:7
there is no r   Lam 5:5
I will give you r   Matt 11:28
no r for my spirit   2 Cor 2:13
not enter My r   Heb 3:11
no r day and night   Rev 14:11

REST (v) *place on, refresh*

the ark r-ed upon   Gen 8:4
glory...LORD r-ed   Ex 24:16
Spirit r-ed upon   Num 11:25
R in the LORD   Ps 37:7
Wisdom r-s in   Prov 14:33
government will r on   Is 9:6
iniquity r-ed on   Ezek 32:27
r-ed on the seventh   Heb 4:4
r from their labors   Rev 14:13

RESTING PLACE

dove found no r   Gen 8:9
This is My r forever   Ps 132:14
Do not destroy his r   Prov 24:15
r will be glorious   Is 11:10

RESTITUTION *reparation*

owner...make r   Ex 21:34
make r in full   Num 5:7
r for the lamb   2 Sam 12:6

RESTORE *reestablish, replace*

son he had r-d to   2 Kin 8:1
they r-d Jerusalem   Neh 3:8
r His righteousness   Job 33:26
He r-s my soul   Ps 23:3
R to me the joy   Ps 51:12
O God, r us   Ps 80:3
the LORD r-s Zion   Is 52:8
R us to Thee   Lam 5:21
his hand was r-d   Mark 3:5
r-ing the kingdom   Acts 1:6

RESTRAIN *hold back*

the rain...was r-ed   Gen 8:2
who can r Him   Job 11:10
He r-ed His anger   Ps 78:38
who r-s his lips   Prov 10:19
Wilt Thou r Thyself   Is 64:12
R your voice from   Jer 31:16
r-ed the crowds   Acts 14:18

RESULT (n) *consequence, effect*

a r of the anguish   Is 53:11
not as a r of works   Eph 2:9

have *its* perfect r   James 1:4
as a r of the works   James 2:22

RESULT (v) *follow, happen*

r-ed In reproach   Jer 20:8
sin r-ing in death   Rom 6:16
proved to r in death   Rom 7:10
r-ing in salvation   Rom 10:10

RESURRECTION

who say...no r   Matt 22:23
r of the righteous   Luke 14:14
being sons of the r   Luke 20:36
r of judgment   John 5:29
the r and the life   John 11:25
r of the dead   Acts 24:21
if there is no r   1 Cor 15:13
power of His r   Phil 3:10
hope through the r   1 Pet 1:3
This is the first r   Rev 20:5

RETRIBUTION *punishment*

days of r have come   Hos 9:7
stumbling block...r   Rom 11:9
dealing out r to   2 Thess 1:8

RETURN *go back, turn back*

to dust you shall r   Gen 3:19
r-ed me evil for   1 Sam 25:21
clouds r after the   Eccl 12:2
a remnant...will r   Is 10:22
ransomed...will r   Is 51:11
r-ed to Galilee   Luke 4:14
Repent...and r   Acts 3:19
not r-ing evil for   1 Pet 3:9

REUBEN

1 *son of Jacob/Leah*   Gen 29:32
2 *tribe*   Ex 6:14; Num 1:21

REVEAL *expose, make known*

God has r-ed Himself   Gen 35:7
He r-s mysteries   Job 12:22
will r his iniquity   Job 20:27
do not r the secret   Prov 25:9
glory...will be r-ed   Is 40:5
r this mystery   Dan 2:47
r them to babes   Matt 11:25
blood did not r *this*   Matt 16:17
Son of Man is r-ed   Luke 17:30
glory...to be r-ed   Rom 8:18
r-ed with fire   1 Cor 3:13
to r His Son in me   Gal 1:16

lawlessness is **r-ed** 2 Thess 2:3
r-ed in the flesh 1 Tim 3:16

REVELATION *divine disclosure*

a **r** to Thy servant 2 Sam 7:27
the **r** ended Dan 7:28
r to the Gentiles Luke 2:32
r of...judgment Rom 2:5
the **r** of the mystery Rom 16:25
awaiting...the **r** 1 Cor 1:7
through a **r** of Jesus Gal 1:12
by **r**...made known Eph 3:3
The **R** of Jesus Rev 1:1

REVENGE *vengeance*

take our **r** on him Jer 20:10
Never take...**r** Rom 12:19

REVERE *adore, venerate*

r My sanctuary Lev 19:30
nations will **r** Thee Is 25:3

REVERENCE *respect, awe*

you do away with **r** Job 15:4
Worship...with **r** Ps 2:11
bow in **r** for Thee Ps 5:7
in **r** prepared an ark Heb 11:7
service with **r** and Heb 12:28

REVILE *use abusive language*

Do you **r** God's high Acts 23:4
are **r-d**, we bless 1 Cor 4:12
r-d for the name of 1 Pet 4:14
r angelic majesties Jude 8

REVIVE *bring back to life*

they **r** the stones Neh 4:2
let your heart **r** Ps 69:32
r us again Ps 85:6
r me in Thy ways Ps 119:37
r-d your concern Phil 4:10

REVOLT *rebellion*

incited **r** within it Ezra 4:15
Speaking...and **r** Is 59:13
stirred up a **r** Acts 21:38

REWARD *prize*

emptiness...his **r** Job 15:31
r for the righteous Ps 58:11
The **r** of humility Prov 22:4
chases after **r-s** Is 1:23

His **r** is with Him Is 62:11
your **r** in heaven Matt 5:12
not lose his **r** Matt 10:42
looking to the **r** Heb 11:26
receive a full **r** 2 John 8

RHODA

Christian servant girl Acts 12:13

RHODES

Mediterranean isle Acts 21:1

RIB *bone*

took one of his **r-s** Gen 2:21
r-s were in its mouth Dan 7:5

RICH (adj) *wealthy*

Abram was very **r** Gen 13:2
LORD makes poor...**r** 1 Sam 2:7
not a **r** man boast Jer 9:23
woe to you who are **r** Luke 6:24
a certain **r** man Luke 16:1
being **r** in mercy Eph 2:4
r in good works 1 Tim 6:18

RICH (n) *wealthy*

r shall not pay more Ex 30:15
the **r** above the poor Job 34:19
r among the people Ps 45:12
The **r** and the poor Prov 22:2

RICHES *wealth*

R do not profit Prov 11:4
who trusts in his **r** Prov 11:28
neither poverty nor **r** Prov 30:8
deceitfulness of **r** Matt 13:22
choked with...**r** Luke 8:14
abounding in **r** Rom 10:12
r of His grace Eph 1:7
r of Christ Eph 3:8
his **r** in glory Phil 4:19
uncertainty of **r** 1 Tim 6:17
Your **r** have rotted James 5:2

RIDDLE *puzzle*

propound a **r** Judg 14:12
my **r** on the harp Ps 49:4
wise and their **r-s** Prov 1:6
propound a **r** Ezek 17:2

RIGHT (adj) *correct* or *direction*

r in the sight of Deut 12:25

r in his own eyes   Judg 17:6
precepts...are r   Ps 19:8
r eye makes you   Matt 5:29
what your r hand is   Matt 6:3
Sit at My r hand   Matt 22:44
the r hand of God   Mark 16:19
at the r time Christ   Rom 5:6
r hand of fellowship   Gal 2:9
whatever is r   Phil 4:8
forsaking the r way   2 Pet 2:15

RIGHT (n) *due, prerogative*

her conjugal r-s   Ex 21:10
r of redemption   Lev 25:32
r of the first-born   Deut 21:17
the r-s of the poor   Prov 29:7
r-s of the afflicted   Prov 31:9
my r in the gospel   1 Cor 9:18

RIGHTEOUS (adj) *virtuous*

Noah was a r man   Gen 6:9
LORD is the r one   Ex 9:27
You are more r   1 Sam 24:17
God is a r judge   Ps 7:11
A r man hates   Prov 13:5
for David a r Branch   Jer 23:5
LORD our God is r   Dan 9:14
ninety-nine r   Luke 15:7
coming of the R One   Acts 7:52
r man shall live by   Rom 1:17
none r, not even one   Rom 3:10
many will be made r   Rom 5:19
prayer of a r man   James 5:16

RIGHTEOUS (n) *moral one*

assembly of the r   Ps 1:5
LORD tests the r   Ps 11:5
LORD loves the r   Ps 146:8
the paths of the r   Prov 2:20
the r will flourish   Prov 11:28
joy for the r   Prov 21:15
way of the r is   Is 26:7
they sell the r for   Amos 2:6
sends rain on *the* r   Matt 5:45
r into eternal life   Matt 25:46

RIGHTEOUSNESS

reckoned it...as r   Gen 15:6
will repay...his r   1 Sam 26:23
I put on r   Job 29:14
in the paths of r   Ps 23:3
judge the world in r   Ps 96:13

declare His r   Ps 97:6
His r endures forever   Ps 111:3
R exalts a nation   Prov 14:34
clouds pour down r   Is 45:8
wrapped me with...r   Is 61:10
The LORD our r   Jer 23:6
to rain r on you   Hos 10:12
to fulfill all r   Matt 3:15
and thirst for r   Matt 5:6
kingdom and His r   Matt 6:33
you enemy of all r   Acts 13:10
through one act of r   Rom 5:18
breastplate of r   Eph 6:14
pursue r, faith   2 Tim 2:22
the crown of r   2 Tim 4:8
peaceful fruit of r   Heb 12:11
not achieve the r   James 1:20
suffer for...r   1 Pet 3:14

RIMMON

1 *a Benjamite*   2 Sam 4:2
2 *Syrian deity*   2 Kin 5:18
3 *town in Simeon*   Josh 19:1,7
4 *city of Zebulum*   Josh 19:13
5 *rock of*   Judg 20:45;21:13

RING *jewelry, ornament*

make four gold r-s   Ex 25:26
took his signet r   Esth 3:10
As a r of gold   Prov 11:22
finger r-s, nose r-s   Is 3:21

RIOT *tumult, uprising*

lest a r occur   Matt 26:5
a r was starting   Matt 27:24
accused of a r   Acts 19:40

RIPE *fully developed*

old man of r age   Gen 35:29
produced r grapes   Gen 40:10
the harvest is r   Joel 3:13
harvest...is r   Rev 14:15

RISE *go up, issue forth*

mist used to r from   Gen 2:6
Cain **rose** up against Gen 4:8
scepter shall r   Num 24:17
witnesses r up   Ps 35:11
children r up   Prov 31:28
nation will r   Matt 24:7

r-n, just as He said   Matt 28:6
children will r up   Mark 13:12
R and walk   Luke 5:23
R and pray   Luke 22:46
Lord has really **r-n**   Luke 24:34

RIVER

r flowed out of Eden   Gen 2:10
the r Euphrates   Josh 1:4
r of Thy delights   Ps 36:8
He changes r-s into   Ps 107:33
the r-s of Babylon   Ps 137:1
A place of r-s and   Is 33:21
r-s in the desert   Is 43:20
peace...like a r   Is 66:12
tears...like a r   Lam 2:18
baptized...Jordan **R**   Mark 1:5
r-s of living water   John 7:38
r of the water of life   Rev 22:1

RIZPAH

concubine of Saul   2 Sam 3:7

ROAD path, way

a lion in the r   Prov 26:13
the rough r-s smooth   Luke 3:5
garments in the r   Luke 19:36
the Lord on the r   Acts 9:27

ROAR (n) loud deep sound

the sound of the r   1 Kin 18:41
young lions' r   Zech 11:3
pass away with a r   2 Pet 3:10

ROAR (v) utter a deep sound

a voice r-s   Job 37:4
Let the sea r   Ps 96:11
LORD will r from   Jer 25:30
a lion r in the   Amos 3:4

ROAST cook

grain r-ed in the fire   Lev 2:14
r-ed the...animals   2 Chr 35:13
slothful man...r   Prov 12:27

ROB steal

bear r-bed of her   Prov 17:12
Do not r the poor   Prov 22:22
Will a man r God   Mal 3:8
do you r temples   Rom 2:22
I r-bed...churches   2 Cor 11:8

ROBBER thief

she lurks as a r   Prov 23:28
become a den of r-s   Jer 7:11
crucified two r-s   Mark 15:27
he fell among r-s   Luke 10:30
a thief and a r   John 10:1
r-s of temples   Acts 19:37

ROBBERY theft

not vainly hope in r   Ps 62:10
I hate r in the   Is 61:8
they are full of r   Matt 23:25
you are full of r   Luke 11:39

ROBE cloak, garment

cut off...Saul's r   1 Sam 24:4
justice was like a r   Job 29:14
r of righteousness   Is 61:10
put a scarlet r on   Matt 27:28
walk...in long r-s   Mark 12:38
wearing a white r   Mark 16:5
bring...the best r   Luke 15:22
washed their r-s   Rev 7:14
a r dipped in blood   Rev 19:13

ROCK stone

the cleft of the r   Ex 33:22
struck the r twice   Num 20:11
R of his salvation   Deut 32:15
LORD is my r   2 Sam 22:2
engraved in the r   Job 19:24
my r and my fortress   Ps 18:2
r and my Redeemer   Ps 19:14
set my feet upon a r   Ps 40:2
a r to stumble over   Is 8:14
an everlasting **R**   Is 26:4
his house upon the r   Matt 7:24
upon this r I will   Matt 16:18
the r-s were split   Matt 27:51
hewn out in the r   Mark 15:46
a r of offense   Rom 9:33

ROD staff, stick

fresh r-s of poplar   Gen 30:37
r of Aaron   Num 17:8
break them with a r   Ps 2:9
Thy r and Thy staff   Ps 23:4
who spares his r   Prov 13:24
The r of discipline   Prov 22:15
r of My anger   Is 10:5
rule them with a r   Rev 19:15

ROLL *move*

sky will be **r-ed** up   Is 34:4
let justice **r** down   Amos 5:24
r-ed away the stone   Matt 28:2
Who will **r** away the   Mark 16:3

ROMANS

citizens of Roman Empire
    John 11:48; Acts 16:21,37
N.T. book   Romans

ROME

Italian city   Acts 2:10
Roman Empire capital Acts 18:2
Paul held there   Acts 28:14,16

ROOF

brought...to the **r**   Josh 2:6
r...woman bathing   2 Sam 11:2
removed the **r** above   Mark 2:4
r and let him down   Luke 5:19

ROOM *chamber*

the ark with **r-s**   Gen 6:14
go into your inner **r**   Matt 6:6
a large upper **r**   Mark 14:15
no **r** for them in   Luke 2:7
r for the wrath   Rom 12:19

ROOT (n) *source*

the **r** of Jesse   Is 11:10
no **r**, it withered   Mark 4:6
if the **r** be holy   Rom 11:16
of money is a **r**   1 Tim 6:10
no **r** of bitterness   Heb 12:15
the **R** of David   Rev 5:5

ROOT (v) *establish* or *tear out*

r out your Asherim   Mic 5:14
r-ed and grounded in   Eph 3:17

ROPE *cord*

them down by a **r**   Josh 2:15
bound...two new **r-s** Judg 15:13
he snapped the **r-s**   Judg 16:12
Instead of a belt, a **r**   Is 3:24

ROSE (n) *flower*

I am the **r** of Sharon   Song 2:1

ROSH

1 *son of Benjamin*   Gen 46:21
2 *place of Gog* Ezek 38:2,3;39:1

ROT *decay*

their flesh will **r**   Zech 14:12
riches have **r-ted**   James 5:2

ROTTENNESS *decay*

passion is **r** to   Prov 14:30
r to the house of   Hos 5:12

ROUGH *jagged, uneven*

r ground become a   Is 40:4
the **r** places smooth   Is 45:2

ROYAL *kingly*

captured the **r** city 2 Sam 12:26
his **r** bounty   1 Kin 10:13
all the **r** offspring   2 Kin 11:1
put on her **r** robes   Esth 5:1
And a **r** diadem   Is 62:3
roof of the **r** palace   Dan 4:29
a certain **r** official   John 4:46
fulfilling the **r** law   James 2:8
a **r** priesthood   1 Pet 2:9

RUDDY *reddish in complexion*

he was **r**   1 Sam 16:12
a youth, and **r**   1 Sam 17:42
beloved is...and **r**   Song 5:10

RUHAMAH

symbolic for Israel   Hos 2:1

RUIN (n) *destruction*

shall be a **r** forever Deut 13:16
become a heap of **r-s** 1 Kin 9:8
the perpetual **r-s**   Ps 74:3
Jerusalem in **r-s**   Ps 79:1
r of the poor is   Prov 10:15
fools mouth is his **r**   Prov 18:7
rebuild its **r-s**   Acts 15:16

RUIN (v) *destroy*

to **r** him without   Job 2:3
the grain is **r-ed**   Joel 1:10
skins will be **r-ed**   Luke 5:37

RULE (n) *authority, government*

to establish his **r**   1 Chr 18:3
against the **r** of   2 Chr 21:8
will walk by this **r**   Gal 6:16
above all **r** and   Eph 1:21
according to the **r-s**   2 Tim 2:5

RULE (v) *govern*

r over the fish	Gen 1:26
Gideon, R over us	Judg 8:22
godless men...not r	Job 34:30
r-s over the nations	Ps 22:28
The sun to r by day	Ps 136:8
By me princes r	Prov 8:16
women r over them	Is 3:12
r over the Gentiles	Rom 15:12
peace of Christ r	Col 3:15
r them with a rod	Rev 2:27

RULER *king, monarch*

Joseph was the r	Gen 42:6
nor curse a r	Ex 22:28
no chief...or r	Prov 6:7
your r-s have fled	Is 22:3
Most High God is r	Dan 4:32
come forth a R	Matt 2:6
r of the demons	Matt 9:34
r-s of the Gentiles	Mark 10:42
the r of this world	John 12:31
Who made you a r	Acts 7:27
be subject to r-s	Titus 3:1

RUMOR *gossip, hearsay*

r will be *added* to r	Ezek 7:26
wars and r-s of wars	Matt 24:6

RUN *move rapidly*

to r his course	Ps 19:5
their feet r to evil	Prov 1:16
streams r-ning with	Is 30:25
r and not get tired	Is 40:31
rivers to r like oil	Ezek 32:14
Peter arose and ran	Luke 24:12
disciple ran ahead	John 20:4
who r in a race	1 Cor 9:24

RUSH *move quickly*

and r upon the city	Judg 9:33
r-s headlong at Him	Job 15:26
herd r-ed down the	Matt 8:32
horses r-ing to battle	Rev 9:9

RUSHES *marshy plant*

Can the r grow	Job 8:11
reeds and r will rot	Is 19:6

RUST *corrosion*

in which there is r	Ezek 24:6
moth and r destroy	Matt 6:19
r will be a witness	James 5:3

RUTH

Moabitess	Ruth 1:4
Naomi's daughter-in-law	
	Ruth 1:14,ff
married Boaz	Ruth 4:13
in Messianic line	Matt 1:5

RUTHLESS *cruel*

Reprove the r	Is 1:17
song of the r is	Is 25:5
most r of the	Ezek 28:7

S

SABAOTH

*Lord of Sabaoth is same as
Lord of Hosts*
Rom 9:29; James 5:4
see also HOST

SABBATH *day of rest*

Remember the s day	Ex 20:8
LORD blessed the s day	Ex 20:11
keep My s-s and	Lev 26:2
Observe the s day	Deut 5:12
new moon nor s	2 Kin 4:23
call the s a delight	Is 58:13
My s-s to be a sign	Ezek 20:12
is Lord of the S	Matt 12:8
S was made for man	Mark 2:27
on the S to do good	Mark 3:4
the cross on the S	John 19:31
a S day's journey	Acts 1:12
are read every S	Acts 13:27
S rest for the people	Heb 4:9

SABBATICAL YEAR

seventh year of rest	Lev 25:5

SABEANS

people of Sheba in SW Arabia
Job 1:15; Is 45:14; Joel 3:8

SACKCLOTH *coarse cloth*

put s on his loins	Gen 37:34
gird on s and lament	2 Sam 3:31
put on s and ashes	Esth 4:1
sewed s over my skin	Job 16:15
with fasting, s, and	Dan 9:3
sun became black as s	Rev 6:12

SACRED *consecrated, holy*

took all the s things   2 Kin 12:18
perform s services   1 Cor 9:13
known the s writings2 Tim 3:15
table and the s bread   Heb 9:2

SACRIFICE (n) *offering of a life*

Jacob offered a s   Gen 31:54
a Passover s to   Ex 12:27
s-s of righteousness   Ps 4:5
The s of the wicked   Prov 15:8
loyalty rather than s   Hos 6:6
compassion...not s   Matt 9:13
a s to the idol   Acts 7:41
a living and holy s   Rom 12:1
an acceptable s   Phil 4:18
by the s of Himself   Heb 9:26
s-s God is pleased   Heb 13:16
offer up spiritual s-s   1 Pet 2:5

SACRIFICE (v) *offer a life*

we may s to the LORD   Ex 5:3
s on it your burnt   Ex 20:24
when you s a sacrifice Lev 22:29
they s-d to the LORD   Judg 2:5
even s-d their sons   Ps 106:37
s-ing to the Baals   Hos 11:2
lamb had to be s-d   Luke 22:7
they s to demons   1 Cor 10:20

SAD *sorrowful, unhappy*

people heard s word   Ex 33:4
Why is your face s   Neh 2:2
heart is s, the   Prov 15:13

SADDUCEES

Jewish religious party Matt 3:7
Matt 16:11,12; Mark 12:18
Acts 5:17;23:6-8

SAFE *free from danger*

houses are s from fear Job 21:9
runs into it and is s Prov 18:10
back s and sound   Luke 15:27

SAIL (n) *canvas for wind*

Nor spread out the s   Is 33:23
s was...embroidered Ezek 27:7

SAIL (v) *proceed by boat*

they s-ed to Cyprus   Acts 13:4
to s past Ephesus   Acts 20:16
set s from Crete   Acts 27:21

SAILOR *mariner, seaman*

s-s who knew the sea 1 Kin 9:27
s-s and your pilots   Ezek 27:27
every passenger and s Rev 18:17

SAINTS *ones faithful to God*

s...in the earth   Ps 16:3
the s of the Highest   Dan 7:22
s...fallen asleep   Matt 27:52
lock up...s in prisons Acts 26:10
intercedes for the s   Rom 8:27
s will judge the   1 Cor 6:2
citizens with the s   Eph 2:19
perseverance of the s Rev 14:12

SALAMIS

city on Cyprus   Acts 13:5

SALEM

short for Jerusalem
Gen 14:18; Ps 76:2; Heb 7:1,2

SALOME

1 *wife of Zebedee*   Mark 15:40
mother of James and John
at open tomb   Mark 16:1
2 *unnamed daughter of*
Herodias
Matt 14:6ff; Mark 6:22-26

SALT *preservative*

became a pillar of s   Gen 19:26
and sowed it with s   Judg 9:45
be eaten without s   Job 6:6
the s of the earth   Matt 5:13
seasoned, ...with s   Col 4:6
can s water produce James 3:12

SALT SEA

the Dead Sea   Gen 14:3
Num 34:3;Deut 3:17;Josh 15:2

SALT, VALLEY OF

S of Dead Sea   2 Sam 8:13
2 Chr 25:11

SALVATION *deliverance*

For Thy s I wait   Gen 49:18
He has become my s   Ex 15:2
scorned...his s   Deut 32:15
S belongs to the LORD   Ps 3:8
my light and my s   Ps 27:1
lift up the cup of s   Ps 116:13

My s shall be forever Is 51:6
helmet of s on His Is 59:17
S is from the LORD Jon 2:9
eyes have seen Thy s Luke 2:30
s in no one else Acts 4:12
power of God for s Rom 1:16
now is the day of s 2 Cor 6:2
take the helmet of s Eph 6:17
work out your s with Phil 2:12
s through our Lord 1 Thess 5:9
that leads to s 2 Tim 3:15
who will inherit s Heb 1:14
neglect so great a s Heb 2:3
S to our God who Rev 7:10

SAMARIA

1 *capital of N kingdom*
1 Kin 16:24; 2 Chr 18:9
2 *another name for N kingdom*
1 Kin 13:32; 2 Kin 17:24
Hos 8:5; Amos 3:9; Obad 19
3 *region of central Palestine*
John 4:4-7; Acts 8:1ff

SAMOTHRACE

N Aegean island Acts 16:11

SAMSON

a Hebrew judge Judg 13:24
weak in character Judg 14:1ff
slave of passion Judg 16:1ff
great strength Judg 16:5,12

SAMUEL

son of Elkanah and Hannah
1 Sam 1:20
dedicated to God 1 Sam 1:21ff
called by God 1 Sam 3:1-18
judge 1 Sam 7:15-17
opposed monarchy 1 Sam 8:6
anointed Saul 1 Sam 10:1
anointed David 1 Sam 16:12
death 1 Sam 25:1

SANBALLAT

man of Beth-horon Neh 2:10
against Nehemiah Neh 6:1ff

SANCTIFICATION *holiness*

resulting in Rom 6:22
righteousness and s 1 Cor 1:30
will of God, your s 1 Thess 4:3
s by the Spirit 2 Thess 2:13

s without which no Heb 12:14

SANCTIFY *set apart to God*

S to Me every Ex 13:2
the LORD who s-ies Lev 22:32
They will s My name Is 29:23
will s the Holy One Is 29:23
And s My sabbaths Ezek 20:20
S them in the truth John 17:17
s-ied by the...Spirit Rom 15:16
husband is s-ied 1 Cor 7:14
s Christ as Lord 1 Pet 3:15

SANCTUARY *place of worship*

construct a s for Me Ex 25:8
revere My s Lev 19:30
utensils of the s 1 Chr 9:29
into the s of God Ps 73:17
Praise God in His s Ps 150:1
beautify...My s Is 60:13
a minister in the s Heb 8:2

SAND

descendants as the s Gen 32:12
treasures of the s Deut 33:19
built...upon the s Matt 7:26
innumerable as the s Heb 11:12

SANDAL *footwear*

s has not worn out Deut 29:5
fit to remove His s-s Matt 3:11
two tunics, or s-s Matt 10:10

SANHEDRIN *see* COUNCIL

SAPPHIRA

wife of Ananias Acts 5:1-10
struck dead for lying

SAPPHIRE *precious stone*

a s, and a diamond Ex 28:18
Inlaid with s-s Song 5:14
foundations...in s-s Is 54:11

SARAH/SARAI

wife of Abraham Gen 11:29
barren Gen 11:30
beautiful Gen 12:11
gave birth to Isaac Gen 21:2,3
death Gen 23:2

SARDIS

city in Asia Minor Rev 1:11
Rev 3:1,4

SARGON

son of Tiglathpileser III Is 20:1
king of Assyria

SATAN

Titles:

Abaddon	Rev 9:11
accuser	Ps 109:6; Rev 12:10
adversary	1 Pet 5:8
Apollyon	Rev 9:11
Beelzebul	Matt 10:25
	Mark 3:22
Belial	2 Cor 6:15
devil	Matt 4:1,5;25:41
John 6:70;13:2; Eph 4:27;6:11	
1 Tim 3:6,7; Heb 2:14; 1 Pet 5:8	
	Rev 2:10;20:2,10
dragon	Rev 12:9
enemy	Matt 13:28,39
evil one	Matt 13:19,38
	John 17:15; Eph 6:16
	1 John 2:13,14;5:18,19
father of lies	John 8:44
god of this world	2 Cor 4:4
liar	John 8:44
murderer	John 8:44
prince of the power of the air	
	Eph 2:2
ruler of the demons	Matt 9:34
	Mark 3:22
ruler of this world	John 12:31
	John 14:30;16:11
serpent of old	Rev 12:9
deceiver of the world	Rev 12:9

SATISFY *be content*

eat and not be **s-ied**	Lev 26:26
s-ied their desire	Ps 78:30
steals To s himself	Prov 6:30
hunger is not **s-ied**	Is 29:8
to s the multitude	Mark 15:15

SATRAPS *Persian officials*

to the king's s	Ezra 8:36
the s, the governors	Esth 8:9
commissioners and s	Dan 6:4

SAUL

1 *son of Kish*	1 Sam 9:1,2
anointed	1 Sam 10:1ff
first king	1 Sam 11:15
rejected as king	1 Sam 15:11ff
jealous of David	1 Sam 18:6ff
death	1 Sam 31:4ff

2 *apostle Paul, see* **PAUL**

SAVE *deliver, rescue*

s-d by the LORD	Deut 33:29
S with Thy right hand	Ps 60:5
He will s you	Prov 20:22
Turn to Me, and be **s-d**	Is 45:22
s you from afar	Jer 30:10
he will s his life	Ezek 18:27
will s His people	Matt 1:21
wishes to s his life	Matt 16:25
Son...has come to s	Matt 18:11
faith has **s-d** you	Luke 7:50
world should be **s-d**	John 3:17
Father, s Me from	John 12:27
by which we...be **s-d**	Acts 4:12
be **s-d** by His life	Rom 5:10
will s your husband	1 Cor 7:16
Jesus came...to s	1 Tim 1:15
One who is able to s	James 4:12
the righteous is **s-d**	1 Pet 4:18

SAVIOR *one who saves*

My s, Thou dost	2 Sam 22:3
forgot God their S	Ps 106:21
send them a S and a	Is 19:20
no s besides Me	Is 43:11
righteous God and a S	Is 45:21
S, who is Christ	Luke 2:11
the S of the world	John 4:42
as a Prince and a S	Acts 5:31
S of all men	1 Tim 4:10
appearing of our S	2 Tim 1:10
our great God and S	Titus 2:13
kingdom of our...S	2 Pet 1:11

SAVORY *appetizing*

prepare a s dish for	Gen 27:4
mother made s food	Gen 27:14

SAWS *cutting tool*

set *them* under s	2 Sam 12:31
cut *them* with s	1 Chr 20:3

SAY *pronounce, speak*

God blessed...**s-ing**	Gen 1:22
not s in your heart	Deut 9:4
to the wicked God **s-s**	Ps 50:16
Do not s to your	Prov 3:28
s-s the Preacher	Eccl 1:2
He will s, Here I am	Is 58:9
Many will s to Me	Matt 7:22

If we s...no sin   1 John 1:8

SAYINGS *statements*

utter dark s of old   Ps 78:2
s of understanding   Prov 1:2
s of the wise   Prov 24:23
anyone hears my s   John 12:47

SCALE *for measuring weight*

with accurate s-s   Job 31:6
false s is not good   Prov 20:23
been weighed on the s   Dan 5:7
with dishonest s-s   Amos 8:5
justify wicked s-s   Mic 6:11
a pair of s-s in his   Rev 6:5

SCAPEGOAT *for removal of sin*

lot for the s fell   Lev 16:10
released the goat...s   Lev 16:26

SCARLET *bright red*

tied a s *thread*   Gen 38:28
s thread in the window Josh 2:18
lips are like a s   Song 4:3
sins are as s   Is 1:18
put a s robe on Him Matt 27:28

SCATTER *spread, sprinkle*

s among the nations Lev 26:33
Brimstone is s-ed on   Job 18:15
storm will s them   Is 41:16
s-ing the sheep of   Jer 23:1
s him like dust   Matt 21:44
sheep...shall be s-ed Matt 26:31

SCEPTER *symbol of authority*

s shall not depart   Gen 49:10
s...rise from Israel   Num 24:17
A s of uprightness   Ps 45:6
The s of rulers   Is 14:5
s of His kingdom   Heb 1:8

SCHEME *plan, plot*

s...he had devised   Esth 9:25
s brings him down   Job 18:7
carries out wicked s-s Ps 37:7
ignorant of his s-s   2 Cor 2:11
the s-s of the devil   Eph 6:11

SCOFF *mock, sneer*

s-ed at His prophets 2 Chr 36:16
The Lord s-s at them   Ps 2:4
s at all the nations   Ps 59:8

were s-ing at Him   Luke 16:14

SCOFFER *mocker*

My friends are my s-s Job 16:20
sit in the seat of s-s   Ps 1:1
He who corrects a s   Prov 9:7
Behold, you s-s   Acts 13:41

SCORCHING *burning*

words are as a s fire Prov 16:27
s heat or sun strike   Is 49:10
appointed a s east wind Jon 4:8
s heat of the day   Matt 20:12

SCORN *treat with contempt*

s-ed...his salvation Deut 32:15
that...s-s a mother Prov 30:17

SCORPION *poisonous spider*

serpents and s-s   Deut 8:15
discipline...with s-s 1 Kin 12:11
tread upon...s   Luke 10:19
not give him a s   Luke 11:12
s-s...have power   Rev 9:3

SCOURGE (n) *whip*

the s of the tongue   Job 5:21
arouse a s against   Is 10:26
He made a s of cords John 2:15

SCOURGE (v) *flog, whip*

s and crucify *Him*   Matt 20:19
having Jesus s-d   Matt 27:26
lawful for you to s   Acts 22:25
He s-s every son   Heb 12:6

SCRAPE *rub, scratch*

plaster that they s   Lev 14:41
s-d the honey into   Judg 14:9
potsherd to s himself   Job 2:8

SCREEN *conceal, separate*

s the ark with the veil Ex 40:3
s-ed off the ark   Ex 40:21

SCRIBE *copier, writer*

and Sheva was s   2 Sam 20:25
then the king's s   2 Chr 24:11
Ezra the s stood   Neh 8:4
lying pen of the s-s   Jer 8:8
chief priests and s-s Matt 2:4
and not as the s-s   Mark 1:22
Where is the s   1 Cor 1:20

SCRIPTURE

understanding...S-s | Matt 22:29
S-s...be fulfilled | Mark 14:49
S has been fulfilled | Luke 4:21
You search the S-s | John 5:39
S cannot be broken | John 10:35
mighty in the S-s | Acts 18:24
what does the S say | Rom 4:3
S is inspired by God | 2 Tim 3:16

SCROLL *parchment*

these curses on a s | Num 5:23
Take a s and write | Jer 36:2
eat this s, and go | Ezek 3:1
like a s...rolled | Rev 6:14

SEA *body of salt water*

waters He called s-s | Gen 1:10
s or the s monster | Job 7:12
founded it upon the s-s | Ps 24:2
to the s in ships | Ps 107:23
the waters cover the s | Is 11:9
rebukes the s and | Nah 1:4
walking on the s | Matt 14:26
s *began* to be stirred | John 6:18
dangers on the s | 2 Cor 11:26
s of glass like crystal | Rev 4:6

SEA OF GALILEE *see*
GALILEE, SEA OF

SEACOAST *seashore*

remnant of the s | Ezek 25:16
inhabitants of the s | Zeph 2:5
s will be pastures | Zeph 2:6

SEAL (n) *mark, stamp*

Your s and your cord | Gen 38:18
the engravings of a s | Ex 28:21
the s of perfection | Ezek 28:12
witness has set his s | John 3:33
s of God on their | Rev 9:4

SEAL (v) *mark, secure*

s-ed...his seal | 1 Kin 21:8
s it...king's signet | Esth 8:8
a spring s-ed up | Song 4:12
to s up vision | Dan 9:24
s up the book until | Dan 12:4

SEARCH *examine, inquire*

LORD s-es all hearts | 1 Chr 28:9
S me, O God, and | Ps 139:23

LORD, s the heart | Jer 17:10
s for the Child | Matt 2:13
You s the Scriptures | John 5:39

SEASHORE *sea coast*

sand that is on the s | Josh 11:4
the s in abundance | 1 Kin 4:20
he stood on...s | Rev 13:1

SEASON *time of year*

rains in their s | Lev 26:4
grain in its s | Job 5:26
its fruit in its s | Ps 1:3
in s *and* out of s | 2 Tim 4:2

SEAT (n) *chair, stool*

mercy s of pure gold | Ex 25:17
sit in the s of scoffers | Ps 1:1
sit in the s of gods | Ezek 28:2
s-s in the synagogues | Matt 23:6
before...judgment s | Rom 14:10

SEAT (v) *sit*

s-ed at His feet | Luke 10:39
coming, s-ed...colt | John 12:15
s-ed at the right hand | Col 3:1

SECRET *what is hidden*

sets *it* up in s | Deut 27:15
the s-s of wisdom | Job 11:6
the s-s of the heart | Ps 44:21
bread *eaten* in s | Prov 9:17
A gift in s subdues | Prov 21:14
have not spoken in s | Is 45:19
alms may be in s | Matt 6:4
Father who sees in s | Matt 6:4
God will judge the s-s | Rom 2:16

SECT *faction, party*

s of the Sadducees | Acts 5:17
s of the Pharisees | Acts 15:5
s of the Nazarenes | Acts 24:5

SECURE *safe, stable*

overthrows the s | Job 12:19
be s on their land | Ezek 34:27
s in the mountain | Amos 6:1
made the grave s | Matt 27:66

SECURITY *certainty, safety*

Israel dwells in s | Deut 33:28
in it living in s | Judg 18:7
provides them with s | Job 24:23
will lie down in s | Is 14:30

will dwell in s   Zech 14:11

SEDUCE *entice, persuade*

if a man s-s a virgin   Ex 22:16
s you from the LORD Deut 13:10
s them to do evil   2 Kin 21:9
lips she s-s him   Prov 7:21

SEE *look, perceive*

I have s-n God face   Gen 32:30
No eye will s me   Job 24:15
s the works of God   Ps 66:5
the blind shall s   Is 29:18
s the glory of the LORD Is 35:2
to s but do not s   Ezek 12:2
s your good works   Matt 5:16
and the blind s-ing   Matt 15:31
s the Son of Man   Matt 16:28
s-ing their faith   Mark 2:5
s-n Thy salvation   Luke 2:30
No man has s-n God John 1:18
you will s Me   John 16:16
s in a mirror dimly 1 Cor 13:12
of things not s-n   Heb 11:1

SEED *descendant or plant*

sow your s uselessly Lev 26:16
establish your s   Ps 89:4
O s of Abraham   Ps 105:6
s to the sower   Is 55:10
like a mustard s   Matt 13:31
went out to sow his s Luke 8:5
s is the word of God Luke 8:11
s which is perishable 1 Pet 1:23
His s abides in him 1 John 3:9

SEEK *pursue, search for*

s the LORD your God Deut 4:29
pray, and s My face 2 Chr 7:14
S peace and pursue it Ps 34:14
s me will find me   Prov 8:17
man s-s only evil   Prov 17:11
s wisdom and an   Eccl 7:25
I will s the lost   Ezek 34:16
time to s the LORD   Hos 10:12
S good and not evil Amos 5:14
s first His kingdom Matt 6:33
s, and you shall find Matt 7:7
s for a sign   Mark 8:12
he who s-s, finds   Luke 11:10
I do not s My glory John 8:50
s-ing the favor of men Gal 1:10

s-ing the things above Col 3:1

SEER *prophet*

prophets...every s 2 Kin 17:13
Who say to the s-s   Is 30:10
Go, you s, flee away Amos 7:12
s-s will be ashamed   Mic 3:7

SEIR

1 *land of Edom* Gen 32:3;36:8,9
           Num 24:18; Ezek 25:8
2 *mountain range within Edom*
       Gen 14:6; Deut 1:2;2:4
3 *on boundary of Judah*
              Josh 11:17;15:10

SEIZE *grasp, take*

mother shall s him Deut 21:19
Babylon has been s-d Jer 50:46
and s her plunder   Ezek 29:19
fields and then s *them* Mic 2:2
seeking...to s Him   John 7:30

SELA

rock city in Edom   Judg 1:36
                 Is 16:1;42:11
also **Joktheel**   2 Kin 14:7
later known as Petra

SELAH

musical or liturgical sign
        Ps 3:2,4,8;20:3;60:4
    Ps 81:7; Hab 3:3,9,13

SELEUCIA

port in N Syria   Acts 13:4

SELF-CONTROL

s and the judgment Acts 24:25
your lack of s   1 Cor 7:5
gentleness, s   Gal 5:23
without s, brutal   2 Tim 3:3
in *your* knowledge, s 2 Pet 1:6

SELFISH *self-centered*

the bread of a s man Prov 23:6
s ambition in your James 3:14

SELL *barter, trade*

s me your birthright Gen 25:31
s me food for money Deut 2:28
s the oil and pay   2 Kin 4:7
sold a girl for wine Joel 3:3

sold all that he had Matt 13:46
s-ing their property Acts 2:45
sold into bondage Rom 7:14

SELLER *merchant, trader*

the buyer like the s Is 24:2
a s of purple Acts 16:14

SENATE

Sanhedrin Acts 5:21
see also **COUNCIL**

SEND *convey, dispatch*

s rain on the earth Gen 7:4
he **sent** out a raven Gen 8:7
Whom shall I s Is 6:8
Lord God has **sent** Me Is 48:16
s-s rain on *the* Matt 5:45
He has **sent** Me Luke 4:18
s-ing His own Son Rom 8:3
not s her husband 1 Cor 7:13
s him...in peace 1 Cor 16:11
God **sent** forth His Son Gal 4:4

SENNACHERIB

king of Assyria 2 Kin 18:13
2 Kin 19:16,20; 2 Chr 32:1-22
Is 36:1;37:17,21

SENSUALITY

deceit, s, envy Mark 7:22
promiscuity and s Rom 13:13
themselves over to s Eph 4:19
the wealth of her s Rev 18:3

SENTENCE *judgment*

s is by the decree Dan 4:17
escape the s of hell Matt 23:33
Pilate pronounced s Luke 23:24
to the s of death Luke 24:20

SEPARATE *divide, set apart*

God s-d the light Gen 1:4
They s with the lip Ps 22:7
s-s intimate friends Prov 16:28
let no man s Matt 19:6
Who shall s us from Rom 8:35

SEPARATION *division, isolation*

of his s to the LORD Num 6:6
his s he is holy Num 6:8
his s was defiled Num 6:12
have made a s Is 59:2

SEPHARAD

*place in Assyria for
Jerusalem exiles* Obad 20

SEPHARVAIM

*place in Aram; people relocated
to Samaria* 2 Kin 17:31
2 Kin 18:34; Is 36:19;37:13

SERAPHIM

celestial beings Is 6:2,6

SERGIUS PAULUS *see*
PAULUS, SERGIUS

SERPENT *snake*

s was more crafty Gen 3:1
they turned into s-s Ex 7:12
viper and flying s Is 30:6
be shrewd as s-s Matt 10:16
will pick up s-s Mark 16:18
Moses lifted up the s John 3:14

SERVANT *helper, slave*

s of s-s He shall be Gen 9:25
Thy s is listening 1 Sam 3:9
to shine upon Thy s Ps 31:16
s-s of a new covenant 2 Cor 3:6
they s-s of Christ 2 Cor 11:23
s of Christ Jesus 1 Tim 4:6

SERVE *help, work for*

shall s the LORD Ex 23:25
s Him with...heart Josh 22:5
s-d as priests 1 Chr 24:2
you shall s strangers Jer 5:19
God whom we s is Dan 3:17
s God and mammon Matt 6:24
If anyone s-s Me John 12:26
s-ing the Lord Rom 12:11
through love s one Gal 5:13

SERVICE *ministry, work*

s of righteousness Is 32:17
spiritual s of worship Rom 12:1
for the work of s Eph 4:12
s with reverence Heb 12:28

SETH

son of Adam Gen 4:25,26
Gen 5:3-8; 1 Chr 1:30

211

SETTLED *arranged or inhabited*

Lot s in the cities Gen 13:12
cloud s over the Num 9:18
assault shall be s Deut 21:5
word is s in heaven Ps 119:89
mountains were s Prov 8:25
s in the lawful Acts 19:39

SEVEN *number*

Jacob served s years Gen 29:20
For s women...one man Is 4:1
will be s weeks Dan 9:25
s other spirits more Matt 12:45
forgive...s times Matt 18:21
John to the s churches Rev 1:4
s golden lampstands Rev 1:12

SEVERE *difficult, hard*

famine was s Gen 12:10
a very s pestilence Ex 9:3
s and lasting plagues Deut 28:59
s judgments against Ezek 14:21
a s earthquake had Matt 28:2

SEW *fasten, join*

s-ed fig leaves together Gen 3:7
s-ed sackcloth over Job 16:15
a time to s together Eccl 3:7
women who s *magic* Ezek 13:18

SEXUAL

not in s promiscuity Rom 13:13
from s immorality 1 Thess 4:3

SHACKLES *fetters*

will tear off your s Nah 1:13
s broken in pieces Mark 5:4
with chains and s Luke 8:29

SHADE *protection*

cover him with s Job 40:22
The LORD is your s Ps 121:5
lived under its s Ezek 31:6
over Jonah to be a s Jon 4:6
nest under its s Mark 4:32

SHADOW *image of shade*

days...like a s 1 Chr 29:15
the s of Thy wings Ps 17:8
in the s...Almighty Ps 91:1
the s-s flee away Song 2:17
his s might fall on Acts 5:15

s of the heavenly Heb 8:5

SHADRACH

friend of Daniel Dan 2:49
Dan 3:12-30
Hebrew: Hananiah Dan 1:7

SHAKE *quiver, tremble*

made all my bones s Job 4:14
s my head at you Job 16:4
peace will not be s-n Is 54:10
s off the dust Matt 10:14
A reed s-n by the Matt 11:7
heavens will be s-n Luke 21:26
he **shook** the creature Acts 28:5
voice **shook** the earth Heb 12:26

SHALLUM

1 *king of Israel* 2 Kin 15:8-15
2 *Huldah's husband* 2 Kin 22:14
3 *son of Josiah* 1 Chr 3:15
   king of Judah 2 Kin 23:31-33
   also **Jehoahaz** 2 Kin 23:30
4 *gatekeeper* 1 Chr 9:17
5 *son of Zadok* 1 Chr 6:12
6 *time of Nehemiah* Neh 3:12
name of nine other men

SHALMANESER

king of Assyria 2 Kin 17:3
2 Kin 18:9

SHAME *disgrace, dishonor*

wicked be put to s Ps 31:17
my reproach and my s Ps 69:19
s to his mother Prov 29:15
wise men are put to s Jer 8:9
unjust knows no s Zeph 3:5
worthy to suffer s Acts 5:41
glory is in their s Phil 3:19
put Him to open s Heb 6:6

SHAMGAR

judge of Israel Judg 3:31;5:6

SHARE (n) *portion*

them take their s Gen 14:24
s from My offerings Lev 6:17
give me the s Luke 15:12
I do my s Col 1:24

SHARE (v) *partake, participate*

stranger does not s Prov 14:10

s in the inheritance   Prov 17:2
s it...yourselves   Luke 22:17
s all good things   Gal 6:6
may s His holiness   Heb 12:10
s the sufferings of   1 Pet 4:13

SHARON

*coastal plain in central
Palestine*   Is 33:9;65:10

SHARP *cutting*

their tongue a s sword   Ps 57:4
S...two-edged sword   Prov 5:4
Put in your s sickle   Rev 14:18

SHATTER *break, burst*

s-ed every tree of the   Ex 9:25
the mighty are s-ed   1 Sam 2:4
s them like earthenware   Ps 2:9
s the doors of bronze   Is 45:2
iron crushes and s-s   Dan 2:40

SHAUL

1 *king of Edom*   Gen 36:37,38
2 *son of Simeon*   Gen 46:10
3 *Kohathite Levite*   1 Chr 6:24

SHAVE *cut or scrape*

he shall s his hand   Lev 14:9
s off the seven   Judg 16:19
s-d off half of   2 Sam 10:4
will s with a razor   Is 7:20

SHEAF *bundle of grain stalks*

s-ves in the field   Gen 37:7
s of the first fruits   Lev 23:10
among the s-ves   Ruth 2:15

SHEARER *wool cutter*

silent before its s-s   Is 53:7
Lamb before its s   Acts 8:32

SHEAR-JASHUB

son of Isaiah   Is 7:3
name symbolizes prophecy

SHEBA

1 *son of Raamah*   Gen 10:7
2 *son of Joktan*   Gen 10:28
3 *grandson of Abraham*Gen 25:3
4 *a Benjamite*   2 Sam 20:1-7
5 *a Gadite*   1 Chr 5:13
6 *Simeonite town*   Josh 19:2
7 *kingdom*   Job 6:19

Ps 72:10,15 Jer 6:20
8 *Queen of*   2 Chr 9:1ff

SHEBAT

*eleventh month of Hebrew
calendar*   Zech 1:7

SHECHEM

1 *city in central Palestine*
Gen 12:6;33:18; 1 Chr 7:28
city of refuge   Josh 20:7
2 *son of Hamor*   Gen 34:2
3 *line of Manasseh*   Num 26:31
4 *son of Shemida*   1 Chr 7:19

SHED *pour out*

Whoever s-s man's   Gen 9:6
s streams of water   Ps 119:136
hasten to s blood   Prov 1:16
will not s its light   Is 13:10
bribes to s blood   Ezek 22:12
swift to s blood   Rom 3:15
s-ding of blood   Heb 9:22

SHEEP *animal*

Rachel came with...s   Gen 29:9
not be like s   Num 27:17
the fleece of my s   Job 31:20
s of His pasture   Ps 100:3
All of us like s   Is 53:6
a s that is silent   Is 53:7
will care for My s   Ezek 34:12
lost s of...Israel   Matt 10:6
s from the goats   Matt 25:32
my s which was lost   Luke 15:6
His life for the s   John 10:11
s hear My voice   John 10:27
Tend My s   John 21:17
Shepherd of the s   Heb 13:20

SHEEP GATE *see* GATES
OF JERUSALEM

SHEEPFOLDS *enclosure*

s for the flocks   2 Chr 32:28
lie down among the s   Ps 68:13
took him from the s   Ps 78:70

SHEEPSKINS *coverings*

they went about in s   Heb 11:37

SHEET

hammered out gold s-s   Ex 39:3
s over *his* naked   Mark 14:51

SHEET

object like a great s Acts 10:11

SHELTER *cover, refuge*

under the s of my Gen 19:8
in the s of Thy wings Ps 61:4
a s to *give* shade Is 4:6
a s from the storm Is 32:2
made a s for himself Jon 4:5

SHEM

son of Noah Gen 5:32;6:10
Gen 9:27;11:11

SHEOL

place of the dead Gen 37:35
Job 7:9; Ps 49:15; Prov 15:11
Is 38:10; Ezek 32:27; Hab 2:5

SHEPHELAH

low hill country 1 Chr 27:28
Obad 19

SHEPHERD (n)

sheep...have no s Num 27:17
The LORD is my s Ps 23:1
Like a s He Is 40:11
s-s after My own heart Jer 3:15
for lack of a s Ezek 34:5
raise up a s Zech 11:16
sheep without a s Matt 9:36
strike down the s Matt 26:31
s-s...in the fields Luke 2:8
I am the good s John 10:11
the great S Heb 13:20
the Chief S 1 Pet 5:4

SHEPHERD (v)

s My people 2 Sam 5:2
s My people Matt 2:6
S My sheep John 21:16
to s the church Acts 20:28
s the flock of God 1 Pet 5:2

SHESHBAZZAR

governor of Judah under
Cyrus Ezra 5:14,16

SHIBBOLETH

test word for identification
Judg 12:6

SHIELD *protection*

Abram, I am a s Gen 15:1
He is a s to all 2 Sam 22:31

My s is with God Ps 7:10
faithfulness is a s Ps 91:4
the s of faith Eph 6:16

SHILOH

1 *Messianic title* Gen 49:10
2 *town N of Bethel* Josh 18:1
site of tabernacle Judg 18:31

SHINAR

Babylonian plain Gen 10:10
Gen 11:2; Josh 7:21; Dan 1:2

SHINE *be radiant, glow*

his face **shone** Ex 34:29
His face s on you Num 6:25
Thy face to s *upon us* Ps 80:3
light s before men Matt 5:16
s-s in the darkness John 1:5
lamp s-ing in a dark 2 Pet 1:19
light is...s-ing 1 John 2:8

SHIP *boat*

a haven for s-s Gen 49:13
like merchant s-s Prov 31:14
to the sea in s-s Ps 107:23
escape from the s Acts 27:30

SHISHAK *see* **PHARAOH**

SHOOT *new growth*

s will spring from Is 11:1
like a tender s Is 53:2
His s-s will sprout Hos 14:6

SHORT *lacking*

Is My hand so s Is 50:2
days shall be cut s Matt 24:22
s of the grace Heb 12:15

SHOULDER *part of body*

He bowed his s Gen 49:15
turned a stubborn s Neh 9:29
relieved his s Ps 81:6
government...on His s-s Is 9:6

SHOUT *cry out loudly*

s with a great s Josh 6:5
the people s-ed with Ezra 3:11
s for joy Ps 35:27
S joyfully to God Ps 66:1

SHOW *manifest, reveal*

land...I will s you Gen 12:1

s me Thy glory Ex 33:18
s you the secrets Job 11:6
s Thy lovingkindness Ps 17:7
S us the Father John 14:9
God s-s no partiality Gal 2:6
s hospitality Heb 13:2
if you s partiality James 2:9

SHOWBREAD

tables of s 1 Chr 28:16
s is *set*...table 2 Chr 13:11

SHOWER *abundant flow*

roar of a *heavy* s 1 Kin 18:41
Like s-s that water Ps 72:6
be s-s of blessing Ezek 34:26
A s is coming Luke 12:54

SHREWD *cunning*

frustrates...the s Job 5:12
be s as serpents Matt 10:16

SHRINE *object of worship*

built yourself a s Ezek 16:24
tear down your s-s Ezek 16:39
who made silver s-s Acts 19:24

SHULAMMITE
title of young woman Song 6:13

SHUNAMMITE *from Shunem*

1 *David's nurse* 1 Kin 1:3,15
1 Kin 2:17,21,22
2 *hostess of Elisha* 2 Kin 4:12ff

SHUR
wilderness in NW Sinai
Gen 16:7;20:1; Ex 15:22
1 Sam 15:7

SHUT *close*

wilderness has s them Ex 14:3
s the lions' mouths Dan 6:22
s your door, pray Matt 6:6
power to s up the sky Rev 11:6

SIBBOLETH
test word for identification
Judg 12:6

SICK *unwell*

strengthen the s Ezek 34:16
lying s with a fever Mark 1:30
Lazarus was s John 11:2

anyone among you s James 5:14

SICKLE *cutting tool*

who wields the s Jer 50:16
sharp s in His hand Rev 14:14
Put in your s Rev 14:15

SICKNESS *illness*

remove from you...s Deut 7:15
every kind of s Matt 4:23
authority over...s Matt 10:1
s is not unto death John 11:4

SIDON

1 *son of Canaan* Gen 10:15
1 Chr 1:13
2 *Phoenician port* Gen 10:19
Is 23:4; Ezek 28:22

SIEGE *encirclement*

city came under s 2 Kin 24:10
their s towers Is 23:13
s against Jerusalem Jer 6:6
build a s wall Ezek 4:2

SIGHT *perception, vision*

pleasing to the s Gen 2:9
acceptable in Thy s Ps 19:14
precious in My s Is 43:4
blind receive s Matt 11:5
three days without s Acts 9:9
by faith, not by s 2 Cor 5:7

SIGN *indication or wonder*

a s for Cain Gen 4:15
s of the covenant Gen 9:12
this shall be the s Ex 3:12
blood shall be a s Ex 12:13
His s-s in Egypt Ps 78:43
Ask a s for yourself Is 7:11
an everlasting s Is 55:13
a s from You Matt 12:38
s of Your coming Matt 24:3
show s-s and Mark 13:22
s-s in sun and moon Luke 21:25
beginning of *His* s-s John 2:11
s of circumcision Rom 4:11
Jews ask for s-s 1 Cor 1:22
tongues are for a s 1 Cor 14:22
s-s...false wonders 2 Thess 2:9

SIGNET *seal*

examine...whose s Gen 38:25
engravings of a s Ex 39:14

s rings of his nobles   Dan 6:17

SILAS

co-worker with Paul
Acts 15:22,32,40;16:19,25
Acts 17:4,10,14
also Silvanus

SILENCE *quietness*

My soul *waits* in s   Ps 62:1
war will be s-d   Jer 50:30
s the ignorance   1 Pet 2:15
s in heaven   Rev 8:1

SILENT *quiet*

LORD, do not keep s   Ps 35:22
A time to be s   Eccl 3:7
But Jesus kept s   Matt 26:63
women keep s   1 Cor 14:34

SILOAM

1 *tower in Jerusalem* Luke 13:4
2 *water pool in Jerusalem*
John 9:7,11

SILVANUS *see* SILAS

SILVER *precious metal*

rich in...s   Gen 13:2
took no plunder in s Judg 5:19
as s is refined   Ps 66:10
in settings of s   Prov 25:11
s has become dross   Is 1:22
The s is Mine   Hag 2:8
not acquire...s   Matt 10:9
thirty pieces of s   Matt 26:15

SIMEON

1 *son of Jacob*   Gen 29:33
2 *tribe*   Num 1:23; Rev 7:7
3 *ancestor of Jesus* Luke 3:30
4 *devout Jew*   Luke 2:25
5 *Christian prophet*   Acts 13:1
6 *Simon Peter*   Acts 15:14

SIMON

1 *apostle*   Matt 4:18
Mark 1:16
see also PETER
2 *the Zealot*   Matt 10:4
Mark 3:18; Luke 6:15
3 *brother of Jesus* Matt 13:55
Mark 6:3
4 *leper*   Matt 26:6; Mark 14:3
5 *a Pharisee*   Luke 7:40,43

6 *of Cyrene*   Matt 27:32
carried Jesus' cross Mark 15:21
Luke 23:26
7 *father of Judas*   John 6:71
John 13:2
8 *Magus*   Acts 8:9,13,18
sorcerer
9 *the tanner* Acts 9:43;10:6,32

SIMPLE *innocent* or *humble*

making wise the s   Ps 19:7
LORD preserves the s   Ps 116:6

SIN (n) *transgression*

please forgive my s   Ex 10:17
atonement for your s   Ex 32:30
purification from s   Num 19:9
s will find you out   Num 32:23
s of divination   1 Sam 15:23
the s-s of my youth   Ps 25:7
s my mother conceived   Ps 51:5
Fools mock at s   Prov 14:9
bore the s of many   Is 53:12
s-s of her prophets   Lam 4:13
an eternal s   Mark 3:29
forgive us our s-s   Luke 11:4
takes away the s   John 1:29
wash away your s-s   Acts 22:16
wages of s is death   Rom 6:23
died for our s-s   1 Cor 15:3
Him who knew no s   2 Cor 5:21
pleasures of s   Heb 11:25
confess your s-s   James 5:16
a multitude of s-s   James 5:20
confess our s-s   1 John 1:9
s is lawlessness   1 John 3:4

SIN (v) *transgress*

When a leader s-s   Lev 4:22
s against the LORD 1 Sam 14:34
Job did not s   Job 1:22
s against Thee   Ps 119:11
Father, I have s-ned Luke 15:18
s no more   John 8:11
all have s-ned   Rom 3:23
that you may not s   1 John 2:1

SIN

1 *wilderness in Sinai* Ex 16:1
Num 33:11,12
2 *Egyptian city* Ezek 30:15,16

SIN OFFERING
see **OFFERINGS**

SINAI

1 *mountain* Ex 19:11; Lev 26:46
Num 28:6

where Law received
Ex 31:18; 34:29
also Horeb
2 *desert wilderness* Ex 16:1
Ex 19:1; Num 1:19; 9:5

SINCERE *without deceit*

be s and blameless Phil 1:10
mindful of the s faith 2 Tim 1:5
s love...brethren 1 Pet 1:22

SINEW *strength or tendon*

with bones and s-s Job 10:11
neck is an iron s Is 48:4
will put s-s on you Ezek 37:6

SINFUL *wicked*

a brood of s men Num 32:14
s generation Mark 8:38
I am a s man Luke 5:8
likeness of s flesh Rom 8:3

SING

s to the LORD Ex 15:1
s-ing and dancing 1 Sam 18:6
I will s praises 2 Sam 22:50
morning stars sang Job 38:7
S to Him a new song Ps 33:3
the righteous s-s Prov 29:6
birds will s Zeph 2:14
after s-ing a hymn Mark 14:26
s-ing...thankfulness Col 3:16
sang a new song Rev 5:9

SINGERS

these are the s 1 Chr 9:33
male and female s Eccl 2:8

SINK *descend, fall*

do not let me s Ps 69:14
so shall Babylon s Jer 51:64

SINNER *wrongdoer*

He instructs s-s Ps 25:8
if s-s entice you Prov 1:10
Adversity pursues s-s Prov 13:21
one s destroys much Eccl 9:18

a friend of...s-s Matt 11:19
one s who repents Luke 15:7
merciful to me...s Luke 18:13
God...not hear s-s John 9:31
while we were yet s-s Rom 5:8
came...to save s-s 1 Tim 1:15

SISERA

1 *Canaanite warrior* Judg 4:2ff
2 *class of Nethinim* Ezra 2:53
Neh 7:55

SISTER

She is my s Gen 12:19
We have a little s Song 8:8
a s called Mary Luke 10:39
commend to you our s-s Rom 16:1
younger women as s-s 1 Tim 5:2

SIT *recline, rest*

Moses sat to judge Ex 18:13
Nor s in the seat Ps 1:1
S at My right hand Ps 110:1
lonely s-s the city Lam 1:34
who s in darkness Luke 1:79
dead man sat up Luke 7:15
where the harlot s-s Rev 17:15

SIVAN

*third month of Hebrew
calendar* Esth 8:9

SKILL *proficiency*

filled them with s Ex 35:35
the heavens with s Ps 136:5
work of s-ed men Jer 10:9
s-ed in destruction Ezek 21:31

SKILLFUL *accomplished*

became a s hunter Gen 25:27
s player on...harp 1 Sam 16:16
praises with a s psalm Ps 47:7

SKIN *covering*

garments of s Gen 3:21
s of his face shone Ex 34:29
Clothe me with s Job 10:11
My s turns black Job 30:30
will burst the s-s Mark 2:22

SKIP *hop, leap*

children s about Job 21:11
Lebanon s like a calf Ps 29:6
go forth and s Mal 4:2

217

SKULL *bony framework of head*

head, crushing his **s** Judg 9:53
the **s** and the feet 2 Kin 9:35
Place of a S Matt 27:33

SKY *heavens*

sun stopped in...**s** Josh 10:13
the **s** grew black 1 Kin 18:45
witness in the **s** Ps 89:37
s will be rolled up Is 34:4
for the **s** is red Matt 16:2
will appear in the **s** Matt 24:30
s was shut up Luke 4:25
gazing...into the **s** Acts 1:10
s was split apart Rev 6:14

SLANDER (n) *defamation*

spreads **s** is a fool Prov 10:18
s-s, gossip 2 Cor 12:20
and **s** be put away Eph 4:31

SLANDER (v) *defame*

He does not **s** Ps 15:3
Whoever secretly **s-s** Ps 101:5
Do not **s** a slave Prov 30:10

SLANDERER *defamer*

s separates...friends Prov 16:28
s-s, haters of God Rom 1:30

SLAUGHTER (n) *brutal killing*

great **s** at Gibeon Josh 10:10
lamb led to the **s** Jer 11:19
as a sheep to **s** Acts 8:32
in a day of **s** James 5:5

SLAUGHTER (v) *kill*

shall **s** the bull Ex 29:11
shall **s** the lamb Lev 14:25
Who **s** the children Is 57:5
s-ed My children Ezek 16:21

SLAVE *bondservant*

The Hebrew **s** Gen 39:17
s at forced labor Gen 49:15
sold *in* a **s** sale Lev 25:42
Is Israel a **s** Jer 2:14
S-s rule over us Lam 5:8
s above his master Matt 10:24
good and faithful **s** Matt 25:21
shall be **s** of all Mark 10:44
is the **s** of sin John 8:34
neither **s** nor free Gal 3:28

as **s-s** of Christ Eph 6:6

SLAVERY *servitude*

from the house of **s** Ex 13:3
ransomed you from...**s** Mic 6:4
received a spirit of **s** Rom 8:15
to a yoke of **s** Gal 5:1

SLAY *destroy, kill*

knife to **s** his son Gen 22:10
s-s the foolish Job 5:2
Though He **s** me Job 13:15
Evil...**s** the wicked Ps 34:21
s her with thirst Hos 2:3
Lamb that was **slain** Rev 5:12

SLEEP (n) *rest*

caused a deep **s** Gen 2:21
Do not love **s** Prov 20:13
a spirit of deep **s** Is 29:10
s fled from him Dan 6:18
overcome by **s** Acts 20:9

SLEEP (v) *slumber*

why dost Thou **s** Ps 44:23
neither slumber nor **s** Ps 121:4
who **s-s** in harvest Prov 10:5
found them **s-ing** Matt 26:43
we shall not all **s** 1 Cor 15:51

SLOW *not quick*

I am **s** of speech Ex 4:10
gracious, **S** to anger Ps 103:8
to hear, **s** to speak James 1:19
Lord is not **s** 2 Pet 3:9

SLUGGARD *lazy one*

to the ant, O **s** Prov 6:6
the **s** craves Prov 13:4
s buries his hand Prov 26:15

SLUMBER *sleep*

s in their beds Job 33:15
He...will not **s** Ps 121:3
None **s-s** or sleeps Is 5:27
Dreamers...love to **s** Is 56:10

SMALL *little*

both **s** and great 2 Kin 32:2
s among the nations Jer 49:15
day of **s** things Zech 4:10

For the gate is s | Matt 7:14
a few s fish | Mark 8:7
he was s in stature | Luke 19:3
tongue is a s part | James 3:5

SMILE grin

I s-d on them | Job 29:24
that I may s again | Ps 39:13
she s-s at the future | Prov 31:25

SMITE hit, strike

s...with frogs | Ex 8:2
smote Job with sore | Job 2:7
sun will not s you | Ps 121:6
righteous s me | Ps 141:5
s the earth | Rev 11:6

SMITH worker of metal

a vessel for the s | Prov 25:4
created the s who | Is 54:16
s-s from Jerusalem | Jer 24:1

SMOKE mist, vapor

s...ascended | Gen 19:28
Sinai was all in s | Ex 19:18
like s they vanish | Ps 37:20
temple was filling with s | Is 6:4
s rises up forever | Rev 19:3

SMOOTH no roughness

I am a s man | Gen 27:11
five s stones | 1 Sam 17:40
Make s...a highway | Is 40:3
the rough roads s | Luke 3:5
s...flattering speech | Rom 16:18

SMYRNA

city in Asia Minor | Rev 1:11;2:8

SNAKE serpent

horned s in the path | Gen 49:17
a s bites him | Amos 5:19
s instead of a fish | Luke 11:11

SNARE trap

gods shall be a s | Judg 2:3
s-s of death | 2 Sam 22:6
laid a s for me | Ps 119:110
his lips are the s | Prov 18:7
caught in My s | Ezek 12:13
table become a s | Rom 11:9
s of the devil | 1 Tim 3:7

SNOW ice flakes

storehouses of the s | Job 38:22
be whiter than s | Ps 51:7
He gives s like wool | Ps 147:16
Like s in summer | Prov 26:1
as white as s | Matt 28:3

SOBER serious, temperate

words of s truth | Acts 26:25
be alert and s | 1 Thess 5:6
Be of s spirit | 1 Pet 5:8

SODOM

city S of Dead Sea | Gen 10:19
home of Lot | Gen 19:1,4
destroyed by God | Gen 19:24

SODOMITE

one guilty of unnatural
sexual practices | 1 Kin 22:46

SOFT kind

speak to you s words | Job 41:3
s tongue breaks the | Prov 25:15

SOIL earth, ground

first fruits of your s | Ex 23:19
he loved the s | 2 Chr 26:10
fell into the good s | Mark 4:8
produce of the s | James 5:7

SOJOURN visit temporarily

S in this land | Gen 26:3
stranger s-s with you | Ex 12:48
s...land of Moab | Ruth 1:25

SOJOURNER

s in a foreign land | Ex 2:22
are s-s before Thee | 1 Chr 29:15
oppressed the s | Ezek 22:29

SOLDIER military man

s-s took Him away | Mark 15:16
s-s also mocked | Luke 23:36
s-s pierced His side | John 19:34
a devout s | Acts 10:7
good s of Christ | 2 Tim 2:3

SOLEMN deeply earnest, serious

sabbath of s rest | Lev 16:31
have a s assembly | Num 29:35
sworn s oaths | Ezek 21:23
bound...a s oath | Acts 23:14

219

SOLOMON

1 *son of David*   2 Sam 12:24
  king of Israel   1 Kin 1:43
  ruled wisely   1 Kin 4:29,34
  built the Temple 1 Kin 6:2;9:1
  international fame 1 Kin 10:1
  ruled foolishly   1 Kin 11:6
  death   1 Kin 11:43
2 *Song of Solomon*
  also **Song of Songs**

SON *male descendant*

the s-s of Noah   Gen 9:18
Take...your only s   Gen 22:2
O Absalom, my s   2 Sam 18:33
to be a s to Me   1 Chr 28:6
s-s of God shouted   Job 38:7
Thou art My S   Ps 2:7
wise s makes a   Prov 10:1
Discipline your s   Prov 19:18
bear a s...Immanuel   Is 7:14
Egypt I called My s   Hos 11:1
she gave birth to a S Matt 1:25
This is My beloved S Matt 3:17
the carpenter's s   Matt 13:55
I am the S of God   Matt 27:43
S of Man...suffer   Mark 8:31
her first-born s   Luke 2:7
If You are the S   Luke 4:3
man had two s-s   Luke 15:11
only begotten S   John 3:16
S also gives life   John 5:21
become s-s of light John 12:36
sending His own S   Rom 8:3
image of His S   Rom 8:29
not spare His own S Rom 8:32
fellowship with His S 1 Cor 1:9
if a s, then an heir   Gal 4:7
shall be a S to Me   Heb 1:5
abide in the S   1 John 2:24
He who has the S   1 John 5:12

SON-IN-LAW

the s of the Timnite Judg 15:6
be the king's s   1 Sam 18:18
s of Sanballat   Neh 13:28

SON OF GOD

Messianic title indicating
deity of Jesus Christ
Matt 4:3;8:29;16:16; Mark 1:20
  Mark 3:11;14:61; Luke 1:35
  John 3:18;11:27; Acts 8:37

SON OF MAN

Messianic title indicating
humanity of Jesus Christ
Matt 8:20;9:6; Mark 2:10;10:33
Luke 12:10;18:31;John 6:27;13:31

SONG *melody, music*

LORD is my...s   Ex 15:2
ministered with s   1 Chr 6:32
gives s-s in the night Job 35:10
s-s of deliverance   Ps 32:7
Sing to Him a new s   Ps 33:3
A s of my beloved   Is 5:1
Praise the LORD in s   Is 12:5
not drink wine with s   Is 24:9
hymns...spiritual s-s Eph 5:19

SORCERER *witch*

interprets...or a s   Deut 18:10
witness against the s-s Mal 3:5
immoral persons...s-s Rev 21:8

SORCERY *witchcraft*

practiced s   2 Chr 33:6
idolatry, s, enmities Gal 5:20
deceived by your s   Rev 18:23

SORDID *filthy*

fond of s gain   1 Tim 3:8
the sake of s gain   Titus 1:11
not for s gain   1 Pet 5:2

SOREK

valley SW of Jerusalem Judg 16:4

SORROW *grief, sadness*

down to Sheol in s   Gen 42:38
life is spent with s   Ps 31:10
man of s-s   Is 53:3
s is beyond healing   Jer 8:18
s...turned to joy   John 16:20
if I cause you s   2 Cor 2:2

SOSTHENES

1 *synagogue leader* Acts 18:17
2 *Corinthian believer* 1 Cor 1:27

SOUL *life, spirit*

her s was departing Gen 35:18

humble your s-s	Lev 16:29
poured out my s	1 Sam 1:15
not abandon my s	Ps 16:10
He restores my s	Ps 23:3
my s pants for Thee	Ps 42:1
Bless the LORD, O my s	Ps 103:1
who is wise wins s-s	Prov 11:30
s who sins will die	Ezek 18:4
unable to kill the s	Matt 10:28
exchange for his s	Matt 16:26
My s is...grieved	Matt 26:38
and forfeit his's	Mark 8:36
My s exalts the Lord	Luke 1:46
your s is required	Luke 12:20
one heart and s	Acts 4:32
an anchor of the s	Heb 6:19
able to save your s-s	James 1:21
save his s from	James 5:20
war against the s	1 Pet 2:11

SOUND (adj) *accurate, stable*

s wisdom...two sides	Job 11:6
I give you s teaching	Prov 4:2
the s doctrine	1 Tim 4:6

SOUND (n) *noise*

s of Thee in...garden	Gen 3:10
s of war in the camp	Ex 32:17
s of a great army	2 Kin 7:6
s of many waters	Ezek 43:2

SOUND (v) *express*

s His praise abroad	Ps 66:8
s an alarm	Joel 2:1
trumpet will s	1 Cor 15:52

SOUR *distasteful, tart*

eaten s grapes	Jer 31:29
offering...s wine	Luke 23:36

SOURCE *origin*

the s of sapphires	Job 28:6
s of eternal salvation	Heb 5:9
s of quarrels	James 4:1

SOVEREIGNTY *authority*

His s rules over all	Ps 103:19
s from Damascus	Is 17:3
s will be uprooted	Dan 11:4

SOW *plant, spread*

you may s the land	Gen 47:23
s your seed uselessly	Lev 26:16

who s in tears	Ps 126:5
who s-s iniquity will	Prov 22:8
they s the wind	Hos 8:7
birds...do not s	Matt 6:26
s good seed	Matt 13:27
s-ed spiritual things	1 Cor 9:11
whatever a man s-s	Gal 6:7

SOWER *planter*

seed to the s	Is 55:10
s went out to sow	Matt 13:3
s sows the word	Mark 4:14

SPAIN

S European land	Rom 15:24,28

SPARE *save or be lenient*

did not s their soul	Ps 78:50
who s-s his rod	Prov 13:24
No man s-s his brother	Is 9:19
not s His own Son	Rom 8:32
I will not s *anyone*	2 Cor 13:2
God did not s angels	2 Pet 2:4

SPEAK *proclaim, tell*

God **spoke** to Noah	Gen 8:15
God s-s with man	Deut 5:24
S of all His wonders	1 Chr 16:9
He who s-s falsehood	Ps 101:7
and a time to s	Eccl 3:7
the dumb to s	Mark 7:37
s that...we know	John 3:11
Never did a man s	John 7:46
s with other tongues	Acts 2:4
we s God's wisdom	1 Cor 2:7
If I s with tongues	1 Cor 13:1

SPEAR *weapon*

leaning on his s	2 Sam 1:6
s-s into pruning hooks	Is 2:4
pruning hooks into s-s	Joel 3:10
pierced...with a s	John 19:34

SPECK *particle*

regarded as a s of	Is 40:15
s out of your eye	Matt 7:4

SPEECH *message, word*

I am slow of s	Ex 4:10
His s was smoother	Ps 55:21
in cleverness of s	1 Cor 1:17
I am unskilled in s	2 Cor 11:6

SPELL

SPELL *incantation*

one who casts a s	Deut 18:11
skillful caster of s-s	Ps 58:5
power of your s-s	Is 47:9

SPICE

s and the oil	Ex 35:28
mix in the s-s	Ezek 24:10
prepared s-s and	Luke 23:56
wrappings with...s-s	John 19:40

SPIES *clandestine persons*

we are not s	Gen 42:31
two men as s	Josh 2:1
David sent out s	1 Sam 26:4
welcomed the s	Heb 11:31

SPIN *make thread*

nor do they s	Matt 6:28
neither toil nor s	Luke 12:27

SPIRIT

S rested upon them	Num 11:26
God sent an evil s	Judg 9:23
My s is broken	Job 17:1
renew a steadfast s	Ps 51:10
my s grows faint	Ps 77:3
a haughty s before	Prov 16:18
the S lifted me up	Ezek 3:14
his s was troubled	Dan 2:1
four s-s of heaven	Zech 6:5
are the poor in s	Matt 5:3
authority over...s-s	Matt 10:1
put My S upon Him	Matt 12:18
blasphemy...the S	Matt 12:31
yielded up *His* s	Matt 27:50
S like a dove	Mark 1:10
s...not have flesh	Luke 24:39
born of...the S	John 3:5
worship in s and	John 4:24
gave up His s	John 19:30
pour forth of My S	Acts 2:17
Jesus, receive my s	Acts 7:59
power of the S	Rom 15:19
taught by the S	1 Cor 2:13
pray with the s	1 Cor 14:15
walk by the S	Gal 5:16
fruit of the S is love	Gal 5:22
one body and one S	Eph 4:4
be filled with the S	Eph 5:18
sword of the S	Eph 6:17
not quench the S	1 Thess 5:19

division of soul and s	Heb 4:12
the s-s *now* in prison	1 Pet 3:19
S who bears witness	1 John 5:7

see also HOLY SPIRIT

SPIRIT OF GOD

the S was moving	Gen 1:2
S came upon him	1 Sam 10:10
a vision by the S	Ezek 11:24
S descending as a	Matt 3:16
being led by the S	Rom 8:14
S dwells in you	1 Cor 3:16
worship in the S	Phil 3:3

see also HOLY SPIRIT

SPIRIT OF THE LORD

S came upon him	Judg 3:10
S departed from	1 Sam 16:14
S gave them rest	Is 63:14
filled with...the S	Mic 3:8
S is upon Me	Luke 4:18

see also HOLY SPIRIT

SPIRITIST *medium*

not turn to...s-s	Lev 19:31
s...be put to death	Lev 20:27
removed...the s-s	2 Kin 23:24

SPIRITUAL *of the spirit*

the Law is s	Rom 7:14
s service of worship	Rom 12:1
raised a s body	1 Cor 15:44
with every s blessing	Eph 1:3
hymns and s songs	Eph 5:19
offer up s sacrifices	1 Pet 2:5

SPIT

began to s at Him	Mark 14:65
and s upon	Luke 18:32
He spat on...ground	John 9:6
I will s you out	Rev 3:16

SPLENDOR *magnificence*

the moon going in s	Job 31:26
displayed Thy s	Ps 8:1
Thy s and Thy majesty	Ps 45:3
clothed with s	Ps 104:1
s covers the heavens	Hab 3:3

SPLIT *divide*

He s the rock	Is 48:21

valleys will be s   Mic 1:4
Mount...will be s   Zech 14:4
sky was s apart   Rev 6:14

SPOIL *booty, pillage*

he divides the s   Gen 49:27
the s of the cities   Deut 2:35
divide the s with   Prov 16:19
widows may be their s   Is 10:2
for s to the nations   Ezek 25:7

SPONGE *absorbent matter*

taking a s, he filled   Matt 27:48
a s with sour wine   Mark 15:36

SPOT *speck*

or the leopard his s-s   Jer 13:23
no s or wrinkle   Eph 5:27

SPOTLESS *no defects*

unblemished and s   1 Pet 1:19
s and blameless   2 Pet 3:14

SPREAD *stretch out*

He s His wings   Deut 32:11
I s My skirt over   Ezek 16:8
death s to all men   Rom 5:12

SPRING (adj) *period, season*

has been no s rain   Jer 3:3
Like the s rain   Hos 6:3
s crop began to sprout   Amos 7:1

SPRING (n) *water source*

went down to the s   Gen 24:16
twelve s-s of water   Ex 15:27
stop all s-s of water   2 Kin 3:19
s-s of the deep...fixed   Prov 8:28
the s-s of salvation   Is 12:3
s of the water of life   Rev 21:6

SPRING (v) *jump, leap*

S up, O well   Num 21:17
Truth s-s from the   Ps 85:11
s-ing up to eternal   John 4:14

SPRINKLE *scatter*

take its blood and s   Ex 29:16
s some of the blood   Lev 4:6
s *it* seven times   Lev 4:17
s some of the oil   Lev 14:16

SPY *investigate*

Moses sent...to s   Num 13:17
to s out Jericho   Josh 6:25
spied out Bethel   Judg 1:23
s out our liberty   Gal 2:4

SQUARE *area or shape*

altar shall be s   Ex 27:1
voice in the s   Prov 1:20
city is...a s   Rev 21:16

STAFF *rod*

s of God in his hand   Ex 4:20
Thy s, they comfort   Ps 23:4
or sandals, or a s   Matt 10:10
a mere s; no bread   Mark 6:8

STAIN *blemish*

s of your iniquity   Jer 2:22
without s or reproach   1 Tim 6:14

STAND *maintain position*

s before the LORD   Deut 10:8
O sun, s still   Josh 10:12
s before kings   Prov 22:29
word of our God s-s   Is 40:8
will s on the Mount   Zech 14:4
love to s and pray   Matt 6:5
s-ing by the cross   John 19:25
why do you s looking   Acts 1:11
s by your faith   Rom 11:20
s before...judgment   Rom 14:10
s firm in the faith   1 Cor 16:13
foundation...s-s   2 Tim 2:19
I s at the door   Rev 3:20

STANDARD *banner or rule*

set up their own s-s   Ps 74:4
set up My s   Is 49:22
s of the Law   Acts 22:12
s of sound words   2 Tim 1:13

STAR *heavenly body*

He made the s-s   Gen 1:16
s shall come forth   Num 24:17
morning s-s sang   Job 38:7
s of the morning   Is 14:12
s-s for light by night   Jer 31:35
His s in the east   Matt 2:2
morning s arises   2 Pet 1:19
wandering s-s   Jude 13
s fell from heaven   Rev 8:10

the bright morning s   Rev 22:16

STATE *position*

s of expectation   Luke 3:15
of our humble s   Phil 3:21
s has become worse   2 Pet 2:20

STATEMENT *assertion*

let your s be   Matt 5:37
trap Him in a s   Mark 12:13
catch Him in...s   Luke 20:20
This is a difficult s   John 6:60

STATURE *height*

was growing in s   1 Sam 2:26
in wisdom and s   Luke 2:52
he was small in s   Luke 19:3
measure of the s   Eph 4:13

STATUTE *law, rule*

My s-s and My laws   Gen 26:5
a perpetual s   Ex 29:9
keep My s-s   Lev 18:5
Teach me Thy s-s   Ps 119:26
not walked in My s-s   Ezek 5:7

STEADFAST *established, firm*

be s and not fear   Job 11:15
renew a s spirit   Ps 51:10
My heart is s   Ps 57:7
s in righteousness   Prov 11:19
be s, immovable   1 Cor 15:58

STEAL *rob, take*

You shall not s   Ex 20:15
be in want and s   Prov 30:9
thieves break in...s   Matt 6:19
Do not s   Mark 10:19

STEPHANAS

Corinthian Christian
          1 Cor 1:16;16:15,17

STEPHEN

deacon   Acts 6:5,8
martyred   Acts 7:59;8:2

STEPS *distance or movements*

dost number my s   Job 14:16
s...bathed in butter   Job 29:6
His s do not slip   Ps 37:31
s lay hold of Sheol   Prov 5:5
in the s of the faith   Rom 4:12
follow in His s   1 Pet 2:21

STEWARD *supervisor*

and sensible s   Luke 12:42
s-s of the mysteries   1 Cor 4:1
reproach as God's s   Titus 1:7

STEWARDSHIP *responsibility*

an account of your s   Luke 16:2
a s entrusted to me   1 Cor 9:17
s of God's grace   Eph 3:2

STIFFEN *make rigid*

s your neck no more   Deut 10:16
do not s your neck   2 Chr 30:8
have s-ed their necks   Jer 19:15

STILL *motionless or quiet*

O sun, stand s   Josh 10:12
the storm to be s   Ps 107:29
Why are we sitting s   Jer 8:14
sea, Hush, be s   Mark 4:39

STIMULATE *excite*

how to s my body   Eccl 2:3
s one another to   Heb 10:24

STING *pain*

where is your s   1 Cor 15:55
s of death is sin   1 Cor 15:56

STIR *agitate*

S up Thyself   Ps 35:23
word s-s up anger   Prov 15:1
man s-s up strife   Prov 29:22
s-red up the water   John 5:4

STOCKS *confinement*

put my feet in the s   Job 13:27
Jeremiah from the s   Jer 20:3
their feet in the s   Acts 16:24

STOMACH *part of body*

s will be satisfied   Prov 18:20
s of the fish   Jon 1:17
Food is for the s   1 Cor 6:13
s was made bitter   Rev 10:10

STONE (n) *rock*

they used brick for s   Gen 11:3
two s tablets   Ex 34:1
do these s-s mean   Josh 4:6
five smooth s-s   1 Sam 17:40
there was no s seen   1 Kin 6:18
Water wears...s-s   Job 14:19
foot against a s   Ps 91:12

in Zion a s	Is 28:16
take the heart of s	Ezek 11:19
serving wood and s	Ezek 20:32
foot against a s	Matt 4:6
will give him a s	Matt 7:9
rolled away the s	Matt 28:2
s-s will cry out	Luke 19:40
six s waterpots	John 2:6
first to throw a s	John 8:7
Remove the s	John 11:39
s-s, wood, hay	1 Cor 3:12
as to a living s	1 Pet 2:4
A s of stumbling	1 Pet 2:8

STONE (v) *throw stones*

people will s us	Luke 20:6
seeking to s You	John 11:8
went on s-ing Stephen	Acts 7:59
they s-d Paul	Acts 14:19

STOP *cease*

the sun s-ped	Josh 10:13
And the oil s-ped	2 Kin 4:6
put a s to sacrifice	Dan 9:27
s weeping for Me	Luke 23:28
s sinning	1 Cor 15:34

STORE *accumulate*

s up the grain	Gen 41:35
His sin is s-d up	Hos 13:12
place to s my crops	Luke 12:17
s-d up your treasure	James 5:3

STOREHOUSE *storage place*

s-s of the snow	Job 38:22
wind from His s-s	Jer 10:13
tithe into the s	Mal 3:10

STORK *bird*

the s, the heron	Lev 11:19
the s in the sky	Jer 8:7
wings of a s	Zech 5:9

STORM *tempest, whirlwind*

A refuge from the s	Is 25:4
will come like a s	Ezek 38:9
a great s on the sea	Jon 1:4
mists driven by a s	2 Pet 2:17

STRAIGHT *direct*

Make Thy way s	Ps 5:8
make your paths s	Prov 3:6
Make His paths s	Matt 3:3

Make s the way	John 1:23

STRANGE *foreign*

offered s fire	Lev 10:1
no s god among you	Ps 81:9
to teach s doctrines	1 Tim 1:3
went after s flesh	Jude 7

STRANGER *alien, sojourner*

s-s in the land	Gen 22:21
a s and a sojourner	Gen 23:4
shall not wrong a s	Ex 22:21
a s in the earth	Ps 119:19
LORD protects the s-s	Ps 146:9
violence to the s	Jer 22:3
I was a s	Matt 25:35
hospitality to s-s	Heb 13:2

STRAW *stalk of grain*

s to make brick	Ex 5:7
s for the horses	1 Kin 4:28
as s before the wind	Job 21:18
wood, hay, s	1 Cor 3:12

STRAY *wander*

not s into her paths	Prov 7:25
no longer s from Me	Ezek 14:11
s-s from the truth	James 5:19
s-ing like sheep	1 Pet 2:25

STREAM *current, flow*

planted by s-s of water	Ps 1:3
The s of God	Ps 65:9
like a rushing s	Is 59:19

STREET *road, way*

Wisdom shouts in...s	Prov 1:20
race madly in the s-s	Nah 2:4
on the s corners	Matt 6:5
s of the city...gold	Rev 21:21

STRENGTH *force, power*

no longer yield its s	Gen 4:12
The LORD is my s	Ex 15:2
was no s in him	1 Sam 28:20
My s is dried up	Ps 22:15
The LORD is my s	Ps 28:7
s in time of trouble	Ps 37:39
God is our refuge...s	Ps 46:1
s of my salvation	Ps 140:7
your s to women	Prov 31:3
s to the weary	Is 40:29
strangers devour his s	Hos 7:9

with all your s — Mark 12:30
s which God supplies — 1 Pet 4:11
sun shining in its s — Rev 1:16

STRENGTHEN *make strong*

please s me — Judg 16:28
David s-ed himself — 1 Sam 30:6
s-ed weak hands — Job 4:3
s the feeble — Is 35:3
s the sick — Ezek 34:16
s your brothers — Luke 22:32
s-ed in the faith — Acts 16:5
Him who s-s me — Phil 4:3
s-ed with all power — Col 1:11
s your hearts — 2 Thess 2:17
who has s-ed me — 1 Tim 1:12

STRETCH *extend*

I will s out My hand — Ex 3:20
He s-s out the north — Job 26:7
S-ing out heaven — Ps 104:2
I s-ed out the heavens — Is 45:12

STRIFE *discord, quarrel*

s between...herdsmen — Gen 13:7
the s of tongues — Ps 31:20
Hatred stirs up s — Prov 10:12
fool's lips bring s — Prov 18:6
of envy, murder, s — Rom 1:29
and s among you — 1 Cor 3:3
enmities, s, jealousy — Gal 5:20

STRIKE *hit*

I will s the water — Ex 7:17
you shall s the rock — Ex 17:6
He who s-s a man — Ex 21:12
s the timbrel — Ps 81:2
you s your foot — Ps 91:12
S a scoffer — Prov 19:25
He will s the earth — Is 11:4
let us s at him — Jer 18:18
S the Shepherd — Zech 13:7
s...the shepherd — Matt 26:31

STRIVE *contend, struggle*

not s with man forever — Gen 6:3
He will not always s — Ps 103:9
and s-ing after wind — Eccl 1:14
s together with me — Rom 15:30
s-ing to please men — Gal 1:10
we labor and s — 1 Tim 4:10
s-ing against sin — Heb 12:4

STRONG *powerful, steadfast*

a very s west wind — Ex 10:19
not drink...s drink — Lev 10:9
Be s and courageous — Deut 31:6
Israel became s — Judg 1:28
God is...s fortress — 2 Sam 22:33
The LORD s and mighty — Ps 24:8
s drink a brawler — Prov 20:1
their Redeemer is s — Prov 23:11
ants are not a s folk — Prov 30:25
love is as s as death — Song 8:6
Their Redeemer is s — Jer 50:34
grew s in faith — Rom 4:20
act like men, be s — 1 Cor 16:13
be s in the Lord — Eph 6:10
weakness...made s — Heb 11:34
I saw a s angel — Rev 5:2

STRONGHOLD *fortress, refuge*

David lived in the s — 2 Sam 5:9
s and my refuge — 2 Sam 22:3
s for the oppressed — Ps 9:9
For God is my s — Ps 59:9
my salvation, My s — Ps 62:2
a s to the upright — Prov 10:29

STRUGGLE (n) *conflict*

the days of my s — Job 14:14
our s is not against — Eph 6:12
have shared my s — Phil 4:3

STRUGGLE (v) *contend*

children s-d together — Gen 25:22
men s...each other — Ex 21:22

STUBBLE *short stumps*

gather s for straw — Ex 5:12
fire consumes s — Is 5:24
give birth to s — Is 33:11
house of Esau...s — Obad 18

STUBBORN *obstinate*

Pharaoh's heart is s — Ex 7:14
you are a s people — Deut 9:6
s...generation — Ps 78:8
house of Israel is s — Ezek 3:7

STUBBORNNESS *intractable*

I know your...s — Deut 31:27
s of their heart — Ps 81:12
s...unrepentant heart — Rom 2:5

STUMBLE *fall, trip*

your foot will not s	Prov 3:23
a rock to s over	Is 8:14
arrogant one will s	Jer 50:32
eye makes you s	Matt 5:29
a stone of s-ing	Rom 9:33
all s in many *ways*	James 3:2

STUMBLING BLOCK *obstacle*

s before the blind	Lev 19:14
s of iniquity	Ezek 44:12
You are a s to Me	Matt 16:23
to Jews a s	1 Cor 1:23
s of the cross	Gal 5:11

STUMP *part of plant*

s dies in the dry soil	Job 14:8
The holy seed is its s	Is 6:13
the s with the roots	Dan 4:26

STUPID *foolish, senseless*

s and the senseless	Ps 49:10
I am more s than	Prov 30:2
they are altogether s	Jer 10:8

STYLUS *marking/writing device*

an iron s and lead	Job 19:24
with an iron s	Jer 17:1

SUBDUE *conquer, overcome*

fill the earth, and s	Gen 1:28
the land was s-d	Josh 18:1
us completely s them	Ps 74:8
s nations before him	Is 45:1

SUBJECT (adj) *under authority*

s to forced labor	Judg 1:30
demons are s to us	Luke 10:17
church is s to Christ	Eph 5:24
s to...husbands	Titus 2:5
be s to the Father	Heb 12:9

SUBJECT (v)

s him to a slave's	Lev 25:39
creation was s-ed	Rom 8:20
them s themselves	1 Cor 14:34
all things are s-ed	1 Cor 15:28

SUBJECTION *under authority*

kingdom...in s	Ezek 17:14
He continued in s	Luke 2:51
s to the governing	Rom 13:1
all things in s	1 Cor 15:27

SUBMISSIVE *yielding*

Servants, be s	1 Pet 2:18
s to...husbands	1 Pet 3:5

SUBMIT *yield to*

Foreigners s to me	Ps 18:44
s yourself to decrees	Col 2:20
S therefore to God	James 4:7

SUBSTITUTE

s shall become holy	Lev 27:10
s darkness for light	Is 5:20
s bitter for sweet	Is 5:20

SUCCESS *accomplishment*

grant me s today	Gen 24:12
hands cannot attain s	Job 5:12
Daniel enjoyed s	Dan 6:28

SUCCESSFUL *having achieved*

make your journey s	Gen 24:40
make Thy servant s	Neh 1:11
make his ways s	Is 48:15

SUCCOTH

1 Israelite camping place
Ex 12:37;13:20
2 Gadite town in Jordan Valley
Josh 13:27; Ps 60:6

SUDDENLY *abruptly*

lest he come s	Mark 13:36
s...from heaven	Acts 2:2

SUFFER *experience pain*

s the fate of all	Num 16:29
Son of Man must s	Mark 8:31
s and rise again	Luke 24:46
worthy to s shame	Acts 5:41
we s with *Him*	Rom 8:17
creation...s-s	Rom 8:22
if one member s-s	1 Cor 12:26
s-ing for the gospel	2 Tim 1:8
Christ also s-ed	1 Pet 2:21

SUFFERINGS *distress*

s of this present	Rom 8:18
sharers of our s	2 Cor 1:7
fellowship of His s	Phil 3:10
rejoice in my s	Col 1:24
share the s of Christ	1 Pet 4:13

SUFFICIENT *enough*

s for its redemption	Lev 25:26

bread is not s — John 6:7
My grace is s — 2 Cor 12:9

SUMMER *season*

fever heat of s — Ps 32:4
Thou hast made s — Ps 74:17
Like snow in s — Prov 26:1
know that s is near — Matt 24:32

SUMMIT *peak, top*

Like the s of Lebanon — Jer 22:6
hide on the s — Amos 9:3

SUMMON *call, gather*

s-ed all Israel — Deut 5:1
s all the prophets — 2 Kin 10:19
He s-s the heavens — Ps 50:4
He s-ed the twelve — Matt 6:7

SUN *heavenly body*

when the s grew hot — Ex 16:21
the s stood still — Josh 10:13
chariots of the s — 2 Kin 23:11
God is a s — Ps 84:11
s will not smite — Ps 121:6
s to rule by day — Ps 136:8
new under the s — Eccl 1:9
s go down at noon — Amos 8:9
shine forth as the s — Matt 13:43
signs in the s — Luke 21:25
not let the s go down — Eph 4:26
clothed with the s — Rev 12:1

SUNRISE *appearance of sun*

toward the s — Num 3:38
Jordan toward the s — Josh 1:15

SUNSET

Passover...at s — Deut 16:6
dawn and the s shout — Ps 65:8

SUNSHINE

Through s after rain — 2 Sam 23:4
dazzling heat in the s — Is 18:4

SUPPER *meal*

made Him a s — John 12:2
eat the Lord's S — 1 Cor 11:20
marriage s of the — Rev 19:9
the great s of God — Rev 19:17

SUPPLICATION *petition*

Make s to the LORD — Ex 9:28
s of Thy people — 1 Kin 8:52

LORD has heard my s — Ps 6:9
poor man utters s-s — Prov 18:23
seek *Him by...*s-s — Dan 9:3
by prayer and s — Phil 4:6

SUPPLY *provide*

He who s-ies seed — 2 Cor 9:10
my God shall s — Phil 4:19
s moral excellence — 2 Pet 1:5

SUPPORT (n) *strength*

the LORD was my s — 2 Sam 22:19
gave him strong s — 1 Chr 11:10
Both supply and s — Is 3:1
worthy of his s — Matt 10:10

SUPPORT (v) *uphold*

Hur s-ed his hands — Ex 17:12
will He s...evildoers — Job 8:20
He s-s the fatherless — Ps 146:9
ought to s such men — 3 John 8

SUR *see* GATES OF
JERUSALEM

SURE *secure, true*

testimony...is s — Ps 19:7
His precepts are s — Ps 111:7
His water will be s — Is 33:16

SURETY *liable, security*

I myself will be s — Gen 43:9
s for Thy servant — Ps 119:122
s for a stranger — Prov 11:15

SURFACE *exterior*

s of the deep — Gen 1:2
ark floated on the s — Gen 7:18
water was on the s — Gen 8:9

SURPASS *excel*

you s in beauty — Ezek 32:19
s-ing riches of His — Eph 2:7
which s-es knowledge — Eph 3:19

SURRENDER *yield*

s me into his hand — 1 Sam 23:11
How can I s you — Hos 11:8

SURROUND *encircle*

s him with favor — Ps 5:12
Sheol s-ed me — Ps 18:5
s me with songs — Ps 32:7
witnesses s-ing us — Heb 12:1

SURVIVE *outlive*

your household will s Jer 38:17
how can we s Ezek 33:10

SURVIVORS *continued to live*

inheritance for...s Judg 21:17
out of...Zion s 2 Kin 19:31
left us a few s Is 1:9
imprison their s Obad 14

SUSA

a Persian capital city
Neh 1:44; Esth 1:2,5;3:15;9:15

SUSTAIN *provide for*

land could not s Gen 13:6
LORD s-s the righteous Ps 37:17
He will s you Ps 55:22
S...with raisin cakes Song 2:5

SWALLOW (n) *bird*

the s nest Ps 84:3
like a s in *its* Prov 26:2

SWALLOW (v) *take in*

earth may s us up Num 16:34
He will s up death Is 25:8
great fish to s Jonah Jon 1:17
s-ed up in victory 1 Cor 15:54

SWARM *collect, gather*

Nile will s with frogs Ex 8:3
which s on the earth Lev 11:29
land s-ed with frogs Ps 105:30

SWEAR *take oath, vow*

s by the LORD Gen 24:3
oath which I swore Gen 26:3
person s-s thoughtlessly Lev 5:4
not s falsely Lev 19:12
sworn by My holiness Ps 89:35
s by My name Jer 12:16
who s-s by heaven Matt 23:22
began to...s Matt 26:74
brethren do not s James 5:12

SWEAT *perspiration*

By the s of your face Gen 3:19
s...like drops of Luke 22:44

SWEET *fresh, pleasant*

waters became s Ex 15:25
s psalmist of Israel 2 Sam 23:1

who had s fellowship Ps 55:14
s are Thy words Ps 119:103
your sleep will be s Prov 3:24
Stolen water is s Prov 9:17
it was s as honey Ezek 3:3

SWIFT *fast, rapid*

horses and s steeds 1 Kin 4:28
s as the gazelles 1 Chr 12:8
race is not to the s Eccl 9:11
riding on a s cloud Is 19:1
s to shed blood Rom 3:15

SWINDLER *cheater*

cursed be the s Mal 1:14
a drunkard, or a s 1 Cor 5:11
revilers, nor s-s 1 Cor 6:10

SWINE *pig*

gold in a s-'s snout Prov 11:22
Who eat s-'s flesh Is 65:4
your pearls before s Matt 7:6
Send us into the s Mark 5:12

SWORD *weapon with blade*

flaming s...turned Gen 3:24
by your s you shall Gen 27:40
the s shall bereave Deut 32:25
A s for the LORD Judg 7:20
s devour forever 2 Sam 2:26
fell on his s 1 Chr 10:5
tongue a sharp s Ps 57:4
as a two-edged s Prov 5:4
teeth are *like* s-s Prov 30:14
s against nation Is 2:4
the power of the s Jer 18:21
abolish...the s Hos 2:18
s-s into plowshares Mic 4:3
perish by the s Matt 26:52
s of the Spirit Eph 6:17
than any two-edged s Heb 4:12
s of My mouth Rev 2:16

SYCAMORE *tree*

olive and s trees 1 Chr 27:28
plentiful as s-s 2 Chr 1:15
grower of s figs Amos 7:14
climbed up into a s Luke 19:4

SYCHAR

town of Samaria John 4:5
also Shechem

SYMPATHY *mutual feeling*

I looked for s — Ps 69:20
s to the prisoners — Heb 10:34

SYNAGOGUE *assembly*

pray in the s-s — Matt 6:5
He went into their s — Matt 12:9
flogged in *the* s-s — Mark 13:9
chief seats in...s-s — Luke 20:46
outcasts from the s — John 16:2
taught in s-s — John 18:20
reasoning in the s — Acts 17:17
but are a s of Satan — Rev 2:9

SYRIA

N of Palestine — Matt 4:24
— Acts 15:23,41;20:3
see also ARAM

T

TAANACH

Canaanite royal city Josh 12:21
Josh 21:25; Judg 5:19

TABERNACLE *assembly and worship area*

*dwelling place of God among
    the Israelites* — Ex 25:8
construction directed by God
— Ex 25:9
contained Ark of the Covenant
— Ex 25:10

**phrases used in connection with
the tabernacle:**
house of the LORD — Ex 23:19
— Ex 34:26; Deut 23:18
*tabernacle of the house
    of God* — 1 Chr 6:48
*tabernacle of the tent of
    meeting* — Ex 39:40;40:6,29
*tabernacle or tent of
    the testimony* — Ex 38:21
— Num 1:50,53
tent of meeting — Ex 38:43
Ex 29:32;30:26;38:30;40:2,6,7

TABITHA *see* DORCAS

TABLE *furniture*

gold t before the LORD — Lev 24:6
Thou dost prepare a t — Ps 23:5
crumbs...masters' t — Matt 15:27
t-s...moneychangers — Matt 21:12
dogs under the t — Mark 7:28
drink at My t — Luke 22:30
in order to serve t-s — Acts 6:2
t of the Lord — 1 Cor 10:21

TABLET *writing surface*

give you the stone t-s — Ex 24:12
t-s of the testimony — Ex 31:18
the t of their heart — Jer 17:1
t-s of human hearts — 2 Cor 3:3

TABOR

1 mountain — Judg 4:6,12
2 city in Zebulun — 1 Chr 6:77
3 oak in Benjamin — 1 Sam 10:3

TAHPANHES

Egyptian city — Jer 2:16
place where Jeremiah escaped
— Jer 43:7-9;44:1

TAHPENES

queen of Egypt — 1 Kin 11:19,20

TAIL

grasp *it* by its t — Ex 4:4
the foxes t to t — Judg 15:4
cuts off head and t — Is 9:14
t-s like scorpions — Rev 9:10

TAKE *get, grasp*

t...the tree of life — Gen 3:22
T My yoke upon — Matt 11:29
T, eat; this is My — Matt 26:26
t up your pallet — Mark 2:9
t-s away the sin — John 1:29
day that He was t-n — Acts 1:22

TALENT

measure of weight — Ex 38:27
— 2 Sam 12:30; 1 Chr 20:2
measure of money — 1 Kin 20:39
— Matt 18:24;25:15,25

TALK (n) *conversation, speech*

argue with useless t — Job 15:3
no...silly t — Eph 5:4
their t will spread — 2 Tim 2:17

TALK (v) *converse, speak*

God t-ed with him   Gen 17:3
lips t of trouble   Prov 24:2
who t about you   Ezek 33:30
Paul kept on t-ing   Acts 20:9

TALL *high*

cut...its t cedars   2 Kin 19:23
a nation t and smooth   Is 18:2
grew up, became t   Ezek 16:7

TAMAR

1 *Judah's daughter-in-law*
            Gen 38:6ff
2 *daughter of David* 2 Sam 13:1
3 *daughter of Absalom*
            2 Sam 14:27
4 *town near the Dead Sea*
    1 Kin 9:18; Ezek 47:19;48:28

TAMARISK *tree*

a t tree at Beersheba Gen 21:33
under the t tree   1 Sam 22:6

TAMBOURINE

accompanied by...t   Is 5:12
gaiety of t-s ceases   Is 24:8

TAMMUZ

Mesopotamian god Ezek 8:14

TARES *weeds*

t...among the wheat Matt 13:25
gather up the t   Matt 13:30
parable of the t   Matt 13:36

TARSHISH

1 *lineage of Japheth* Gen 10:4
2 *ships of*   1 Kin 10:22;22:48
    2 Chr 9:21; Ps 48:7
3 *line of Benjamin* 2 Chr 7:6-10
4 *Persian official* Esth 1:14
5 *city*   Is 66:19; Jon 1:3

TARSUS

birthplace of Paul Acts 21:39
capital of Cilicia   Acts 22:3

TASKMASTERS *overseers*

appointed t over them Ex 1:11
Pharaoh commanded...t Ex 5:6

TASTE *test flavor*

As the palate t-s   Job 34:3

O t and see   Ps 34:8
shall not t death   Matt 16:28
t death for everyone   Heb 2:9
t-d...heavenly gift   Heb 6:4

TASTELESS *without taste*

Can something t be   Job 6:6
salt has become t   Matt 5:13

TAUNT *object of ridicule*

a t among all   Deut 28:37
I have become their t Job 30:9

TAX *charge, tribute*

levy a t for the LORD Num 31:28
money for the king's t Neh 5:4
sitting in the t office Matt 9:9
pay t-es to Caesar Luke 20:22
t to whom t *is due* Rom 13:7

TAX-GATHERER *tax collector*

t-s do the same   Matt 5:46
many t-s and sinners Matt 9:10
Matthew the t   Matt 10:3
a friend of t-s   Matt 11:19
he was a chief t   Luke 19:2

TEACH *instruct*

t you what...to say   Ex 4:12
t them the good way 1 Kin 8:36
Can anyone t God   Job 21:22
T me Thy paths   Ps 25:4
T me to do Thy will Ps 143:10
would He t knowledge Is 28:9
He *began* to t them Matt 5:2
t-ing...in parables   Mark 4:2
Lord, t us to pray   Luke 11:1
Spirit will t you   Luke 12:12
He will t you all   John 14:26
t strange doctrines   1 Tim 1:3
allow a woman to t 1 Tim 2:12
she t-es and leads   Rev 2:20

TEACHER *instructor*

will behold your T   Is 30:20
T, I will follow You Matt 8:19
not above his t   Matt 10:24
why trouble the T   Mark 5:35
the t of Israel   John 3:10
call Me T and Lord John 13:13
t of the immature   Rom 2:20
as pastors and t-s   Eph 4:11
t of the Gentiles   1 Tim 2:7

false **t-s** among you   2 Pet 2:1

TEACHING (n) *instruction*

t drop as the rain   Deut 32:2
your mother's **t**   Prov 1:8
amazed at His **t**   Matt 7:8
My **t** is not Mine   John 7:16
contrary to sound **t**   1 Tim 1:10

TEAR *crying*

have seen your **t-s**   2 Kin 20:5
my **t-s** in Thy bottle   Ps 56:8
sow in **t-s** shall reap   Ps 126:5
drench you with my **t-s**   Is 16:9
eyes a fountain of **t-s**   Jer 9:1
His feet with her **t-s**   Luke 7:38
God...wipe every **t**   Rev 7:17

TEBETH

*name of the tenth month
in Hebrew calendar*   Esth 2:16

TEL-ABIB

place in Babylonia   Ezek 3:15
Jewish exiles located there

TELL *relate, speak*

not **t** the riddle   Judg 14:14
T of His glory   1 Chr 16:24
t of Thy righteousness   Ps 71:15
t-s lies will perish   Prov 19:9
t you great and mighty   Jer 33:3
See that you **t** no one   Matt 8:4
t you about Me   John 18:34
t you the mystery   Rev 17:7

TEMA

1 *son of Ishmael*   Gen 25:15
2 *town in Arabia*   Job 6:19
    Is 21:14

TEMPER *anger*

always loses his **t**   Prov 29:11
the ruler's **t** rises   Eccl 10:4

TEMPEST *storm*

bruises me with a **t**   Job 9:17
stormy wind *and* **t**   Ps 55:8
t of destruction   Is 28:2
on the day of **t**   Amos 1:14

TEMPLE *structure for worship*

doorpost of the **t**   1 Sam 1:9
t is not for man   1 Chr 29:1

LORD is in His holy **t**   Ps 11:4
meditate in His **t**   Ps 27:4
t of the LORD   Jer 7:4
pinnacle of the **t**   Matt 4:5
will destroy this **t**   Mark 14:58
veil of the **t**   Luke 23:45
Destroy this **t**, and   John 2:19
you are a **t** of God   1 Cor 3:16
t of the Holy Spirit   1 Cor 6:19
his seat in the **t**   2 Thess 2:4
the Lamb, are its **t**   Rev 21:22

TEMPT *test, try*

And **t-ed** God in the   Ps 106:14
being **t-ed** by Satan   Mark 1:13
lest Satan **t** you   1 Cor 7:5
t-ed beyond what   1 Cor 10:13
Himself does not **t**   James 1:13

TEMPTATION *testing, trial*

not lead us into **t**   Matt 6:13
not enter into **t**   Matt 26:41
time of **t** fall away   Luke 8:13
t has overtaken you   1 Cor 10:13
the godly from **t**   2 Pet 2:9

TEN *number*

T Commandments   Deut 10:4
it had **t** horns   Dan 7:7
has the **t** talents   Matt 25:28

TEND *take care of*

t his father's flock   1 Sam 17:15
He will **t** His flock   Is 40:11
T My lambs   John 21:15
T My sheep   John 21:17

TENDER *gentle, young*

t and choice calf   Gen 18:7
your heart was **t**   2 Kin 22:19
like a **t** shoot   Is 53:2
t mercy of our God   Luke 1:78

TENT *mobile shelter*

Abram moved his **t**   Gen 13:18
man, living in **t-s**   Gen 25:27
your **t-s**, O Israel   1 Kin 12:16
t-s of the destroyers   Job 12:6
dwell in Thy **t** forever   Ps 61:4
grumbled in their **t-s**   Ps 106:25
Like a shepherd's **t**   Is 38:12

TENT OF MEETING
see **TABERNACLE**

TENT OF TESTIMONY
see **TABERNACLE**

TERAH
father of Abraham Gen 11:24
Num 33:27; Luke 3:34

TERAPHIM
household gods 2 Kin 23:24
Zech 10:2

TERRIBLE *dreadful*
and t wilderness Deut 8:15
t day of the LORD Mal 4:5
into t convulsions Mark 9:26

TERRIFY *frighten*
t-ied by the sword 1 Chr 21:30
t me by visions Job 7:14
t them with Thy storm Ps 83:15
t you by my letters 2 Cor 10:9

TERRITORY *country, land*
smite your whole t Ex 8:2
God enlarges your t Deut 19:8
t of...inheritance Josh 19:10
will possess the t Obad 19

TERROR *intense fear*
Sounds of t are in Job 15:21
t-s of thick darkness Job 24:17
t-s of Sheol came Ps 116:3
meditate on t Is 33:18
t-s and great signs Luke 21:11

TERTIUS
Paul's scribe Rom 16:22

TEST (n) *trial*
put God to the t Ps 78:18
put Him to the t Luke 10:25
you fail the t 2 Cor 13:5

TEST (v) *try*
God t-ed Abraham Gen 22:1
Why do you t the LORD Ex 17:2
she came to t him 1 Kin 10:1
T my mind and my Ps 26:2
word of God is t-ed Prov 30:5
Spirit...to the t Acts 5:9

fire itself will t 1 Cor 3:13
t the spirits to see 1 John 4:1

TESTIFY *give witness*
nor shall you t Ex 23:2
them t against him 1 Kin 21:10
I will t against you Ps 50:7
our sins t against us Is 59:12
Jesus Himself t-ied John 4:44

TESTIMONY *witness*
into the ark the t Ex 25:16
two tablets of the t Ex 31:18
t of the LORD is sure Ps 19:7
t-ies are righteous Ps 119:144
Bind up the t Is 8:16
t against Jesus Matt 26:59
t of two men is true John 8:17
t concerning Christ 1 Cor 1:6
ashamed of the t 2 Tim 1:8
This t is true Titus 1:13

TETRARCH
governor of a region Matt 14:1
Luke 3:1,19; Acts 13:1

THADDAEUS
apostle Matt 10:3; Mark 3:18

THANK (v) *express gratitude*
my song I shall t Him Ps 28:7
God, I t Thee Luke 18:11
I t God always 1 Cor 1:4

THANKS (n) *gratitude*
give t to the LORD 1 Chr 16:7
It is good to give t Ps 92:1
giving t, He broke Matt 15:36
a cup and given t Matt 26:27
But t be to God Rom 6:17
not cease giving t Eph 1:16
always to give t 2 Thess 1:3

THANKSGIVING *gratitude*
the sacrifice of t Lev 7:12
with the voice of t Ps 26:7
His presence with t Ps 95:2
supplication with t Phil 4:6
t and honor and Rev 7:12

THEBES
Egyptian city Jer 46:25
Ezek 30:14-16

233

THEFT

THEFT *robbery*
be sold for his t   Ex 22:3
t-s, murders   Mark 7:21

THEOPHILUS
addressee of Luke's gospel
and Acts   Luke 1:3
    Acts 1:25

THESSALONICA
Macedonian city   Acts 27:2
    Phil 4:16
visited by Paul   Acts 17:1,11,13

THICKET *underbrush*
ram caught in the t   Gen 22:13
the t of the Jordan   Jer 50:44

THIEF *robber*
that t shall die   Deut 24:7
partner with a t   Prov 29:24
companions of t-ves   Is 1:23
enter...like a t   Joel 2:9
t comes...to steal   John 10:10
a t in the night   1 Thess 5:2

THIGH *part of leg*
hand under my t   Gen 24:2
socket of Jacob's t   Gen 32:25
Thy sword on *Thy* t   Ps 45:3
on His t...a name   Rev 19:16

THIN *lean*
t ears scorched   Gen 41:27
t yellowish hair   Lev 13:30
streams...will t out   Is 19:6

THINK *ponder, reflect*
as he t-s...so he is   Prov 23:7
not t...to abolish   Matt 5:17
not to t more highly   Rom 12:3
t as a child   1 Cor 13:11
t-s he is something   Gal 6:3
beyond all that we...t   Eph 3:20

THIRD *number*
morning, a t day   Gen 1:13
raised...the t day   Matt 16:21
raised on the t day   1 Cor 15:4
to the t heaven   2 Cor 12:2

THIRST (n) *craving, dryness*
for my t...vinegar   Ps 69:21

donkeys quench...t   Ps 104:11
not hunger or t   Is 49:10
in Me shall never t   John 6:35
no more, neither t   Rev 7:16

THIRST (v) *have a craving*
My soul t-s for God   Ps 42:2
Everyone who t-s, come   Is 55:1
t for righteousness   Matt 5:6

THIRSTY *lacking water*
satisfied the t soul   Ps 107:9
In a dry and t land   Ezek 19:13
I was t, and you   Matt 25:35
If any man is t   John 7:37
one who is t come   Rev 22:17

THOMAS
apostle   Matt 10:3; Mark 3:18
    Luke 6:15
doubted Jesus' resurrection
    John 20:24-28

THORN *sharp point*
Both t-s and thistles   Gen 3:18
as t-s in your sides   Num 33:55
as a hedge of t-s   Prov 15:19
lily among the t-s   Song 2:2
have reaped t-s   Jer 12:13
fell among the t-s   Matt 13:7
a crown of t-s   Matt 27:29
a burning t bush   Acts 7:30
t in the flesh   2 Cor 12:7

THOUGHT *concept, idea*
t-s of his heart   Gen 6:5
knows the t-s of man   Ps 94:11
My t-s are not your t-s   Is 55:8
Jesus knowing...t-s   Matt 9:4
heart come evil t-s   Matt 15:19
every t captive   2 Cor 10:5

THREAD *string*
cord of scarlet t   Josh 2:18
lips...a scarlet t   Song 4:3

THREE *number*
Job's t friends   Job 2:11
or t have gathered   Matt 18:20
deny Me t times   Matt 26:34
t days I will raise   John 2:19

THRESH *beat out*

ox while he is t-ing   Deut 25:4
like dust at t-ing   2 Kin 13:7
will t the mountains   Is 41:15
Arise and t   Mic 4:13

THRESHING FLOOR

winnows...at the t   Ruth 3:2
David bought...t   2 Sam 24:24
clear His t   Matt 3:12

THROAT *part of neck*

t is an open grave   Ps 5:9
my t is parched   Ps 69:3
has enlarged its t   Is 5:14
t is an open grave   Rom 3:13

THRONE *seat of sovereign*

sitting on His t   1 Kin 22:19
LORD'S t is in heaven   Ps 11:4
Thy t is established   Ps 93:2
it is the t of God   Matt 5:34
sit upon twelve t-s   Matt 19:28
Thy t...is forever   Heb 1:8
to the t of grace   Heb 4:16
a great white t   Rev 20:11

THRUST *cast, push*

He shall t them out   Josh 23:5
t away like thorns   2 Sam 23:6
Nor to t aside   Prov 18:5
LORD has t them down   Jer 46:15

THUMMIN

*kept in high priest's breastplate
for determining will of God*
   Ex 28:30; Lev 8:8; Deut 33:8
   Ezra 2:63; Neh 7:65

THUNDER (n)

LORD sent t and hail   Ex 9:23
But His mighty t   Job 26:14
the hiding place of t   Ps 81:7
be punished with t   Is 29:6
sound of loud t   Rev 14:2

THUNDER (v)

t in the heavens   1 Sam 2:10
you t with a voice   Job 40:9
LORD also t-ed   Ps 18:13

THYATIRA

city in Asia Minor

home of Lydia   Acts 16:14
early church   Rev 1:11;2:18,24

TIBERIAS

*city on W shore of Sea
  of Galilee*   John 6:1,23
Sea of   John 21:1
also **Sea of Galilee**

TIBERIUS

Roman emperor   Luke 3:1
see also **CAESAR**

TIDINGS *information, news*

t of His salvation   1 Chr 16:23
not fear evil t   Ps 112:7
bring glad t of good   Rom 10:15

TIGLATH-PILESER

Assyrian king   2 Kin 15:29
   2 Kin 16:7,10

also **Pul**
also **Tilgath-Pilneser**

TIGRIS

Mesopotamian river   Gen 2:14
   Dan 10:4

TILGATH-PILNESER

Assyrian king   1 Chr 5:6,26
   2 Chr 28:20

also **Pul**
also **Tiglath-Pileser**

TILLER *cultivator*

Cain was a t   Gen 4:2
a t of the ground   Zech 13:5

TIMBER *wood*

cedar and cypress t   1 Kin 9:11
whatever t you need   1 Chr 2:16
t of Lebanon   Song 3:9

TIMBREL *musical instrument*

with songs, with t   Gen 31:27
strike the t   Ps 81:2
Praise Him with t   Ps 150:4

TIME *day, period, season*

in t-s of trouble   Ps 9:9
t-s are in Thy hand   Ps 31:15
for a t, t-s, and half   Dan 12:7
t to seek the LORD   Hos 10:12

signs of the t-s Matt 16:3
My t is at hand Matt 26:18
deny Me three t-s Luke 22:61
My t is not yet John 7:6
not...you to know t-s Acts 1:7
is the acceptable t 2 Cor 6:2
grace...in t of need Heb 4:16
for the t is near Rev 1:3

TIMOTHY

companion of Paul Acts 17:15
Acts 18:5; Phil 1:24
Col 1:23; Heb 13:23

TIRED *weary*

I am t of living Gen 27:46
run and not get t Is 40:31

TIRZAH

1 *daughter of Zelophedad*
Num 26:33;27:1;36:11
2 *royal Canaanite city*
1 Kin 14:17; 2 Kin 15:14

TISHBITE

town identity of Elijah
1 Kin 17:1;21:17; 2 Kin 1:3,8

TITHE (n) *tenth*

all the t of the land Lev 27:30
a t of the t Num 18:26
the t of your grain Deut 12:17
t into the storehouse Mal 3:10
t-s of all that I get Luke 18:12
mortal men receive t-s Heb 7:8

TITHE (v) *pay a tithe*

shall surely t all Deut 14:22
you t mint and dill Matt 23:23

TITUS

co-worker with Paul
2 Cor 2:13;8:23; Gal 2:1

TODAY *present time*

t you...be with Me Luke 23:43
same yesterday and t Heb 13:8

TOGARMAH

grandson of Japheth
Gen 10:1-3
1 Chr 1:6

TOIL (n) *labor, work*

the t of our hands Gen 5:29
t is not *in* vain 1 Cor 15:58

TOIL (v) *work hard*

I have t-ed in vain Is 49:4
they do not t nor Matt 6:28

TOMB *grave, sepulchre*

from womb to t Job 10:19
you have hewn a t Is 22:16
like whitewashed t-s Matt 23:27
laid Him in a t Mark 15:46
Lazarus out of the t John 12:17
outside the t John 20:11

TOMORROW *future time*

not boast about t Prov 27:1
for t we may die Is 22:13
not be anxious for t Matt 6:34

TONGUE *speech, talk*

speech and slow of t Ex 4:10
flatter with their t Ps 5:9
their t a sharp sword Ps 57:4
a lying t Prov 6:17
t of the wise Prov 12:18
soft t breaks...bone Prov 25:15
His t is like...fire Is 30:27
t is a deadly arrow Jer 9:8
impediment of his t Mark 7:35
cool off my t Luke 16:24
no one...tame the t James 3:8

TONGUE *language*

speak with new t-s Mark 16:17
speak with other t-s Acts 2:4
t-s of men...angels 1 Cor 13:1
if I pray in a t 1 Cor 14:14
every tribe and t Rev 5:9

TOOL *work instrument*

among your t-s Deut 23:13
nor any iron t 1 Kin 6:7
iron into a cutting t Is 44:12

TOOTH

teeth white from Gen 49:12
eye for eye, t for t Ex 21:24
and a t for a t Matt 5:38

TOPAZ *precious stone*

ruby, t, and emerald Ex 39:10
t of Ethiopia Job 28:19
the ninth, t Rev 21:20

TOPHETH

site of Baal worship in
Hinnom Valley   2 Kin 23:10
          Jer 7:31,32;19:6,12,14

TORMENT (n) *pain, torture*

this place of t   Luke 16:28
their t was like   Rev 9:5
the fear of her t   Rev 18:15

TORMENT (v) *annoy, harass*

long will you t me   Job 19:2
t us before the time Matt 8:29
do not t me   Luke 8:28

TORRENT *flood*

The ancient t   Judg 5:21
t-s of destruction 2 Sam 22:5
t-s of ungodliness   Ps 18:4
like an overflowing t Is 30:28

TOUCH *feel, handle*

not eat...or t it   Gen 3:3
an angel t-ing him 1 Kin 19:5
evil will not t you   Job 5:19
not t My anointed Ps 105:15
T nothing unclean   Is 52:11
t the fringe of His Matt 14:36
not to t a woman   1 Cor 7:1

TOWER *fortress structure*

t whose top *will reach* Gen 11:4
Count her t-s   Ps 48:12
name...strong t   Prov 18:10
and built a t   Matt 21:33

TOWN *city, village*

many unwalled t-s Deut 3:5
founds a t with   Hab 2:12
except in his home t Matt 13:57

TRADE (n) *business, occupation*

abundance of your t Ezek 28:16
of the same t   Acts 18:3

TRADE (v) *buy or sell*

may t in the land Gen 42:34
t-ed with them   Matt 25:16

TRADERS *merchants*

Midianite t passed Gen 37:28
king's t procured 2 Chr 1:16
in a city of t   Ezek 17:4
increased your t   Nah 3:16

TRADITION *custom*

sake of your t   Matt 15:3
hold to the t of men Mark 7:8
hold...to the t-s 1 Cor 11:2
my ancestral t-s   Gal 1:14

TRAIN *guide, instruct*

T up a child   Prov 22:6
will they t for war Mic 4:3
t-ed to discern good Heb 5:14
heart t-ed in greed 2 Pet 2:14

TRAMPLE *crush, hurt*

t-s down the waves Job 9:8
let him t my life   Ps 7:5
didst t the nations Hab 3:12
Jerusalem...t-d Luke 21:24

TRANCE *daze, dream*

he fell into a t Acts 10:10
in a t I saw a vision Acts 11:5
fell into a t   Acts 22:17

TRANSFIGURED *changed*

He was t before them Matt 17:2

TRANSFORM *change*

t-ed by the renewing Rom 12:2
t-ed into the same 2 Cor 3:18
who will t the body Phil 3:21

TRANSGRESS *break, overstep*

you t the covenant Josh 23:16
rulers also t-ed   Jer 2:8
they t-ed laws   Is 24:5
disciples t the   Matt 15:2

TRANSGRESSION *trespass, sin*

forgives iniquity, t Ex 34:7
I am pure, without t Job 33:9
I know my t-s   Ps 51:3
removed our t-s from Ps 103:12
love covers all t-s Prov 10:12
pierced...for our t-s Is 53:5
not forgive your t-s Matt 6:15
dead in our t-s   Eph 2:5

TRANSGRESSOR *sinner*

teach t-s Thy ways Ps 51:13
numbered with the t-s Is 53:12
a t of the law   James 2:11

TRANSLATED

t and read before me Ezra 4:18
Immanuel...t means Matt 1:23

237

Golgotha, which is t   Mark 15:22
Messiah...t means   John 1:41

TRAP (n) *snare*

a snare and a t   Josh 23:13
hidden a t for me   Ps 142:3
table become...a t   Rom 11:9

TRAP (v) *catch*

they might t Him   Matt 22:15
in order to t Him   Mark 12:13

TRAVAIL *intense pain*

t-ed nor given birth   Is 23:4
woman is in t   John 16:21

TRAVEL *journey*

t by day and by night Ex 13:21
who t on the road   Judg 5:10
Jesus...*began* t-ing   Luke 24:15

TREACHEROUS *traitorous*

I behold the t   Ps 119:158
t will be uprooted   Prov 2:22
way of the t is hard Prov 13:15

TREAD *walk on*

They t wine presses   Job 24:11
as the potter t-s clay   Is 41:25
t upon serpents   Luke 10:19
t-s the wine press   Rev 19:15

TREASURE (n) *valuable thing*

t-s of the sand   Deut 33:19
the LORD is his t   Is 33:6
opening their t-s   Matt 2:11
for where your t is   Matt 6:21
have t in heaven   Matt 19:21
t in earthen vessels   2 Cor 4:7
stored up your t   James 5:3

TREASURE (v) *value greatly*

I have t-d the words Job 23:12
Thy word have I t-d Ps 119:11
t my commandments   Prov 7:1

TREASURY *place of valuables*

t of the LORD   Josh 6:19
paid from the royal t Ezra 6:4
fill their t-ies   Prov 8:21
into the temple t   Matt 27:6

TREATY *agreement, contract*

Let there be a t   1 Kin 15:19

go, break your t   2 Chr 16:3

TREE *woody plant*

fruit t-s bearing   Gen 1:11
t of life   Gen 2:9
gave me from the t   Gen 3:12
hang him on a t   Deut 21:22
said to the olive t   Judg 9:8
t *firmly* planted   Ps 1:3
she is a t of life   Prov 3:18
Beneath the apple t   Song 8:5
like a t planted by   Jer 17:8
under his fig t   Mic 4:4
good t bears good   Matt 7:17
the fig t withered   Matt 21:19
a sycamore t   Luke 19:4
autumn t-s without   Jude 12
eat of the t of life   Rev 2:7

TREMBLE *shake*

T before Him   1 Chr 16:30
pillars of heaven t   Job 26:11
T, and do not sin   Ps 4:4
make the heavens t   Is 13:13
His soul t-s   Is 15:4
my inward parts t-d Hab 3:16

TREMBLING (n) *fear, reverence*

rejoice with t   Ps 2:11
eat...with t   Ezek 12:18
with fear and t   Phil 2:12

TRESPASS *fault, sin*

Saul died for his t 1 Chr 10:13
caught in any t   Gal 6:1
dead in your t-es   Eph 2:1

TRIAL *testing*

if we are on t today   Acts 4:9
which was a t to you   Gal 4:14
perseveres under t James 1:12

TRIBE *common ancestry*

twelve t-s of Israel   Gen 49:28
a man of each t   Num 1:4
t-s of the LORD   Ps 122:4
judging...twelve t-s Luke 22:30
men from every t   Rev 5:9

TRIBULATION *affliction*

will be a great t   Matt 24:21
world you have t   John 16:33
exult in our t-s   Rom 5:3

my t-s on your behalf   Eph 3:13
out of the great t   Rev 7:14

TRIBUNAL *court*

before Caesar's t   Acts 25:10

TRIBUTE *tax*

sons of Israel sent t   Judg 3:15
impose a...t or toll   Ezra 7:24
exact a t of grain   Amos 5:11

TRIGON *musical instrument*

sound of...lyre, t   Dan 3:5

TRIUMPH *victory*

the righteous t   Prov 28:12
His t in Christ   2 Cor 2:14
mercy t-s over   James 2:13

TROAS

city in Asia Minor   Acts 16:8,11
visited by Paul   Acts 20:5
    2 Cor 2:12

TROPHIMUS

companion of Paul   Acts 20:4
    2 Tim 4:20
Ephesian Christian   Acts 21:29

TROUBLE (n) *affliction*

forget all my t   Gen 41:51
man is born for t   Job 5:7
Look upon...my t   Ps 25:18
very present help in t   Ps 46:1
remember his t no   Prov 31:7
t is heavy upon him   Eccl 8:6
day has enough t   Matt 6:34

TROUBLE (v) *bother, disturb*

t you in the land   Num 33:55
t-s his own house   Prov 11:29
also t the hearts   Ezek 32:9
Herod...was t-d   Matt 2:3
why t the Teacher   Mark 5:35
your heart be t-d   John 14:1

TROUBLED (adj) *disturbed*

songs to a t heart   Prov 25:20
soul has become t   John 12:27

TRUE *actual, real, reliable*

gets a t reward   Prov 11:18
There was the t light   John 1:9
gives you...t bread   John 6:32

let God be found t   Rom 3:4
signs of a t apostle   2 Cor 12:12
This testimony is t   Titus 1:13
t grace of God   1 Pet 5:12
faithful and t Witness   Rev 3:14

TRUMPET *wind instrument*

t-s of rams' horns   Josh 6:6
t-s...empty pitchers   Judg 7:16
Praise Him with t   Ps 150:3
do not sound a t   Matt 6:2
at the last t   1 Cor 15:52
voice like...a t   Rev 1:10

TRUST (n) *confidence, hope*

whose t a spider's web   Job 8:14
In God...put my t   Ps 56:11
put My t in Him   Heb 2:13

TRUST (v) *commit to*

t in the LORD   Ps 4:5
Than to t in man   Ps 118:8
t-s in his riches   Prov 11:28
not t in a neighbor   Mic 7:5
not t in ourselves   2 Cor 1:9

TRUSTWORTHY *reliable*

who can find a t   Prov 20:6
It is a t statement   1 Tim 3:1

TRUTH *genuineness, honesty*

walk before Me in t   1 Kin 2:4
speaks t in his heart   Ps 15:2
Thy word is t   Ps 119:160
Buy t, and do not   Prov 23:23
judge with t   Zech 8:16
full of grace and t   John 1:14
worship in...t   John 4:24
t shall make you free   John 8:32
the way, and the t   John 14:6
exchanged the t of   Rom 1:25
t of the gospel   Gal 2:5
speaking the t in love   Eph 4:15
the word of t   2 Tim 2:15
the t is not in us   1 John 1:8

TUBAL

1 son of Japheth   Gen 10:2
2 land ruled by Gog   Ezek 38:3
    Ezek 39:1

TUBAL-CAIN

son of Zillah   Gen 4:22

239

inventor of cutting tools

TUMULT *disturbance*

t of the peoples	Ps 65:7
A sound of t	Is 13:4
t of waters	Jer 51:16

TUNIC *cloak, garment*

a varicolored t	Gen 37:3
the holy linen t	Lev 16:4
or even two t-s	Matt 10:10

TURBAN *headdress*

a t of fine linen	Ex 28:39
justice was like...a t	Job 29:14
Remove the t	Ezek 21:26

TURMOIL *tumult*

treasure and t with	Prov 15:16
rest from your...t	Is 14:3
ill repute, full of t	Ezek 22:5

TURN *change or move*

not t to mediums	Lev 19:31
leave you *or* t back	Ruth 1:16
T from your evil	2 Kin 17:13
forget, nor t away	Prov 4:5
T to Me, and be saved	Is 45:22
t-ed to his own way	Is 53:6
t their mourning into	Jer 31:13
t...shame into praise	Zeph 3:19
t from darkness to	Acts 26:18
he who t-s a sinner	James 5:20
t away from evil	1 Pet 3:11

TURTLEDOVE *bird*

t for a sin offering	Lev 12:6
the voice of the t	Song 2:12

TUTOR *teacher*

t-s in Christ	1 Cor 4:15
Law...become our t	Gal 3:24

TWELVE *number*

t tribes of Israel	Gen 49:28
summoned His t	Matt 10:1
t legions of angels	Matt 26:53
when He became t	Luke 2:42
a crown of t stars	Rev 12:1

TWILIGHT *darkness, dusk*

lamb...offer at t	Ex 29:39
waits for the t	Job 24:15

midday as in the t	Is 59:10

TWINKLING *flicker*

in the t of an eye	1 Cor 15:52

TWINS *pair, two*

t in her womb	Gen 25:24
T of a gazelle	Song 4:5

TWO-EDGED *with two edges*

than any t sword	Heb 4:12
His mouth...t sword	Rev 1:16

TYRE

Phoenician seaport Josh 19:29
Ezek 27:3; Matt 15:21; Acts 21:3

U

UGLY *unsightly*

u and gaunt cows	Gen 41:4
seven lean...u cows	Gen 41:27

UNBELIEF *lack of faith*

wondered at their u	Mark 6:6
help my u	Mark 9:24
continue in their u	Rom 11:23

UNBELIEVER *non-believer*

a place with the u-s	Luke 12:46
wife who is an u	1 Cor 7:12
ungifted men or u-s	1 Cor 14:23
bound...with u-s	2 Cor 6:14
worse than an u	1 Tim 5:8

UNBELIEVING *doubting*

O u generation	Mark 9:19
u husband is	1 Cor 7:14
blinded the...u	2 Cor 4:4
evil, u heart	Heb 3:12

UNBLEMISHED *without defect*

shall be an u male	Ex 12:5
u and spotless	1 Pet 1:19

UNCEASING *continuous*

u complaint in his	Job 33:19
sorrow and u grief	Rom 9:2

UNCHANGEABLENESS

the u of His purpose	Heb 6:17

UNCIRCUMCISED

But an u male	Gen 17:14
u heart...humbled	Lev 26:41
the nations are u	Jer 9:26
who is physically u	Rom 2:27
the gospel to the u	Gal 2:7

UNCIRCUMCISION

has become u	Rom 2:25
who are called U	Eph 2:11
the u of your flesh	Col 2:13

UNCLEAN *not clean or not holy*

touches any u thing	Lev 5:2
u in their practices	Ps 106:39
man of u lips	Is 6:5
authority over u	Matt 10:1
u spirits entered	Mark 5:13
eaten anything...u	Acts 10:14
nothing is u in itself	Rom 14:14

UNCONTENTIOUS

| gentle, u, free from | 1 Tim 3:3 |
| be u, gentle | Titus 3:2 |

UNCOVER *expose*

to u her nakedness	Lev 18:7
u his feet and	Ruth 3:4
head u-ed while	1 Cor 11:5

UNDEFILED *uncorrupted*

holy, innocent, u	Heb 7:26
marriage bed *be* u	Heb 13:4
pure and u religion	James 1:27
imperishable and u	1 Pet 1:4

UNDERGARMENTS

| u next to his flesh | Lev 6:10 |
| linen u shall be on | Ezek 44:18 |

UNDERGO *experience*

Holy One to u decay	Ps 16:10
should not u decay	Ps 49:9
did not u decay	Acts 13:37

UNDERSTAND *comprehend*

u-s every intent	1 Chr 28:9
To u a proverb	Prov 1:6
do not u justice	Prov 28:5
Who can u it	Jer 17:9
u that the vision	Dan 8:17
Hear, and u	Matt 15:10
to u the Scriptures	Luke 24:45
Why do you not u	John 8:43

| none who u-s | Rom 3:11 |
| things hard to u | 2 Pet 3:16 |

UNDERSTANDING

a wise and u people	Deut 4:6
servant an u heart	1 Kin 3:9
Holy One is u	Prov 9:10

UNDISCIPLINED

| in an u manner | 2 Thess 3:7 |
| leading an u life | 2 Thess 3:11 |

UNDISTURBED *peaceful*

| land was u for forty | Judg 8:28 |
| an u habitation | Is 33:20 |

UNFADING *lasting*

| u crown of glory | 1 Pet 5:4 |

UNFAITHFUL

u to her husband	Num 5:27
very u to the LORD	2 Chr 28:19
u to our God	Ezra 10:2

UNFAITHFULNESS *faithless*

u...they committed	Lev 26:40
to Babylon for their u	1 Chr 9:1
the u of the exiles	Ezra 9:4

UNFATHOMABLE

| How...u His ways | Rom 11:33 |
| u riches of Christ | Eph 3:8 |

UNFRUITFUL *not productive*

the land is u	2 Kin 2:19
my mind is u	1 Cor 14:14
u deeds of darkness	Eph 5:11

UNGODLINESS *sinfulness*

torrents of u terrified	Ps 18:4
remove u from Jacob	Rom 11:26
lead to further u	2 Tim 2:16

UNGODLY *sinful, wicked*

who justifies the u	Rom 4:5
Christ died for the u	Rom 5:6
destruction of u men	2 Pet 3:7
their own u lusts	Jude 18

UNHOLY *not holy*

| no *longer* consider u | Acts 10:15 |
| for the u and profane | 1 Tim 1:9 |

UNINTENTIONALLY

| If a person sins u | Lev 4:2 |
| who kills a person u | Num 35:15 |

UNITED *joined, union*

u as one man	Judg 20:11
become u with *Him*	Rom 6:5
love, u in spirit	Phil 2:2
not u by faith	Heb 4:2

UNITY *united, union*

dwell together in u	Ps 133:1
perfected in u	John 17:23
all attain to the u	Eph 4:13
perfect bond of u	Col 3:14

UNJUST *unfair*

u man is abominable	Prov 29:27
For God is not u	Heb 6:10
the just for *the* u	1 Pet 3:18

UNKNOWN *not known*

To An U God	Acts 17:23
as u yet well-known	2 Cor 6:9

UNLEAVENED *non-fermented*

and baked u bread	Gen 19:3
you shall eat u bread	Ex 12:15
first day of U Bread	Matt 26:17
you are *in fact* u	1 Cor 5:7

**UNLEAVENED BREAD,
FEAST OF** *see* **FEASTS**

UNLOVED *not loved*

that Leah was u	Gen 29:31
loved and the u	Deut 21:15
Under an u woman	Prov 30:23

UNMARRIED *single*

I say to the u	1 Cor 7:8
let her remain u	1 Cor 7:11

UNPRINCIPLED *unscrupulous*

conduct of u men	2 Pet 2:7
error of u men	2 Pet 3:17

UNPROFITABLE *without value*

u and worthless	Titus 3:9
grief...u for you	Heb 13:17

UNPUNISHED *not punished*

not leave him u	Ex 20:7
shall go u	Ex 21:19
not let him go u	1 Kin 2:9

UNQUENCHABLE

burn...with u fire	Matt 3:12
into the u fire	Mark 9:43

UNRESTRAINED *uncontrolled*

the people are u	Prov 29:18
with u persecution	Is 14:6

UNRIGHTEOUS *evil, wicked*

u man his thoughts	Is 55:7
rain on...*the* u	Matt 5:45
u in a...little thing	Luke 16:10
God...is not u	Rom 3:5
u shall not inherit	1 Cor 6:9
u under punishment	2 Pet 2:9

UNRIGHTEOUSNESS *evil*

have no part in u	2 Chr 19:7
no u in Him	Ps 92:15
not rejoice in u	1 Cor 13:6
cleanse us from all u	1 John 1:9
All u is sin	1 John 5:17

UNRULY *disorderly*

admonish the u	1 Thess 5:14
who leads an u life	2 Thess 3:6

UNSEARCHABLE *inscrutable*

His greatness is u	Ps 145:3
u are His judgments	Rom 11:33

UNSKILLED *lack of training*

I am u in speech	Ex 6:12
u in speech, yet I	2 Cor 11:6

UNSTABLE *unreliable*

Her ways are u	Prov 5:6
u in all his ways	James 1:8
enticing u souls	2 Pet 2:14

UNWILLING *reluctant*

u to move the ark	2 Sam 6:10
they were u to come	Matt 22:3
He was u to drink	Matt 27:34
u to be obedient	Acts 7:39

UNWISE *foolish*

foolish and u people	Deut 32:6
walk, not as u men	Eph 5:15

UNWORTHY *not deserving*

u of...lovingkindness	Gen 32:10
We are u slaves	Luke 17:10
u of eternal life	Acts 13:46

UPRIGHT *honest, just*

the death of the u	Num 23:10
blameless and u man	Job 1:8

u will behold His face Ps 11:7
led you in u paths Prov 4:11
God made men u Eccl 7:29
no u...among men Mic 7:2
Stand u on your feet Acts 14:10

UPROAR *loud noise*

Why...such an u 1 Kin 1:41
nations in an u Ps 2:1
there arose a great u Acts 23:9

UPROOT *tear out*

He will u Israel 1 Kin 14:15
He has u-ed my hope Job 19:10
u-ed and be planted Luke 17:6

UR

1 *city in S Mesopotamia*
    Gen 11:31;15:7
  original home of Abraham
    Gen 11:28; Neh 9:7
2 *son of Eliphal* 1 Chr 11:35

URBANUS

Roman Christian Rom 16:9

URGE *entreat*

Do not u me to leave Ruth 1:16
hunger u-s him *on* Prov 16:26
I u you therefore Rom 12:1

URIAH

1 *husband of Bathsheba*
    2 Sam 11:3;12:9
2 *priest under Ahaz* Is 8:2
  also Urijah 2 Kin 16:10ff
3 *priest under Ezra* Neh 8:4
4 *time of Jeremiah* Jer 26:20

URIM

*kept in high priest's breast-
plate for determining the will
of God*
    Lev 8:8; Num 27:21
    Ex 28:30

USE *utilization*

be of u to God Job 22:2
for common u Ezek 48:15
for honorable u Rom 9:21
not make full u of 1 Cor 7:31

USEFUL *beneficial*

man be u to himself Job 22:2
u to me for service 2 Tim 4:11

USELESS *worthless*

they have become u Rom 3:12
without works is u James 2:20

USURY *interest*

leave off this u Neh 5:10
by interest and u Prov 28:8

UTENSILS *vessels*

table also and its u Ex 31:8
u of the sanctuary 1 Chr 9:29

UTTER *express*

righteous u-s wisdom Ps 37:30
Let my lips u praise Ps 119:171
He u-s His voice Jer 10:13
u words of...truth Acts 26:25

UTTERANCE *expression*

was giving them u Acts 2:4
in faith and u 2 Cor 8:7
u may be given Eph 6:19
through prophetic u 1 Tim 4:14

UZ

1 *grandson of Shem* Gen 10:23
2 *son of Nahor* Gen 22:21
3 *son of Dishan* Gen 36:28
4 *home of Job* Job 1:3
  land of Uz Jer 25:20
    Lam 4:21

V

VAIN *empty or profane*

name of...God in v Ex 20:7
devising a v thing Ps 2:1
labor in v who build Ps 127:1
our preaching is v 1 Cor 15:14

VALIANT *brave, strong*

these...v warriors Judg 20:46
be a v man for me 1 Sam 18:17
even all the v men 1 Chr 28:1
He drags off the v Job 24:22

VALLEY *ravine*

v of the Jordan Gen 13:10
the v of Aijalon Josh 10:12
v of the shadow of Ps 23:4
The lily of the v-s Song 2:1

v of the dead bodies Jer 31:40
v...full of bones Ezek 37:1
the v of decision Joel 3:14

VALLEY GATE see GATES OF JERUSALEM

VALOR *bravery*

mighty man of v 1 Sam 16:18
mighty men of v 1 Chr 12:8

VALUE *worth*

you are of more v Matt 10:31
one pearl of great v Matt 13:46
v of knowing Christ Phil 3:8

VANISH *disappear*

When a cloud v-s Job 7:9
sky will v like smoke Is 51:6
v-ed from...sight Luke 24:31

VANITY *futility, pride*

will reap v Prov 22:8
V of v-ies! All is v Eccl 1:2
arrogant *words* of v 2 Pet 2:18

VAPOR *smoke*

causes the v-s to Ps 135:7
Is a fleeting v Prov 21:6
You are *just* a v James 4:14

VARICOLORED *multicolored*

made him a v tunic Gen 37:3

VARIOUS *different*

v diseases and pains Matt 4:24
led on by v impulses 2 Tim 3:6
encounter v trails James 1:2
distressed by v trials 1 Pet 1:6

VASHTI

deposed queen of Ahasuerus
Esth 1:19;2:4

VAULT *arched cover*

the v of heaven Job 22:14
the v of earth Is 40:22

VEGETABLES *plant*

like a v garden Deut 11:10
Better...dish of v-s Prov 15:17
weak eats v-s *only* Rom 14:2

VEGETATION *plant life*

earth brought forth v Gen 1:12
ate up all v Ps 105:35

wither all their v Is 42:15

VEIL *cover, curtain*

a v over his face Ex 34:33
v of the sanctuary Lev 4:6
Remove your v Is 47:2
v of the temple Matt 27:51
enters within the v Heb 6:19

VENGEANCE *revenge*

not take v Lev 19:18
V is Mine Deut 32:35
God...executes v 2 Sam 22:48
LORD takes v on His Nah 1:2
V is Mine, I will Heb 10:30

VESSEL *utensil*

Go, borrow v-s 2 Kin 4:3
I am like a broken v Ps 31:12
v-s of wrath Rom 9:22
treasure in...v-s 2 Cor 4:7
be a v for honor 2 Tim 2:21
as with a weaker v 1 Pet 3:7
v-s of the potter Rev 2:27

VESTURE *apparel*

v *was* like...snow Dan 7:9

VIAL *small container*

alabaster v of Matt 26:7
she broke the v Mark 14:3

VICTORIOUS *triumphant*

A v warrior Zeph 3:17
v from the beast Rev 15:2

VICTORY *triumph*

LORD brought...v 2 Sam 23:10
had given v to Aram 2 Kin 5:1
the glory and the v 1 Chr 29:11
gained the v for Him Ps 98:1
v belongs to the LORD Prov 21:31
He leads justice to v Matt 12:20
swallowed up in v 1 Cor 15:54
v that has overcome 1 John 5:4

VIGOR *vitality*

nor his v abated Deut 34:7
grave in full v Job 5:26
his youthful v Job 20:11

VILLAGE *small town*

land of unwalled v-s Ezek 38:11
Go into the v Matt 21:2

entered a certain v   Luke 10:38

VINDICATE *justify*

will v His people   Deut 32:36
V the weak   Ps 82:3
wisdom is v-d by   Matt 11:19

VINE *stem of plant*

trees said to the v   Judg 9:12
every man...his v   1 Kin 4:25
like a fruitful v   Ps 128:3
the v-s in blossom   Song 2:13
mother was like a v   Ezek 19:10
Israel is a luxuriant   Hos 10:1
The v dries up   Joel 1:12
fruit of the v   Matt 26:29
I am the true v   John 15:1

VINEDRESSER *gardener*

v-s and plowmen   2 Kin 25:12
My Father is the v   John 15:1

VINEGAR *sour liquid*

he shall drink no v   Num 6:3
bread in the v   Ruth 2:14
gave me v to drink   Ps 69:21
Like v to the teeth   Prov 10:26

VINE-GROWERS

rented it out to v   Matt 21:33
and destroy the v   Mark 12:9

VINEYARD *grapevines*

Noah...planted a v   Gen 9:20
Nor...glean your v   Lev 19:10
Hewn cisterns, v-s   Neh 9:25
shelter in a v   Is 1:8
ruined My v   Jer 12:10
laborers for his v   Matt 20:1
Who plants a v   1 Cor 9:7

VIOLATE *assault or break*

shall not v his word   Num 30:2
do not v me   2 Sam 13:12
who v-d the ban   1 Chr 2:7
If they v My statutes   Ps 89:31

VIOLENCE *destructive action*

earth was filled with v   Gen 6:11
implements of v   Gen 49:5
such as breathe out v   Ps 27:12
drink the wine of v   Prov 4:17
He had done no v   Is 53:9

not mistreat *or* do v   Jer 22:3

VIOLENT *destructive*

a v, wicked man   Ps 37:35
v men attain riches   Prov 11:16
a v, rushing wind   Acts 2:2

VIPER *snake*

v-'s tongue slays him   Job 20:16
hand on the v-'s den   Is 11:8
v and flying serpent   Is 30:6
You brood of v-s   Matt 3:7

VIRGIN *unmarried maiden*

very beautiful, a v   Gen 24:16
if a man seduces a v   Ex 22:16
could I gaze at a v   Job 31:1
the v shall rejoice   Jer 31:13
v shall be with child   Matt 1:23
kept her a v   Matt 1:25
comparable to ten v-s   Matt 25:1
v-'s name was Mary   Luke 1:27
if a v should marry   1 Cor 7:28

VISIBLE *manifest, seen*

He should become v   Acts 10:40
becomes v is light   Eph 5:13
things which are v   Heb 11:3

VISION *dream, foresight*

to Abram in a v   Gen 15:1
v-s were infrequent   1 Sam 3:1
Where there is no v   Prov 29:18
prophets find No v   Lam 2:9
I saw v-s of God   Ezek 1:22
in a night v   Dan 2:19
young men...see v-s   Joel 2:28
Tell the v to no one   Matt 17:9
young men...see v-s   Acts 2:17

VISIT *come* or *go to see*

v-ing the iniquity of   Ex 20:5
Thou dost v the earth   Ps 65:9
you did not v Me   Matt 25:43
For He has v-ed us   Luke 1:68
v orphans...widows   James 1:27

VOICE *sound, speech*

have obeyed My v   Gen 22:18
listen to His v   Deut 4:30
v of singing men   2 Sam 19:35
Thou wilt hear my v   Ps 5:3

the v of my teachers Prov 5:13
v of the turtledove Song 2:12
Give ear...hear my v Is 28:23
A v is calling Is 40:3
v came from heaven Dan 4:31
v...heard in Ramah Matt 2:18
v...out of the cloud Mark 9:7
v of one crying in Luke 3:4
v of the Son of God John 5:25
v has gone out Rom 10:18
v of the archangel 1 Thess 4:16
His v shook...earth Heb 12:26
if anyone hears My v Rev 3:20
with a v of thunder Rev 6:1

VOID *empty, invalid*

was formless and v Gen 1:2
make v the counsel Jer 19:7
faith is made v Rom 4:14
cross...be made v 1 Cor 1:17

VOMIT *throw up*

will v them up Job 20:15
returns to its v Prov 26:11
staggers in his v Is 19:14
and it v-ed Jonah Jon 2:10
returns to its own 2 Pet 2:22

VOTIVE *dedicated*

his offering is a v Lev 7:16
choice v offerings Deut 12:11

VOW *solemn promise*

Jacob made a v Gen 28:20
v of a Nazirite Num 6:2
I shall pay my v-s Ps 22:25
not make false v-s Matt 5:33
he was keeping a v Acts 18:18

VOYAGE *journey*

v was now dangerous Acts 27:9

VULTURE *bird*

not eat...the v Deut 14:12
the v-s will gather Matt 24:28
the v-s be gathered Luke 17:37

W

WAFER *thin cake of bread*

w-s with honey Ex 16:31
one unleavened w Num 6:19

WAGE *salary*

God has given...w-s Gen 30:18
w-s of the righteous Prov 10:16
w is not reckoned Rom 4:4
the w-s of sin Rom 6:23
worthy of his w-s 1 Tim 5:18

WAIL *lament, mourn*

w with a broken spirit Is 65:14
w, son of man Ezek 21:12
I must lament and w Mic 1:8
W, O inhabitants of Zeph 1:11
weeping and w-ing Mark 5:38

WAIT *expect*

For Thee I w Ps 25:5
I w for Thy word Ps 119:81
who w for the LORD Is 40:31
creation w-s eagerly Rom 8:19
w-ing for the hope Gal 5:5

WALK *follow, go along*

w-ing in the garden Gen 3:8
W before Me Gen 17:1
w in My instruction Ex 16:4
w in My statutes Lev 26:3
w-ed forty years Josh 5:6
w before Me in truth 1 Kin 2:4
W about Zion Ps 48:12
I will w at liberty Ps 119:45
fool w-s in darkness Eccl 2:14
w in the light Is 2:5
w and not...weary Is 40:31
w-ed with Me in peace Mal 2:6
Rise, and w Matt 9:5
w-ed on the water Matt 14:29
w in newness of life Rom 6:4
we w by faith 2 Cor 5:7
w by the Spirit Gal 5:16
w in love Eph 5:2
w as children of light Eph 5:8
if we w in the light 1 John 1:7
w by its light Rev 21:24

WALL *structure*

living on the w Josh 2:15
So we built the w Neh 4:6
I can leap over a w Ps 18:29
w-s of Jerusalem Jer 39:8

built a siege w   Jer 52:4
you whitewashed w   Acts 23:3
w-s of Jericho fell   Heb 11:30
a great and high w   Rev 21:12

WANDER *roam*

w in the wilderness Num 32:13

I would w far away   Ps 55:7
w...Thy statutes   Ps 119:118
people w like sheep   Zech 10:2
w-ed...from the faith 1 Tim 6:10
w-ing stars, for whom   Jude 13

WANDERER *roamer*

a w on the earth   Gen 4:12
an exile and a w   Is 49:21
w-s among...nations   Hos 9:17

WAR *battle, conflict*

when they see w   Ex 13:17
sound of w in...camp   Ex 32:17
land...rest from w   Josh 11:23
He makes w-s to cease   Ps 46:9
the weapons of w   Ps 76:3
A time for w   Eccl 3:18
will they learn w   Is 2:4
w-s...rumors of w-s   Matt 24:6
w against the law   Rom 7:23
w in your members   James 4:1
w against the soul   1 Pet 2:11
judges and wages w   Rev 19:11

**WARS OF THE LORD,
    BOOK OF**

ancient Hebrew literature
    Num 21:14

WARM *heat*

could not keep w   1 Kin 1:25
the child became w   2 Kin 4:34
can one be w *alone*   Eccl 4:11
no one is w *enough*   Hag 1:6

WARN *give notice*

w the people   Ex 19:21
not...w the wicked   Ezek 33:8
w-ed...in a dream   Matt 2:12
w you whom to fear   Luke 12:5
Moses was w-ed   Heb 8:5

WARRIOR *soldier*

The LORD is a w   Ex 15:3

O valiant w   Judg 6:12
w from his youth 1 Sam 17:33
w-s will flee naked   Amos 2:16

WASH *bathe, clean*

w your feet, and rest Gen 18:4
w in the Jordan   2 Kin 5:10
w...in innocence   Ps 26:6
W...from my iniquity   Ps 51:2
w-ed off your blood Ezek 16:9
do not w their hands Matt 15:2
ceremonially w-ed Luke 11:38
w in the pool of   John 9:7
w the disciples' feet John 13:5
w away your sins   Acts 22:16
w-ed...saints' feet   1 Tim 5:10
w-ed with pure   Heb 10:22
who w their robes   Rev 22:14

WASTE (n) *wilderness*

land was laid w   Ex 8:24
land into a salt w   Ps 107:34
lay w the mountains   Is 42:15
laid w like a desert   Jer 9:12
altars may become w Ezek 6:6
Egypt...become a w   Joel 3:19

WASTE (v) *destroy, use up*

he w-d his seed   Gen 38:9
w away the eyes   Lev 26:16
sick man w-s away   Is 10:18
perfume been w-d   Mark 14:4

WASTE PLACE *barren*

w-s of the wealthy   Is 5:17
Seek Me in a w   Is 45:19
like the ancient w-s Ezek 26:20
w-s will be rebuilt   Ezek 36:10

WATCH (n) *guard*

at the morning w   Ex 14:24
in the night w-es   Ps 63:6
His eyes keep w   Ps 66:7
keep w with Me   Matt 26:38
w over their flock   Luke 2:8
w over your souls   Heb 13:17

WATCH (v) *observe*

LORD w between you Gen 31:49
dost w all my paths Job 13:27
W over your heart   Prov 4:23
who w-es the wind   Eccl 11:4

w...for the LORD   Mic 7:7

WATCHMAN *one who guards*

w keeps awake in vain   Ps 127:1
w-men for...morning   Ps 130:6
W, how far gone is   Is 21:11
I set w-men over you   Jer 6:17
Ephraim *was* a w   Hos 9:8

WATER (n) *flood, liquid*

moving over...the w-s   Gen 1:2
flood of w came   Gen 7:6
w-s *were like* a wall   Ex 14:22
w of bitterness   Num 5:18
the clouds dripped w   Judg 5:4
W wears away stones   Job 14:19
poured out like w   Ps 22:14
beside quiet w-s   Ps 23:2
Stolen w is sweet   Prov 9:17
bread on the...w-s   Eccl 11:1
come to the w-s   Is 55:1
fountain of living w-s   Jer 2:13
eyes run...with w   Lam 1:16
knees...like w   Ezek 7:17
baptize you with w   Matt 3:11
a cup of cold w   Matt 10:42
walked on the w   Matt 14:29
no w for My feet   Luke 7:44
one is born of w   John 3:5
given you living w   John 4:10
John baptized with w   Acts 1:5
of w with the word   Eph 5:26
formed out of w   2 Pet 3:5
by w and blood   1 John 5:6
sound of many w-s   Rev 19:6

WATER (v) *make moist*

to w the garden   Gen 2:10
I will w your camels   Gen 24:46
w their father's flock   Ex 2:16
that w the earth   Ps 72:6
Apollos w-ed   1 Cor 3:6

WAVES *billows*

w of death   2 Sam 22:5
tramples down the w   Job 9:8
Thy w have rolled   Ps 42:7
w were breaking   Mark 4:37
wild w of the sea   Jude 13

WAX *paraffin*

My heart is like w   Ps 22:14

Like w before the fire   Mic 1:4

WAY *manner or path*

guard the w   Gen 3:24
all His w-s are just   Deut 32:4
blameless...His w   2 Sam 22:33
from your evil w-s   2 Kin 17:13
joy of His w   Job 8:19
w of the righteous   Ps 1:6
Commit your w to   Ps 37:5
your w-s acknowledge   Prov 3:6
is the w of death   Prov 14:12
Clear the w   Is 40:3
w of the wicked   Jer 12:1
Make ready the w   Matt 3:3
Pray...in this w   Matt 6:9
w is broad that leads   Matt 7:13
teach...w of God   Mark 12:14
into the w of peace   Luke 1:79
I am the w   John 14:6
belonging to the W   Acts 9:2
the w of salvation   Acts 16:17
unfathomable...w-s   Rom 11:33
the w of escape   1 Cor 10:13
new and living w   Heb 10:20
the w of the truth   2 Pet 2:2

WEAK *feeble*

I shall become w   Judg 16:17
Rescue the w   Ps 82:4
but the flesh is w   Matt 26:41
must help the w   Acts 20:35
who is w in faith   Rom 14:1
God...chosen the w   1 Cor 1:27

WEAKNESS *fault*

Spirit...helps our w   Rom 8:26
bear the w-es   Rom 15:1
w of God is stronger   1 Cor 1:25
it is sown in w   1 Cor 15:43
perfected in w   2 Cor 12:9

WEALTH *riches*

power to make w   Deut 8:18
a man of great w   Ruth 2:1
who trust in their w   Ps 49:6
Honor...from you w   Prov 3:9
W adds many friends   Prov 19:4
a w of salvation   Is 33:6
the w of all nations   Hag 2:7
w of their liberality   2 Cor 8:2
rich by her w   Rev 18:19

WEAPON *armament*

girded on his w-s   Deut 1:41
flee from the iron w   Job 20:24
turn back the w-s   Jer 21:4
w-s of righteousness   2 Cor 6:7

WEARY *tired*

the people were w   1 Sam 14:28
the w are at rest   Job 3:17
w with my crying   Ps 69:3
water to a w soul   Prov 25:25
and not become w   Is 40:31
sustain the w one   Is 50:4
all who are w   Matt 11:28
w of doing good   2 Thess 3:13

WEAVE *interlace*

Thou didst w me   Ps 139:13
w the spider's web   Is 59:5
after w-ing a crown   Matt 27:29

WEB *woven work*

loom and the w   Judg 16:14
trust a spider's w   Job 8:14

WEDDING *marriage*

had no w songs   Ps 78:63
day of his w   Song 3:11
come to the w feast   Matt 22:4
a w in Cana   John 2:1

WEEK *period of time*

Complete the w of   Gen 29:27
Seventy w-s   Dan 9:24
first *day* of the w   Matt 28:1
I fast twice a w   Luke 18:12

WEEKS, FEAST OF
   see FEASTS

WEEP *cry, sorrow*

sought *a place* to w   Gen 43:30
do not mourn or w   Neh 8:9
My eye w-s to God   Job 16:20
widows could not w   Ps 78:64
Let me w bitterly   Is 22:4
w day and night   Jer 9:1
Rachel w-ing for her   Matt 2:18
w-ing and gnashing   Matt 13:42
he...wept bitterly   Matt 26:75
saw the city...wept   Luke 19:41
w for yourselves   Luke 23:28

Jesus **wept**   John 11:35
why are you w-ing   John 20:13
w with...who w   Rom 12:15

WEIGH *measure out*

actions are w-ed   1 Sam 2:3
LORD w-s the motives   Prov 16:2

WEIGHT *heaviness*

a full and just w   Deut 25:15
w to the wind   Job 28:25
bag of deceptive w-s   Mic 6:11
eternal w of glory   2 Cor 4:17

WELCOME *gladly receive*

no prophet is w   Luke 4:24
multitude w-d Him   Luke 8:40
who fears Him...w   Acts 10:35
she...w-d the spies   Heb 11:31

WELL *water shaft*

sat down by a w   Ex 2:15
w of Bethlehem   1 Chr 11:17
Like...a polluted w   Prov 25:26
A w of fresh water   Song 4:15
Jacob's w was there   John 4:6

WELL-PLEASED *satisfied*

in whom I am w   Matt 3:17
in Thee I am w   Luke 3:22
God was not w   1 Cor 10:5

WEST *direction*

very strong w wind   Ex 10:19
east is from the w   Ps 103:12
gather you from the w   Is 43:5

WHEAT *grain*

days of w harvest   Gen 30:14
first fruits of the w   Ex 34:22
plant w in rows   Is 28:25
gather His w into   Matt 3:12
to sift you like w   Luke 22:31
unless a grain of w   John 12:24

WHEEL *circular disk*

the w...is crushed   Eccl 12:6
w-s like a whirlwind   Is 5:28
one w were within   Ezek 1:16
rattling of the w   Nah 3:2

WHIRLWIND

take...Elijah by a w   2 Kin 2:1

249

comes on like a w   Prov 1:27
chariots like a w   Jer 4:13
they reap the w   Hos 8:7

WHISPER *talk quietly*

who hate me w   Ps 41:7
w a prayer   Is 26:16
your speech shall w   Is 29:4

WHISTLE *shrill sound*

And will w for it   Is 5:26
LORD will w for the fly   Is 7:18
I will w for them   Zech 10:8

WHITE *color*

teeth w from milk   Gen 49:12
w of an egg   Job 6:6
be as w as snow   Is 1:18
make one hair w   Matt 5:36
clothing *became* w   Luke 9:29
fields...w for harvest   John 4:35
clothed in w robes   Rev 7:9

WHITEWASHED *wall covering*

like w tombs   Matt 23:27
you w wall   Acts 23:3

WHOLE *entire*

water the w surface   Gen 2:6
w earth...populated   Gen 9:19
leavens the w lump   1 Cor 5:6
keeps the w law   James 2:10

WICK *candle thread*

extinguished like a w   Is 43:17
a smoldering w   Matt 12:20

WICKED *evil, ungodly*

condemn the w   Deut 25:1
w ones are silenced   1 Sam 2:9
counsel of the w   Ps 1:1
the w spurned God   Ps 10:13
The w strut about   Ps 12:8
devises w plans   Prov 6:18
When a w man dies   Prov 11:7
no peace for the w   Is 48:22
turn from his w way   Jon 3:8
taking...some w men   Acts 17:5
righteous and the w   Acts 24:15

WICKEDNESS *evil*

w of man was great   Gen 6:5
if I regard w   Ps 66:18
eat the bread of w   Prov 4:17

inclines toward w   Is 32:6
w of My people   Jer 7:12
You have plowed w   Hos 10:13
repent of this w   Acts 8:22
spiritual *forces* of w   Eph 6:12

WIDOW *husband dead*

Remain a w   Gen 38:11
not afflict any w   Ex 22:22
sent w-s away empty   Job 22:9
judge for the w-s   Ps 68:5
Plead for the w   Is 1:17
devour w-s' houses   Matt 23:14
w put in more   Mark 12:43
Honor w-s   1 Tim 5:3
visit orphans...w-s   James 1:27

WIFE *married woman*

cleave to his w   Gen 2:24
man and his w hid   Gen 3:8
shall not covet...w   Ex 20:17
w of your youth   Prov 5:18
An excellent w   Prov 31:10
who divorces his w   Matt 5:32
Remember Lot's w   Luke 17:32
have his own w   1 Cor 7:2
head of the w   Eph 5:23
husband of one w   1 Tim 3:1
w-ves, be submissive   1 Pet 3:1
w of the Lamb   Rev 21:9

WILD *untamed*

w donkey of a man   Gen 16:12
horns of the w ox   Num 23:22
locusts and w honey   Mark 1:6
being a w olive   Rom 11:17

WILDERNESS *barren area*

water in the w   Gen 16:7
journey into the w   Ex 5:3
to die in the w   Ex 14:11
forty years in the w   Deut 29:5
pastures of the w   Ps 65:12
roadway in the w   Is 43:19
Have I been a w   Jer 2:31
preaching in the w   Matt 3:1
into the w...tempted   Matt 4:1
crying in the w   Mark 1:3
manna in the w   John 6:31

WILL *attitude, purpose*

delight to do Thy w   Ps 40:8

Thy w be done   Matt 6:10
the w of My Father   Matt 7:21
not My w, but   Luke 22:42
nor of the w of man   John 1:13
who resists His w   Rom 9:19
what the w of God   Rom 12:2
knowledge of His w   Col 1:9
come to do Thy w   Heb 10:9
an act of human w   2 Pet 1:21

WIN *succeed*

wise w-s souls   Prov 11:30
we will w him over   Matt 28:14
that I might w Jews   1 Cor 9:20
won without a word   1 Pet 3:1

WIND

caused a w to pass   Gen 8:1
scorched by...w   Gen 41:27
will inherit w   Prov 11:29
prophets are *as* w   Jer 5:13
they sow the w   Hos 8:7
reed shaken by...w   Matt 11:7
w and the sea obey   Mark 4:41
He rebuked the w   Luke 8:24
violent, rushing w   Acts 2:2
every w of doctrine   Eph 4:14
driven by strong w-s   James 3:4

WINDOW *opening*

enter through the w-s   Joel 2:9
open...w-s of heaven   Mal 3:10
sitting on the w sill   Acts 20:9
basket through a w   2 Cor 11:33

WINE *strong drink*

eyes...dull from w   Gen 49:12
Do not drink w   Lev 10:9
overflow with new w   Prov 3:10
W is a mocker   Prov 20:1
love is better than w   Song 1:2
new w into old   Matt 9:17
gave Him w to   Matt 27:34
made the water w   John 4:46
full of sweet w   Acts 2:13
not get drunk with w   Eph 5:18
not addicted to w   1 Tim 3:3

WINESKINS *animal skin bag*

these w...were new   Josh 9:13
Like new w   Job 32:19
wine into fresh w   Matt 9:17

WINGS

bore you on eagles' w   Ex 19:4
He spread His w   Deut 32:11
under whose w   Ruth 2:12
under His w...refuge   Ps 91:4
with w like eagles   Is 40:31
healing in its w   Mal 4:2
chicks under her w   Matt 23:37

WINK *blink*

w maliciously   Ps 35:19
w-s with his eyes   Prov 6:13

WINNOW *scatter*

king w-s the wicked   Prov 20:26
You will w them   Is 41:16
His w-ing fork   Matt 3:12

WINTER *season*

And summer and w   Gen 8:22
the w is past   Song 2:11
even spend the w   1 Cor 16:6

WIPE *pass over, rub*

GOD will w tears   Is 25:8
w-d His feet   John 11:2
sins...w-d away   Acts 3:19
w away every tear   Rev 21:4

WISDOM *discernment*

the spirit of w   Ex 28:3
w has two sides   Job 11:6
the beginning of w   Ps 111:10
Fools despise w   Prov 1:7
w to fear Thy name   Mic 6:9
w given to Him   Mark 6:2
kept increasing in w   Luke 2:52
made foolish the w   1 Cor 1:20
any of you lacks w   James 1:5

WISE *judicious, prudent*

not find a w man   Job 17:10
making w the simple   Ps 19:7
w in your own eyes   Prov 3:7
the words of the w   Prov 22:17
He is not a w son   Hos 13:13
Who...you is w   James 3:13

WITCHCRAFT *magic, sorcery*

who practices w   Deut 18:10
practiced w and   2 Kin 21:6

WITHER *dry up*

its leaf does not w	Ps 1:3
w...like the grass	Ps 37:2
earth mourns *and* w-s	Is 24:4
the leaf shall w	Jer 8:13
with a w-ed hand	Mark 3:1
the fig tree w-ed	Mark 11:20

WITNESS (n) *testimony*

This heap is a w	Gen 31:48
is w between us	Judg 11:10
my w is in heaven	Job 16:19
a w to the LORD	Is 19:20
w to all the nations	Matt 24:14
He came for a w	John 1:7
My w is true	John 8:14
you shall be My w-es	Acts 1:8
For God is my w	Phil 1:8
w of God is greater	1 John 5:9
Christ, the faithful w	Rev 1:5

WITNESS (v) *testify*

not bear false w	Ex 20:16
w against you today	Deut 4:26
John bore w	John 1:32
bear w of Me	John 15:26
Spirit...bears w	Rom 8:16
three that bear w	1 John 5:8

WOLF *animal*

w will dwell with	Is 11:6
the midst of w-ves	Matt 10:16
w snatches them	John 10:12

WOMAN *female, lady*

she shall be called W	Gen 2:23
w...not wear man's	Deut 22:5
a w of excellence	Ruth 3:11
Man...born of w	Job 14:1
gracious w attains	Prov 11:16
a contentious w	Prov 25:24
like a w in labor	Is 42:14
looks on a w to lust	Matt 5:28
w-en...grinding	Matt 24:41
Blessed among w-en	Luke 1:42
W, behold, your son	John 19:26
not to touch a w	1 Cor 7:1
w is the glory of	1 Cor 11:7
w to speak in	1 Cor 14:35
His Son, born of a w	Gal 4:4
w clothed with...sun	Rev 12:1

WOMB

nations...in your w	Gen 25:23
LORD...closed her w	1 Sam 1:5
from w to tomb	Job 10:19
formed you from the w	Is 44:2
baby leaped in...w	Luke 1:41

WONDER *marvel, sign*

consider the w-s of	Job 37:14
tell of all Thy w-s	Ps 9:1
His w-s in the deep	Ps 107:24
w-s in the sky	Joel 2:30
were filled with w	Acts 3:10

WONDERFUL *marvelous*

His w deeds	1 Chr 16:12
name will be called W	Is 9:6

WOOD *cut tree*

ark of gopher w	Gen 6:14
other gods, w and	Deut 28:36
children gather w	Jer 7:18
stones, w, hay	1 Cor 3:12

WOOL *cloth* or *hair*

of w and linen	Deut 22:11
put a fleece of w on	Judg 6:37
They will be like w	Is 1:18
hair...like pure w	Dan 7:9
white like white w	Rev 1:14

WORD *message, speech*

to the w of Moses	Lev 10:7
declare to you the w	Deut 5:5
Joshua wrote...w-s	Josh 24:26
proclaim the w of	1 Sam 9:27
Thy w...confirmed	2 Chr 6:17
no limit to windy w-s	Job 16:3
w-s of my mouth	Ps 19:14
Thy w is a lamp	Ps 119:105
harsh w stirs up	Prov 15:1
w of God is tested	Prov 30:5
despised the w	Is 5:24
w-s of a sealed book	Is 29:11
speak My w in truth	Jer 23:28
conceal these w-s	Dan 12:4
every w that proceeds	Matt 4:4
these w-s of Mine	Matt 7:24
sower sows the w	Mark 4:14
the W was God	John 1:1
the W became flesh	John 1:14

w-s of eternal life　John 6:68
abide in My w　John 8:31
glorifying the w　Acts 13:48
too deep for w-s　Rom 8:26
hearing by the w　Rom 10:17
the w of the cross　1 Cor 1:18
fulfilled in one w　Gal 5:14
no unwholesome w　Eph 4:29
sanctified by...w　1 Tim 4:5
the w of truth　2 Tim 2:15
the faithful w　Titus 1:9
w of God is living　Heb 4:12
doers of the w　James 1:22
pure milk of the w　1 Pet 2:2
the W of Life　1 John 1:18
The W of God　Rev 19:13

WORK (n) *act, deed, labor*

God completed His w　Gen 2:2
You shall w six days　Ex 34:21
His w is perfect　Deut 32:4
the w of His hands　Ps 19:1
see the w-s of God　Ps 66:5
Commit your w-s to　Prov 16:3
let Him hasten His w　Is 5:19
His w on Mount Zion　Is 10:12
see your good w-s　Matt 5:16
the w-s of Christ　Matt 11:2
the w of the Law　Rom 2:15
faith apart from w-s　Rom 3:28
not...a result of w-s　Eph 2:9
for the w of service　Eph 4:12
began a good w　Phil 1:6
fruit in...good w　Col 1:10
rich in good w-s　1 Tim 6:18
faith without w-s　James 2:20

WORK (v) *perform, produce*

has w-ed with God 1 Sam 14:45
those who w iniquity　Ps 28:3
Who...w-s wonders　Ps 72:18
not w for the food　John 6:27
w together for good　Rom 8:28
So death w-s in us　2 Cor 4:12
w out your salvation　Phil 2:12
anyone will not w 2 Thess 3:10

WORKER *laborer*

O w of deceit　Ps 52:2
w-s of iniquity　Prov 10:29
w is worthy of his　Matt 10:10
God's fellow w-s　1 Cor 3:9

beware...evil w-s　Phil 3:2
pure, w-s at home　Titus 2:5

WORKMAN *craftsman*

a skillful w　Ex 38:23
approved...as a w　2 Tim 2:15

WORKMANSHIP *craftsmanship*

we are His w　Eph 2:10

WORLD *earth, humanity*

foundations of...w　2 Sam 22:16
He will judge the w　Ps 9:8
first dust of the w　Prov 8:26
the light of the w　Matt 5:14
the field is the w　Matt 13:38
Go into all the w　Mark 16:15
gains the whole w　Luke 9:25
God so loved the w　John 3:16
Savior of the w　John 4:42
w cannot hate you　John 7:7
the light of the w　John 8:12
overcome the w　John 16:33
have upset the w　Acts 17:6
sin entered...the w　Rom 5:12
reconciling the w　2 Cor 5:19
unstained by the w　James 1:27
flood upon the w　2 Pet 2:5
Do not love the w　1 John 2:15

WORLDLY *earthly*

w fables fit only　1 Tim 4:7
avoid w...chatter　2 Tim 2:16

WORM *creeping animal*

But I am a w　Ps 22:6
w-s are your covering　Is 14:11
God appointed a w　Jon 4:7
their w does not die Mark 9:48
he was eaten by w-s Acts 12:23

WORMWOOD

1 *a bitter plant*　Deut 29:18
2 *used figuratively*　Prov 5:4
　　　　Amos 6:12; Rev 8:11

WORSHIP *bow, revere*

not w any other god　Ex 34:14
you shall w Him　Deut 6:13
W the LORD　Ps 2:11
earth will w Thee　Ps 66:4
in vain do they w　Matt 15:9
w in spirit and truth John 4:24

w in the Spirit — Phil 3:3
w Him who lives — Rev 4:10
who w the beast — Rev 14:11

WORTHLESS *useless*

all w physicians — Job 13:4
w man digs up evil — Prov 16:27
your w offerings — Is 1:13
your faith is w — 1 Cor 15:17
w for any good — Titus 1:16
man's religion is w — James 1:26

WORTHY *having merit*

sin w of death — Deut 21:22
w of his support — Matt 10:10
is not w of Me — Matt 10:37
is w of his wages — Luke 10:7
manner w of the — Rom 16:2
w of the gospel — Phil 1:27
world was not w — Heb 11:38
W is the Lamb — Rev 5:12

WOUND *injury*

My w is incurable — Job 34:6
binds up their w-s — Ps 147:3
Your w is incurable — Jer 30:12
bandaged...his w-s — Luke 10:34
by His w-s you were — 1 Pet 2:24
fatal w was healed — Rev 13:3

WRAPPINGS *cloth coverings*

bound...with w — John 11:44
linen w lying *there* — John 20:5

WRATH *anger, indignation*

and in great w — Deut 29:28
Nor chasten...in Thy w — Ps 6:1
Pour out Thy w — Ps 79:6
turns away w — Prov 15:1
Lest My w go forth — Jer 4:4
spent My w upon — Ezek 5:13
from the w to come — Matt 3:7
w of God abides on — John 3:36
God who inflicts w — Rom 3:5
children of w — Eph 2:3
w of God will come — Col 3:6
the w of the Lamb — Rev 6:16

WRETCHED *miserable*

in to this w place — Num 20:5
W man that I am — Rom 7:24

WRITE *enscribe*

Moses, W this in a — Ex 17:14
W them on a tablet — Prov 3:3
he wrote the dream — Dan 7:1
w a certificate — Mark 10:4
with His finger **wrote** — John 8:6
w...King of the Jews — John 19:21
W in a book — Rev 1:11

WRITINGS *literary work*

not believe his w — John 5:47
known the sacred w — 2 Tim 3:15

WRITTEN *enscribed*

w by...God — Ex 31:18
w in the law — 2 Chr 23:18
remembrance was w — Mal 3:16
w by the prophet — Matt 2:5
about whom it is w — Matt 11:10
Law w in...hearts — Rom 2:15
name has not been w — Rev 13:8
w in the Lamb's — Rev 21:27

WRONG *do evil, harm*

not w a stranger — Ex 22:21
not w one another — Lev 25:14
I...have done w — 2 Sam 24:17
Love does no w — Rom 13:10

WROUGHT *accomplished*

He w wonders — Ps 78:12
been w in God — John 3:21

Y

YAHWEH *see* YHWH *and*
LORD

YEAR *period, time*

atonement...every y — Lev 16:34
fiftieth y...jubilee — Lev 25:11
the y of remission — Deut 15:9
crowned the y with — Ps 65:11
length of...y-s — Prov 3:2
favorable y of the LORD — Is 61:2
thirty y-s of age — Luke 3:23
y of the LORD — Luke 4:19
priest *enters*, once a y — Heb 9:7
sacrifices y by y — Heb 10:1

| y-s as one day | 2 Pet 3:8 |
| reign...thousand y-s | Rev 20:6 |

YEARLING *one year old*

| a y eye lamb | Lev 14:10 |
| With y calves | Mic 6:6 |

YEARNS *deeply moved*

| my flesh y for Thee | Ps 63:1 |
| My heart y for him | Jer 31:20 |

YESTERDAY *past*

we are *only* of y	Job 8:9
thousand years...y	Ps 90:4
same y and today	Heb 13:8

YHWH

Hebrew tetragrammaton for name of God, probably pro-nounced Yahweh

Derived from Hebrew verb meaning "to be"
Translated usually as Lord
see also **LORD**
see also introductory material to NASB

YIELD *produce*

no longer y its	Gen 4:12
land...y its produce	Lev 25:19
Which y-s its fruit	Ps 1:3
y-ed up *His* spirit	Matt 27:50
not y in subjection	Gal 2:5
y-s the peaceful	Heb 12:11

YOKE *wooden bar*

break his y from	Gen 27:40
iron y on...neck	Deut 28:48
made our y hard	1 Kin 12:4
the y of their burden	Is 9:4
Take My y upon	Matt 11:29
to a y of slavery	Gal 5:1

YOUNG *early age, youth*

he sent y men	Ex 24:5
or two y pigeons	Lev 15:29
glory of y men is	Prov 20:29
y men stumble	Is 40:30
like a y lion	Hos 5:14
finding a y donkey	John 12:14
y men...visions	Acts 2:17
urge the y men	Titus 2:6

YOUTH *young*

evil from his y	Gen 8:21
fresher than in y	Job 33:25
the sins of my y	Ps 25:7
confidence from my y	Ps 71:5
your y is renewed	Ps 103:5
the wife of your y	Prov 5:18
y-s grow weary	Is 40:30
the reproach of my y	Jer 31:19
life from my y up	Acts 26:4

Z

ZACCHEUS

tax collector who followed Jesus Luke 19:2,5,8

ZACHARIAS

father of John the Baptist
Luke 1:5,12,18;3:2

ZARAPHATH

scene of miracle by Elijah
1 Kin 17:9,10

| *Phoenician town* | Obad 20 |
| | Luke 4:26 |

ZEAL *fervor, passion*

kill them in his z	2 Sam 21:2
my z for the Lord	2 Kin 10:16
z has consumed me	Ps 119:139
Thy z for the people	Is 26:11
have a z for God	Rom 10:2
your z for me	2 Cor 7:7

ZEALOT

member of radical Jewish nationalist party Matt 10:4
Mark 3:18; Luke 6:15; Acts 1:13

ZEALOUS *fervent*

z for the Lord	1 Kin 19:10
all z for the Law	Acts 21:20
z of...*gifts*	1 Cor 14:12
z for good deeds	Titus 2:14
be z...and repent	Rev 3:19

ZEBEDEE

father of James and John
Matt 4:21;27:56; Mark 1:19

255

ZEBEDEE

Mark 10:35; Luke 5:10; John 21:2

ZEBULUN

1 *son of Jacob*   Gen 30:20
2 *tribe* Num 34:25; Josh 21:34
3 *territory of the tribe,
    located in N Palestine*
        Josh 19:27; Judg 12:12
        Is 9:1; Ezek 48:27

ZECHARIAH

1 *line of Saul*   1 Chr 9:35-37
2 *priest with ark*   1 Chr 15:24
3 *son of Isshiah*   1 Chr 24:25
4 *father of Iddo*   1 Chr 27:21
5 *son of Benaiah*   2 Chr 20:14
6 *son of Jehoshaphat*
                        2 Chr 21:2
7 *son of Jehoida*   2 Chr 24:20
8 *prophet*   2 Chr 26:5
9 *priest under Ezra* Neh 12:41
10 *minor prophet*   Zech 1:1

ZELOPHEHAD

Manassite, son of Hepher
                        Num 26:33
daughters became his heirs
                     Num 27:1;36:2

ZEPHANIAH

1 *priest*   2 Kin 25:18
2 *Kohathite Levite*   1 Chr 6:36
3 *minor prophet*   Zeph 1:1
4 *father of Josiah*   Zech 6:10

ZERUBBABEL

line of David   1 Chr 3:1-19
helped rebuild temple Ezra 3:8

ZERUIAH

*mother of Joab, Abishai, and
    Asahel*   2 Sam 2:18
David's half-sister 1 Chr 2:16

ZIKLAG

town in S Judah   Josh 15:31
            1 Sam 27:6; 1 Chr 12:1

ZILPAH

concubine of Jacob Gen 29:24
            Gen 30:10;46:18

ZIN

wilderness in Negev Num 13:21
            Deut 32:51; Josh 15:1,3

ZION

1 *hill/Temple Mount in
    Jerusalem*   2 Sam 5:7
        1 Kin 8:1; 1 Chr 11:5
2 *applied to all of Jerusalem*
        Ps 126:1; Is 1:26,27;33:20
3 *applied to the heavenly
    Jerusalem*
    Is 60:14; Heb 12:22; Rev 14:1

ZIPORRAH

wife of Moses   Ex 2:21;4:25

ZIV

*name of the second month in
    Hebrew calendar* 1 Kin 6:1,37

ZOAN

Egyptian delta city Num 13:22
    Ps 78:12; Is 19:11; Ezek 30:14

ZOAR

*city of the plain near the
    Dead Sea* Gen 13:10;19:23,30
            Deut 34:3; Jer 48:34
also **Bela**

ZOPHAR

one of Job's friends   Job 2:11
            Job 11:1;20:1;42:9

ZUZIM

*pre-Israelite tribe in
    Palestine*   Gen 14:5